# The Russian Cosmists

# THE RUSSIAN COSMISTS

*The Esoteric Futurism of Nikolai*
*Fedorov and His Followers*

GEORGE M. YOUNG

OXFORD
UNIVERSITY PRESS

# OXFORD
## UNIVERSITY PRESS

Oxford University Press, Inc., publishes works that further
Oxford University's objective of excellence
in research, scholarship, and education.

Oxford    New York
Auckland    Cape Town    Dar es Salaam    Hong Kong    Karachi
Kuala Lumpur    Madrid    Melbourne    Mexico City    Nairobi
New Delhi    Shanghai    Taipei    Toronto

With offices in
Argentina    Austria    Brazil    Chile    Czech Republic    France    Greece
Guatemala    Hungary    Italy    Japan    Poland    Portugal    Singapore
South Korea    Switzerland    Thailand    Turkey    Ukraine    Vietnam

Published by Oxford University Press, Inc.
198 Madison Avenue, New York, NY 10016

www.oup.com

Oxford is a registered trademark of Oxford University Press

Library of Congress Cataloging-in-Publication Data
Young, George M.
The Russian cosmists : the esoteric futurism of Nikolai Fedorov and his followers / George M. Young.
p.   cm.
Includes bibliographical references and index.
ISBN 978-0-19-989294-5 (hardcover : alkaline paper) — ISBN 978-0-19-989295-2 (ebook)
1. Philosophy, Russian—History. 2. Cosmology—Philosophy. 3. Fedorov, Nikolai Fedorovich, 1828–1903.
4. Philosophers—Russia. 5. Philosophers—Soviet Union. I. Title.
B4235.C6Y68   2012
197—dc23       2011041924

1  3  5  7  9  8  6  4  2
Printed in the United States of America
on acid-free paper

# Contents

# *Preface*

THIS STUDY BEGAN some years ago, in 1964, in a Yale graduate school seminar on Dostoevsky taught by Robert Louis Jackson. As I recall, ten or twelve of us were in the seminar, and early in the term Professor Jackson gave us a list of some ten or twelve topics for weekly reports. We chose by our order in the class roll, and I watched in dismay as one after another all the best "Dostoevsky-and" topics were chosen: Bakhtin, Vyacheslav Ivanov, the Elder Amvrosy, Dickens, Pushkin, Images of Childhood, the Ideal of Beauty. When the choice reached me, as last in the alphabet, two topics were left, neither of which I had ever heard of. So, having no idea what I was in for, I chose Nikolai Fedorov. The first information I found about him came from a footnote to Dolinin's edition of Dostoevsky's letters, and reading that footnote again and again I began to think to myself: this is a big idea! When the week for my report came, I gave it and have been thinking and writing about Fedorov and topics related to him since.

This study presents several corrections and a great many updates, and is an adventurous outgrowth of my 1979 book, *Nikolai Fedorov: An Introduction*. When I wrote that work, I was not a proponent of Fedorov's teachings but admired the strength and boldness of his philosophical imagination. Over the years, my attitude to Fedorov's ideas has not changed significantly, and in writing the present book I find that I view the thoughts of most of the other Cosmists much in the same way I view Fedorov's: hugely fascinating, inspiring, stimulating, but not ideas I would insist that friends and readers drop everything to live by. Mental health warning: fascinating as they are, at least to me, all the Cosmists were and are highly controversial—some would say even kooky—thinkers, recommended for mature audiences only.

In mechanical matters, the translations are mine unless otherwise noted. In the notes and bibliography I have used a standard system of transliteration, but in the body of the text I have used familiar English spellings rather than consistent transliterations for certain Russian words and names. In quoting other commentary in English, I have used that author's spelling of Russian names instead of changing them to be consistent with my spellings.

Over the years, many people, some no longer alive, have supported and helped my writing in general and my work on Fedorov and the Cosmists in particular. I would like to express my gratitude to all of them, but will mention only a few teachers, colleagues, friends, and editors: Gale Carrithers, William Blackburn, Reynolds Price, Fred Chappell, Wallace Kaufman, Robert Louis Jackson, Victor Erlich, Richard Gustafson, Rene Wellek, Michael Holquist, John Dunlop, Gordon Livermore, George Zimmar, George L. Kline, William F. Buckley, Jeffrey Hart, Peter Jarotski, Walter Arndt, Robert Siegel, James Tatum, Charles Stinson, Anouar Majid, Matthew Anderson, Susan McHugh, Lee Irwin, Maria Carlson, Kristi Groberg, Bernice Rosenthal, Betty Bland, Richard Smoley, John Algeo, David London, Svetlana Semenova, Anastasia Gacheva, Valery Borisov, Julie Scott, Steven Armstrong, Cynthia Read, and Ben Sadock. I am grateful to the University of New England librarians for help in research, and to the Center for Global Humanities of the University of New England for generous financial assistance to complete research and writing. Most important of all to me over these many years has been the love and support of my wife Patricia, son Roy, daughter Susannah, and son-in-law Patrick. Always in my mind, I wish to dedicate this book to the memory of my parents, George and Mary Ella Young, and my sister Patricia Pryor.

*The Russian Cosmists*

# I

## The Spiritual Geography of Russian Cosmism

*There is that in the Russian soul which corresponds to the immensity, the vagueness, the infinitude of the Russian land, spiritual geography corresponds with physical. . . . Two contradictory principles lay at the foundation of the structure of the Russian soul, the one a natural, Dionysian, elemental paganism and the other ascetic monastic Orthodoxy. The mutually contradictory properties of the Russian people may be set out thus: despotism, the hypertrophy of the State, and on the other hand anarchism and licence: cruelty, a disposition to violence, and again kindliness, humanity and gentleness: a belief in rites and ceremonies, but also a quest for truth: individualism, a heightened consciousness of personality, together with an impersonal collectivism: nationalism, laudation of self, and universalism, the ideal of the universal man: an eschatological messianic spirit of religion, and a devotion which finds its expression in externals: a search for God, and a militant godlessness: humility and arrogance: slavery and revolt. But never has Russia been bourgeois.*
—NIKOLAI BERDYAEV, *The Russian Idea*

SINCE THE COLLAPSE of the Soviet Union in 1991, Russian intellectuals have directed much of what Berdyaev describes as their traditional prodigious, contradictory, but creative mental energy toward bringing back into focus—and finding new signs of vitality in—writers, artists, thinkers, and intellectual currents suppressed, degraded, or merely ignored during the Soviet period. One of the most vigorous and productive of these rediscovered intellectual tendencies is Russian Cosmism, a highly controversial and oxymoronic blend of activist speculation, futuristic traditionalism, religious science, exoteric esotericism, utopian pragmatism, idealistic materialism—higher magic partnered to higher mathematics.

## General Characteristics

Main themes in Cosmist thought include the active human role in human and cosmic evolution; the creation of new life forms, including a new level of humanity; the unlimited extension of human longevity to a state of practical immortality; the physical resurrection of the dead; serious scientific research into matters long considered subjects fit only for science fiction, occult, and esoteric literature; the exploration and colonization of the entire cosmos; the emergence on our biosphere of a new sphere of human thought called the "noosphere"; and other far-reaching "projects," some of which may no longer seem as impossible or crazy as they did when first proposed in the late nineteenth and early twentieth centuries.

Sufficiently contradictory and compelling to serve as a living example of Berdyaev's definition of the "Russian soul," Cosmism has today entered the curriculum of Russian schools and universities, is discussed and debated in large crowded halls at frequent academic conferences around the country, and is the subject of a multiplying number of academic articles, dissertations, and scholarly books, presented in both print and electronic media. Once dismissed and derided, Cosmist ideas are now regarded as a main tendency in Russian culture and thought.

Several factors contribute to the high degree of interest in Cosmism among today's Russian intellectuals.[1] First, the Cosmists, like many Russians, are expansive thinkers: their worldview attempts to comprehend all humanity, all time, all space, all science, art, and religion. Moreover, this view is totalitarian in the sense that it must apply to all, without exception. As Berdyaev has suggested, half solutions do not satisfy the "Russian soul." And as we shall see, the Cosmists do not favor half solutions.

Second, the Cosmists emphasize their Russianness: the adjective they frequently use in referring to both early and recent Cosmist thought is *otechestvennyi*, "native"—"patriotic" without the Latinate flavor it carries in English, "fatherlandish," without Teutonic connotations. *Otechestvennyi* is the word used in referring to World War II as the Great Patriotic War and, when applied to Cosmist thought, can suggest that even the most unorthodox speculations are grounded in the rich, damp Russian soil. The Cosmist thinkers would probably be placed outside or on the periphery of the modern Western philosophical tradition with its rationalist or empiricist principles, its narrowing into specialized interests, and its emphasis on epistemology, whereas in the Russian god-seeking but human-centered philosophical tradition, emphasizing the existential, the historiosophic, and the eschatological, the Cosmists are well within the mainstream.

Third, and connected to the previous point, the Cosmists are at least slightly—some of them even more than slightly—anti-Western, and in Russia, today as yesterday, this resonates. To the Cosmists, the intellectual culture of the West is isolative, individualistic, arrogant, divisive, uncentered, and self-destructive. Cosmism is presented as a robust native alternative to the fashionable but shallow and overrated Western intellectual currents of deconstruction, ecosophism, species egalitarianism, and other alien abominations. To its adherents, Cosmism is a continental, Eurasian antidote to the growing threat of cultural and intellectual Atlanticism.

Fourth, the Cosmists were banned during the Soviet period. Their works could not be published, and the thinkers themselves were either forced into emigration or sent to the gulag, where many were executed and others died from disease, starvation, or hard labor. After the fall of Communism, the writings that had been most strenuously prohibited understandably became the most immediately appealing. Locked trunks and secret drawers began to open: manuscripts hidden or ignored for thirty, forty, even a hundred years reemerged, fresh and new. This rediscovery of such a rich hidden past has become a major part of the Russian vision of the distant future, so that thinkers who appeared out of step with their own time are now considered all the more in step with ours and with times that will come after ours.

Fifth, many of the Cosmists were polymaths, not only interested in but highly competent in two, three, or half a dozen specialized disciplines. As philosophers, artists, natural scientists, theologians, and social activists, individually and collectively, they tended to be encyclopedic in their erudition, jacks of all intellectual trades and masters of most. Each was so highly respected in at least one recognizable field that his Cosmist speculations—even if unorthodox—borrowed at least the possibility of legitimacy.

Sixth, like much Russian religious and spiritual writing, Cosmism has a profoundly mystical, occult, esoteric dimension. As George Vernadsky documents, in *The Origins of Russia*, the practice of magic and exercise of shamanistic supernatural powers dominate the earliest records of Russian spiritual life,[2] a tendency that continues to our day. A study of Russian publications in the 1990s found that some 39 percent of all nonfiction books published in Russia in that decade had something to do with the occult.[3] And a trip through any large bookstore in Russia today would probably produce a similar, if not even larger unofficial tally. The air of intellectual legitimacy that Cosmism lends to certain occult, or semi-occult speculations accounts for some of the appeal of the movement today. Cosmism provides a forum for serious modern academic or intellectual consideration of topics normally associated with occult or prescientific investigation. As we shall see further along in this study, Cosmism does meet the four necessary and two optional criteria suggested in Antoine Faivre's definition of esotericism,[4] but if a narrower and more specific label is necessary, one I would propose, if it were not such a mouthful, would be "exoteric thaumaturgy"—wonderworking conducted in an open, intellectually respectable form.

Seventh, the Cosmists offer far-sighted and carefully considered answers to the most frequently asked question in Russian intellectual history, *Chto delat'?*—"What Is To Be Done?" The answer to this perennial Russian question is inevitably a "plan," and the plan offered by the Cosmists is, if no more workable or realizable, at least bolder and more comprehensive than those offered by most other thinkers at most other times in Russian history.

Eighth, even in the face of formidable challenges, and in no way turning aside from the problems to be faced, the Cosmists offer a positive, hopeful outlook. Despite the odds, they remain optimistic and do not succumb to what they see as today's Western doom and gloom. They convey the traditional Russian sense that no matter how bad a situation may look at the moment, no matter how great a threat that any Batu Khan, Napoleon, Hitler, or other human or nonhuman forces may present, history has repeatedly shown that Russia—and under its leadership humanity—will eventually prevail.

But if Cosmism is viewed by its prominent adherents as *the* most Russian and therefore most significant current of thought running from the nineteenth through the twenty-first century, outside Russia the movement and the figures associated with it are all but unknown. The Western transhumanists, the cryonicists, the immortalists, and certain new age spiritual movements share some Cosmist ideas and practices and present the closest foreign analog, but by and large, futuristic Russian and Western thinkers remain separated by a curtain perhaps no longer made of iron but of language, culture, and other materials invisible, intangible, but very durable.

As mentioned above, and elsewhere frequently noted, Russia has long been fertile ground for esotericism. Major individual figures in earlier Russian esotericism, such as the eighteenth-century Rosicrucians Nikolai Novikov and Iohann Schwartz, are still little known outside Russia. But in more recent times, since the late nineteenth century, some of the best known figures in the history of Western esotericism have spent their early years—and some more than their early years—in Russia. H. P. Blavatsky, George Gurdjieff, P. D. Ouspensky, Nicholas and Helena Roerich, Rasputin, and more recently Vissarion of the "Last Testament" and Anastasia of the "Ringing Cedars" are names that immediately come to mind.

But at the same time that these names were becoming so familiar in and beyond esoteric circles worldwide, the all but unnoticed Cosmists were devoting serious philosophical, theological, and scientific attention to matters usually considered topics for esoteric speculation, such as self-directed evolution toward higher levels of humanity; human attainment of virtual omniscience, omnipotence, and immortality; the restoration of life to the dead; the influence of astral forces on human affairs; the human attainment of superhuman powers; the radical alteration and spiritualization of the material world. The major figures usually listed as Cosmists include many names little known in the West: the eccentric librarian and religious thinker Nikolai Fedorov; the mystical poet and idealist philosopher Vladimir Solovyov; the legendary physicist and lecturer Nikolai Umov; the rocket pioneer and theosophical writer Konstantin Tsiolkovsky; the geochemist Vladimir Vernadsky; the religious philosophers Sergei Bulgakov, Nikolai Berdyaev, and Pavel Florensky; the diplomat and Soviet government official Valerian Muravyov; the Fedorovian activists Alexander Gorsky and Nikolai Setnitsky; the Soviet scientists Alexander Chizhevsky, Nikolai Kholodny, Vasily Kuprevich, and Aleksei Maneev. Individually, these thinkers have not considered themselves part of an intellectual school of any kind, especially an esoteric school, but regarded together, their contributions to separate fields of study exhibit many points in common with each other as well as with the works of such earlier figures in the Western esoteric tradition as Marsilio Ficino, Pico della Mirandola, Cornelius Agrippa, Giordano Bruno, and Francis Bacon. As Frances Yates noted in *The Rosicrucian Enlightenment*, nowhere in *The New Atlantis* does Bacon mention the Rose and Cross, but the entire work is full of Rosicrucian ideas.[5] So it is with the Russian Cosmists: seldom do any of them acknowledge occult sources or inclinations, but their works are replete with theosophical and esoteric ideas couched in the rhetoric of mainstream intellectual discourse. Indeed, their major contribution to the Western tradition of esotericism may in fact lie in their transformation of esoteric into exoteric investigations, the renewal of legitimate research into topics academically discredited or avoided since the seventeenth-century dawn of the Age of Reason.

## Recent Definitions of Cosmism

Early references to Russian Cosmism as a school of thought came in the first decades of the twentieth century,[6] but the first retrospective scholarly attempts to define who the Cosmists were and what distinguished the Cosmist from other schools of thought came in the late 1980s and early 1990s, when ideas, texts, and materials suppressed through the Soviet period began to reappear. Svetlana Semenova, today's leading proponent and authority on the movement, has found the "defining genetic mark" of Cosmist thought to be "active evolution." In her introduction to a valuable anthology of Cosmist thought published in 1993, she wrote:

> To avoid an unwieldy and limitless extension of this philosophical current is possible, if, from the start, we designate a principally new kind of relationship to the world, displaying a defining genetic mark. This is the idea of *active evolution*, i.e., the necessity for a new conscious stage of development of the world, when humanity directs it on a course which reason and moral feeling determine, when man takes, so to say, the wheel of evolution into his own hands. . . . Man, for actively evolutionary thinkers, is a being in transition, in the process of growing, far from complete, but also consciously creative, called upon to overcome not only the outer world but also his own inner nature.[7]

Thus, in Semenova's definition, Cosmism not only shifts our perspective from an earth-centered to a cosmos-centered view, not only shifts our self-image from earth dweller to cosmic citizen, but emphasizes that present humanity is not the end point of evolution, that in addition to its long past the evolutionary process also has a long future, and that humanity is now in a position to direct and shape its own future evolution.

In an article from a collection devoted to the broad topic of Russia and the occult, a leading Western scholar of Russian intellectual history, Michael Hagemeister, adds more "genetic marks" to the definition:

> "Russian cosmism" and "Russian cosmist thinking" are terms indicative of a broad intellectual movement in contemporary Russia which has scarcely been noticed in the West. . . . Stated briefly, Russian cosmism is based on a holistic and anthropocentric view of the universe which presupposes a teleologically determined—and thus meaningful—evolution; its adherents strive to redefine the role of humankind in a universe that lacks a divine plan for salvation, thus acknowledging the threat of self-destruction. As rational beings who are evolving out of the living matter . . . of the earth, human beings appear destined to become a decisive factor in cosmic evolution—a collective, cosmic self-consciousness, active agent,

and potential perfector. Cosmic evolution is thus dependent on human action to reach its goal, which is perfection or wholeness. By failing to act, or failing to act correctly, humankind dooms the world to catastrophe. According to cosmism, the world is in a phase of transition from the "biosphere" (the sphere of living matter) to the "noosphere" (the sphere of reason). During this phase the active unification and organization of the whole of humankind . . . into a single organism is said to result in a higher "planetarian consciousness" capable of guiding further development reasonably and ethically . . . changing and perfecting the universe, overcoming disease and death, and finally bringing forth an immortal human race.[8]

Active or self-directed evolution, then—holistic, anthropocentric, and teleologically determined effort—are some of the terms that scholars have applied to all the Russian Cosmist thinkers, whether the given Cosmist is a poet, an artist, a theologian, a philosopher, or a natural scientist. To these marks, I would add a few more general characteristics. One is the previously mentioned tendency, which will be a primary focus of the present study, to transform esoteric knowledge into exoteric, to turn elements of traditional occult wisdom into new directions in philosophy, theology, literature, art, and science, a tendency that has allowed some critics of Cosmism to dismiss it as mere pseudoscience, pseudotheology, and pseudophilosophy. But as we shall see a bit further along, the lines between intellectual categories are perhaps more often blurred in the Russian tradition than in Western European traditions of speculation. A better way to describe Russian Cosmism than to call it pseudo this or pseudo that might be to regard it as occupying a unique borderland, a crossover area between science and magic: a back-and-forth process in which thaumaturgy finds academic legitimacy, and academic knowledge becomes thaumaturgical.

As also mentioned above, and as many commentaries, including my own,[9] have often observed, the Cosmists also characteristically display an emphasis on the "Russianness" of their projects, a suggestion—sometimes even an insistence—that being Russian has something to do with the cosmic scope of their creative thought, that a Slavic instinct for expansiveness, wholeness, unity, and total solutions underlies the global, and beyond-global character of their investigations and projects. In several of the Cosmists, we see a neo-Slavophile, neo-Eurasian, or even a Russian nationalist tendency that does not necessarily contradict or interfere with the international, interplanetary, intergalactic scope of their vision. Borrowing Peter Chaadaev's memorable phrase, "with one elbow resting on Germany and the other on China," Russia, according to Cosmist (following the Slavophile) thinking, is in a position to offer a broader outlook, a healthy middle way between the extremes of East and West, and a fresh synthesis of the best features from many traditions.

In the passage from *The Russian Idea*, quoted at the head of this chapter, Nikolai Berdyaev writes of the immensity, the vagueness, the infinitude of the Russian land, the spiritual geography which corresponds with the physical. And many others, besides Berdyaev, have noted the expansive and seemingly bipolar character of Russian literature and thought, the tendency, most evident in a writer like Dostoevsky, to push to the extremes psychological and spiritual characteristics which are present but less sharply pronounced in other traditions of literature and thought. To many of today's Russian students of Cosmism, the Cosmist approach to world problems—seeking unity, wholeness, and universality by facing and attempting to overcome a multitude of apparent contradictions—represents Berdyaev's characterization of the "Russian soul" at its best, in action. Most of the Russian Cosmists were encyclopedic geniuses who were able to work at the highest level in apparently mutually contradictory intellectual directions. Fedorov, for example, was simultaneously a futuristic visionary of unsurpassed boldness and an archconservative spokesman for ideas usually branded reactionary, a man with a twenty-first-century mind and a medieval heart. Solovyov, the great philosopher who inspired Russia's "Silver Age" of literature and art (successor to the earlier nineteenth-century "Golden Age" of Pushkin and Gogol), was a model of rational clarity, a master of lucid prose, and at the same time a mystic poet of foggy lake crossings, sophiological raptures, and ardent longing for otherworldly caresses. Tsiolkovsky was a raw youth from the Russian countryside who, under Fedorov's personal direction, began a course of self-education that eventually allowed him to calculate the first mathematical formulas for orbiting artificial satellites, becoming the honored grandfather of Soviet rocket science and space exploration, and at the same time he was the author of innumerable booklets and brochures of what to many readers may seem sophomoric occult fantasies and science fiction tales. Vernadsky, an internationally honored scientist, took his original inspiration from the study of ancient Greek history and literature, was then trained in mineralogy, made significant contributions to several additional highly specialized fields of science, founded such new cross-disciplinary fields of investigation as geochemistry, biogeochemistry, and radiogeology, and, most important for the purposes of our study, developed the theory of the biosphere in transition to noosphere. And Florensky, sometimes called the "Russian Leonardo," was a groundbreaking mathematician, inventor, aesthetician, electrical engineer, philosopher, social worker, priest, theologian, gulag prisoner, and martyr, best known today as author of *The Pillar and Ground of the Truth*, a classic of Russian spirituality. This breadth not only of interest, then, but of competence as well is one of the more important "genetic marks" of the Russian Cosmists, and is a reflection of the expansiveness and ability to contain apparent contradictions that Berdyaev includes in his definition of "Russianness."

What, then, in the last analysis, makes a Cosmist a Cosmist? After all, nearly all Christians believe in transformation of the world; Marxists and Romantics of all kinds believe in thought as action; Utopians believe in ideal worlds. In a nutshell, what is different about the Cosmists?

Cosmism is a loose, diverse, and complex tendency, so rather than attempt another simple one- or two-sentence answer, I would prefer to look more closely, first, at the Russian context out of which Cosmist thought emerged, then at the major individual Cosmist thinkers one by one, then at what further tendencies and consequences developed from their lines of thought, and gradually, by the end of this study, we will have gained a clearer sense of what makes a Cosmist a Cosmist, what positions the individual thinkers in the tendency share and on what positions they differ, and what followed or failed to follow the ideas they proposed.

## 2

# Forerunners of Russian Cosmism

THE SEMINAL THINKER, whom Berdyaev considered "the most Russian" of Russian thinkers, and from whom the Cosmist movement took its major themes and directions, was Nikolai Fedorovich Fedorov (1829–1903, pronounced and sometimes transliterated "Fyodorov"), an eccentric, abstemious nineteenth-century Moscow librarian who published only a few anonymous newspaper pieces in his lifetime, but whose writings, posthumously edited and published by disciples, have been derided as crazed fantasies by some and hailed by others as—literally—the philosophical equivalent of the second coming of Christ. Since we shall shortly devote separate chapters of this study to Fedorov's life and thought, we shall not discuss details of his "project" here, but in order to gain a fuller sense of what we do and do not term "Cosmist," we shall turn instead to brief sketches of a few other Russian thinkers who explored the territory between science and magic before and during the time of Fedorov.

## Vasily Nazarovich Karazin (1773–1842)

One of the major divisions in humanity that Fedorov wished to heal—even wider and more destructive, he believed, than the division between rich and poor—was the division between the learned elite, who had the knowledge but not the will to act, and the unlearned masses, who had the will to act but not the knowledge. Nevertheless, several times in his writings, he presents, as a model for the rare person with both the knowledge and will to act, Vasily Karazin, a Russian-Ukrainian intellectual prodigy, who published important works on agriculture, pharmacology, chemistry, meteorology, and physics, and in 1802, at the age of twenty-nine, founded the University of Kharkov. Of him, Fedorov wrote: "We shall speak of Karazin, that many-sided man, as a meteor-*urgist*, not as a meteor-*ologist*. The difference between meteorology and meteorurgy might be defined as follows: the former has as its *ultimate goal the forecasting of famine*, whereas the latter has the goal—and in that an *initial* goal only—of *salvation from famine*." Evidently fearing that his words could be mistaken for an endorsement of an esotericism which he either did not recognize or to which he could not admit his intellectual debt, Fedorov immediately assures us that his use of the suffix -*urgy* is entirely benign. "Unfortunately, the word *urgy* has been degraded by mystics and has acquired from them a connotation of *wizardry*, secret, irrational activity, influence of a blind force of the soul, and not an open, transparent, joint activity of reason upon the blind forces of nature."[1] The specific "activity of reason" for which Fedorov praised Karazin was his establishment in 1810 of the first weather station in Ukraine, and in 1814, while experimenting with the use of weather balloons to conduct electrical currents as part of a procedure in the production of saltpeter, he wrote to Alexander I's advisor Arakcheev outlining the enormous potential of electrical power for both military and peaceful purposes. Fedorov quotes from Karazin's letter:

> If the experiment, as I hope, definitely confirms my hypothesis about bringing electricity down from the upper levels of the atmosphere, then man will obtain a *new* implement which he has not previously possessed. Water, air, fire, animal power, gravity, and the expansion of certain bodies are until now the forces by the control of which we operate machines. Consider, Your Excellency, what new results will follow, if we control the mass of electrical power extending through the atmosphere, if we will be in a position to distribute it according to our will . . . and man attains the ability to manage atmospheric conditions, to make it rain or shine as he wishes.[2]

According to Fedorov, Karazin was the first in Russia to call for systematic, rational, human "management" of nature. The complete proposal that Karazin eventually put before the tsar was for experimentation on a large scale, involving not only balloons but great explosive projectiles, with the ultimate goal of maximum human control over all meteorological phenomena. Although the emphasis in all his "meteorurgical" proposals was on the potential benefit to humanity, implicit was the potential for military use and the warning that if the Russians did not develop this technology now, some enemy would surely do so in the future. Karazin's proposal was referred to, and eventually rejected by, a commission headed by the academician Nikolai Fuss, a mathematician and designer of scientific instruments who, perhaps not coincidentally, also advised the editorial rejection of the first book written by the future non-euclidian geometer Nikolai Lobachevsky, later generally recognized as the foremost mathematician in Russian history.[3] The Fuss commission found that

while the potential benefit of electrical power was well known, Karazin's proposals were based on unproven hypotheses and impractical procedures and
therefore should not be awarded the relatively modest amount of financial
support requested. Fedorov's complaint is that minds like Fuss's dominate the
world of "the learned," in the world "as it is," but that truly learned men like
Karazin, who propose projects to benefit the unlearned, represent hope for
the world "as it ought to be." Karazin, then, represents one important feature
of Cosmist thought—the insistence that present sciences of observation and
discovery become sciences of action, transformation, and creation, that every
discipline now as "-ology" become an "-urgy."

## Alexander Nikolaevich Radishchev (1749–1802)

Karazin, so far as we know, said nothing about active evolution. But another
forerunner of the Cosmist movement did. Alexander Radishchev was hailed
from the middle of the nineteenth century through the Soviet period primarily
for his role as a radical social critic and political thinker; he was arrested, tor-
tured, and exiled under Catherine the Great for having depicted the brutish
conditions under which most Russians lived in his 1790 classic *Journey from St.
Petersburg to Moscow*. But in addition to presenting indisputable evidence of the
drastic need for social change, Radishchev, in a 1792 work, *On Man, His Mortality and Immortality*, presents a literary preview of the idea that man is an
unfinished, evolving creature. While arguing his major point, that man is
endowed with an immortal soul that lives beyond the death and disintegration
of the mortal body, he writes: "But can man really be the crown of creation?
Can these wondrous, splendid, gradual increments, having led up to him, break
off, cease, and come to nothing? Impossible!"[4] Radishchev further explores various hypotheses of what happens to us after the death of the body, but he does
not offer detailed suggestions concerning what might lie beyond our current
stage of evolution. So while Karazin offers, at least in Fedorov's representation
of him, a pre-Cosmist example of *-ology* becoming *-urgy*, Radishchev offers a
flash preview of the idea that humanity is in an ongoing process of evolution.

## Two Poets: Mikhail Vasilyevich Lomonosov (1711–1765) and
## Gavrila Romanovich Derzhavin (1743–1816)

Two other important eighteenth-century figures of genius, Mikhail Lomonosov, a poet and pioneer in many scientific fields who, in Pushkin's apt phrase,
not only founded but "*was himself* our first university," and Gavrila Derzhavin,

ranked by the dean of Russian literary historians, Prince D. S. Mirsky, as one of the supreme poets in the language, also prefigured some Cosmist tendencies, but did not develop them fully. In his astronomical poems "Evening Meditation on the Divine Majesty on the Occasion of the Great Northern Lights" and "Morning Meditation on the Greatness of God,"[5] Lomonosov uses sonorous, majestic, skillfully rhymed verse to present accurate, original scientific observations about the northern lights and firestorms on the sun. The son of a peasant fisherman from the far north, Lomonosov was a passionate, prodigious early learner who ran away from home as a teenager to study in Moscow and, taking up one subject after another, mastered everything he put his mind to. As a many-sided genius from a humble village who wrote advanced science in verse and who directed his reader's attention to the wonders of the cosmos, Lomonosov certainly shared personal biographical traits and intellectual inclinations with the later Cosmists, but his spiritual outlook was more deistic than thaumaturgical, more contemplative than active, and his unification of art and science was closer to that of a poetic astronomer than of a visionary astrurgist. In his poems, the wonders of the universe are already wonderful enough—we don't need to improve on them, as Fedorov and some of the later Cosmists will suggest we should.

Similarly, Derzhavin is more a great man of his age, comfortable with himself and his time, resigned to his own mortality, rather than a restless visionary whose ideas and hopes must wait for future ages. His poem "God" is a majestic celebration of the deistic universe, and of the inner spark of the divine that joins each person to the absolute, the part to the whole. Especially famous are the lines:

> I am the link to worlds existing everywhere,
> I am the very last stage of matter,
> I am the focal point of everything living,
> And the starting point of the divine;
> Though into dust my body will disintegrate,
> My mind will command the thunder:
> I am tsar—I am slave—I am worm—I am God!

Throughout the rest of the poem, however, and in the worldview expressed in Derzhavin's other philosophical poems, the emphasis is always on almighty God's power at work through our feeble, transitory frames, rather than a Cosmist emphasis on the new, creative, godlike people we can become and the new universe we can create with our godlike powers.

## Prince Vladimir Fedorovich Odoevsky (1803–1869)

A writer, philosopher, musicologist, and philanthropist who is closer to Fedorov and the Cosmists in time and spirit is Prince Vladimir Odoevsky.[6] For some years he was, with Pushkin, coeditor of *The Contemporary*, the leading "thick journal" of the early nineteenth century, and was the host and driving force behind the Lovers of Wisdom, a semisecret society of prominent young thinkers and men of letters, including both future Slavophiles and Westernizers, who gathered regularly until the 1825 Decembrist uprising and resulting crackdown, to discuss the works of Schelling, Boehme, Tieck, Goethe, Byron, and other Western writers of idealist, romantic, or mystical orientation. In his later years he directed major libraries, first in St. Petersburg, and then in Moscow at the Rumiantsev Museum, where Fedorov would work in the last decades of the century. Odoevsky's own stories and novellas earned him the nickname "the Russian Hoffmann" for their esoteric and macabre subjects. But his major literary work, and the one that establishes him as a forerunner of the Cosmists, is an unfinished epistolary novel, a remarkable futuristic fantasy, *The Year 4338*. The world, by that year, is divided between the two great powers, Russia and China. Bankrupt Britain has sold itself at auction; America is little more than a shell for individual speculators and isolated exploitive capitalists; and the rest of the world belongs to one or the other of the two great powers. Pneumatic air travel, sky hotels, controlled weather, electric illumination for homes and covered gardens, magnetic baths that induce candid confessions and repel hostile vibrations, magnetic communication devices, plastics, even something like blogs are all common in Russia, the center of world culture and advanced technology in 4338. Due to a natural law of accelerated time sense, the citizens of that world know less about ours, 2,500 years before them, than we know about the ancient civilizations 2,500 years before ours. Almost nothing from our time has survived into theirs. The few negative relics of our basic human nature that remain include insecurity, vanity, flirtation, and procrastination. More serious flaws, such as selfishness, poverty, ignorance, competition, war, and tragedy are all things of the past. Life is comfortable, interesting, cooperative, and good—better in Russia than in China or anywhere else. The only problem is that within a year a giant comet is expected to destroy the planet. The letters describing Russian life during the year before the comet is predicted to strike are written by a visiting student from China to a fellow student back home in Beijing. In a further narrative framing device, a Russian man in the year 1839 has perfected self-mesmerism to the degree that he can choose to project his consciousness to enter any mind at any point in time, past or present. Russian astronomers of 1839 have predicted the great comet collision of 4339, so out of curiosity to learn just how far humankind will have advanced before the world ends, our self-mesmerizing Russian time traveler projects his consciousness into the mind of the visiting Chinese student. Odoevsky's projected novel is, in part, a futuristic variation on the "last days" theme made internationally popular at the time by Karl Briullov's celebrated 1830–1834 painting, *The Last Days of Pompeii*, and by the esotericist Lord Edward Bulwer-Lytton's enormously popular novel of the same title published in 1834. Odoevsky died before he could finish his work, so we do not know whether he intended to have the world be destroyed by the comet or saved by science. The visiting Chinese student reports that the leading Russian scientists are confident that new technological devices they are developing will save the planet, but ordinary citizens fear that the world is doomed. Literary historian Victor Terras suggests that Odoevsky implies that the world will be destroyed because the Russians of 4338 have forgotten God and have put all their faith in science.[7] This would put Odoevsky in the Slavophile camp in the long debate over whether Russia's future should follow the path of Orthodox spirituality or Western science. Svetlana Semenova, however, suggests that *The Year 4338* is more utopian than dystopian, and the visiting student's raptures over the wonders of advanced technology outweigh the anxieties of the ordinary citizens. She also points out, however, that in another work, "The Final Suicide," Odoevsky does clearly warn that technology alone, unguided by religion, can only lead us to self-destruction. The solution, which Odoevsky proposes in his essay "Russian Nights, or The Need for a New Science and New Art," lies in a new, comprehensive worldview that combines science, art, and religious faith—a position that Fedorov and the Cosmists will build on.[8]

## *Aleksander Vasilyevich Sukhovo-Kobylin (1817–1903)*

Another precursor of Cosmism is the acerbic dramatist and almost misanthropic playwright and thinker Aleksander Sukhovo-Kobylin.[9] A fabulously wealthy aristocrat who was accused and arrested, but later acquitted, of the murder of his French mistress, Sukhovo-Kobylin was at the center of a notorious, protracted, scandalizing court case that embittered him for life but inspired the dramas that constitute his literary legacy: *Krechinsky's Wedding*, *The Case*, and *The Death of Tarelkin*, a savage comic trilogy that still plays to appreciative audiences in Russia. It was his enormous wealth, Sukhovo-Kobylin argued, that drew the false accusations against him, and only the bribes that his wealth enabled him to pay secured his acquittal. His dramatic trilogy vigorously satirizes the greed, corruption, and bureaucratic stupidity that have long plagued Russia, among other places. After his ordeal, he withdrew entirely from his previously active role in Russian high society, and devoted himself to translating and explicating Hegel, advocating vegetarianism and the abstemious life, and, in the surviving fragments of an original philosophical manuscript destroyed by fire, he developed his own eccentric but visionary version of spiritual Darwinism. The negative side of his thought focuses on the "law of selection," which he interprets as God's wise and unflinching wrathful judgment, allowing the strong and rational to flourish, and the weak and foolish to destroy themselves. "It is obvious," he writes, "that by means of this wrathful judgment of divine wisdom, mankind advances in its progress, i.e., approaches the eternal idea of rationality, in that the weak perish and disappear *by the fire of selection*, while the strong develop, thrive, and advance."[10]

On the positive side of his thought, more consonant with later Cosmism, Sukhovo-Kobylin posits three stages in the development of humanity: telluric, or earthbound man, confined to the planet we inhabit; solar man, inhabiting our solar system; and sidereal man, inhabiting all worlds throughout the entire universe. Only the third, sidereal stage of humanity brings the absolute freedom that is the goal and perfection of all human movement and development. Human evolution operates between two extremes: from the lowest, herdlike, bestial state to the human angels fit to inhabit the infinite City of God: "From the horde or the 'mob of savages,' from the human herd, begins that sociological series of steps, i.e., the advance of human society, that advance which is the process of the spiritualization of mankind, and only in infinity does that spiritualization reach its conclusion in the supreme reality of divine reason, i.e., in the Kingdom of God, the *Civitas Dei*."[11]

Important steps in the process of turning ourselves from human animals into human angels include becoming vegetarians, developing lighter and smaller rather than more massive bodies, and gradually acquiring the ability to fly. And flight for Sukhovo-Kobylin does not mean merely the invention of flying machines but the growth of wings and attainment of the birdlike, insectlike skill of aerial self-propulsion. He writes: "The entire theory of humanity and its infinite development, i.e., the philosophy of the history of mankind, is the process of its freedom from spatial constraint, in other words, its passing into spirit; the result of spiritualization (or subjectivization) is perfection, pointedness [*tochechnost'*]. The history of spiritualization is the history of self-propulsion, the autokinesis of mankind."[12] The steam locomotive and the bicycle were, in his time, the most advanced mechanical expressions of the human wish to fly. The bicycle, especially, represented "horizontal flight."

> But all these contemporary devices are nothing other than steps taken by humanity along the path of its subjectivization, or spiritualization. A person flying horizontally on a bicycle—this is already motion toward the form of the angel, the highest human. Through the invention of these machines of horizontal flight, mankind moves closer to an angelic state, or toward *ideal humanity*. Every thinking human being can understand that the bicycle represents precisely those mechanical wings, the starting point or kernel of the future *organic* wings, by means of which humanity will undoubtedly break the fetters confining it to the telluric world, and humanity will escape by means of mechanical inventions into the solar world around it.[13]

Humanity in its present telluric stage is too much a captive of gravity and the senses. To develop the ability to fly, we need to develop more lung capacity, to reconfigure our body's ratio of air to solid mass.

> If God is spirit, and spirit is spaceless, then man, approaching God, *should consume his spaciousness*, i.e., *reduce his body*, and by this reduction of the body become more and more spiritual, i.e., free himself from the burden and fetters of space. We see this in the animal world in the form of flying insects, who, owing precisely to their reduced size, i.e., their proximity to spirit, are wonderfully mobile. A fly in one second flies over approximately one hundred times its own length. If a man could attain that same degree of physical freedom which a fly has attained, he could move with great speed *one hundred times his length*, race almost two hundred meters in one second, i.e., move through space with the velocity of a cannon ball.[14]

To approach a state of absolute freedom, perfection, or divinity, then, mankind must reduce the size and weight of the human body, and negate space and extension. "Extension constitutes the spatial fetters of man's spirit, which from birth set the boundaries of his movements—i.e., initially in the savage state keep him tied to the place he inhabits."[15]

Given the many millions of stars that recently had become visible through telescopes at this time, and given the astronomical evidence that the laws and natural processes apparent on earth are also apparent elsewhere in the universe, Sukhovo-Kobylin, writing at a time when the universe still seemed a single, unified field, reasons that our planet cannot be the only one that is habitable or inhabited: "In one word, if a sphere or planet, whose chemical composition of matter is identical with the composition of other planets, finds itself under the same forces, then their [the planets'] processes will also be identical, and their origins and development will be the same. In a word, reason is one and matter is one, and therefore their products will be identical."[16] But in order to inhabit the entire universe, we must evolve beyond our present, earthbound state. Sukhovo-Kobylin's unique contribution to pre-Cosmist thought is his idea that the further we evolve, the smaller our bodies should become, and that as we approach divinity we will also approach a vanishing point of spaceless invisibility. God is invisible, and we shall also become invisible, essentially bodiless, as we approach the goal of perfect, spiritualized, universal humanity.

These pre-Cosmist thinkers, then, project several of the lines that Fedorov, Solovyov, Bulgakov, Vernadsky, Tsiolkovsky and others will extend further. Radishchev's keen social concern and belief that evolution cannot have ended with man in his present state finds ultimate development in Cosmist projects to reconstitute and thus save all humanity. Odoevsky's futuristic vision of an advanced technological world culture led by Russia finds its extensions in the scientific Cosmist speculations about control over nature and the reshaping of the universe. Sukhovo-Kobylin's thoughts about the stages of human evolution and the changes needed in the human body and spirit point toward the Cosmist concepts of the noosphere and emergence of the godman.

How the Cosmist tendency relates not only to a few pre-Cosmist thinkers but to the entire tradition of Russian philosophical speculation is what we shall now consider.

# 3

## The Russian Philosophical Context

UNLIKE RUSSIAN LITERATURE, Russian music, or even Russian art, Russian philosophy is little known outside its homeland. This is not because Russians have neglected philosophical speculation but because they have gone about it in their own way, usually avoiding paths favored by followers of Descartes, Kant, and Mill.

### Philosophy as Passion

Since for most of the nineteenth century, the study of philosophy in Russian universities was either prohibited or, when permitted, allowed to range only from Plato to Aristotle, discussion of the "accursed questions" remained an extracurricular activity. Philosophy in Russia could not be a profession, so it had to be an irrepressible passion, something for small groups behind closed doors or, when conducted openly, done so in the form of letters, poems, stories, novels, and essays in literary criticism. The major contributions to Russian thought, then, as reflected in the standard anthologies, have been made not by trained academicians but by gifted amateurs: imaginative writers (Dostoevsky, Tolstoy), literary and social critics (Belinsky, Chernyshevsky, Pisarev, Dobroliubov), wealthy landowners (Kireevsky, Samarin), former horse guardsmen (Khomiakov), certified madmen (Chaadaev), spiritual pilgrims (Skovoroda), expelled teachers (Solovyov), and frocked and unfrocked priests (Bulgakov, Florensky, Berdyaev). Moreover, not only in the nineteenth century but throughout the history of Russian thought, even into the present century, the line between literature and philosophy has never been as sharply drawn as in other traditions. Philosophical *belles lettres* and belletristic philosophy in Russia have more often been the rule than the exception. From Pushkin, Baratynsky, Gogol, Tiutchev, Dostoevsky, and Tolstoy on through Blok, Biely, Ivanov, Pasternak, and Solzhenitsyn, writers whose talents are primarily literary have made contributions to Russian thought significant enough to justify innumerable studies titled: "So-and-so, Writer As Thinker." And from

Chaadaev, Kireevsky, Belinsky, Herzen, and Khomiakov through Solovyov, Leontiev, Shestov, and Rozanov, thinkers whose chief gift is for speculation have also demonstrated considerable literary talent. And even when the thinker has lacked genuine literary talent, as in the case of Chernyshevsky, that thinker has still often preferred the novel, poem, or play to the treatise as the vehicle for his or her ideas. And we recall that it was not any of Russia's academic philosophers but Dostoevsky from whom Nietzsche said he could learn something. Thus, whereas in the Western intellectual tradition, of all Russia's best known thinkers perhaps only Solovyov and Berdyaev would be considered genuine philosophers, in Russia being a "lover of wisdom" is still often sufficient to qualify.

## The Destiny of Russia

As V. V. Zenkovsky, Berdyaev, and many others who have written on the intellectual history of Russia have observed, in the Russian tradition of speculation, epistemology and pure rationalism have not been preeminent. Instead, Russian philosophy has tended to be unacademic, existential, historiosophic, prophetic, reform minded, and man centered.[1] The major questions have been: What are the lessons of history? What is Russia's special role in the world? What is the nature and destiny of man? Who or what is to blame for man's fate? Which is more important, beauty or utility? And, as mentioned before, the most frequently asked question of all has been: *Chto delat'?*— What is to be done? Berdyaev could have been describing Russian thinkers in general when he wrote of himself: "Despite the established and venerable tradition of confining philosophy to logic and epistemology, I was never able to conform my mind to such a limitation or to see any possibility of true philosophical knowledge along these lines. On the contrary, knowledge appeared to me as creative understanding, involving a movement of the spirit, a direction of will, a sensitivity, a search for meaning, a being shaken, elated, disillusioned, and imbued with hope."[2]

The great century of Russia's "accursed questions" began with Pyotr Chaadaev (1794–1856), who asked, in his first "Philosophical Letter" of 1836, what Russia had ever contributed to world civilization, and feared that the answer was that Russia had contributed nothing of value and had presented only a negative example, a living demonstration of how a civilization ought not to evolve. For this, the journal that published the letter was shut down, the publisher was exiled to the farthest north, and Chaadaev was officially declared insane. Although further publication of Chaadaev's work was prohibited, his ideas were thoroughly discussed and debated in salons and intellectual circles in both Moscow and St. Petersburg. Out of these debates emerged the long running argument between the Slavophiles, such as Alexander Khomiakov, Ivan Kireevsky, and Yuri Samarin, who emphasized what Russia could teach the West, and the Westernizers, such as Vissarion Belinsky, Nikolai Ogarev, and Alexander Herzen, who emphasized what Russia should learn from the West. Fedorov and the Cosmists eventually offer a synthesis of Westernizer and Slavophile positions, welcoming Western scientific and technological advances, but turning them toward Slavophile goals of communal wholeness, unifying activity, and spiritual consensus—all contained in the well-known Slavophile concept of *sobornost'*. In his unfinished work *Apology of a Madman*, Chaadaev suggests that Russia does have an historic mission, but in order to fulfill that mission she must follow some inner path of development of her own instead of attempting to imitate and overtake the West. Fedorov and the later Cosmists believe that their projects, combining science and spirituality, represent precisely that inner, integrative path that Russia should follow in order to be true to her historic mission.

After Chaadaev in the 1830s and the original Slavophiles and Westernizers in the 1840s, the dominant intellectual forces to emerge were the neo-Westernist radical socialists and populists in the 1860s and 1870s, and the neo-Slavophile Pan-Slavists and revanchist Orthodox monarchists in the 1880s and 1890s. And, again, the Cosmists share goals with all these earlier groups and attempt to resolve the apparent contradictions. Fedorov, Solovyov, and Bulgakov, for example, all propose models of an all-embracing communal life more radical than the socialist communes proposed by Dmitri Pisarev, Nikolai Dobroliubov, Nikolai Chernyshevsky, or any of the other radicals of the 1860s. Similarly, the awakening of the Russian people that Fedorov and other Cosmist thinkers call for is more profound than anything dreamed by Peter Lavrov and the agrarian populist *narodniki* (from the word *narod*, "people") movement, of the 1870s and 1880s—the difference between a total moral, spiritual, physical rebirth, as advocated by the Cosmists, and an appeal to join a mass movement for mere regime change and social reform, as advocated by the *narodniki*. The appeal for a universal Christianity with Russia at the center, as developed by Fedorov and other Cosmists, reaches farther and is more radically inclusive than the late nineteenth-century Pan-Slavist calls for Russia to ride to the aid of their Balkan ethnic cousins and defend Slavic Christendom from the Turk; and Fedorov's defense of "Orthodoxy, Autocracy, and Nationality" presents a profound and radical extension of the revenant slogan most often associated with those archenemies of all Russian progressives, then and now, Sergei Uvarov and Konstantin Pobedonostsov.[3] For Fedorov and the Cosmists who follow his lead, all humans—even temporary political enemies—are related, share the single common goal of eternal life, and have one and only one common enemy: death. And the Russian autocrat and the Russian Orthodox Church destined to save the world are not those now in existence, not those exalted by Pobedonostsov and the neo-Slavophile revanchists, but the *Samoder-zhavets*, the Russian autocrat "as he ought to be," the distant future autocrat—a model of regulation of nature and self-control—and the Orthodox Church "as it ought to be" in the distant future—the sponsoring institution for the activity of restoring wholeness and unity to the living and life to the dead.

## *Thought as a Call for Action*

A constant feature of the Russian tradition of speculation, linking it to Cosmism, is its emphasis on *thought as a call for action*. It is no accident that the Russians adopted and attempted to implement the ideas of Marx more immediately and thoroughly than did other Europeans, or that Bakunin, the apostle of anarchistic action throughout Europe, came from the high Russian aristocracy. From the early exchange of philosophical letters between Ivan IV (the Terrible) and his renegade former friend and subject Prince Ivan Kurbsky, through Chaadaev's agonized meditations on Russia's mission, through the Slavophile-Westernizer debates on which direction Russia should follow, through Dostoevsky's dialectics on freedom and subjugation, through Tolstoy's search for a truth to live by, and up to Solzhenitsyn's philosophical letters "To the Rulers of Russia," the focus has characteristically been not on the theoretical nature of this or that concept but on the actions required by this or that ideal—not the nature of reality but the consequences of any given model of reality. In the Russian tradition, it is not enough to ask "What is true?"; we must go on to ask "What must we do about it?" Thus, long embedded in Russian philosophy, as we have seen in Fedorov's view of science, is a tendency to view every *-ology* as an opportunity for an *-urgy*, every discussion of "what is" as an invitation to consider "how to accomplish what ought to be." And this insistence on not merely observing and defining, but radically transforming the given world is a further example of Cosmism's thaumaturgical tendencies, of an eschatological historiosophy that links Russian Cosmism of the nineteenth and twentieth centuries to the age-old practice of magic and alchemy.

## The Totalitarian Cast of Mind

Another feature of Russian thought relevant to Cosmism is its totalitarian cast, its tendency toward total, universal solutions. With exceptions, such as Dostoevsky's *Underground Man* and most of Berdyaev, Russian thinkers—whether Westernist or Slavophile, liberal or conservative in orientation—tend to place the good of the whole community above the freedom of the individual to go his or her own independent way. Chaadaev, for example, argues in his "First Letter" that unity is paramount, and that one virtue of Christianity is that it can "captivate" our being whether we wish it to do so or not. "Nothing more clearly indicates the divine origin of this religion than this aspect of absolute universality which allows it to penetrate people's souls in all possible ways, to possess souls without their being aware of it, to dominate them, to subjugate them, even when they resist it the most."[4] And in his "Third Letter," he goes so far as to suggest that our goal as creatures endowed with reason should be to rid ourselves of freedom.

> There is no reason which is not obedient reason. But that is not all. Does man do anything his life long but seek to submit to something?... What would happen if man could make himself so submissive that he wholly rid himself of freedom? Clearly, according to what we have said, this would be the highest degree of human perfection. Every movement of his soul would then be produced by the principle which produced all other movements of the world. Thus, instead of being separated from nature, as he now is, man would fuse with it. Instead of the feeling of his own will, which separates him from the general order of things, which makes him a being apart, he would find the feeling of universal will, or, what is the same thing, the intimate feeling, the profound awareness of his real relation to the whole of creation.[5]

To Russian thinkers, Western notions of individual freedom often seem more like willfulness and license than genuine freedom. For Russians, the individual completes himself, becomes whole, and finds true freedom only by becoming part of a greater whole. In Russian thought, as in Russian opera, the dominant sound is more often that of the mighty chorus than of one like

Thoreau's solitary, independent American hero "marching to a different drummer." And like other Russian thinkers, the Cosmists, as we shall see in detail later in this study, are for the most part not interested in compromise positions and partial solutions. The emphasis is nearly always on the universal applicability of the given idea, the totality of the given project, inner and outer nature as a unified cosmic whole.

*4*

# *The Religious and Spiritual Context*

HISTORIANS HAVE OFTEN emphasized the special character of Russian spirituality and the role it has played in shaping traditional Russian culture. In this chapter, we shall examine some of the features of Russian religion and spirituality that have played a particularly important role in the development of Russian Cosmism.

## *The Kingdom of God on Earth*

As within the Russian tradition of philosophy, so within the tradition of Russian spirituality the Cosmists find themselves closer to the center than to the periphery. Berdyaev discusses at some length both the religious and sociopolitical manifestations of the Russian emphasis on eschatology,[1] a preoccupation with the kingdom at the end of history. Whether it will be the Kingdom of God or of perfect Communism, Russians have traditionally believed with special intensity that something awaits them at the end of linear time—and awaits not just individuals but the entire human race. And that kingdom is to come, emphatically, not in some sweet by-and-by up yonder, but in our time and here on earth. For the Russian Orthodox, the profound ritual of the annual Easter celebration with its special foods and music and services prepares the believer for the universal Resurrection that will follow human time and history. Orthodox Holy Week is a reminder to the faithful that the time we live in is the time between Christ's resurrection and ours. As Father Alexander Schmemann explained in a brief, eloquent guide to the meaning of each day of Holy Week,

> Every year, on Great Saturday, after this morning service, we wait for the Easter night and the fullness of Paschal joy. We know that they are approaching—and yet how slow is this approach, how long is this day! But is not the wonderful quiet of Great Saturday the symbol of our very life in this world? Are we not always in this "middle day," waiting for the Pascha of Christ, preparing ourselves for the day without evening of His Kingdom?[2]

As we shall see, the sense that the entire world is waiting for a resurrection and will not be what it is intended to be until that resurrection takes place is a theme that links Russian Cosmism to the entire history of Russian spirituality. The originality of Cosmism is its insistence that the resurrection that the world anticipates will not come about on its own but must be a universal project of all human intelligence and labor.

## Hesychasm; Two Great Russian Saints

In addition to its eschatologism, Russian spirituality has traditionally shown similarities to certain elements in Indian spirituality, particularly in the often noted resemblances between the hesychastic repetition of the Jesus Prayer ("Lord Jesus Christ, Son of God, have mercy on me, a sinner") as in the nineteenth-century anonymous Russian classic *Way of a Pilgrim*[3] and the repetition of a mantra in Hindu yogic practice and Buddhist meditation. Though they did not originate in Russia, the meditative practices described in the *Philokalia*[4] and *The Way of the Pilgrim* had by the nineteenth century become a special feature of Russian monastic life and underlay some of the miraculous events—similar to yogic *siddhis*—attributed to such Russian saints as Sergius of Radonezh in the fourteenth century and Seraphim of Sarov in the late eighteenth and early nineteenth.

In addition to miracles of healing, clairvoyance, visions of the Mother of God, divine illumination, pacification of wolves and bears, and raising the dead, Saint Sergius is particularly noted for establishing, through disciples, more than four hundred monasteries throughout Russia. For Fedorov and religious Cosmists, it was for this constructive activity, the spreading of monastic Christianity through the wilderness, a prefiguration of the task of spiritualizing (or in Fedorov's words, "patrifying") the empty cosmos—for this even more than for his other miracles—that Sergius deserves the title "Wonderworking Abbot of Russia."[5] A traditional feature of Russian spirituality that Fedorov links to Saint Sergius is the northern village practice of constructing *obydennye tserkvy*, churches built in a single day, thanks to the joint labor of everyone in the community. Fedorov finds this to be a perfect example of the collaborative spirit that will someday allow Russians to lead the universal task of resurrecting the dead, an example of a realistic, non-magical "miracle"—a church standing today where yesterday stood only trees—secular space turned into sacred not by any supernatural action but only by collective human will, knowledge, and labor. And though not built in a single day, the more than four hundred monasteries that Saint Sergius built or inspired were also "natural" miracles of ordinary people working together.

Saint Seraphim is particularly noted for *siddhi*-like miracles of divine illumination, levitation, appearing in more than one place at the same time, and healing the blindness that his unbearable luminescence has caused in beholders. But where Sergius directed his illumination outward, spreading light through the darkness, establishing communities of worship where there had been none, Seraphim directed his constructive effort toward the individual's inner life, showing the highly motivated seeker the way to receive divine grace and attain greater illumination. One of his followers, Nikolai Motovilov, left an often-cited account of how he received illumination from the saint.[6] Since this narrative, set in the 1830s, was said to have been discovered in 1902 in a derelict rural attic under a heap of rubbish covered in bird droppings by S. A. Nilus, the same man who "discovered" the notorious *Protocols of the Wise Elders of Zion*, questions of authenticity have naturally arisen but have not prevented wide distribution, institutional endorsement, and popular acceptance of the account. It begins:

> It was Thursday. The day was gloomy. The snow lay eight inches deep on the ground; and dry, crisp snowflakes were falling thickly from the sky when Father Seraphim began his conversation with me in a field adjoining his near hermitage, opposite the River Sarovka, at the foot of the hill which slopes down to the river bank. He sat me on the stump of a tree which he had just felled, and he himself squatted opposite me.

Father Seraphim begins the conversation by stating immediately and directly, without any prompting from his listener, that God has revealed to him that since childhood Motovilov has had "a great desire to know the aim of our Christian life" and has constantly but unsuccessfully sought answers from various spiritual advisers. Following a pattern familiar to students of initiation narratives, Father Seraphim reviews with Motovilov the prescriptions that other spiritual advisors have given—go to church, follow the Ten Commandments, do good works—and then tells Motovilov that this is not the truer, deeper answer he seeks. The advisors may have been good Christians. "But they did not speak as they should. And now poor Seraphim will explain to you in what this aim really consists." In the traditional manner in esoteric literature, the guru has now accepted the disciple and will guide him from false starts onto the path of true enlightenment. First, Seraphim explains, familiar Christian disciplines and practices are necessary but not sufficient steps along the path.

Prayer, fasting, vigil and all other Christian activities, however good they may be in themselves, do not constitute the aim of our Christian life, although they serve as the indispensable means of reaching this end. The true aim of our Christian life consists in the acquisition of the Holy Spirit of God. As for fasts, and vigils, and prayer, and almsgiving, and every good deed done for Christ's sake, they are only means of acquiring the Holy Spirit of God. But mark, my son, only the good deed done for Christ's sake brings us the fruits of the Holy Spirit. All that is not done for Christ's sake, even though it be good, brings neither reward in the future life nor the grace of God in this.

This is a point that Fedorov will repeat many times in his writings: good deeds, good intentions, good habits, good technologies—all will remain ineffectual if not directed toward one very precise and specific Christian goal, which for Seraphim is acquisition of the Holy Spirit of God and for Fedorov the resurrection of the dead. But as the conversation continues, Motovilov remains puzzled. How, exactly, can one acquire the Holy Spirit of God? Addressing Motovilov as "Your Godliness," emphasizing the undeveloped divine spark within, Seraphim tries again and again to explain, using illustrations from Scripture and from daily business life, the parable of the wise and foolish virgins, and shrewd commercial sense he developed in his own boyhood as the son of a merchant, quotations from the Old Testament and New, examples from the desert fathers and from the great Byzantine preachers, even quoting how Christ opened the understanding of his disciples—and still Motovilov remains in the dark:

"Nevertheless," I replied, "I do not understand how I can be certain that I am in the Spirit of God. How can I discern for myself His true manifestation in me?"

Father Seraphim replied: "I have already told you, your Godliness, that it is very simple and I have related in detail how people come to be in the Spirit of God and how we can recognize His presence in us. So what do you want, my son?"

"I want to understand it well," I said.

Then Father Seraphim took me very firmly by the shoulders and said: "We are both in the Spirit of God now, my son. Why don't you look at me?"

I replied: "I cannot look, Father, because your eyes are flashing like lightning. Your face has become brighter than the sun, and my eyes ache with pain."

Father Seraphim said: "Don't be alarmed, your Godliness! Now you yourself have become as bright as I am. You are now in the fullness of the Spirit of God yourself; otherwise you would not be able to see me as I am."

Seraphim then utters a silent "prayer of the heart" to complete the initiation, allowing Motovilov to share the saint's moment of total enlightenment.

After these words I glanced at his face and there came over me an even greater reverent awe. Imagine in the center of the sun, in the dazzling light of its midday rays, the face of a man talking to you. You see the movement of his lips and the changing expression of his eyes, you hear his voice, you feel someone holding your shoulders; yet you do not see his hands, you do not even see yourself or his figure, but only a blinding light spreading far around for several yards and illumining with its glaring sheen both the snow-blanket which covered the forest glade and the snow-flakes which besprinkled me and the great Elder. You can imagine the state I was in!

We cannot help but note how similar this passage is to the one describing the enlightenment Arjuna receives from Krishna in Book 12 of the Bhagavad Gita. It is as if the master, after lengthy attempts to explain and reason his pupil to enlightenment, finally accomplishes the task by switching on all his own inner lights, in the process all but blinding the pupil. Krishna provides Arjuna with a third "wisdom" eye allowing him to withstand the illumination. Motovilov, who with Seraphim's help apparently was able to bear "the ineffable glow" of the saint's light without benefit of an extra eye, experienced a great inner calm, a sweet taste in his mouth though he had ingested nothing material, a sense of great warmth though the snow was still accumulating on their heads and shoulders, and a wonderful fragrance despite the frozen earth and frigid air. Saint Seraphim explains that the sensations Motovilov experiences are more exquisite than those of earth because Motovilov has discovered the Kingdom of God:

The Lord said: *The Kingdom of God is within you* (Lk. 17:21). By the Kingdom of God the Lord meant the grace of the Holy Spirit. This Kingdom of God is now within us, and the grace of the Holy Spirit shines upon us and warms us from without as well. It fills the surrounding air with many fragrant odours, sweetens our senses with heavenly delight and floods our hearts with unutterable joy. Our present state is that of which the Apostle says; *The Kingdom of God is not food and drink, but righteousness and peace and joy in the Holy Spirit* (Rom. 14:17). Our faith consists not in the plausible words of earthly wisdom, but in the demonstration of the Spirit and power (cp. I Cor. 2:4). That is just the state that we are in now. Of this state the Lord said: *There are some of those standing here who shall not taste of death till they see the Kingdom of God come in power* (Mk. 9:1). See, my son, what unspeakable joy the Lord God has now granted us!

We see, then, two approaches to the traditional Russian spiritual tendency to seek the Kingdom of God here on earth. For Sergius, it meant the lifelong labor of building monasteries throughout previously uninhabited Russian space, setting monks to the task of constructing the *civitas dei* in the middle of the wilderness, converting profane space to sacred space, praying for the salvation of a world occupied by demons, wolves, and bears. For Seraphim, and, we might note, for Father Zosima in *The Brothers Karamazov*, the kingdom is already present, internal, accessible to the earnest seeker through properly directed religious disciplines and through personal, individual initiation by an enlightened master. Both these approaches will be further developed in the works of the religious Cosmists: the conversion of profane space and culture to sacred in Bulgakov's *Philosophy of Economy*, and the discovery of the kingdom within by Solovyov and Berdyaev.

## *The Third Rome*

Another important feature of the Russian spiritual tradition is what can only be considered its chauvinistic, even nationalistic tendencies. Probably every ethnic or national entity has at one time or another considered itself a people chosen for a special destiny. The Russian version of the "chosen people" narrative is spiritually rooted in two closely related medieval texts: the anonymous fifteenth century "Tale of the White Cowl," and the doctrine of "Moscow, the Third Rome," as formulated by the monk Philotheus. In the anonymous tale, the White Cowl, the radiant symbol of resurrection and Orthodox Christianity, was moved from Rome to Constantinople when the popes began to distort the original teachings of Christ. And when later the Byzantine Greeks also began to corrupt Christianity, and God sent the Turk as punishment upon them, the White Cowl was passed on to Russia, which, a century before the fall of Constantinople, had been designated by God to become the true seat of Orthodox Christianity. The Third Rome doctrine states, in Philotheus's words: "All Christian realms will come to an end and will unite into the one single realm of our sovereign, that is, into the Russian realm, according to the prophetic books. Both Romes fell, the third endures, and a fourth there will never be."[7]

Russia's special role in world history, then, is to embody, preserve, defend, and put into action God's absolute, Orthodox truth. As Fedorov and the Cosmists would contend, Russia was fortunate to receive Christianity at a relatively late date, after the major Byzantine disputes over dogma had been resolved and the disputes over liturgy, the active embodiment of dogma, were still going on. Thus Russia and the other Slavs entered Christendom and adopted Orthodoxy at precisely the right moment, when the new converts were able to participate in and bring back to their homelands new developments in liturgical practice instead of debates over dogma itself. The Fathers of the Russian Orthodox Church, consequently, were more concerned with creating artistic and didactic guides to the practice of living a Christian life than with developing a scholastic theology designed to appeal more to the intellect alone than to the whole person. The strength of medieval Orthodoxy, in the traditional Russian view, is that the Eastern church has historically attended to the spiritual life and health of the entire community, and has best expressed its "theology in color,"[8] in icons painted on wood, accessible models of Christian life that hang in every Russian church and home and speak to all, highly educated or illiterate, whereas medieval Christianity in the West became more and more an intellectual exercise of the rational (Aquinas) and imaginative (Dante) faculties of clever individuals on the one hand and unthinking mass obedience to the dictates of the papal hierarchy on the other. To Fedorov and most of the religious Cosmists (Solovyov the exception), Catholicism stands for unity without freedom, Protestantism for freedom without unity, and Orthodoxy for *sobornost'*, the synthesis of freedom and unity, wholeness, communality, spiritual consensus.

## Pre-Christian Antecedents

Even in looking back to pre-Christian pagan Russia, Fedorov and the Cosmists find spiritual ideas and practices that provide bases for their constructs. Fedorov devotes special attention to the ancient Slavic veneration of *rod*,[9] originally a god of fertility and light, eventually becoming the root for words denoting the basic kinship unit, the common Slavic equivalent to the *gens* of Greek and Latin. The veneration of *rod* is seen in the Slavic customs of burying one's dead ancestors with heads pointed toward the sunrise, ready for the new day, and including articles needed for the soul's journey, such as coins, food, water, and extra clothing, and at regular intervals afterward and on certain holidays leaving special portions of food out for departed ancestors. Veneration of the ancestors, the *rod*, is also evident in the ancestral house spirit that shares one's dwelling in most Slavic lands, usually perched near the oven, known as the "*domovoi*" in Russian (from *dom*, "house"). Considered a member of the family, he guards the house, performs little useful services, but is often peevish and must be addressed and treated with respect. If ignored or mistreated, he can behave like a poltergeist. He almost never leaves the house, except in brief fits of displeasure, in which case he must be invited back with words such as: "Grandfather, grandfather domovoi, please come back and tend your sheep." When moving to another house, one should make an offering to the *domovoi* and say: "Grandfather, grandfather domovoi, don't stay here but come with us."[10]

Russian is one of the few Indo-European languages to retain the active use of the patronymic in everyday speech, so that the common, polite way to address or refer to another adult is to use the first name and patronymic: Ivan Ivanovich, "Ivan, son of Ivan," or Vera Ivanovna, "Vera, daughter of Ivan." One's father, then, is a permanent part of every Russian's name and identity to a degree once common but no longer known in most other modern European languages and cultures (Iceland being the main exception). And even those who are not parents but who occupy a position of authority or respect, such as a priest or the tsar, are honored with the title *batiushka*, "dear father," or *matiushka*, "dear mother," and among Russians any stranger wrinkly and kindly enough to qualify may be addressed familiarly as *dedushka*, "dear grandfather," or *babushka*, "dear grandmother." *Rod*, then, the morpheme of kinship, is what links us not only to other people and other generations but to nature and the earth as well. In poetry and song, the adjective *rodnaia*, "native," relates us intimately to our rivers, our meadows, our birch trees, our mountains, our furrowed earth. Boris Pasternak titled his great collection of early poems *Sestra moia zhizn'* (My sister life), a family relationship that Russian readers found easy to understand and identify with.

Russian folklore, with its mixture of pagan roots and Christian overlays, is especially rich in spells, tales, and wonders involving human control over nature and the exercise of supernormal powers: a *bogatyr* hero can make his horse fly from Chernigov to Kiev in one mighty leap; the witch Baba Yaga flies up on a mortar and broomstick from her hut with chicken legs; and the *volkhv* (wizard) operates in dimensions of space and time inaccessible to his neighbors. The folklorist brothers Boris and Yuri Sokolov[11] documented the feared and respected presence of *kolduny*, sorcerers, in Russian village life as recently as the nineteenth and early twentieth century. Reputed to have the ability to change people into animals, spoil wells, and cause sudden illness, *kolduny* were notorious for turning up uninvited at weddings, all but guaranteeing an unhappy marriage for the unlucky couple. A *bogatyr* would almost always be successful in his struggles with dragons, robber nightingales, and other natural and supernatural opponents. But the poor peasant or ordinary Russian often found him- or herself overcome by the ubiquitous nature spirits: *leshi*, the forest spirits, are waiting in the woods to trick the unwary traveler, whom the *leshi* turn mute and wild-eyed and cover with moss; at rivers, women and girls must beware of *bereginy*, nymphs who hide by the banks to steal human babies and leave changelings in their place; in the river itself lurk *rusalki*, drowned maidens who like to bewitch and entangle young men. Other forces behind nature that one has to contend with include *bolotny*, female spirits of the bog; *divozhenky*, wild, beautiful female spirits who can use certain plants to make themselves invisible or visible as they wish, and can effortlessly make a good man lose his way; *lugoviki*, male meadow spirits who can be the ruin of young girls picking berries or working in the fields; *mora*, a shape changer who brings bad dreams and suffocates sleepers, especially children; and *vodyanoy*, a male water spirit who likes to drown people, especially anyone who swims after sunset or on a holy day. This is not even mentioning the vampires and werewolves who have haunted the Slavic lands since at least the time of Herodotus, and who serve as a frightening warning that we are not necessarily always and permanently human—we can slide backward in evolution at the change of the moon or the setting of the sun. The hope of Fedorov and the Cosmists is that on our self-directed evolutionary journey, we can also metamorphose forward.

# 5

# *The Russian Esoteric Context*

A MAIN FEATURE of Russian Cosmism is its grounding in traditions of occult or esoteric knowledge. Some of these traditions are specific to Russia; others are common to Western civilization; and still others seem to be shared by many cultures. Of the Cosmists, only a few—Solovyov, Berdyaev, Florensky, and Tsiolkovsky—openly admitted at least a temporary immersion in esoteric literature or practices. But as we shall see, Russians from all social classes and intellectual tendencies have for centuries found occult teachings profoundly attractive, and by transforming matter usually considered esoteric into new theology, philosophy, and science, the Cosmists add to, rather than depart from, a long Russian tradition.

## *Early Searches for "Deep Wisdom"*

In *The Origins of Russia*, George Vernadsky cites one of the early accounts of practice of magic in Slavic lands, *The Meadows of Gold and the Mines of Gems* by the tenth-century Arab historian and geographer Abu al-Hasan Ali ibn al-Husayn ibn Ali al-Mas'udi:

> The Slavs believed that the course of the sun affected the fortunes of mankind. Masudi relates that among the Slavic temples there was one situated on a high mountain, so built that it was easy, through special openings, to observe the points of sunrise. Precious stones were inserted in various parts of the building and magic signs carved in stone. By co-ordinating the data on the course of the sun and magic meaning of the precious stones and of the signs, Slavic high priests prophesied future events.[1]

As we shall see later, in our discussion of Alexander Chizhevsky, belief in a direct correlation between the course of the sun and the course of human events was not confined to prescientific seekers of knowledge.

As W. F. Ryan demonstrates in his indispensable account of the early history of magic in Russia, *The Bathhouse at Midnight*, the practice of folk magic and sorcery was common and accepted at all levels of society even after the coming of Christianity, but learned, hermetic, and neo-Platonic esotericism made only fragmentary appearances.[2] At the end of the fourteenth and beginning of the fifteenth century, the first Russian medical, scientific, and proto-scientific texts begin to appear, modeled on, if not translated from, Greek originals. These include presentations of the four humors, explanation of the microcosm and macrocosm, astrological advice on the best and worst days for certain activities such as planting, pruning, slaughtering livestock, letting blood, and cutting hair.[3] In one of the earliest such books, *Glubinnaia kniga* (The book of deep wisdom),[4] Prince Vladimir and King David engage in dialogues on the power of light, the divinity of the sun, and other theurgical themes drawing on both pagan and Christian views of the world. In the fifteenth century, *Secretum Secretorum*, originally an Arabic work that had been translated into Hebrew, and which purported to be secret instructions given to Alexander the Great by Aristotle, began to appear in Old Russian translations. Ryan explains: "The *Secretum* is notable in that it is not only a work which would appeal to Russians because of its association with the popular Alexander stories, but also because of its advocacy of astrology, and the fact that it contained an onomantic table for predicting the outcome of battles, the first alchemical text in Old Russian, a description of the magical properties of precious stones and magical talismans, and two separate works of physiognomy."[5]

Two well known works of medieval literature, the *Stoglav* (Hundred chapters) and *Domostroi* (Domestic order) offer further evidence of magical practice in pre-Petrine Russia. In *Stoglav*, produced by a council called by Ivan the Terrible to identify and proscribe superstitions and irreligious practices of the time, the list of activities to be forbidden includes various forms of divination, numerology, astrology, and spell casting. Of particular relevance to our study of Cosmism is a passage in chapter 41: "On Thursday of Passion Week people burn straw and call up the dead, and on this day ignorant priests put salt under the altar, which they then keep until the seventh Thursday after Easter, when it becomes a cure for sick men or beasts. The Council replies that this is a Hellene seduction and heresy and any priest involved in this is to be excluded from the priesthood."[6] Here we have, as heretical superstition, two thaumaturgical impulses that will reappear as "projective science" in Cosmist writings: the hope of calling the dead back to life and the hope that faith and time will transform a natural element of ordinary daily use, like salt, into a cure for diseases in animals and people. The *Domostroi*, the earliest versions of which probably predate the *Stoglav*, lists many of the same practices to be avoided in domestic life, warning especially that women should not be allowed to associate with witches or wizards or to practice magic themselves. As for most other offenses by women, the *Domostroi* recommends that the husband, not the church or state, should beat or otherwise punish the wife who ventures into the supernatural. Fortunately for the Cosmists, and others who might later conduct ventures into the supernatural, by the nineteenth century the *Domostroi* had lost at least some of its influence.

Ryan tells us that from the time of Ivan III (1540–1605) "all the rulers of Muscovy for the next two centuries up to Peter the Great seem to have had, or were accused of having, some knowledge of magic, alchemy, or astrology, or all three."[7] This knowledge came primarily from Westerners invited to serve in the Muscovite court as physicians, scientists, or general advisers, such as Jacob Boehme's follower, the mystical poet and utopian thinker Quirinus Kuhlmann, who came to Moscow's German Quarter in 1689 looking to attract adherents to his utopian ideals, but who was burned at the stake with one of his local hosts for heresy in October of that year.[8] One of those who rejected an invitation to serve in Moscow was the famous magus of Elizabeth I of England, Dr. John Dee, although his son Arthur Dee would serve as personal physician to Tsar Michael Romanov between 1621 and 1635.[9] Westerners such as Count Cagliostro, Count St. Germain, and Douglas Home would serve the esoteric needs of eighteenth- and nineteenth-century Russian high society, and by the early twentieth century, homegrown talents such as Grigory Rasputin would make importation less necessary.

## *Popular Magic*

In Russia as elsewhere in premodern times, interest in and practice of magic was generally of two kinds: the popular use of spells, charms, casts, and the like by the uneducated, and the learned study of Greek, Hebrew, and Western European texts by rulers, members of the court, and learned clergy—though sometimes the line between high and low magic was blurred, as with the educated, literate Tsar Alexei Mikhailovich (1629–1696), who, despite his cultivation, had the hut of a recently deceased witch searched for roots, plants, scraps of writing, and anything else that could be put to magical use, and who ordered the gathering of magical herbs at midsummer.

Several other examples of the practice of popular magic in pre-Petrine Russia point forward in time toward the Cosmists. One is the idea that a clear footprint in the mud or snow can be used in hostile magic against the person who left it,[10] demonstrating the belief that an absent person can still be considered present and affected through traces left behind of him- or herself. Fedorov would propose that all matter contains the dust of ancestors, and that traces of ancestral dust could be extracted and used not to do hostile magic but scientifically, to restore life to the departed. The purpose is different but the principle is similar—employing the trace to arrive at the whole person.

Another transformation of medieval popular magic is in the protective devices one must use when attempting to perform magic. Even the act of performing beneficial magic can open the door to powerful evil forces, so to protect oneself, one should hold or wear a cross, or if working without a cross, draw a magic circle into which nothing evil can intrude.[11] In Cosmism the danger is the unintended damage that can occur from powerful technology applied with even the best intentions. As in medieval magic, the best protection for Cosmists is the cross, the conviction that all technological advance must be pursued not for its own sake but for the sake of, and in the name of, the Christian task of resurrection.

In one folk tale cited by Ryan, a young woman feigning illness asks that doctors and *volkhvy*, "wizards," be summoned to treat her, indicating that in the popular mind the practice of medicine and magic, the physician and the wizard may at times have been considered more or less the same thing.[12] The Church Slavonic Gospel uses the same word, *volkhvy*, for the figures we call the Three Kings or Three Wise Men at the Nativity, and in a sixteenth-century document, Plato and Aristotle, the Greek philosophers who were believed to have foretold the coming of Christ, are also referred to as *volkhvy*. In the West, and in the learned circles of Muscovy, the line between *volkhvy* on one side and scientists and philosophers on the other was being drawn, and at least among the learned would remain more or less clearly drawn until the Cosmists would, effectively if unintentionally, blur it once again, so that, as in old Russian popular culture, the wizard and the scientist could once more be one and the same.

## Higher Magic in the Time of Peter the Great

The study of higher magic from ancient and foreign esoteric texts was, as noted above, fragmentary and sporadic until the time of Peter the Great. Learned esotericism, then, as opposed to popular magic and superstition, began to have its most significant impact in Russia with the coming in the eighteenth century of Freemasonry, with its emphasis on the craft of constructing a better man and better world. The claim sometimes made that Peter himself was initiated, possibly by Sir Christopher Wren, on his visit to London in 1697–1698,[13] has not been proved, but recent research by Robert Collis has at least demonstrated Peter's lively interest in alchemy, the attempt not only to produce gold from base metals but to forge higher men from common mortals. Collis cites an account of Peter's meeting on March 28, 1698, with the Oxford "chymist and physician" Moses Stringer.

> The Czar sent some days since for Mr Stringer, an Oxford Chymist, to shew him some of the Choicest Secrets and Experiments known to England; accordingly Mr Stringer drew up a Class (or Number) of Experiments, viz, Some in Separating and Refining of Metals and Minerals, some Geometrical, some Medicinal, others Phylosophical, to the number of 24 Experiments; when they were drawn up, the Czar elected one to be done first; and it seems it was one of the most difficult Operations, which shews that the Czar is skill'd in Natural Philosophy. However he desired to see the Experiment done, which was performed to his satisfaction, It was to Melt Four Metals, with a destroying Mineral together: the Gold, Silver, Copper, and Iron with Antimony, into one Lump, then to dissolve them all, and then to separate each Metal distinct again, without destroying any one of them: It chanced after he had made him some Lead out of its Ore, and Silver out of that Lead, and called the Gold from the rest of the Metals mixt, being transported into a merry Vein, told the Czar, if his Majesty would wear that Gold in a Ring for his sake, he would make him an Artificial Gem of what colour he pleased to name, to set in it, out of an Old Broom staff and a piece of Flint, that lay by them; His Majesty being pleased with the Fancy, ordered it to be done, he staying by part of the time, and his Secretary the rest till it was done, and then it proved so hard, that it cut glass.[14]

Although there is no evidence that Peter himself practiced alchemy, he maintained a lifelong interest in the subject, holding major alchemical texts in his private library, including Basil Valentine's *The Twelve Keys* and *The Triumphal Chariot of Antimony*, and including among his closest Masonic associates and advisors three men deeply involved in alchemical and other esoteric researches.

The first of these three, Jacob Bruce (1669–1735), called by Pushkin "the Russian Faust," was the Russian-born son of William Bruce, a direct descendent of Robert I ("The Bruce"), King of Scotland, and one of a number of Scots, many of them Freemasons, who came to Russia just before, during, and after the failure of the Jacobite movement. Over a long, distinguished military, diplomatic, and administrative career, Jacob Bruce was recognized as one of the most brilliant representatives of Petrine Russia. His outstanding achievements won him many public honors, but during and long after his brilliant career legends of his "sorcery" continued to circulate, including stories of "his ability to create a mute housemaid from flowers, his invention of a concoction which when poured from a vial brought a dead dog back to life and a similar concoction which restored youth to an old man."[15] But as Robert Collis notes,

> The most remarkable evidence of Bruce's deep interest in alchemy can undoubtedly be found in his private library collection. Astonishingly, it is certainly on a par with the confiscated library of Nikolai Novikov, in its range of alchemical, hermetic and occult content. Indeed, the claim that Rosicrucianism and Rosicrucian texts were only brought to Russia in the 1770s and 1780s by I. G. Schwarz, an associate of Novikov's, is severely undermined by the nature of Bruce's library which contains many significant Rosicrucian-inspired volumes.[16]

Collis goes on to list many of the more than 140 occult texts in that library. Bruce, then, could well have served Peter the Great as a magus on the order of Elizabeth I's Dr. John Dee. The second close associate of the tsar was an ecclesiast of encyclopedic erudition, Feofan Prokopovich (1681–1736). An eloquent ideologist for Petrine absolutism, and chief panegyrist of the emperor's glorious military and diplomatic achievements, Prokopovich, as Collis notes, "became the spearhead for a programme of radical ecclesiastic reform."[17] In clear opposition to the old Muscovite clergy, Prokopovich, who before coming to St. Petersburg had taught a wide variety of subjects at the Kiev Academy, advocated scientific as well as spiritual education. His profound interest in all branches of knowledge included a defense of alchemical research and what the Soviet historian V. M. Nichik terms "Prokopovich's 'Neo-Platonic' ideas about the origin of the world by the path of divine emanation."[18] Although Prokopovich's library was not as rich as Bruce's in alchemical literature, he did assemble a substantial collection of some three thousand volumes, primarily theological, but containing "a significant number of alchemical tomes, written by at least thirty-four separate authors, including Daniel Sennert, and many other works of a distinctly occult nature."[19] The collection included standard esoteric works by Cornelius Agrippa, Paracelsus, Robert Fludd, the Emerald Tablets of Hermes Trismegistus, and dozens of rare works on alchemical and other prescientific methods of transforming base elements, whether mineral or human, into incorruptible gold.

As an archbishop, Prokopovich probably did not participate in Peter's drunken revelry with the notorious "All-Mad, All-Jesting, All-Drunken Assembly," a secretive, bawdy fraternal group similar to eighteenth-century London's "Hell-Fire Club," but he was an important member of the more serious scientific and alchemical research group "The Neptune Society."

Another member of this group, and the third of Peter's closest Masonic associates, was Robert Erskine (1677–1718), a Scottish physician who established the first scientific botanical garden in Russia and was later appointed director and chief librarian of Peter's Kunstkamera, a special collection of natural oddities still open to viewers in St. Petersburg. Unlike Bruce and Prokopovich, Erskine was not a prominent public figure during his lifetime, but he was highly esteemed by Peter, and during his relatively brief life of forty-one years, he managed to amass

one of the most extensive private alchemical collections in Europe for its day. In a collection of over 2,300 tomes, one can find at least 287 alchemical works by 157 separate authors, which accounts for over 12 percent of the total collection. This total compares favourably with the contemporaneous (and nowadays renowned) collections of Sir Isaac Newton and Sir Hans Sloane, who held 169 and 204 separate alchemical tomes respectively.[20]

In addition to many of the same works in the two previously described libraries, Erskine's collection featured an especially strong collection of Rosicrucian literature, the first clear instance of the presence of this movement in Russia. As Collis relates, Erskine was at the center of a "Jacobite network" that significantly influenced Peter's designs for a new Russia and helped to direct Peter's reforms along lines parallel to Masonic ideals. Peter's personal seal, depicting a Pygmalion-like sculptor creating an idealized human figure from rough stone, featured Masonic imagery and emblems. His creation of fraternal and mock fraternal hierarchical organizations, from the bureaucratic table of ranks to the secretive, scientific Neptune Society and the bawdy "All-Mad, All-Jesting, All-Drunken Assembly" may owe as much to Masonic as to ecclesiastical models of hierarchy. As Collis demonstrates, even if Peter himself was not officially a Mason, his goals and policies for reshaping Russia into a forward-looking Westernized empire bear a strong resemblance to those of early eighteenth-century Freemasonry.[21] The goal common to Peter and to eighteenth-century Russian Freemasonry of "hewing the rough stone," reshaping both the individual Russian and Russian culture as a whole, also lays a solid foundation for later, more radical "hewings" and reshapings to be proposed by Fedorov and the Cosmists.

## *Esotericism after Peter the Great*

If, as Collis submits, Freemasonry played a significant and previously underestimated role in the Petrine reforms of the first quarter of the eighteenth century, the importance of Masonic ideas and activities later in the century, particularly under Catherine the Great (1729–1796, ruled from 1762) has long been recognized. The major figure in the movement was Nikolai Novikov (1744–1818), a writer, editor, and publisher who was instrumental in propagating not only Rosicrucianism and Martinism but also Shakespeare and other enlightening literature then new to Russia. Shortly after the French Revolution, however, he was arrested by Catherine and saw his press smashed and his inventory destroyed. Novikov was the force behind what Rafaella Faggionato has called Russia's "Rosicrucian Utopia,"[22] in which the ideals of Rosicrucian Christianity, with its secret inner teachings supposedly reaching back before Christ to ancient Egyptian and Chaldean sources, were becoming so appealing to the cream of Russia's younger aristocracy that Catherine—despite having cultivated international admiration for her "enlightened" principles and policies—perceived the movement as a serious threat to the state and ruthlessly suppressed it.

Though feared as a political threat—a fear that has periodically resurfaced, and not only in Russian history—the Rosicrucian movement was essentially utopian, otherworldly, and had no musket sights targeted directly at Catherine's empire. As Tatiana Artemyeva has demonstrated, the utopia offered by Novikov and his circle promises not only a perfect man but a perfect world as well, a world without slavery, poverty, taxes, despotism, or churches, a world of free believers purified from Adam's Fall by free adoption of Masonic practices. The only step needed to create this perfect world is for everyone to become true, practicing Masons.[23] The totality of this utopia, the unity of pedagogical, social, ontological, spiritual, technological, and cosmological orders again points toward the comprehensive, multidisciplinary impulses embodied in the Fedorovian and Cosmist worldviews. In the early twentieth century, when the Cosmist worldview was forming, the same impulses were

at work as in the eighteenth century, when Freemasonry prevailed. As Berdyaev put it, referring to his intellectual contemporaries, "They all wanted to be
Rosicrucians."[24]

## Theosophy and Anthroposophy

As Maria Carlson has shown, in her masterful study of the Theosophical
movement in Russia,[25] by the end of the eighteenth and beginning of the
nineteenth century, Russian interest in all things esoteric was only just beginning. The general European turn away from positivism and materialism,
leading to the investigation and embrace of innumerable varieties of mysticism, supernaturalism, and esotericism, found special resonance throughout
nineteenth- and early twentieth-century Russia. Whether coming from such
native sons as Alexander Pushkin, Nikolai Gogol, M. N. Zagoskin, and A. K.
Tolstoy, or from foreign writers such as Swedenborg, Eliphas Levi, Louis
Constant, and Papus, esoteric literature found a very receptive audience in
Russia. The culmination came in the writings and activities of Madame Blavatsky (Helena Petrovna Blavatskaya), who, though born in Russia, spent
most of her life abroad and published first in English all the seminal Theo-
sophical works that would later be translated back into Russian. Although the
Cosmists hardly ever cite her writings, or mention them only in disparaging
terms, echoes from her *Isis Unveiled* (first published in English 1877) and *The
Secret Doctrine* (1888), as we shall see, find their way into the Cosmists' works
more often than the Cosmists would care to admit. One of the early Russian
Theosophists, Elena Pisareva, translated, and with her husband published,
Russian versions of the major Theosophical works not only by Madame Bla-
vatsky, but also by her English and Indian followers Annie Besant, Charles
Leadbeater, Mabel Collins, and Curuppumullage Jinarajadasa.

Another major conduit for Blavatsky's Theosophical teachings, not only
for the twentieth century Cosmists but for late nineteenth- and early twentieth-century Silver Age Russian intellectuals as a whole, was Rudolf Steiner's
offshoot of Theosophy, which he called Anthroposophy. Through his wife,
Maria von Sivers, a Russian Theosophist, Steiner, both in his early role as leader
of German Theosophists and later as head of his own movement of Anthroposophy, enjoyed close contacts with many influential Russian intellectuals,
particularly the Symbolist poet and thinker Andrei Biely and Biely's wife, the
artist Asya Turgeneva. The major difference between Anthroposophy and
Theosophy was one of emphasis: where Blavatsky and the later Theosophists,
particularly Annie Besant, emphasized the Indian and Tibetan roots of their

esotericism, Steiner based his Anthroposophy on Western hermetic, Gnostic, Manichean, and Rosicrucian sources. And where Theosophy was often characterized as "esoteric Hinduism" or "esoteric Buddhism," Steiner himself often described Anthroposophy as "esoteric Christianity." Russians were attracted to both Theosophy and Anthroposophy, but perhaps due in part to the scandalous reputation of Madame Blavatsky, and the contrasting academic credentials of the strenuously upright Steiner, Russian intellectuals who acknowledged esoteric sources tended to cite Steiner rather than Blavatsky. In Russia, however, thanks mainly to the talent and energy of the president of the Russian section, Anna Kamenskaia, the Russian Theosophical movement went on to thrive for two decades despite the controversies surrounding the earlier activities of Madame Blavatsky. According to Elena Pisareva, author of a vivid personal memoir of the early years of the Russian Theosophical Society,[26] major activities of the Russian Theosophists included, in addition to publishing Russian versions of important Theosophical and other esoteric literature, the running of vegetarian kitchens in major cities, the sewing of undergarments and other supplies for Russian soldiers during World War I, the sponsoring of public debates on leading social questions, the opening of kindergartens and day care centers, and the presentation of cultural events including free public concerts of classical music arranged especially for workers and peasants.

One of the leading figures in the Masonic movement of the late eighteenth and early nineteenth century, Prince Ivan Alekseevich Gagarin (1771–1832), was the grandfather of the chief Russian Cosmist, Nikolai Fedorov. As an illegitimate child, both part of and not part of the Gagarin family, and only three years old when his grandfather died, Fedorov could not have had much direct contact with the great Mason. But whether from the family library or from his later work as a librarian in the Rumiantsev Museum, which housed an extensive collection of Masonic and other esoteric literature, or from whatever other sources, as Zenkovsky, Bulgakov, and others have noted, Fedorov's ideas have much in common with, and perhaps owe much to, Russian esoteric Freemasonry of the eighteenth and early nineteenth century. To understand this better, it is now time for us to take a longer and closer look at Fedorov and his idea. Since recent research by scholars in Russia has brought to light biographical information previously unavailable or misreported, we shall present Fedorov's life in more detail and, we hope, more accurately than has previously been possible in English.

*6*

---

# Nikolai Fedorovich Fedorov (1829–1903), the Philosopher of the Common Task

*"Now there's a saintly man," said Lev Nikolaevich. "He owns nothing; any book that he buys or that is given him he at once donates to the library. At home he sleeps on a trunk on newspapers in a tiny little room he rents from some old woman. He is, of course, a vegetarian, but is bashful and doesn't like to talk about it. But do you know, he has his own theory!"*

*And Tolstoy began to tell us something strange: Fedorov can in no way reconcile himself with the thought that men are dying and that people now very dear to us will vanish without a trace, and he has developed a theory that science, by a giant step forward, will discover a means to extract from the earth the remains—the particles of our forefathers, in order then to restore them again to living form.*
—FROM THE NOTEBOOK OF V. F. LAZURSKY, *July 13, 1894.*

THROUGHOUT HIS LIFE and for much of the century after his death, Fedorov was all but unknown. Since the end of the Soviet period, however, he has become, at least in his own country, one of the best known figures in the history of Russian thought. While probably only a few very serious students have read through much of his work, everyone who knows anything about Russian intellectual history knows one very important thing about this eccentric, once obscure Moscow librarian.

## The One Idea

Like the hedgehog in the well-known dichotomy (which Sir Isaiah Berlin borrows from a fragment attributed to Archilochus) between foxes, who know many things, and hedgehogs, who know one big thing, Nikolai Fedorov was a thinker with one vast idea.[1] He believed that all known problems have a single root in the problem of death, and that no solution to any social, economic, political, or philosophical problems will prove adequate until we have solved the problem of death. But if a solution to the problem of death can be found, then solutions to any and all other problems will follow.

All his writings, collected under the title *Filosofiia obshchego dela* (*The Philosophy of the Common Task*), are devoted to a solution to the problem of death. He believed that any question, no matter how apparently trivial, is under the surface literally a question of life and death. A consideration of the development of handwriting, of female attire, or of the entire history of the human race will lead to one and the same conclusion: that disintegration is the universal rule, and that reintegration is the human task. No matter where Fedorov looks he sees manifestations of the natural principle of disintegration and death, and yet, with unfailing optimism, he views every instance of disintegration as a fresh opportunity for us to begin the common task of reintegration.

"All philosophies," Fedorov wrote, "while disagreeing about all else, agree on one thing—they all recognize the reality of death, its inevitability, even when recognizing, as some do, nothing real in the world. The most skeptical systems, doubting even doubt itself, bow down before the fact of the reality of death." Fedorov, then, would establish his position against the entire history of philosophy, arguing that death is not an inevitable certainty but conditional. "Death is a property, a condition . . . but not a quality without which man ceases to be *what he is and what he ought to be*."[2] To Fedorov, man "as he ought to be" is not only himself immortal but engaged in the task of bringing immortality to all others.

Fedorov speaks of two kinds of death. The one he devotes most attention to is death as disintegration. Whether in the physical universe, in society, in the family, or within the individual, particle is separated from particle, the inner ties dissolve, the whole is shattered. The task of all humanity is to restore to wholeness and life all that nature would disaggregate and drive to death. The opposite of disintegration, in the world as it presently exists, is not wholeness but fusion. This also is a kind of death, in which each unit loses its individuality and particularity, and all discrete parts are amalgamated into a lifeless mass. Fedorov finds death by fusion, like death by disintegration, present everywhere: in mass movements, in blind allegiance to the war cry, and in the swallowing of the lives of individual villages by cities. The task here is to decentralize, to turn the lifeless, shapeless mass back into living units. The world "as it is" operates under the principles of disintegration and fusion;

everything is either disaggregated into unconnected particles or amalgamated into huge, lifeless, corporate entities. The "common task" is to reverse the natural flow of life toward death as disintegration and death as fusion, and to restore everywhere a wholeness that insures both the integrity of the unit and the unity of the whole. The model—or icon—for the universe "as it should be" is the mystical consubstantiality of the Holy Trinity, in the words of the Orthodox liturgy, *ni sliianno ni razdel'no*, "neither fused nor disaggregated," perfect as both three and one. In today's terms, Fedorov's project might be described as an attempt to turn the universe of the big bang into one of a steady state. In Fedorov's utopia (which he did not consider a utopia but simply the world "as it ought to be"), there will be neither birth nor death but a gradual restoration of life to all—literally all—who have ever lived. The life in unity of all humankind must include those now dead. To stop the task of unification after only the living have been united and freed from death would be, Fedorov insists, an act of selfishness and immaturity. Maturity—and morality—require that sons and daughters not only take life from their parents but return it. "The duty of resurrecting unites both 'memento mori' as a most lamentable fact, and 'memento vivere' as a necessary, inevitable goal."[3]

By uniting all people alive in a task to overcome the only true enemy of all people alive, namely death, the project of literal, active, physical resurrection would represent a great step toward the solution of many other problems which seem insoluble today. Energies and resources now directed toward war would be directed toward resurrection. Historical enemies would find mutual assistance not only possible but necessary. Unbelievers, who in theory might find Christianity unacceptable, would, by resurrecting the dead, become in practice followers of Christ.

The resurrection of the dead would be a long and gradual, but ultimately universal, project. The philosopher Vladimir Solovyov once estimated to Fedorov that it might take several thousand years. But as Fedorov explains:

> The difficulty for each generation of restoring the generation that immediately preceded it will be absolutely equal; for the attitude of the present generation toward its fathers, and of that generation which will first acquire the art of restoration toward its fathers is exactly the same as the attitude of our great grandfathers toward their fathers. Although the first resurrectee will be, in all likelihood, resurrected almost immediately after death, hardly even having died, and after him will follow those in whom very little decomposition is evident, nevertheless each new experience in this task will make subsequent steps

easier. With each new person resurrected, knowledge will be growing; it will peak in its task just when the human race arrives at the first person who died. Moreover, for our great-great-grandchildren it will be incomparably more difficult to resurrect their fathers than for us and for our great-great-grandfathers; for in the resurrection of our fathers we shall make use not only of all previous experiences in the task, but shall even have the collaboration of our resurrectors; in this way it will be easiest of all for the first son of man to resurrect his father, the father of all people.[4]

Thus the first steps might consist of little more than the brief, temporary resuscitation of a person who had just died. But as all scientific technology, sociopolitical organization—indeed all human knowledge and action—gradually became directed toward the goal of resurrection, more than brief and temporary resuscitation would in time be possible. Eventually the synthesizing of bodies should be possible, and ultimately, Fedorov believed, whole persons could be re-created from the least trace of recovered ancestral dust. To recover particles of disintegrated ancestors, Fedorov projected, research teams would have to travel to the moon, to the planets, and to distant points throughout the universe. Eventually these outer points of the cosmos would be colonized by the resurrected ancestors, whose bodies might be reengineered so they could live under conditions that could not now support human life as it is known. This would both extend the realm of spirituality and rationality to areas of the universe now presumed to be lifeless and solve the Malthusian problem of an overpopulated Earth. Space exploration thus should not be undertaken simply for itself, out of curiosity or as an adventure or conquest, but for a specific purpose: life over death for all humanity.

We shall discuss some of the details of Fedorov's project in greater depth further along in this study. For now, it is perhaps sufficient to say that while Fedorov may be considered a thinker with one idea, his single idea was extremely complex and comprehensive. He includes any number of individual projects within his one grand project of resurrection. Some of these subsidiary projects, such as the gathering of all nations into one political unit governed by a Russian autocrat, constitute in themselves vast and complex—not to mention improbable—undertakings. Other projects, such as the establishing of small, local museums, are more realizable and less grandiose in scale. But an important point to be made, even from the start, is that all Fedorov's projects are interrelated, all are directed toward the ultimate goal of resurrecting the dead, and, in Fedorov's mind at least, all are necessary in order for any to succeed. The scientific projects cannot be understood in isolation from the religious, political, sociological, artistic, and economic projects. In contrast to some of his followers, Fedorov repeatedly emphasizes that technological advance, if pursued independently from advances in morality, the arts, government, and spirituality, and if pursued for its own sake or for purposes other than the resurrection of the ancestors, could end only in disaster. And further, also in contrast to some of the other Cosmist thinkers, he believed that spiritual development alone, without scientific technology, could also lead only to a dead end. Many thinkers before and after Fedorov have proposed one or more of the ideas that Fedorov puts forward. But only Fedorov rolls them all into hedgehog-like unity.

Fedorov was convinced that his project was practical and realizable. To the objection that all human knowledge and effort could never be directed toward a single goal, he simply said: look around. "At the present time everything serves war; there is not one discovery which the military does not study with the aim of applying it to warfare, not one invention which they do not attempt to turn to military use."[5] A world order and economy pointed toward a single goal already exists—all we have to do is to change our present orientation and goal. One of his favorite examples, repeated several times in the thousands of pages of his writings, is of American experiments to bring rain in time of drought by shooting cannons into the air: a simple reorientation of aim from horizontal to vertical, from weapons of destruction to instruments of salvation. And this simple but radical change in orientation, from horizontal to vertical, returns throughout his writings to symbolize the reorientation needed in every field of activity: from a horizontal "zoomorphic" culture of human animals to a vertical, fully human stance of broad rational perspective; from a Ptolemaic, earth-centered worldview to a Copernican, cosmos-centered worldview; from the horizontal position of a body lying in its grave to the vertical position of the monument and mourner standing over that grave; from the horizontality of the railroad track to the verticality of the air balloon now and the spaceship tomorrow.

He insisted that his projects were in no way utopian fantasies but reasonable, necessary, practical, feasible tasks. He does not himself claim to know how, for instance, future biologists will create synthetic bodies. But he does insist that if future biologists take the creation of synthetic bodies as their task, as they should, they can and will find the solution. Fedorov believes that humanity's creative potential is unlimited. In the long run, people can accomplish whatever they set out to accomplish—whether a better way to exterminate or to preserve, extend, and restore all human life. In the course of his writings, Fedorov points out hundreds of different ways in which we are now at work on our own destruction, and argues that in each case the only way that we can not destroy ourselves is by radically transforming our goal of conscious and unconscious self-annihilation into the goal of conscious self-perfection. And the only way to do this is—urgently and immediately—to switch our orientation in every way from horizontal to vertical, to stop doing whatever we are now doing, and to begin the attempt to resurrect the dead.

## *The Unacknowledged Prince*

From the first obituaries to the most recent full biography, a phrase often used to characterize Fedorov is *Moskovskii Sokrat*, the "Moscow Socrates."[6] And in many ways Fedorov did lead a Socratic life—indifferent to status and comfort, preferring oral to written transmission of his ideas, relying on friends and disciples to propagate his teachings, using his place of work in the library as a teaching space, in the way that Socrates used the Athenian agora—but the difference in what they taught is crucial. We can recall that toward the end of his *Apology*, Socrates argues that death is not to be feared, that we do not know what death is, and therefore to fear death is a form of hubris, to pretend that we know what we do not know—for all we know, perhaps death is even a good thing. His last words in court are: "The hour of departure has arrived, and we go our ways—I to die, and you to live. Which is better God only knows."[7] In Fedorov, we definitely do know what death is, and it is not good. As we shall see, the awareness of death, the one enemy of all humankind, enters into his earliest memories.

Fedorov was born May 26, 1829, in the village of Kliuchi in Tambov Province in the south of Russia, the illegitimate son of Prince Pavel Ivanovich Gagarin (1798–1860s?), who was a black sheep from one of Russia's oldest and most illustrious families. Fedorov's mother was Elizaveta Ivanova, a local woman about whom very little is presently known.[8] From Fedorov's friend and follower Vladimir Kozhevnikov, the religious philosopher Pavel Florensky learned a few details about the family which he wrote down in a short biographical note about Fedorov.

> He was the son of Prince *Pavel Gagarin*. But just what kind of person this Pavel Gagarin was, it hasn't been possible to make out. By him

Fedorov's mother had four children—two sons and two daughters. At first it was thought that she was a peasant, but later it turned out that she was the daughter of a minor official—something like a collegiate register clerk....

At first she lived with Gagarin. But when [Pavel's] father—the old Gagarin—decided to marry off his son, they took the children away from her, surreptitiously loaded them in a coach, and took them off to one of the other family estates. Fedorov remembered how she ran after the coach and cried....

Fedorov rarely visited his mother. They weren't on good terms. But he evidently loved his father and spoke well of him.

That's all that Vladimir Alexandrovich Kozhevnikov told me.

Along with these details, Florensky offers a keen insight into Fedorov's philosophical work:

It's not difficult to understand what a deep connection this *past* of Nikolai Fedorovich has with his philosophical family, where there are a father, brothers and sisters, but no mother, where the earthly has such a specific aroma, where the feminine principle is so degraded.[9]

As many commentators have noted, Fedorov's thought is extremely patriarchal. He emphasizes rigor, duty, the task, abstention, the responsibility of sons toward fathers, and rails against the eternal temptress, the desire for trivial consumer goods, the "feminine" ideals of worldly pleasure and comfort. Whether due to early memories of his own mother, as Florensky suggested, or to other reasons, unlike many Russian writers and thinkers, Fedorov in all his writings honors the archetypal Great Father, "Lord of the Four Corners," rather than the Magna Mater.[10]

As was the custom at the time for illegitimate children, Fedorov was given his surname and patronymic, Fedorovich Fedorov, from the godfather at his christening. From Fedorov's father, the distinguished Gagarin line has been traced back as far as Riurik, the legendary founder of Russia. As noted above, Fedorov's grandfather, Ivan Alekseevich Gagarin, was a leading dignitary and Freemason from the late eighteenth century through the period of the Napoleonic wars. He could have been one of the pillars of a lodge very much like the one Pierre Bezukhov is initiated into in *War and Peace*. Ivan Alekseevich's second wife was the noted actress Katerina Semenova, considered by Pushkin to have been the greatest tragic actress of her time. Through marriage, the

Gagarin family was related to the Kropotkin family, and thus Fedorov was the unacknowledged second cousin of the famous anarchist P. A. Kropotkin. Another, closer relative of Fedorov's was Ivan Sergeevich Gagarin, a leading Slavophile of the 1830s and 1840s who later converted to Roman Catholicism. Of the Gagarin family in general, P. A. Kropotkin once wrote that it was after the infusion of Gagarin blood that the Kropotkin family first began to display literary talent and social concern.

Among Fedorov's papers, the editors of his posthumous works found only one torn sheet of autobiographical material. It reads:

> From the years of childhood three memories remain clear to me: I saw black, very black bread, on which (I heard people say) the peasants fed in what was probably some year of famine. From childhood I heard an explanation of war (to my question about it) that put me into terrible confusion: "In war people shoot *each other*!" And finally, I learned that some people are not one's kin but strangers, and even among one's kin some are not kin but strangers.[11]

These three memories, recalled near the end of a long life of activity and thought, point to three of Fedorov's abiding concerns: the problems of hunger, war, and the absence of feelings of kinship (*rodstvo*) among people. His project of resurrection would eventually include proposals that people regulate nature to provide adequate but not excessive harvests in order to end hunger, that implements of war be turned into instruments of salvation, and that Christianity become a project of universal sonship and kinship, and a labor to restore life to the ancestors. The memory that "even among one's kin some are not kin but strangers" is Fedorov's only recorded reference to his own illegitimate birth. But Fedorov's entire work can, in part, be understood as an attempt to deal, on a universal scale, with a problem that he first had to confront when he became fully aware of the circumstances of his birth. In a sense, Fedorov views all people as illegitimate children: the issue not of true, Christlike love but of blind natural force; offspring who have no true knowledge of even their mortal fathers—much less the divine Father; brothers and sisters unaware, or unwilling to acknowledge, that they are of one family.

And although Fedorov never uses the word "illegitimate," the role that he always assumes for himself in his writings is that of the outsider looking in, the unlearned man addressing an audience of the learned, the practical, down-to-earth working man talking to philosophers. As a nobleman without a title, an educated man without a degree, and a teacher without an academic appointment, Fedorov was able to discuss "learned" questions from an unusual perspective. His ideas, he believed, were not particularly original but were simply ideas that have long been common among the simple people. By giving these ideas philosophical expression, Fedorov was merely making them accessible to intellectuals. As an "unlearned" man addressing "the learned," Fedorov insisted that he was not trying to create a new philosophy but was merely pointing out problems of life and death which those who lacked privilege and comfort could not afford to ignore.

Fedorov's father, Prince Pavel Ivanovich Gagarin, followed what appear to have been artistic, perhaps bohemian inclinations, not living and working at the family estate but founding and directing theatrical companies in Odessa, Kishinev, and various other towns and cities in the south of what was then Russia (now Ukraine and Moldova). Pavel Ivanovich's passion was not limited to the theater itself but apparently extended also to a number of the actresses who graced his stages. The theatrical offerings, sometimes productions of high culture like Shakespeare and Schiller, other times vaudeville and slapstick comedies, all delighted his audiences, provided a steady flow of scandals for the newspapers, led Prince Pavel into bankruptcy, and estranged him from the rest of the Gagarin family. In addition to the four illegitimate children Prince Pavel Ivanovich fathered with Fedorov's mother, he later sired at least four more with another woman he did not marry, between which liaisons he fathered a legitimate family of three sons and two daughters with a lawful wife. Fedorov's much younger half brother from Pavel Ivanovich's second illegitimate family has left a touching account of the prince's melancholy isolation after the collapse of his theaters, when he would stay up alone late at night improvising beautiful but sad airs on the violin. Pavel Ivanovich continued to love and admire his distinguished brothers despite their scornful treatment of him. Fedorov's half brother tells us that he once sat with his father all afternoon outside their home waiting for one of Pavel Ivanovich's brothers, a distinguished government official, to ride by in an elegant carriage. At last the carriage did drive by, but the figure inside neither waved nor even glanced at his waiting brother and nephew. This event echoes Fedorov's scribbled memory that "even among one's kin some are not kin but strangers." Fedorov is known to have had at least two sisters, with whom he kept in contact over the years; a full brother, Alexander Fedorovich Fedorov, with whom he attended school as a boy and whose funeral he took rare time off from the library to attend; and the half brother already mentioned, Alexander Pavlovich Lensky, who became one of the leading stars of the late nineteenth-century Russian stage and whose autobiography does not mention Fedorov but provides a valuable account of a boyhood in the Gagarin household that must have been similar to the boyhood Fedorov had known twenty years earlier. Throughout his life, Fedorov kept in touch with, and sometimes visited, his half sisters from his father's legitimate family. On those visits, he was always addressed as Nikolai Pavlovich rather than Nikolai Fedorovich. N. P. Peterson, a friend and disciple who accompanied Fedorov on one of those visits, was too inhibited at the time to inquire about Fedorov's relationship to these aristocrats or why they called him Nikolai Pavlovich.

In the absence of Fedorov's father, an uncle, Konstantin Ivanovich Gagarin, assumed responsibility for the estate after the death of Fedorov's grandfather in 1832, and he generously provided for Fedorov's schooling, first at the Tambov Gymnasium, from which he graduated in 1848, and then at the Richelieu Lyceum, which for unknown reasons Fedorov left in 1854 without taking his degree. According to Peterson, Fedorov left the lyceum just before graduation, when, during an oral examination, he fell into a heated dispute with one of his instructors and refused to stand for further examination. Later, to a colleague at the Rumiantsev Museum, Fedorov mentioned that he had not obtained his degree because of an act of insubordination. But an additional reason was that Konstantin Ivanovich Gagarin, uncle and guardian to Fedorov and his brother, had died the year before, leaving no one to pay for the two boys' further education.

Although he did not attend a university, Fedorov's education was a good one for a young man of the time. That he studied at the respected Richelieu Lyceum indicates that his uncle Konstantin had provided him not only with the financial means but also the encouragement and confidence to pursue a sound education. That, in Peterson's version, Fedorov left in a huff before receiving his degree may suggest that quite early in life he had acquired some of the stubbornness, self-assurance, and intellectual independence that characterize his later writings and that seem to have been traits of the Gagarin line.

## *The Village Teacher*

After the lyceum, Fedorov began his years of wandering through southern and central Russia. From 1854 to 1868, he moved from one town or provincial village to another, serving as a teacher of elementary history and geography in such places as Lipetsk, Bogorodsk, Uglich, Odoeva, Bogoroditsk, Borovsk, and Podolsk. As a teacher, Fedorov seems to have been loved by his pupils and regarded by his superiors as a nuisance and a crank. His later friend, editor, and biographer Vladimir Kozhevnikov tells us that Fedorov's frequent removals were due to his unwillingness to limit his work to prescribed activities.

Apparently he caused constant friction by going beyond the duties officially assigned to teachers. In later years, Kozhevnikov tells us, Fedorov's former pupils continued to seek his advice on major decisions and answers to questions that troubled them in life. Fedorov believed that a teacher should treat his pupils like sons, and that his role as teacher should not be to discipline pupils but to set them working on joint projects of discovery. Believing that the entire family should take part in the children's education, Fedorov encouraged his pupils to tackle problems which could only be solved with help from home.

One of the stories that Kozhevnikov tells indicates the depth of Fedorov's love for his pupils. Like other provincial school teachers in Russia at the time, Fedorov received a salary that only a hermit could live well on. Nevertheless, Fedorov's greatest concern seems to have been not how to increase his income but how to give the largest part of his meager salary away. Once when a pupil's father fell ill and could not pay for a doctor, Fedorov gave the boy all his money to defray the father's medical expenses. When the pupil's father died, Fedorov sold his only teacher's uniform and donated the proceeds to the orphan to pay for the burial. When Fedorov appeared in school without his uniform, wearing the shabby clothing that was the only other clothing he owned, a school inspector severely reprimanded him for having dared appear in class in dress not befitting the station of teacher and demanded an immediate explanation. Fedorov stubbornly refused to offer any explanation and apparently indicated that he would rather resign than say a word in his own defense. Fortunately, on this occasion, the principal evidently learned the whole story and persuaded Fedorov not to resign. But from this incident one can perhaps begin to understand why Fedorov seldom stayed at any school for more than one year.

Documents recently uncovered by a Russian researcher further show how in his very first teaching job, Fedorov sorely irritated the headmaster of the village school at Lipetsk. In a formal complaint to the director of Tambov District schools, the Lipetsk headmaster writes:

> For some time now Mr. Fedorov, the teacher of geography and history at the school under my direction, has begun to display characteristics of impudence, willfulness, and insubordination, and more than once has directed insults not only at his comrades but also at people outside the school. The complaints that have come to me concerning his crude and insubordinate conduct on more than one occasion have forced me to report on him, and in order to curtail these bad inclinations of his, I

have employed every means to draw him into society, but all my efforts have turned out to be in vain.

Displaying a crude mentality, he looks down on everyone, and ignores decorum to such a degree that he even appears before me simply in galoshes, without boots, and through the entire past winter, heedless to my warnings, he wore a beard. Recently he was so impudent as to start instructing other teachers on how to conduct their classes; he berated the Russian language teacher Stepanov for wishing to punish a pupil, and later on the 23rd of last May not only berated but threatened to beat the teacher at another school, Erkov, for the sole reason that following my instructions he told a pupil that he could not dare come to school without proper clothing. For this offense I had to issue him a severe reprimand, but he, after uttering some rude comments, at once ceased teaching the class and forthwith quit his post, to which to this day he has stubbornly refused to return.

In presenting all this for Your Excellency's consideration, I would make bold to submit that Mr. Fedorov, owing to the coarseness and impudence of his character, as well as to the nature of his thoughts, nourished by the harmful false doctrines of the West: equality, liberty, and the rejection of authority and absolute indifference toward official obligations, can no longer be tolerated in his present position. For he, dreaming about equality, encourages his pupils to make insubordinate demands, he pays no attention whatsoever to advice or direction, he stubbornly wears a beard, and dresses in such a slovenly manner that he even brings shame to his comrades; and he treats the teaching of his subject carelessly, like mechanical labor, just to earn a living. As a result, the pupils in history and geography are left in an unsatisfactory situation.

As a green, supremely idealistic teacher, Fedorov could not have been an easy colleague to work with, much less supervise, but in his report to the district director, the headmaster of the Lipetsk school goes out of his way to disparage Fedorov. As we shall see from his friend Peterson's account of their first meeting, Fedorov's attitude toward the "harmful false doctrines" of equality, liberty, and other Western imports was not at all the attitude that the headmaster attributed to him—indeed, as we shall see later, Fedorov's view toward "progressive" ideas was even more negative than the headmaster's. Fedorov's shabby dress was less a gesture of insubordination than an indifference to all external appearance. He wore a beard because he was extremely conservative and identified with the patriarchs of old, not because he was an unkempt radical from the Parisian barricades eager to indoctrinate Lipetsk ten-year-olds in revolutionary politics. And, most important, as he explains in his response to the charges, his negative behavior toward his colleagues was in response to their mistreatment of both his and their pupils. Fedorov responded to the charges:

> As a result of your communication to me of August 7, I have the honor to offer you a brief explanation regarding the four points specified in your communication: (1) concerning the inappropriate and impudent behavior during the class lessons of comrades Misters Stepanov and Erkov. In your report to the director of the Tambov District schools concerning my inappropriate behavior toward comrades, you doubtless forgot to mention the bad behavior of these same comrades toward pupils. It is difficult to be an indifferent observer of the kind of behavior that Misters Stepanov and Erkov permit themselves toward their pupils, and I have not always managed to constrain myself within the limits of civility, and thus my involuntary displeasure came across as impudence. In order to ward off similar unpleasant situations, I have proposed to you, Mister Headmaster, that you put into effect a resolution, the force of which would be to assign the right to establish punishment for students to the District Pedagogical Council, and not to the whim of every teacher. You, Mister Headmaster, not only rejected my just demand, but even vowed to carry out the punishment of pupils yourself. After that, my further presence in the school could only serve to intensify the punishments. That is the reason for my voluntary termination of duties. The bad behavior of Misters Stepanov and Erkov toward their pupils was so unpleasant (and sad) for me to observe that I consider the teaching of geography and especially of history in light of such behavior to be absolutely impossible. If to this is also added the circumstance that in the entire district school there are only sixteen pupils, very few of whom regularly attend class, and entire classrooms have been standing empty, then it should be clear whether under such conditions successful instruction in the subjects I have been teaching is indeed even possible. But your expression "the pupils of all classes showed no successes whatsoever" forces me to doubt the accuracy of your investigations. As for the beard, I can only say that I actually wore it only two or three months over the course of the current year.[12]

Contrary to the charges brought against him, the later testimony of former students indicates that Fedorov was an exceptionally good teacher, always emphasizing practical applications of knowledge rather than simple memorization and accumulation of facts. As Kozhevnikov noted, years after Fedorov had left teaching to work in the Moscow libraries, former pupils continued to turn to him for advice. And as we shall see, whenever anyone came to him with a serious desire to learn, whether in school or in the library, Fedorov went to extraordinary lengths to encourage, assist, and if possible, properly direct that person's researches.

The years that Fedorov spent as a village teacher were critical years in the life of Russia. The Crimean War, the emancipation of the serfs, the decline of village life and the growth of cities, and the emergence of a radical intelligentsia all combined to make this period one of the most controversial and decisive in the history of the country. The Russia that Fedorov knew during these years of enormous change was not the Russia of Moscow and Petersburg but the Russia of Lipetsk, Bogorodsk, Uglich, and Podolsk. The people he knew and identified with were not those who were making decisions for all Russia but those who had to live with whatever decisions were made. In the towns and villages, where Fedorov lived, war meant peasants returning without arms or legs and families without fathers or sons. Emancipation too often simply meant being uprooted. Education meant learning to remove oneself from the common people and the common life. He would later suggest that emancipation had been a great mistake, that instead of freeing the serfs, the Tsar should have enserfed the free. And education, as currently practiced, produced only learned idlers—future education should become universal active research into the causes and solutions to the problem of death.

As noted before, Fedorov would later write that the most serious and destructive division between people was not between rich and poor but between the learned and the unlearned. Those of the learned class, he argued, had separated themselves from the unlearned masses, from the soil, from their origins, from their fathers, and, ultimately, from nature, God, and life. The learned, who had the knowledge to control the blind, destructive forces of nature, did not feel the need to do so. Living in cities, insensible to nature's brute power, the learned viewed nature merely from an aesthetic standpoint. The unlearned, on the other hand, who knew and had to bear the brunt of nature's blind force every day, had the desire but lacked the knowledge to exercise control. To the learned, nature was a matter of beauty or ugliness, to the unlearned, a matter of life and death. The idea of nature at its purest, as wilderness, for Fedorov, would always be the opposite of the Romantic ideal, still common in America today, of pristine, sacred space unspoiled by humans. In describing the Russian natural landscape, Fedorov writes that it is better for the soul that Russia has no spectacular scenery, no Alpine grandeur or charming Italianate vistas to lull the Russian into complacency, to tempt him toward aesthetic delight, lead him to sublime repose, and distract him from his transformative task. In Fedorov any form of nature worship is viewed essentially as a death wish.

Moreover, by pursuing knowledge for its own sake and scorning all practical application of knowledge, Fedorov argued, the learned merely aided those who would wage war. The learned contribute to the waging of war either directly, by discoveries which can be turned into weapons, or indirectly, by allowing their discoveries to be turned into articles of commerce, which leads to competition, which then inevitably leads to war. The only solution was for the learned to form themselves into a "temporary task force" whose assignment would be to find practical means to regulate nature. In the war against nature, all armies of the world would collaborate to liberate mankind from blind force, and all military weapons would be turned into instruments for the benefit of humanity. Just as in war, "people shoot each other," so in the task of regulation people would shoot their cannons not at each other but at the natural forces they wish to control. This simple but radical shift in direction seemed to Fedorov the first step toward the solution of the problem of how to turn mankind from self-destruction. By shifting the orientation from horizontal to vertical, initially in the aiming of cannons and later in other redirections of effort, man could begin the task of his own resurrection.

## First Disciple; Dostoevsky and Tolstoy

In the early 1860s, a book that all young Russian intellectuals were talking about was Chernyshevsky's long, turgid didactic novel, *What Is to Be Done?* In his hero, Rakhmetov, and his heroine, Vera, Chernyshevsky attempted to create positive models to be emulated by Russian youth. In deliberate contrast to the line of attractive, talented, but ineffectual "superfluous men" notorious to all students of Russian literature, Rakhmetov is an upright, faultless, unwavering "new man" selflessly dedicated to his "cause," the establishing of utopian communes and the eventual revolutionary transformation of Russian society. Vera, the model for the new Russian woman, launches as her part in the transformation of Russia a sewing cooperative in which three young girls gradually become aware of the benefits of communal life and labor.

This book, and the writings of Chernyshevsky's two younger fellow "nihilists," Nikolai Dobroliubov and Dmitri Pisarev, had an enormous impact on the student generation of the 1860s. Living in tiny, filthy, book-cluttered rooms, underlining pages of Mill, Comte, Darwin, and Buchner's *Kraft und Stoff*, calling themselves "socialists," "scientists," "determinists," "Nihilists," or simply "new people," thousands of sometime students all over Russia were discussing, planning, and sporadically attempting to take actual steps toward the radical transformation of Russia into a vaguely socialist, materialist, utopian society. Some of these young revolutionaries and would-be revolutionaries met in more or less secret groups to discuss ideas, exchange literature, and lay plans for future action. Early in 1864, one such ex-student, Nikolai Pavlovich Peterson, then twenty years old and a member of a Moscow based group which would later be known as "The Organization," came to Bogorodsk, ostensibly to teach mathematics, but chiefly to spread revolutionary propaganda. He writes:

One of my fellow members in the circle informed me that in Bogorodsk there was a teacher at the district school, a certain Nikolai Fedorovich Fedorov, a selfless man who by his life reminded one of Rakhmetov, a man of unusual intelligence and honesty; and at that time we thought that an intelligent and honest man could not help but be on our side. And so arriving in Bogorodsk on March 15, 1864, I went at once to see Nikolai Fedorovich, who turned out to be a man about forty years old, i.e., about four years older than Lev Nikolaevich;[13] he was a bachelor and lived as an ascetic: he not only did without a bed, but without even a pillow; he ate whatever his landlords, simple merchants, put out for him, the healthful, but simple food that they themselves ate; during Lent N. F. ate Lenten dishes, and on Wednesdays, Fridays, and other days of fasting, he fasted. N. F. never made any special demands and was always content with whatever he was given. In my first meeting with N. F. I immediately blurted out everything about myself and explained the purpose for which I had become a teacher at the district school. To this N.F. said: "I don't understand what you're troubling yourself about. After all, you won't be able to give those for whom you're troubling yourself anything except material well-being, since you don't admit to any other well-being; but meanwhile, working to obtain material well-being for others, you renounce it for yourself and indeed are prepared even to sacrifice your life for the sake of this. But what if material well-being is no more important to those for whom you're troubling yourself than it is for you? To what end is all your bother?" In the course of our conversation I heard from N. F. that the so-called great principles of the great French Revolution—*freedom, equality, and brotherhood*—are the product of extremely shallow thought, or even of thoughtlessness, since *brotherhood cannot result from freedom to fulfill one's whims or from the envious desire for equality;* only brotherhood leads to freedom, for brothers who love one another will not envy one brother who is elevated above others, and will not try to lower him to their own level; and the brother who has raised himself above the others will try to bring all his brothers up to his level. For that reason, we must seek brotherhood first and not put it at the tail, after freedom and equality, as did the proponents of freedom, equality, and brotherhood—we must seek brotherhood first, and the rest will follow. But there cannot be brotherhood without fatherhood and a fatherland—for only by fathers are we brothers, and therefore filial and paternal love must be placed at the head, and from this fraternal love will issue. Conversing in this manner, N. F. gradually unfolded an entire world outlook which was perfectly new to me, and which called for the unification of all people in a labor of universal resurrection. I was committed at once and, already, forever. Nikolai Fedorovich did not stay long in Bogorodsk while I was there, no more than about three months; but these three months enriched me more than my entire life had before and gave me a firm base for the remainder of my life.[14]

A young revolutionary thus became Fedorov's first disciple. But two years later, in 1866, Fedorov's association with this young disciple led to his arrest in connection with the student Dmitri Karakozov's unsuccessful attempt to assassinate Tsar Alexander II. Peterson, before meeting Fedorov, had belonged to the same revolutionary circle as Karakozov, and shortly after the attempted assassination, Peterson, Fedorov, and a handful of Karakozov's other associates were brought in for questioning. During the interrogation, Peterson and the other young revolutionaries all testified that Fedorov had met with them, but that in those meetings the older man had argued strenuously against their convictions and had tried in every way possible to convince them to give up their revolutionary activities. As a result all charges against Fedorov were dismissed and he was quickly freed. Karakozov was hanged, the other conspirators received prison sentences of varying length, Peterson's being six months.

As Peterson's Bogorodsk account indicates, and as the testimony of the Karakozov circle confirms, Fedorov had already worked out the main lines of his entire project by 1864. Indeed, in an article about Tolstoy from 1892, Fedorov writes that the idea of active resurrection awakened in him in 1851, when he was still at the lyceum.[15] But he may not have begun to develop his ideas in writing until Peterson joined him as amanuensis and began to take down Fedorov's dictation. Although work kept them apart for most of the year, Fedorov and Peterson would meet on vacations and during the summers, and it was during these periods, over many years, that Fedorov's ideas were committed to writing. As Peterson acknowledges, it was he who first brought Fedorov's ideas to the attention of Dostoevsky and Tolstoy.

It was in 1876, in his capacity as editor of the journal *Diary of a Writer*, that Dostoevsky first received a manuscript from Peterson. For years, Peterson had been trying without success to persuade Fedorov to submit some of his dictated writings for publication. Finally, without Fedorov's knowledge, Peterson decided to take matters into his own hands, and early in 1876 he sent Dostoevsky a manuscript of his own that contained a number of ideas that he could only have gotten from Fedorov. In the March 1876 issue of *Diary of a Writer*, Dostoevsky, without mentioning Peterson's name, published some extracts from the manuscript and offered comments to the effect that he found the ideas interesting but "isolated," and in fact although the unnamed author advocated a "genuine communion among men," the author's thoughts were examples of the very "isolation" and "chemical decomposition of our society into its component parts" that both Dostoevsky and the unnamed author abhorred. Dostoevsky, then, found the manuscript to be symptomatic of the very condition it purported to diagnose.[16] A year later, when he received another manuscript from Peterson, this one containing a more detailed account of Fedorov's idea, Dostoevsky sent a much different response:

> The first matter is a question: who is this thinker whose thoughts you have sent me? If possible, let me know his real name. He has aroused my interest more than enough. By all means do tell me something more detailed about him as a person—all this if you can.
>
> Let me tell you that essentially I am in complete agreement with these ideas. I have read them as if they were my own. Today I read them (anonymously) to Vladimir Sergeevich Solovyov, our young philosopher who is now delivering lectures on religion, lectures that nearly a thousand attend. I waited for him on purpose to read him your account of your thinker's ideas, since I found in his view

much that is similar. We spent a beautiful two hours at this. He finds your thinker's ideas much to his liking and had wished to say almost the same things in his next lecture (of twelve lectures he still has four to give). But now I have a friendly, if difficult question, one that I've wanted to put to you since December.

In your account of this thinker, the most essential thing, without a doubt, is the duty to resurrect the ancestors who lived before. If this duty were fulfilled, then childbirth would cease, and what the Gospels and the Book of Revelation have designated as the first resurrection would begin. But what you have not stated at all in your account is just how you understand this resurrection of ancestors—in just what form you envision and believe in it. That is, do you understand it somehow mentally or allegorically, like, for example, Renan, who understands it to be something like a total illumination of human consciousness at the end of the life of mankind, an illumination of such intensity that it will be clear to the mind of those future people how great was, for example, one of their ancestor's influence on mankind, how and in what manner his influence was exerted, and so forth, and of such intensity that the role of every person who lived before will be seen with perfect clarity, his contribution will be divined . . ., so intense that we shall even recognize the influence that all those who have lived before have exerted on us and the extent to which they are reincarnated in us; and will all this come to pass among those last people, who will know everything and be in utter harmony, those last people in whom humanity will reach its conclusion—

or:

does your thinker intend this to be taken directly and literally, as religion implies, and that the resurrection will be real, that the abyss that divides us from the spirits of our ancestors will be filled, will be vanquished by vanquished death, and that the dead will be resurrected not only in our minds, not allegorically, but in fact, in person, actually in bodies. (N.b. Not of course in their present bodies, for when immortality begins, marriage and the birth of children will end, and that alone is testimony that in the first resurrection, designated to be on earth, the bodies will perhaps be like Christ's body in the fifty days between his resurrection and ascension?)

An answer to this question is essential—otherwise it will all be impossible to understand. I warn you that we here, that is, Solovyov and I at least, believe in a real, literal, personal resurrection, and one that will come to pass on earth. Do let me know, then, if you can and will, esteemed N. P., what your thinker thinks about this, and, if possible, let me know in more detail.[17]

Fedorov would later sharply attack both Dostoevsky and Solovyov for having envisioned a "mystical," "esoteric," "occult" form of resurrection accessible only to initiates and adepts.[18] But his first reaction on reading this extraordinary letter was to begin to prepare what Fedorov and Peterson hoped would be a clear and adequate response to the great writer's questions. They worked at it off and on over the next two years, resulting eventually in the first and longest essay published in the first volume of Fedorov's posthumously collected works, titled "The question of brotherhood, or kinship, of the reasons for the unbrotherly, unkindred, i.e., unpeaceful state of the world, and of the means for the restoration of kinship: A note from the unlearned to the learned; Clergy and laity, believers and unbelievers."[19] But before the manuscript was sufficiently finished to send it off, Dostoevsky had died.

As many scholars have noted,[20] Fedorov's ideas are clearly reflected in *The Brothers Karamazov*. As I have argued elsewhere,[21] Dostoevsky had read many of the same books and shared many ideas, and even without Fedorov's manuscript, Dostoevsky was keenly aware of the complex nature of father-son competition. Fedorov's contribution probably was to clarify and point out the consequences of some of the thoughts that Dostoevsky had not thought through to the end. Fedorov may not have formulated his idea as brilliantly or as dramatically as Dostoevsky did, but the manuscript that Peterson sent was probably behind Ivan's question "Who does not desire the death of his father?" And Fedorov's arguments that we are all guilty of patricide probably helped Dostoevsky see that all four brothers, even saintly Alyosha, were to one degree or another responsible for the death of Fedor Karamazov.

Although Dostoevsky never did meet or even learn the name of the author of the ideas he had read "as if they were my own," the manuscript prepared as an answer to Dostoevsky's questions served to introduce both Fedorov and his idea to Lev Nikolaevich Tolstoy. As Peterson tells it:

I cannot but relate here that in the summer of 1878 Nikolai Fedorovich spent only two weeks at my house. In the same summer I came to see him in Moscow, and on the Syzran-Morshansk railroad, on the half between Penza and Morshansk, I met L. N. Tolstoy; he was returning with all his family from the Samara estate to Yasnaya Polyana, and I

rode with him as far as Riazhsk. On the way I told him about Nikolai
Fedorovich and my communications with Dostoevsky. I read him
Dostoevsky's letter and what I had written from Nikolai Fedorovich's
dictation in reply to that letter during the two weeks that Nikolai
Fedorovich had just spent with me. After he had heard me through,
Lev Nikolaevich told me that he didn't like the idea. Nevertheless, that
same autumn Lev Nikolaevich went to see Nikolai Fedorovich at the
museum and told him that he knew me, and from that time they began
their acquaintanceship.[22]

Dostoevsky and Solovyov were attracted to Fedorov's ideas before they
knew anything at all about the man. But Tolstoy, characteristically, had to find
out what kind of life Fedorov lived before becoming interested in his ideas.
And even after he had long known both Fedorov and his thought, Tolstoy
remained more impressed by the idea that Fedorov slept on a humpback
trunk than by the entire project of universal resurrection.

Through the decade of the 1880s and into the early 1890s, Tolstoy and
Fedorov met many times, and Tolstoy frequently refers to him in his letters
and notebooks. For Tolstoy these were years of spiritual unrest. Never a complacent person unaware of his own self-development, Tolstoy in the late 1870s
and early 1880s was passing through a stage of especially intense spiritual tor-
ment and particularly ruthless self-examination. His earlier religious faith,
never terribly strong, had collapsed utterly, and he was seeking a new faith to
live by. That he could not live a life strictly consistent with his deeply felt (and
widely publicized) principles had always troubled him, and now tormented
him. He had turned against the ideal of family life that he had so memorably
depicted in *War and Peace*, but he still lived as—and at times very much
enjoyed being—a family man. Theoretically he had turned against his own
social class and against all art that did not illustrate some simple moral
truth—and yet his biographers give us a charming picture of Tolstoy at age
fifty and his old aesthetic and ideological enemy Turgenev, age sixty, sitting at
opposite ends of a child's teeter-totter, seesawing up and down as children
from the neighborhood laugh and applaud. Even during his famous "peasant"
phase, in which he allowed himself to be portrayed by the artist Repin *à la
moujik* behind a plow, we learn from his wife's diary that under his peasant
smock he always wore silk underwear.

In the early 1880s, then, Tolstoy was searching for, among other things, a
person whose life was in full accordance with whatever principles he
espoused. And chief among those who, in Tolstoy's judgment, passed that

test was Fedorov. Eyewitnesses to their meetings describe Tolstoy's unusual deference toward Fedorov, as if he viewed Fedorov as his moral superior, and in his behavior with Fedorov sometimes acted more like a son in the presence of a stern father than like a contemporary and equal. Professor I. A. Linnichenko, who observed the two together many times, tells us that Tolstoy "not only highly valued N. F.'s moral qualities, he even openly bowed down before him, seeing in him one of the best personifications of his theory about loving what is close at hand and living life simply."[23] The director of the Tretiakov Gallery, Chernogub, tells us that he once heard Tolstoy say: "If I didn't have my own teaching, I would become a follower of Nikolai Fedorovich's teaching."[24]

The deference, however, was not reciprocal. People who often observed them talking together tell us that when Fedorov spoke, Tolstoy would listen respectfully and nod his agreement, but when Tolstoy spoke Fedorov would usually scowl sternly and shake his head in strong objection. Fedorov was apparently one of the few people who dared tell Tolstoy to his face that he was an utter fool. N. N. Gusev relates that once while walking with Fedorov through the library stacks, Tolstoy looked at the books piled everywhere and remarked: "Ech, they ought to dynamite here!" Fedorov apparently never forgave him for this remark. In another version of what may have been the same incident, Tolstoy said: "So many stupid things are written; it all ought to be burned!" Fedorov, as if stung, seized him by the head. "I've seen many stupid men in the world, but never one like you!" The witness reports that the author of *War and Peace* looked shocked, embarrassed, and confused. And once when they were arguing some philosophical point, Tolstoy began to refer to something he had written earlier on the matter under discussion. Fedorov replied: "Very well, but at that time you, Lev Nikolaevich, were not only a distinguished writer, you were an intelligent person as well."[25]

Fedorov's objections to Tolstoy's late-period writings were chiefly that Tolstoy loved death and that while claiming to offer a simpler, truer form of Christianity, he was actually preaching neo-Buddhism. Tolstoy's doctrine of nonresistance was, to Fedorov, a total capitulation to the forces of nature, disintegration, and death. As Tolstoy himself told a young listener who began to smile as Tolstoy explained Fedorov's theory:

Yes, if you had tried to smile in his presence he would have let you have it. Once I happened to catch sight of a little book in the Rumiantsev Museum—a list of colonels for some certain number of years—and I smiled. Did he scold me! "All this is needed: all these are reminiscences of our ancestors." Now he can't abide me: in the first place because I don't share his theory; in the second place, because I love death.[26]

## *The Moscow Librarian*

Besides Peterson's help in presenting Fedorov's ideas to his great contemporaries, it was also through Peterson that Fedorov became a librarian. Either because of conflicts with superiors, such as the ones described earlier, or because of personal wishes, Fedorov hardly ever taught for more than a year in the same school. Each year he petitioned his superiors to allow him a ten-day leave to come to Moscow, usually walking on foot, for the Easter season. And when he resigned from one teaching position to move on to another, the official reason given was usually "on account of illness." In 1868, Fedorov quit his last teaching job and came to Moscow without specific plans for future employment. Peterson, who had been serving as librarian at the beautiful Chertkov Library, a wealthy collector's private institution devoted to collecting every known book related to Russia, had just accepted a position with the district court system and recommended Fedorov as his replacement at the library. It was a perfect position for Fedorov, who threw himself wholeheartedly into the work, and his services were immediately recognized and appreciated. In 1873 the entire Chertkov Library, and with it Fedorov, was absorbed into the larger Rumiantsev Museum. This institution, where Fedorov would work for the next twenty-five years, was Moscow's leading public library, and today forms a wing of the vast Russian State (formerly Lenin) Library. In Fedorov's day, the library contained some 85,000 books and pamphlets, and some 18,000 broadsides, maps, and other unbound materials. Fedorov, in his capacity as cataloguer and circulation clerk, was reputed to know not only the location but also the contents of every item in the library. Whenever a reader submitted a list of books to be brought from the stacks, he would often receive not only the items requested but also several additional materials which the reader had never heard of, yet which would prove extremely useful, sometimes even essential, for his study. When the fortunate reader asked where the extra books had come from, he or she was told simply that Nikolai Fedorovich had sent them. And sometimes, after receiving repeated "extras" from Nikolai Fedorovich, the reader would be delivered an invitation to visit Fedorov in his office. Then, it was said, the reader's real education would begin.

During his long life in Moscow, Fedorov lived alone, frequently changing addresses, but usually renting a small, closet-sized room for around six rubles a month.[27] He slept on a humpback trunk, sometimes bare, sometimes covered with newspapers, placing under his head not a pillow but some hard object, usually a book. The only coat he wore every day, summer or winter, was more rag than coat, and strangers easily mistook him for a beggar on the streets. He had no furniture, and each time he moved to new quarters he gave away whatever objects the room had accumulated. He spent nothing on entertainment, diversion, or any conveniences, and he refused to take cabs even in the coldest winter months. He drank only tea, ate hard rolls, sometimes accompanied by a piece of old cheese or salt fish, and lived for months without a hot meal. One of Fedorov's landlords asked visitors if Fedorov ate with them, for he had never taken the board that was included in the price for the rent of the room. Sometimes, almost by force, friends would settle him in decent, comfortable quarters, arrange with the landlord for a daily meal with at least two courses, and furnish the room with at least a bed and pillow. If the friends returned in a week, however, they would find that the room was again bare, that Fedorov had already given away the bed and pillow, and that at Fedorov's insistence the landlord would again be serving him only bread and tea.

According to Kozhevnikov, Fedorov had a fear of money and considered it poisonous, infectious, and vile. If he found any change in his pockets at night he would curse himself for not having managed to give it away. He was obsessed with the fear that someday he might be found dead with two or three kopecks left in his pocket.

Fedorov never married, and until recently he was not known to have had a romantic interest in any woman. But in researching archival materials, the Russian scholar Anastasia Gacheva discovered and published a surprising series of letters that Fedorov wrote to Ekaterina Stepanova Nekrasova, a young, pretty journalist. In most of these letters Fedorov speaks only of books ordered or delivered, but in one dated April 6, 1880, he expresses sentiments that give a very different picture from the stern, patriarchal misogynist that some commentators have made him out to be.

I have written you, deeply and sincerely esteemed Ekaterina Stepanovna, at least ten letters—you may see them if you wish—but could not make up my mind to send them. Now I shall say the same thing in two or three words, only take them literally, with all the force of their meaning. I shall say straight out that I nourish toward your person a boundless, exclusive feeling of attraction. I am devoted to you with all my heart, all my mind, all my soul. Of all this, I hope, you will be convinced, as soon as you change your anger to kindness, which I implore you to do. It is unbearably painful for me to see you unhappy, but even more painful not to see you at all.

Sincerely devoted to you,

Nikolai Fedorov

I'll keep hoping that you do not leave my letter unanswered.[28]

With all its arch diction, this is as near a "love letter," as Fedorov would ever write. He was past fifty, she was nearly twenty years younger. He knew that she regarded him as a wise and true friend, but he wished he could be more. What must have hurt Fedorov most was that the man Ekaterina Nekrasova preferred to him, but who did not return her love, was Gleb Uspensky, a writer of limited talent and scope whose then extremely popular but now largely overlooked novels about the brutality of Russian peasant life reflect a shattered idealism and a bitter outlook on life. Nekrasova was hopelessly in love with Uspensky, and for some time they had an on-again, off-again relationship, but in 1885 she had to accept that their latest break-up would be final. After a series of literary successes alternating with failures, Uspensky spent his last years in a mental institution, and in 1902 at the age of fifty-nine committed suicide. After Fedorov's letter of April 6, 1880, the only letters from him to her that have survived are brief, official messages on library matters. After Fedorov's death, Nekrasova wrote a warm obituary for one of the leading Moscow newspapers, in which she presented intimate details of his life and library work in Moscow but made no mention of his philosophy or of any relationship other than that between a kind, considerate librarian and a grateful researcher.

During Fedorov's last years, his daily working schedule, as chronicled by Nekrasova and many others, remained essentially the same as always. He would arrive at the library an hour or so before it opened, to make certain that books ordered late the previous day would be ready when the reader called. He would stay at the library after closing time to take care of any jobs that he had not been able to complete during business hours. He had no sympathy for those who were demanding an eight-hour workday, which he called "sixteen-hour idleness." At home, he would have a light meal and talk with any friends who dropped by. He would sleep for two or three hours, until about midnight, then he would read and write until almost dawn. Then, after another short sleep of about two or three hours, he would set off for the library to start a new day.

# Last Years: Askhabad; The Only Portrait

In 1899 Peterson was transferred to the District Court in Ashkhabad, Turkestan, and in the summer of that year Fedorov visited him to continue their long joint project of writing. This visit to Turkestan brought a new theme into Fedorov's thought and helped to open a new topic for thinkers who would come after him: the task of uniting East and West, Asia and Europe, the special continental Eurasian nature of Russia's historic mission. The question of Asia's future role in the world was the subject of much popular speculation at the time. In different ways and on different intellectual levels, Madame Blavatsky's theosophical writings proclaiming new wisdom from Asia, Vladimir Solovyov's apocalyptic visions of "Panmongolism," and the journalists who wrote of the "yellow peril" all contributed to the fin de siècle assumption that in Russia as well as in Europe, the time of Western dominance was coming to an end and a period of Asian supremacy was about to begin. But Fedorov took quite a different view. Turkestan, the vast territory both joining and separating Russia and China, a sparsely inhabited wasteland dominated by the Pamir mountains and the surrounding desert, became in Fedorov's thought a major focal point for the task of regulating nature and resurrecting the dead. Formerly, Fedorov learned, the wasteland had been fertile and inhabited and, according to local legend, was even the site of the original Eden. Only man's failure to regulate nature had permitted the former paradise to become an uninhabitable wasteland. Legend held that the bones of Adam, the father of all fathers, were buried somewhere in these desolate mountains. And, as Fedorov once wrote to Kozhevnikov, the landscape of the Pamir region reminded him of a "pyramid of skulls." At that time, also, the Pamir region was thought to be one of the most likely candidates for the hypothetical homeland of the original Indo-European people. From here the first fathers of all Indo-European language speakers had supposedly dispersed to what would become India, Persia, and Europe. In later times, the Pamir region had been the center from which the Mongol hordes had overrun Russia, the Middle East, and Eastern Europe. Pamir, then, represented to Fedorov the world's center of repulsion. Adam and Eve, the Aryans, and the Mongols had all fled from this lost paradise. On either side of the Pamir region now lived representatives of the major races and religions of the world: Turan and Aryan; Buddhist, Hindu, Zoroastrian, Muslim, and Christian. Fedorov believed that it was of more than political significance that in a recent treaty with England, Russia had gained control over the Pamir region. The duty of the Russian Tsar, as the one sitting in Pamir, the "father place" and "forefather place" (*otsov-mesto i praotsov-mesto*), would now be to start the restoration of Pamir by building in the high, absolutely clear air of one of the peaks an observatory for advanced research in astronomy, a first step toward regathering dispersed particles of ancestral dust and eventually establishing settlements beyond earth. He also proposed that Ashkhabad become a site for international scientific research conferences, where specialists from all fields could collaborate as a special task force devoted to the restoration of life to the region, and, eventually, to all the dead. In the 1920s, the "Eurasian" movement of Russian émigrés would adopt Fedorov as a cofounder of their movement, and in the mid-twentieth century Kazakhstan and Turkmenistan would indeed become major centers for the astronomical and space-industry activities that had been among Fedorov's signature ideas.

It was during his visit to Peterson in Ashkhabad that a detailed presentation of Fedorov's project first provoked a strong reaction from members of the general public.[29] First Peterson, then Fedorov himself published, under various pseudonyms, a series of articles in the local newspaper, *Askhabad*, and while there was no immediate reaction to the first articles, as more items appeared a lively polemic ensued. Between September 1899 and March 1903, at least fifty articles appeared presenting or reacting to Fedorov's ideas. In a typical sequence, Peterson, under the initials "N. P.," would write an article on a Fedorovian theme, then a regular columnist named Tsirkunov would respond with qualified interest and sympathy, another columnist who wrote under the name "Pensoso" would ridicule it mercilessly, Peterson would then write, under a different pseudonym, a defense of his initial "N. P." article, then two or three other writers would state their opinions, ranging from interested curiosity to puzzlement to outright disapproval, and then Fedorov himself would enter the polemic with a definitive clarification, further exposition, and defense of the idea, sometimes adding for good measure a sharp putdown of "Mr. Pensoso." Then everyone would write back, and the polemic would enter another cycle. Of all the *Askhabad* writers, only Peterson, with his several pseudonyms, fully endorsed Fedorov's project. Of the rest, even the most positive expressed serious reservations about the more radical sides of the project, and several simply found the whole idea preposterous. Probably the most important thing that Fedorov gained from the *Askhabad* polemic was a sense that neither was his project ready for the world nor was the world ready for his project. He had always been reluctant to publish his ideas, and this experience vindicated his reservations. Although he despised the notion of esotericism, Fedorov was now fated to become an unintentionally esoteric writer whose ideas would be known to only a small coterie of friends and disciples and, when eventually published, would for many years find only a small, if devoted and highly influential, readership.

One of the ideas that Fedorov retained through life was that even the most menial and mundane job could become a sacred task. In the Chertkov Library and the Rumiantsev Museum, he often said that "behind the book, a man is hidden," and treated even the most trivial assignments as opportunities to resurrect dead knowledge. In his last position, as desk clerk in the hall of archives for the Ministry of Foreign Affairs, which he assumed after retiring from the Rumiantsev Museum, he transformed his actual humble duties into a project for discovering and preserving documents pertaining to present worldwide disunity and future, Russian-directed worldwide unity. In the records of Russia's foreign relations, he found innumerable confirmations of his conviction that Russia had a special destiny in the world. His late writings show that he had done considerable research on the historical meaning of the title "Tsar" (derived from "Caesar"), and that he had looked carefully at the wording of treaties under which Russia had acquired new territories. He found, essentially, that Russia's territorial growth had resulted from a series of acts that had both sacred and worldly, both hidden and open, significance. The Russian Tsar was divinely intended to be the father of all living peoples, and to represent the interests of the dead among the living. The true task of the Tsar was to gather all lands into one land and to make all peoples one people. Building on the medieval doctrine of "Moscow, the Third Rome," Fedorov was convinced that in the archives of the foreign affairs ministry lay documents of paramount importance for the history of mankind. Russia's history was the world's history: dividing all in history as fact, uniting all in history as project.

In letters to his friend Vladimir Kozhevnikov, written during the last five years of his life, Fedorov often expressed doubt that his lifelong project would find immediate acceptance and recognition. "I have no hope that in our age of unthought and inaction the problem of the universal task, of the regulation of nature by human reason and will, can possibly attract attention to itself." Fedorov was writing, he confessed, "under the influence of complete hopelessness," knowing that "no one has any use for these writings," and that "the teaching on the active relationship to nature, with all its consequences, will be rejected by some as a diatribe from an age of ignorance, and by others as unbelief." But, he also wrote, "my certainty and boldness grow together with the negative reactions and nonrecognition accorded my convictions."[30] As Kozhevnikov writes:

He knew that it is not the grain that appears before all others that grows longest and bears the most abundant crop; he was even convinced that a doctrine too far advanced above the general level of its time would be condemned to temporary failure, that it would have to be buried, perhaps for a long time, but that in time it was also certain to be resurrected, and that it would be recognized and accepted in the very place where once it had elicited only mockery or a smile of doubt.[31]

The only portrait that we have of Fedorov was made in stealth by the well-known painter Leonid Pasternak, father of the poet Boris Pasternak. Pasternak tells us that once while working in the Rumiantsev Museum, he became intrigued by the appearance and manner of the old man who served in the reading room. He began to make a sketch, but noticed that the old man suspected what Pasternak was doing and obviously did not like the idea of being drawn. So for several days in a row, Pasternak sat behind a mountainous stack of books and tried to appear to be busy reading them. He would look up only infrequently, so as not to arouse the old man's suspicion. He kept his sketches, and only later learned that the old man was the philosopher Fedorov. He later used these sketches as the basis for his portrait, now in the Tolstoy Museum in Moscow, of Fedorov, Tolstoy, and Solovyov together. In it, Fedorov is an old man with a full, white beard and a high, bare brow. He is sitting at his desk with his hands crossed before him inside the large, loose sleeves of his shirt. Behind him is a shelf full of books. Although he is looking in Tolstoy's direction, his eyes seem to be staring intently at something behind the portrait's frame. In the death mask, also done by Pasternak, and printed in the journal *Vesy*, the face carries the same intense but meditative expression, but now the eyes are closed.[32]

Fedorov died in December of 1903. As Alexander Gorsky, writing under the pseudonym Ostromirov, tells us, Fedorov had been healthy in even the harshest Moscow winters of previous years, but in this particularly severe winter friends persuaded him to wear a warm coat instead of the light outer rag he had always worn summer and winter, and got him to start taking a cab instead of walking to work. Not long after he had begun to follow this well-meant advice, he contracted pneumonia and died.

Kozhevnikov, who was at Fedorov's deathbed, tells us that during the last, painful hours, Fedorov said nothing of himself or of his pain, or even of death itself, but continued to talk as long as he had strength about the contents of the last two articles he had written, and that even after he could no longer speak, his lips continued to tremble as if he were trying to express the unuttered thoughts that were still burning in his eyes. He was buried in the Skorbiashchenskii Zhenskii Monastery where, when Gorsky wrote in 1928, his grave could still be found, marked by a cross engraved with the words "Christ Is Risen." Not many years after Gorsky's visit, the monastery was closed, the site was razed, and a playground now stands in its place.

# 7

## The "Common Task"

*People, earthbound men, you who have surrendered yourselves to drunk-
enness and sleep and ignorance of God, make yourselves sober and end your
drunken sickness, for you are bewitched in unreasoning sleep.*

*Why have you surrendered yourselves to death, earthbound men, since you
have the right to share in immortality? You who have journeyed with error,
who have partnered with ignorance, think again: escape the shadowy light,
leave corruption behind and take a share in immortality.*
—THE POIMANDRES OF HERMES TRISMEGISTUS

OF THE COSMIST thinkers, Fedorov was the most direct in his rejection of
anything connected with esotericism. But as with the other Cosmists, esoteric
teachings underlie much of Fedorov's thought.

### The Esoteric Dimension of the "Common Task"

From the first reviews of *The Philosophy of the Common Task*, commentators
have called attention to an esoteric dimension present in Fedorov's thought,
but only a few pieces of commentary have gone beyond noting that dimension's existence.[1] The role that esotericism plays, however, in the thought of
Fedorov and, consequently, in the thought of the Cosmists who followed
him, deserves more than a mention or even a brief paragraph, so we shall now
turn to a more detailed examination of that role.

Scholars of the history of Western esotericism have devoted considerable
attention to the important question of just what the term "esotericism" means,
and how it relates to "hermeticism," "occultism," "Neoplatonism," and other
terms frequently encountered in literature on the subject. Antoine Faivre has
offered a useful six-point list of characteristics or components present in the
form of thought traditionally identified as "esoteric." As Faivre explains: "Four
are 'intrinsic,' meaning that they must all be present for a given material to be

classified under the rubric of esotericism. By nature they are more or less inseparable, as we shall see, but methodologically it is important to distinguish them. To them two more components are added that we shall call secondary, i.e., not fundamental, but frequently found in conjunction with the others."[2] The four "intrinsic" characteristics are: "correspondences," "living nature," "imagination and mediations," and "experience of transmutation." The two secondary characteristics are: "the praxis of the concordance" and "transmission."[3] Despite Fedorov's frequent dismissals of esoteric knowledge, all six of Faivre's characteristics can be found in Fedorov's thought. But rather than attempting to demonstrate a point-by-point correlation between Fedorov's formulations and Faivre's definition, we shall discuss what seem to be some of the more obviously esoteric features of Fedorov's thought, and bring in points from Faivre and other scholars of esotericism along the way.

As we noted earlier, *Rodstvo*, usually translated as "kinship" or "relatedness," is a concept central to Fedorov's thought. In Russian the root *rod-* is more or less the equivalent of Greek and Latin *gen-*. But where our English *gen-* words can sound slightly bookish or artificial, the Russian *rod-* words are commonly used in everyday life and include the most ordinary words for "to give birth," "to be born," "parents," "relative," "homeland," "nation-people-folk," "relationship," etc. *Rodstvo*, then, is that which joins one to life, to parents, to relatives, to homeland, and is the basis for most of the unchosen, ineradicable, enduring relationships that one carries through life. "*Nerodstvo*" (unkinship) is, to Fedorov, the present condition of man and the world, and the restoration of *rodstvo* is central to the common task. In Fedorov's thought, *rodstvo* serves the function of Faivre's "correspondence," the hermetic "as above, so below." It is *rodstvo* in Fedorov that joins the one to the many, the inner to the outer, the personal to the universal, each one of us to everything in the entire cosmos. In Fedorov, distant countries and their inhabitants, distant planets, even distant galaxies are not alien to us, but *rodnye*, "native." We are, literally, "at home" anywhere and everywhere in the universe—not now in the "world as it is," but "projectively" in the "world as it ought to be." *Rodstvo*, then, is what links us to "the other." A formula repeated throughout his writings, and the title of one of his brief articles, is "Neither Egoism nor Altruism, but Kinship" (*rodstvo*).

Under what conditions, will *I* no longer mean *domination* or negation of *all* except oneself, and altruism no longer mean *servitude* or *self-negation*? Or: when will *I* (=egoism) no longer mean *isolation* (solipsism), and *other* (=altruism) no longer mean *alienation, discord* (separatism)?

The synthesis of egoism (individualism, solipsism) and altruism can be expressed by the joining of two words: "we" and "all." That would be the fulfillment of kinship: instead of the solitary, uncoordinated existence of individuals—coexistence; instead of the succession of generations—fullness of life, the negation and abolition of death!

Kinship is we: with kinship there are no others in the sense of strangers: with kinship all means both I and my kindred [*rodnye*], naturally, organically related, and not artificially, mechanically, externally affiliated.

When all will feel and recognize *themselves in all*, and thereby become even *more closely* related, then will come *multi-unity* [*mnogoedinstvo*]. . . .

Fullness of kinship now exists only in the Divine Trinity, and not in human multi-unity.

The church also stands for multi-unity, but only in the future, and not in present reality.[4]

In Fedorov, any particle of matter in the universe may contain the dispersed dust of one or more of our ancestors. Thus *rodstvo* is, literally, what joins us to everything in the universe. And, Fedorov tells us in a brief essay called "Parents and Resurrectors," as we begin to collect these particles of ancestral dust in the resurrection project, some kind of vibration between the particle and us will allow us to recognize which particle does and which does not belong to one of our ancestors. "The reverberation and quivering (vibration) of which the molecules and dust of the dead are not incapable, and which so far have not been detected by any microphone, since that is still a crude organ of hearing—this reverberation and quivering will find a responding echo in the shuddering of particles in living beings connected by kinship with the dead to whom the particles belong."[5] Each particle, it seems, contains its own hidden vibration that identifies it, simultaneously distinguishing it from and linking it to others. This vibration of life in all things—a sort of esoteric precursor of DNA—is part of Fedorov's sense of what Faivre terms "living nature."

In many passages throughout *The Philosophy of the Common Task*, Fedorov calls nature "our temporary enemy but permanent friend."[6] By virtue of our reason, we are intended to regulate blind nature, a duty which, from Adam's time to now, through weakness, we have failed to exercise. As fallen humanity, we are now nature's slaves, and our common task is to become nature's masters, after which we shall have recreated paradise and nature will truly be our eternal friend. The secret to mastery of nature is to know and utilize rational counterforces of which we are now only dimly and passively aware. As mentioned above, Fedorov saw the redirection of implements of war from horizontal to vertical aim as a symbol of the shift needed in all human action, a shift which he describes in other passages as "from meteorology to meteorurgy," and generally from any and all *-ology* to *-urgy*. He speculated that someday, by erecting great cones on the earth's surface, people might be able to control the earth's electromagnetic field in such a way as to turn the whole planet into a spaceship under human control. We would no longer slavishly have to orbit our sun but could freely steer our planet wherever we wished, as, in the phrase he used as early as the 1870s, "captain and crew of spaceship earth." The barely understood forces, macro and micro, that we are now subject to in our mortal existence will gradually fall more and more into the realm of what is known and mastered. Scientists and others will have longer lifetimes in which to explore and solve mysteries that now outlive their investigators. The great energy—whatever it is—that informs everything that exists in the cosmos, that brings life to and takes life from matter, that provides for what we in our feeble, limited way can only refer to as "spirit" and "soul," and "mind"—all this, Fedorov says, will be understood, and eventually will be directed by humanity. We and nature are kindred manifestations of the same living energy, but so far we are not acting in full consciousness of that kinship.

Fedorov's view that true knowledge is neither subjective nor objective, but "projective" (*proektivnoe*) is his version of what Faivre termed "imagination and mediations." Properly understood, the universe, not only of human interactions but of physical and chemical interactions as well, is not an "object" whose existence is dependent on or independent of our existence as "subjects," but is a "project" which we shall either direct or fail to direct, yet for which we must bear ultimate responsibility.

"Projectivism" is Fedorov's bridge between, and alternative to, idealism and materialism; it is the task of realizing ideas in the material world. Projectivism is an epistemology for artists rather than for critics, for engineers rather than for theoretical scientists, for -urgists rather than for -ologists. The projective imagination, then, is creative in the most literal sense. Imagination in Fedorov not only allows us to perceive the essence of the universe but provides an image, an icon, a model for our project of refashioning the cosmos.

For Fedorov and the later Russian religious cosmists, holy icons serve as projective models and intermediaries between the world as it is and the world as it ought to be. These icons, "theology in color" in Prince Eugene Trubets-koi's felicitous phrase,[7] serve the sensitive believer as portals to higher reality and offer models for the transformation of mortal flesh into immortal substance. Orthodox liturgy and ritual and the celebration of church holidays also serve as models for the world it is our task to realize. Fedorov writes about the possibility of realizing the prayer, "give us this day our daily bread," through the scientific technology of regulating climate to insure sufficient rain for adequate grain harvests.[8] He presents liturgy in the cathedral as an incomplete initial blessing for the completion of "liturgy outside the cathedral" (*vnekhramovaia liturgiia*), by which he means the regulation of nature and the resurrection of the ancestors.[9] The Orthodox Church, then, and all the rites, celebrations, and symbols associated with it, are not so important in and of themselves, but rather are potentially the prime mediations between the world we now have and the world we are meant to create.

The goal of Fedorov's "common task" is the transformation of both humanity and the cosmos, which is as close as Fedorov gets to Faivre's "experience of transmutation." Fedorov's transformation is to be both inner and outer, spiritual and physical, microcosmic and macrocosmic. The "gnosis" that will lead to this transmutation is knowledge that is active rather than passive, practical rather than theoretical, thaumaturgic rather than contemplative, communal rather than private. The transmutation is to be a total metamorphosis; not sudden, but over time as radical as any previous evolutionary development. Our eventual descendants, and our resurrected selves, Fedorov suggests, may be as different from what we are today as we now are from our prehuman ancestors. But what is most essential in Fedorov's transmutation is that we shall be both the transmuters and the transmuted. We shall not be trying to work magic in the traditional sense but shall be using all future, advanced knowledge and activity—religious, scientific, and artistic—to accomplish the kinds of transmutations that have traditionally been attempted through magic.

In a brief article, "The End of Orphanhood, Limitless Kinship," Fedorov outlines the transmutation he envisions:

> The awaited day, the day longed for through the ages, the jubilation of the immense heavens, will arrive only when the earth, having swallowed generations in darkness, moved and directed by heavenly filial love and knowledge, will begin to return those swallowed by her and with them begin to populate the heavenly, starry worlds that are now without souls and that are now coldly and as if with sadness gazing

down at us; when, gathering and giving life to the dust of those who gave—or more truly—gave up life to us, we will no longer be turning that dust into nourishment for ourselves and our descendents, which we have been forced to do because of the isolation of worlds and the necessity to live by the means that can be accumulated on our small planet. By their knowledge of matter and of the powers of restoring it, succeeding generations will already have found it possible to create their own bodies from the basic elements, and will populate the worlds and eliminate their tendencies toward discord. Then indeed the sun will begin to palpitate, as even now simple people believe they see it do on the Easter morning of Holy Sunday; then indeed even the multitudinous choirs of stars will begin to rejoice. The illusion of poets, which has personified, or "patrified" these worlds, will have become the truth. But personification, or, more precisely, patrification, will be done no longer by thought, no longer by imagination, but in fact, by an active task [*delo*]. Premature patrification, alive in folk poetry and other poetry, clearly testifies that the awaited day is the hope of all ages and peoples, awaited from time immemorial. That day, the one which *the Lord shall accomplish through us*, will be brought about not by the apparent movements of the sun, and not by the actual movement of the earth, but by the joint activity of sons who have loved the God of their fathers and who have been filled with great compassion for all those departed. The earth will be the first star in heaven to be moved not by the blind force of gravity but by reason, which will have countered and prevented gravity and death. Nothing will be remote when in the integrated totality of worlds we shall see the integrated totality of all past generations. [*Fedorov's Note:*] (The universal meeting. This, then is the great future which awaits the past, if the present will comprehend its function, its task, its goal.) *All will be kindred, nothing alien*; nevertheless, for all an immense breadth, depth, and height will be opened, but this will not be overwhelming, or terrifying, but will have the capacity to satisfy the boundless desire, life without limits, which so frightens the present, emaciated, sickly, Buddhist-tending generation. This will be life ever new, regardless of its antiquity, spring without fall, morning without evening, youth without old age, resurrection without death. However, at that time there will also be not only autumn and evening, there will also be dark night, as the hell of suffering remains, in the present and past life of the human race, but it will remain only as a representation, like grief that has been lived through, and will raise higher the value of the bright day of resurrection. This day will be divine, awesome, but not miraculous, for *resurrection will be a task not of miracle but of knowledge and common labor.*

The awaited day, the day longed for through the ages, *will be God's command and man's fulfillment.*[10]

Like Theosophy, Anthroposophy, and other esoteric doctrines, Fedorov's teaching contends that all religions are essentially derived from one, which for Fedorov is the cult of departed ancestors. All earth, properly understood, is a graveyard, and all churches, temples, mosques, and other places of worship arose as sacred space in which to commemorate the dead and, through words, pictures, song, and ritual, to bring something of the dead—at least in our minds—back to life. The "common task" is to make real and lasting what is now only imaginary and temporary. Of all religions, only Christianity now celebrates the idea, and will in the future celebrate the fact, of resurrection. Thus true, active Orthodox Christianity will replace all today's conflicting religions, and all people will voluntarily join the common task of resurrecting their ancestors, becoming Christian in deed regardless of nominal creed or religious upbringing.

In the year 988, at the dawn of Russian history, according to the Kievan Primary Chronicle, Prince Vladimir, in order to select a new religion for Russia to replace traditional pagan worship and to allow Russia to assume its proper place in the civilized world, sent emissaries to Constantinople to perform a "test of the faiths." After attending Jewish, Islamic, and other religious services, the emissaries were overwhelmed by the majesty and beauty of the Greek Christian services in the Hagia Sophia, and on their recommendation Vladimir dumped all the wooden and stone idols of the old Slavic gods into the Dnieper River and decreed that henceforth Russia would be an Orthodox Christian kingdom. Nine hundred years later, Fedorov repeated Vladimir's test of the faiths and, not surprisingly, confirmed the wisdom of Vladimir's choice. Thus all mankind's religions, once one, now broken into disparate and often inimical factions, will again become one in Fedorov's version of Faivre's "praxis of concordance."

Like many esoteric thinkers, Fedorov finds that some ancient and, to Europeans, exotic religions retain more that is worth worshiping than do today's fallen and broken versions of the one original faith. For Madame Blavatsky, for example, that religion is Tibetan Buddhism; for Rudolph Steiner, Gnostic Christianity. For Fedorov, it is the Zoroastrianism of the ancient Iranians. In contrast to the ancient Hebrews, who for Fedorov represent the principle of passive optimism, believing that God, rather than their own efforts, will always see them through, and in further contrast to the ancient Indians, who represent the principle of passive pessimism, submission to the turning of the great wheel, accepting death as an equal good to life—in contrast to them, Fedorov finds in the ancient Iranians the principle of optimistic activism, the struggle of absolute good against absolute evil, the attitude which, he believes, has been inherited by the Slavs. The Avesta, in which all are urged to join the "beautiful task" (*frasho karete*) against the forces of evil and death, offers an ancient precedent for the "common task." The ancient Iranians, to whom Fedorov believes the Slavs are related, were continental rather than insular or peninsular in outlook, land tillers rather than land seekers, and in their close relationship to the earth recognized that life is won only by constant struggle against nature. Evil, for the Zendo-Slavic peoples, is not an inescapable condition of existence, as in India, but can be overcome by concerted human effort. In modern times, Indian pantheism is represented by the Germans, Hebrew monotheistic passivism is represented by Islam, and Zendic active optimism is represented by the Slavs. The Zendo-Slavic principle is the "reconciling link" between the Indo-Germanic and Judeo-Islamic Semitic extremes. In his view that Russia is the heir of ancient Iran, Fedorov follows the Slavophile historiosophy of Khomiakov, who wrote of the eternal opposition between Iran and Turan, and anticipates the views of the twentieth-century Eurasianist school of Russian thought. George Vernadsky, for example, sees Russian pre-Christian pagan religion as a development from both Zoroastrianism and Mithraism.[11] And Alexander Dugin and other current Russian neo-Eurasianists and neonationalists point to ancient Russia's religious and cultural kinship with ancient Iran to support their calls for a new Russo-Iranian Eurasian continental alliance to counter NATO power and culture.

Though he never cites them, Fedorov's works are solidly grounded in the earliest bodies of Western esoteric wisdom as reflected in the writings of Pythagoras, Parmenides, Empedocles, and Plato. True science, in the esoteric, initiatory tradition, teaches us to control nature and achieve immortal life. As formulated in verse by Empedocles:

And all the remedies that exist as defence against sufferings and old age:
These you will learn, because for you alone will I make all these things come true.
　And you'll stop the force of the tireless winds that chase over the earth
　And destroy the fields with their gusts and blasts;

But then again, if you so wish, you'll stir up winds as requital.
Out of a black rainstorm you'll create a timely drought
For men, and out of a summer drought you'll create
Tree-nurturing floods that will stream through the ether.
And you will fetch back from Hades the life-force of a man who has died.[12]

Here, control of the weather, the aging process, human health, and the force of life itself are all proper fields of activity for the enlightened initiate. And as C. G. Jung, Mircea Eliade, and many others have observed, the practice of Western alchemy, from the Alexandrian period through the Renaissance, the Rosicrucian Enlightenment, and into the modern period, has continued the ancient initiatory process. As Eliade summarizes: "Without a shadow of a doubt, the Alexandrian alchemists were from the very beginning aware that in pursuing the perfection of metals they were pursuing their own perfection. The *Liber Platonis quartorum* . . . gives great importance to the parallelism between the *opus alchymicum* and the inner experience of the adept. . . . The adept must transform himself into a Philosopher's Stone."[13] In Christian alchemy, the Christ–Philosopher's Stone parallel turns the alchemical operation into an imitation of Christ's death and resurrection, and the transmutation of matter into a sacred act. Citing the seventeenth-century Rosicrucian alchemist, Gichtel, Eliade writes:

> "We receive not only a new Soul with this regeneration but also a new body. This body is extracted from the Divine Word or from the heavenly Sophia. . . . It is more spiritual than the Air, akin to the rays of the Sun which penetrate all bodies, and as different from the old body as the resplendent Sun is from the dark earth; and although it remains in the old Body, this Body cannot conceive it even though it may sometimes feel it." In short, the Western alchemist, in his laboratory, like his Indian or Chinese colleague, worked upon himself—upon his psycho-physiological life as well as on his moral and spiritual experience.[14]

Thus Zenkovsky, Bulgakov, and others who have suggested Fedorov's unacknowledged debt to eighteenth-century Masonic, Rosicrucian, and other occult and alchemical literature are certainly correct. Fedorov's resurrection project parallels both the Masonic task of rebuilding oneself as one rebuilds the world and the alchemist's transmutation of himself while transmuting matter.

As we have mentioned before, Fedorov cites esoteric writers and texts only in order to dismiss them, or to point out their limitations. In at least one passage in *The Philosophy of the Common Task*, Fedorov does admit that his rejection of occult methods is not about their efficacy or lack of it but about their exclusivity.[15] Even if they worked, esoteric practices were wrong because they were not open and available to all. Nevertheless, in the narrowest, most literal sense of "esoteric," meaning material kept secret, hidden, "occult," not open to all but accessible only to a select few, Fedorov, without intending to be so, was himself a highly esoteric writer. During his lifetime, he was known to most of his colleagues and acquaintances primarily as an erudite, saintly librarian, the one turned to when help was needed in research. But only a few people close to him knew of his ideas. He thought that every scrap of information about everyone who ever lived should be preserved—except about himself. Only a few of his friends knew anything at all about his life before Moscow, and the only autobiographical note found after his death is the one cited earlier, about black bread, people shooting each other in war, and relatives who are and are not related. The few items he published were done so anonymously, and when he referred to his ideas he wrote of them not as his own but as the unarticulated ideas of all simple people, not at all original, but common. His hope was that someone else, perhaps someone already well known like Dostoevsky, Tolstoy, or Solovyov, would become a spokesman for the ideas he had presented to them, and his criticisms of all three are harsh and perhaps touched with bitterness for their failure to become complete advocates of the "common task."

The 480 copies of *The Philosophy of the Common Task* that Peterson and Kozhevnikov edited and paid for were published without copyright, stamped "Not For Sale," and distributed without charge to libraries, select institutions, and individuals who requested copies. Correspondence between the editors and various individuals indicate that not all the copies were distributed, and of those distributed not many were actually read. For example, in 1908 Peterson sent Tolstoy a copy of the first volume and asked if Tolstoy would write something that might bring the book to the attention of the general public. Tolstoy did not reply to that letter, but in a later letter of October 5, 1910, shortly before his death, Tolstoy wrote that he did not have a copy of Fedorov's book and asked Peterson to send him one. From this letter it would seem that either the first copy that Peterson sent did not reach Tolstoy or that it reached him and he misplaced it without having read it. And this was probably not an isolated instance.

The publication and attempted distribution of *Philosophy of the Common Task* in 1906 and 1913 came in the midst of troubled times: the destruction of the Russian fleet by Japan and the revolution of 1905, the coming of war in 1914, the February and October Revolutions in 1917, civil war into the 1920s, the collapse of the ruble and eventually of the entire Russian economy, and the financial ruin and severe, progressive illnesses of the editors, with Kozhevnikov's death in 1917 and Peterson's in 1919. It is a wonder, then, that anyone learned of Fedorov's project.

Unintentionally, but in classic esoteric form, transmission at first seems to have been primarily oral, from person to person. Fedorov's literary style, while often very expressive, is difficult, repetitious, and unsystematic. Many have found him all but unreadable. Sergei Bulgakov, who admired many of Fedorov's ideas, wrote: "I have never encountered a writer more unliterary, more intricate, more abstruse, or unsystematic."[16] It may be that only Bulgakov, Berdyaev, and a few others had actually read much of *Philosophy of the Common Task*, but thanks to their detailed reviews, and to a culture of constant discussion, argument, and debate, every prominent figure in Silver Age Russia had at least a capsule notion of Fedorov's main idea. The poets Andrei Biely, Valery Briusov, Alexander Blok, Anna Akhmatova, Vladimir Mayakovsky, Boris Pasternak, and Osip Mandelstam all knew of him, as did the artists Malevich, Kandinsky, and Chekrygin, the composer Scriabin, and the great short story writer Andrei Platonov. Though intended as a practical task for all humanity, Fedorov's ideas were primarily of interest to artists and intellectuals oriented toward the mystical and the esoteric. These major figures of the Silver Age, like Dostoevsky, Tolstoy, and Solovyov earlier, incorporated certain ideas from Fedorov into their own works, but none became full-fledged advocates of the "common task." As we shall see later, that role would fall to others: small groups of devoted Fedorovians who in some cases gave up their own lives to keep Fedorov's name and ideas alive. For now, the point is that a few served as adepts and Faivre's "transmitters" of Fedorov's teachings, not to a mass audience but to other members of the Russian intellectual elite, who, in turn, would pass the teachings further along. Gradually, despite the rarity of the original texts, and despite some seventy years of official suppression by the Soviet government, Fedorov's unorthodox ideas have begun to reach a wider audience. In the first republication of selections from his works in 1982, the edition of 50,000 sold out before the publishers, embarrassed over the uproar the publication caused, could carry out orders from above to collect and destroy all remaining copies. In the 1990s the five volumes of the scholarly edition of his collected works were published in an edition of 5,000 copies, and again, all quickly sold. Thus, as a result of scholarly works, documentary films, and mass media stories and articles, Fedorov's name and the main outline of his idea are probably now known to most educated Russians. The exoteric Fedorov—the five-hundred-word summary—can now be found in standard Russian encyclopedias and intellectual histories. But the real Fedorov, the complete project with all its variations, subprojects, analogies, surprises, and contradictions, is available only in some two thousand pages of difficult, dense, and sometimes syntactically impenetrable Russian—as esoteric in result as it is exoteric in intention.

## Fedorov's Legacy

The headmaster of the school in Lipetsk where Fedorov taught could not have been further from the truth when he accused Fedorov of indoctrinating young minds with "progressive" ideas from the West. As Peterson reported, Fedorov reordered the French Revolution's priorities to put brotherhood before freedom and equality, and fatherhood before all three. He was probably as far-sighted and futuristic a thinker as any who ever lived, but here are Fedorov's own thoughts about the nineteenth-century ideal of "progress":

> The triumph of the younger generation over the older—that is the essential feature of progress. Biologically, progress is the younger swallowing the older, the sons crowding out the fathers; psychologically it is the replacing of love for the fathers by a soulless exaltation over them, hatred for them; it is the moral, or, more truly, the immoral ousting of the fathers by the sons. Sociologically, progress expresses itself as the attainment of the fullest measure of freedom accessible to man (not in the greatest participation of each in the common task of restoring life to the fathers) since society, which is the same as the absence of brotherhood, demands that the freedom of each individual be limited; then the demand of sociology will be a demand for the greatest freedom and the least unity and association, i.e., sociology is the science not of association but of dissociation and subjugation if society is permitted to swallow up the individual; as the science of dissociation for some and subjugation for others, sociology sins against both that which cannot be divided and that which cannot be confused, against the Triune God. Progress is precisely that form of life in which the human race is able to taste the greatest sum of suffering while striving to attain the greatest sum of delight. Progress is not satisfied with recognizing the activity of evil but wants the activity of evil to have full representation, and revels in it in realistic art; while in ideal art progress struggles

toward a firm conviction that the good is impossible and unreal, it revels in a representation of nirvana. Although stagnation is death and regression is no paradise, progress is veritable hell, and the truly divine, truly human task is to save the victims of progress, to take them out of hell.[17]

For Fedorov, the nineteenth-century ideal of progress simply meant acceleration toward death and destruction. A more, not less, radical ideal was required, and Fedorov's solution was to transform rather than to accelerate history. In international thought, Fedorov shares a place with radical traditionalists such as Rene Guenon, Frithjof Schuon, and Ananda Coomaraswami.[18] But in Russia, Fedorov's traditionalism has usually been dismissed as an embarrassing aspect of an otherwise valuable "native" body of thought.

Another part of Fedorov's project usually considered best to dismiss or ignore is his insistence that only an Orthodox Russian autocrat can initiate and lead the "common task." In arguing that an autocrat would serve all mankind better than a constitution, Fedorov writes:

> Autocracy is the duty to the dead of all the living, while a constitution is the right of the living who are holding onto life, guarding it, but lack the power. Autocracy is the common task, the objective of which is to serve the life of the whole human race as an expression of maturity; a constitution, however, is the rejection of maturity and the seizing onto and preservation of immaturity, the recognition of amusement and play as the goal of life.[19]

In Fedorov, constitutions are the handiwork of "Prodigal Sons." Autocracy, on the other hand, "in its fundamental meaning is a dictatorship, called for by a danger not from other people like ourselves but from a blind force, threatening death to all without exception."[20] A constitution, however, "in its fundamental aspect, is a work of sons who have forgotten the fathers, a work of prodigal sons, or of profligates who have no memories of kinship [rodstvo], who are among those who regard their ruler not as a father but as a stranger."[21]

In his letter to Peterson, Dostoevsky noted that seldom had he encountered any argument more "logical" than Fedorov's—grant him that one statement is true, and everything else, including the universal duty to physically resurrect the dead, necessarily follows. In politics, grant Fedorov that kinship, rodstvo, is essential to the common task, and eventually Fedorov's logic leads to an ideal Russian autocrat sitting in Pamir, the "father place" (*otsov-mesto*). As we shall see, few later Cosmist thinkers went with Fedorov that far along his steep, narrowing path.

In Fedorov's "projectivism," the bridge between the "world as it is" and the "world as it ought to be," the difference on a universal scale between chaos and cosmos is *delo*, a word which can mean "business," "affairs," "matter," "activity," "cause," and even "things" in the colloquial Russian phrase "*kak dela?*"—"how are things?" But as Fedorov uses it, *delo* usually means "task," the work that needs to be done to turn the given world of natural disorder into the rationally ordered world that God initiated but intended humanity to complete. It is *delo* applied to fields of knowledge that will transform every current *-ology* into *-urgy*. It is *delo* that will turn Christianity from ineffectual, passive commemoration to the activity of restoring life to the dead. It is Fedorov's emphasis on ideal Orthodox Christianity as a radically active cosmic project of resurrecting, a common task (*delo*), rather than as simply a conservative preservation and defense of eternal truth, that pointed a new way to Solovyov and the later religious Cosmists like Bulgakov, Berdyaev, and Florensky. In Fedorov, they saw an active, forward-looking interpretation of Orthodoxy that could serve as a Christian alternative to either Marxism or a secular culture dominated by the erotic instinct, which before the advent of Freudianism Fedorov called "pornocracy." "The triumph of Easter, of filial and brotherly love—this is a conscious, natural task; and, on the other hand, the victory of pornocracy, i.e., of animal and bestial passion, masked by civilized falsification—this is the anti- or contra-Easter, an unconscious natural task becoming unnatural."[22]

In Fedorov's "pornocracy," erotic force drives everything. Eros transforms the faithful daughter into the temptress who lures the faithful son from his father and transforms loving brothers into competitors and enemies—leading eventually to war. In pornocracy, healthy rural agricultural culture becomes urban misery so that factories, replacing farms, can manufacture trinkets and seductive garments that will enable temptresses, even as they age, to attract more suitors. In pornocracy, childless marriage does not mean that men and women will devote themselves to their parents' welfare, but that they will grow old trying to remain sexually attractive—the age of permanent immaturity, of the "eternal bride and bridegroom." Glorifying everything "natural" and "instinctive," humanity will sink back into a zoomorphic state. "Having recognized themselves as animals, they will turn themselves into animals."[23]

The aspect of *delo* that will save us from the horrors of a pornocratic "anti-Easter" is "regulation" (*reguliatsiia*). Regulating eros will mean the end not only of sexual exploitation but also of conjugal relations and childbirth. All time and energy that now goes into attracting and holding onto a spouse and to bringing new life into the world will be devoted to restoring life to those who gave it to us. Another feature of regulation will be "autotrophy"— learning to take nourishment from the sun, the air, and rays of cosmic energy instead of cannibalizing the ancestors from whom, both literally and figuratively, we now take life. Fedorov writes: "At the present time we are living on the account of our ancestors, from whose dust we derive our food and clothing; thus all history may be divided into two periods: a first period of direct, immediate cannibalism, and a second period of covert people eating, which continues to this day, and which will continue as long as man does not find a way out of his imprisonment on earth. But after this second period a third must necessarily follow—a period of universal resurrection as the single effective expiation for the sin of cannibalism."[24]

Several of Fedorov's most radical proposals of regulation come near the end of his long "Brotherhood" essay, in a section innocuously called "The Problem of Sanitation" (*Sanitarnyi vopros*).[25] It is here that he tells us that it is not the earth but the heavens that will answer the prayer "give us our daily bread." We must become "captain and crew of spaceship earth," overcoming gravity to guide our planet out of the orbit nature has forced it into, and steering it onto paths selected by human reason. We will reconstruct the human organism, a kind of benign suicide in which we end our own lives as we live them today, and resurrect ourselves as part of the process of resurrecting our ancestors. "Our entire earth is too small and insignificant; we must search for the means to live in other worlds." Our cosmic duty is to "instill spirit" into the lifeless matter of the universe. "Here it must be recognized that the very cosmic force itself is helpless against death, because it contains within itself neither consciousness nor feeling"—humanity, with its consciousness and feeling, was created to provide the cosmos with what it lacks. "It only seems that it is fantastic to propose the possibility of a genuine transition from one world to another; that such a transition is necessary, however, cannot be doubted by anyone who takes a sober, clear view of the subject."[26]

In Fedorov's day, the parts of his thought that seemed boldest, most challenging and original, were these technological proposals for space travel, attainment of immortality, regulation of nature, and the like. But today, as these sides of Fedorov's project draw closer to the realms of possibility, even probability, what does Fedorov's most important contribution, his legacy, now seem to be?

As Svetlana Semenova has suggested, the one major idea that runs from Fedorov through all the Cosmists is the idea of active evolution, the idea that we now bear the responsibility for our future development on this planet and eventually throughout the cosmos. As individuals we have the ability and the responsibility to make ourselves whole again, to heal our inner dividedness, to grow as integrated personalities, with mind, soul, and body functioning as one. Socially, we have the ability and responsibility to live primarily as sons and daughters, sisters and brothers, rather than each person living predominantly for himself or herself, figuratively cannibalizing our parents so that we in turn may be cannibalized by our children. The idea of the organic wholeness of all can be our guide: *rodstvo*—the feeling of family, extended infinitely, the relationship, the kinship of all that is alive and has been alive. We are, Fedorov tells us, immature creatures, or, in one of his favorite comparisons, we are all like the Biblical prodigal son, still swilling with the hogs, not yet realizing that we can and should return home. We shall mature only when we cease to view ourselves as the Ptolemaic center of the universe and recognize that we are part of a larger, Copernican whole. But, as Fedorov repeats, recognition is only the first step. We must not only think but act Copernically, extending our sphere of activity farther and farther outward. Fedorov does not cite the *Poimandres* of Hermes Trismegistus, but every section of *The Philosophy of the Common Task* echoes the ancient hermetic invitation:

> People, earthbound men, you who have surrendered yourselves to drunkenness and sleep and ignorance of God, make yourselves sober and end your drunken sickness, for you are bewitched in unreasoning sleep. Why have you surrendered yourselves to death, earthbound men, since you have the right to share in immortality? You who have journeyed with error, who have partnered with ignorance, think again: escape the shadowy light, leave corruption behind, and take a share in immortality.[27]

In its "bewitched" condition, humanity needs to be awakened by a higher magic. In their ideas of "active Christianity" and "active science," Fedorov and the Cosmists attempt to provide that higher magic.

## 8

## *The Religious Cosmists*

FOUR OF THE leading figures in what has often been called the "Russian Religious Renaissance" of the late nineteenth and early twentieth century shared enough of the concerns central to Fedorov's thought that in Russia today their works are usually included in discussions of Russian Cosmism. As we shall see, each differed from the other three in important ways, and each created a body of work prominent on its own without regard to Cosmism or other schools of thought. Nevertheless, a common thematic thread does link them, and it is this common thread that we shall emphasize in our discussion.

### *Vladimir Sergeevich Solovyov (1853–1900)*

*Vladimir Solovyov must be recognized as one of the greatest thinkers and spiritual leaders of the nineteenth century, a philosopher, a perfectly original mystic, a man of the "prophetic" type, a political thinker, a poet and literary critic. The first thing that strikes one in all of Solovyov's writings and opens out new horizons to the reader, transferring him into a different atmosphere, is the keenness and clarity with which Solovyov sees the invisible, the spiritual world. Solovyov shows the spiritual path which alone can lead humanity out of its present impasse.*
—S. L. FRANK

As the thinker whom probably all but the strictest Marxist-Leninist historians regard as the foremost Russian philosopher, Vladimir Solovyov cannot be described solely, or perhaps even primarily, as a religious Cosmist. Indeed, most biographies and analytical studies make little or no reference to his association with Fedorov, treating their relationship at most as a footnote to the development of Solovyov's thought in the early 1890s. The emphasis is almost always on Solovyov's synthesizing of previous tendencies in Russian thought, his reaction against positivism, his debt to Schelling and Hegel, his attempts to reconcile Eastern and Western Christianity, his immersion in Kabbalah and the mysteries of Divine Sophia, his ideas of godmanhood, all-unity, and incarnate love, his influence on the Symbolist poets and on religious thinkers of the twentieth century. But in addition to all the other sides of his work, Solovyov did also have a Cosmist side. And, as we shall see, his association with Fedorov played a more important role than is often realized in the development and expression of ideas for which Solovyov, and not Fedorov, is best known. For this study, then, we shall say little about Solovyov's sophiology or about other aspects of his work, and focus primarily on his Cosmist side and his relationship to Fedorov.

Solovyov was born January 28, 1853, and died at the young age of forty-seven on August 13, 1900. His father was an eminent historian, author of a classic twenty-nine-volume history of Russia, and his mother was a deeply religious woman of mystical inclination, a descendent of the eighteenth-century Ukrainian pilgrim, bard, prophet, and philosopher Grigory Skovoroda. Unlike Fedorov, Solovyov was born a conspicuously legitimate member of Russia's intellectual elite, a model for academic promise, a prodigy who from an early age was expected to become a major figure in Russian intellectual history. His life developed in part into a series of exits and detours from the straight and narrow academic road for which he had seemed destined. Again and again in life, he would first adhere to and then turn away from whatever intellectual current he was expected to follow. Raised in a traditional Orthodox Christian family, with a profoundly devout mother and conventionally pious father, he converted to atheistic materialism at about age thirteen, and adopted the positivist-nihilist views of the student generation of the 1860s so memorably depicted in the character of Bazarov in Turgenev's *Fathers and Sons*. He began his university studies in 1869 in the natural sciences, with a special interest in biology. After a couple of promising years in this direction, however, he dropped out of his science courses, audited courses in history and philology, and after a year of mostly independent study received the highest marks in his class on the state examinations for his degree in 1873. But instead of continuing to the next logical rung on the academic ladder, advanced study of history or philosophy in France or Germany, he took what must have seemed a step backward for a budding nihilist, attending lectures at the Theological Academy of the famous Monastery of the Holy Trinity, founded by Saint Sergius. But at the monastery too, as previously at the university, he did not follow the expected course of studies. As an archbishop at the monastery later wrote: "Soloviev came to the lecture wearing a great-coat, felt boots, a beaver hat and muffler wound about his neck. He spoke to nobody. He merely walked to the window, stood there for a while, drummed with his fingers on the glass, turned round and went away."[1] At this time, Solovyov was in the process of rediscovering Orthodox Christianity, but his intellectual focus while at the monastery was on Western philosophy and spirituality, especially on the works of Plato, Schelling, and Boehme. While living among monks and seminarians, he was writing, revising, and publishing sections of his earliest philosophical works, his candidate's essay, "The Mythological Process in Ancient Paganism," and his master's thesis, "The Crisis in Western Philosophy: Against the Positivists."

In 1874, after a brilliant defense of his thesis, leading the eminent historian Bestuzhev-Ryumin to declare: "Russia is to be congratulated on a man of genius,"[2] Solovyov began to lecture on philosophy at the University of Moscow and also at the newly founded Women's University College. This work occupied him for less than a year. At the suggestion, apparently, of Dostoevsky,[3] with whom he had recently become acquainted, Solovyov applied for a year's leave to study "the Gnostic, Indian, and Medieval philosophies" in London. Thus in June of 1875, Solovyov took lodgings in a rooming house on Great Russell Street, and spent his days poring over *Splendor Solis*, *Kabbala Denudata*, and other similar Rosicrucian, alchemical, and hermetic texts in the grand reading room of the nearby British Museum.

In "Three Meetings," a poem written in 1898, more than twenty years after his months in London, Solovyov vividly describes a mystical experience that he considered a major event in his life. He was fascinated by the idea of the En Soph, the Infinite One of Kabbalistic literature. According to a Russian friend of his in London, L. I. Yanzhul, Solovyov would sit for hours in the reading room, staring at one page. As Solovyov himself explains in his poem, he was meditating on the name and presence of Divine Sophia.

> In the reading room, I was alone most often
> And whether you believe or not—God sees
> Powers hidden from me were making choices
> Sending everything about Her I could read.
>
> When sometimes I succumbed to a temptation
> To read "from another opera," as they say,
> The stories would produce only confusion
> And I would trudge home, feeling guilty all the way.

But then it happened once—it was in autumn—
I said to Her: "I sense You, know You're here—
Oh why, divinity's full flower, since childhood
Have You been so reluctant to appear?"

This thought, inside my head, had just been uttered
When suddenly the golden azure shone
Filling all space around, and She was present,
Her face glowing—only Her face, alone.

And that moment of bliss was long extended,
And once more to this world my soul turned blind,
And if my speech had been heard by someone "serious"
It would have seemed babble from a feeble mind.

I said to Her: "Your face appears before me,
But I now wish to behold all of You.
Why to a child would You reveal entirely
What to a young man You withhold from view?"

"Then be in Egypt!" rang a voice inside me.
First Paris! then off by steam toward the south.
My feelings could not quarrel with reason,
For reason, like an idiot, sat close-mouthed.[4]

    This was an offer Solovyov could not refuse. In one line of the poem, Sophia commands him to go to Egypt, and in the next line he is on his way. In actual fact, he may have taken a bit longer to get on his way, but by late October, Solovyov was in Cairo, staying at the Hotel Abbat and enjoying philosophical and other conversations with another Russian in Egypt, General Rostislav Fadeev, who happened to be the uncle of Helena Petrovna Blavatskaya.[5] At this point in his life, Solovyov may have known nothing about Madame Blavatsky and her occult researches. Years later, Solovyov would write disparaging encyclopedia entries about her and her Theosophical Society, and his older brother Vsevolod Solovyov would notoriously denounce her as a fraudulent occultist and secret police spy.[6] But while in London, Vladimir Solovyov had himself delved deeply into the same esoteric literature that would be Blavatsky's sources, and had frequented séances and other gatherings of occultists, just as Madame Blavatsky had done and was doing in New

York. And in addition to answering the summons from Sophia, one of the reasons for Solovyov's trip to Egypt in 1875 was to seek contact with an esoteric brotherhood, possibly the Hermetic Brotherhood of Luxor, into which Blavatsky, then unknown to Solovyov, would claim to have been initiated. In London and in Egypt, then, Solovyov was attempting to immerse himself in the same esoteric lore and experience that, unknown to him, Madame Blavatsky, niece of his dinner companion General Fadeev, was probably writing about at that very moment and would soon publish as *Isis Unveiled.*

In "Three Meetings," he tells us that after he had been in Cairo a short time, Sophia, by means of an inner voice, summoned him into the desert for a third, definitive meeting. So, at night, dressed in a European frock coat and top hat, he walked out into the desert and waited. He tells us that he nearly froze in the cold, a jackal threatened to eat him, and a gang of Bedouins suddenly captured him, but after a closer examination the desert folk released him, thinking he was a devil. Then, finally, Sophia appeared to him, granting him the illumination that would last a lifetime. Paul Marshall Allen calls this Solovyov's "Damascus experience."[7] And indeed, even though Solovyov treats it half humorously, it was a profound event that would provide the sophiological basis for all his subsequent work. For the remainder of his relatively brief life, Solovyov's writings, whether in verse or prose, heavy or light, would present a unique fusion of rationality and mysticism. Berdyaev writes of a "day Solovyov" and a "night Solovyov,"[8] the former a formidably erudite master of order and clarity, and the latter a seer of profound intuition and dark, complex spirituality—critical analyst by day, visionary poet by night. His gift was for crystalline, systematic elucidation of the most elusive ideas and perceptions, a rare ability to rationalize the irrational and articulate the ineffable. Both the letters he wrote in 1875 and the poem he wrote twenty years later show as well a remarkable ability to depict a life-changing experience in a tone that is both sincere and self-deprecatingly humorous and ironic. He could apparently detach himself at will from his own most serious pursuits—could act and simultaneously view himself acting without forfeiting sincerity or credibility.

On his return to Russia in 1876, Solovyov resumed his teaching duties at the university, but again, only for a short time. In the spring of 1877 he moved to St. Petersburg, where he became a member of the Scholarly Committee in the Ministry of Education and later that year began the series of twelve important public addresses known as the Lectures on Godmanhood. In March of 1881, following the assassination of Alexander II, Solovyov concluded one of his public lectures on the Enlightenment with a condemnation of the assassination and at the same time an appeal to the new Tsar Alexander III to set before Europe a bold example of compassionate Christian leadership by forgiving his father's assassins and renouncing capital punishment. This courageous and principled but rash appeal provoked such an uproar that Solovyov was forced to retire from teaching at the university and was henceforth forbidden to give public lectures or make public statements, officially curtailing his academic career. For the remaining eighteen years of his life he had no settled home or occupation but subsisted primarily on the charity of friends supplemented by meager earnings from his scholarly and journalistic writings.

As noted earlier, Solovyov first learned of Fedorov's ideas without knowing whose ideas they were from Dostoevsky in 1878, between the eighth and ninth godmanhood lectures. As Dostoevsky wrote in his letter to Fedorov's disciple Peterson, he waited for Solovyov after the eighth of the twelve lectures to read him Peterson's account of Fedorov's ideas, for Dostoevsky had found in their ideas "much that is similar." Dostoevsky and Solovyov spent "a beautiful two hours at this. [Solovyov] finds [Fedorov's] ideas much to his liking and had wished to say almost the same things in his next lecture."[9] And indeed, in the ninth godmanhood lecture, Solovyov takes up some of the same themes that Fedorov had written about in the manuscript sent to Dostoevsky: the isolation of the modern individual; the natural world of everyday reality as a state that ought not to be; humanity as the potential active, reifying agent of divine will; and all-unity as the goal of Christian, divine-human action. Although the two thinkers had independently arrived at similar positions on several points—positions which were not unique to them but shared with other nineteenth-century Russian thinkers—a major difference between the two is evident even here, before they met: for Fedorov, the activity that will lead to all-unity is the common task of resurrecting all the dead; for Solovyov it is active godmanhood, Christ the Logos and Sophia the World Soul working together in us in unspecified divine-human activity. At this point, Solovyov does not yet emphasize the idea of universal resurrection as a task and active project for humanity.

The personal relationship between the two thinkers, and the development of the Cosmist side of Solovyov's work, began with their meeting at Tolstoy's Moscow residence in the autumn of 1881. In a fragment first published in 2000 as part of the fourth volume of his collected works, Fedorov writes:

At the end of September 1881, I became acquainted with Tolstoy, and listened to the reading of his "Gospel." There I also met Solovyov. In the autumn of that year a Moscow correspondence was carried on, in which Tolstoy took part. In that same year began Tolstoy's conversion from a great writer to a bad philosopher. At that time also, the Preface[10] was brought to the attention of Solovyov, Tolstoy, and Strakhov. They [Tolstoy and Solovyov] defended it against Strakhov, who didn't like it. In the beginning of the following year, Solovyov read the project of resurrection itself,[11] about which he expressed his opinion in the letter of January 12, 1882. . . . I remember well that at the end of January, on the twentieth, Solovyov left [for St. Petersburg to deliver a series of lectures] in a state of enthusiasm. On the eve of departure, he read the first lecture which he intended to deliver. And on the very day of his departure he visited me at my apartment in the same enthusiastic state, but later he came back very dejected. He told me that at the conclusion of the lecture he talked with the students and observed that resurrection not as an idea but as a fact wasn't being grasped by them. In the next year, he became a Catholic.[12]

The letter that Solovyov wrote to Fedorov in January 1882 clearly confirms the younger thinker's initial enthusiasm.

I read your manuscript avidly and with a delight of spirit, devoting all night and part of a morning to the reading, and for the next two days, Saturday and Sunday, thought much about what I had read. I accept your "project" completely and without any discussion; what must be talked about is not the project itself but several of the underlying theoretical assumptions or suppositions, and also the first practical steps toward its realization. On Wednesday I'll bring the manuscript to you at the museum, and at the end of the week we will somehow have to get together in the evening. I have a great deal to tell you. But in the meantime, I will say only that since the time of the appearance of Christianity, your "project" is the first forward movement of the human spirit along the way of Christ. For my part, I can only recognize you as my teacher and spiritual father. Your goal is not to proselytize, however, or to found a sect, but to save all mankind by a common task, and for the sake of that it is necessary, first of all, that your project be made known and be recognized by all. The means by which this might be accomplished—that is the main thing I would like to talk about with you when we meet.

Be well, dear teacher and comforter![13]

Over the next several years Fedorov and Solovyov met often, and through what Prince Trubetskoy[14] and others have called Solovyov's "theocratic utopian" period, Solovyov was essentially attempting to rework Fedorov's project into a coherent philosophical, metaphysical system. As an example, an 1882 lecture, possibly the one Fedorov refers to in the fragment quoted above, later published as "Vladimir Sergeevich Solovyov's Last Lecture at St. Petersburg University," is replete with Fedorovian-Cosmist declarations: "The resolution of the worldwide conflict between private and public lies not in the destruction of what naturally exists but in its resurrection and eternal life. And this resolution will be achieved through the rational and free activity of the human will." "Mankind is obligated not to contemplate divinity but to make itself divine. . . . The new religion cannot be merely passive divine veneration—or divine worship—but must become active divine works [*aktyvnym bogodeistvom*], that is, the joint activity of Divinity and humanity for the transformation of the latter from carnal or natural into spiritual and divine." "In its entire structure the reunited and healed world will be a true and complete image and likeness of the Triune God."[15]

But as Fedorov noted in his criticism of this lecture, and in his later critiques on all Solovyov's writings on resurrection, the idea is presented only in the most general terms, with none of the scientific or other specific details that Fedorov considered the most important parts of the project. The closest they came to a real collaborative statement that would attempt to make Fedorov's project known and "recognized by all" was in 1891, when Solovyov was preparing an address to be delivered at an October 19 meeting of the Moscow Psychological Society, which the cream of Russia's intellectual society was expected to attend. Fedorov's disciple Peterson writes: "Solovyov attempted to persuade Nikolai Fedorovich to present the call to the common task jointly with him, and for this reason proposed to write down what Fedorov would dictate to him. When he refused, Solovyov said to him: 'What's the matter, do you think Peterson can present your thoughts better than I can?' Finally, Fedorov agreed to Solovyov's proposition—a time was set, but Solovyov did not come."[16]

The paper that Solovyov read to the Psychological Society was "The Collapse of the Medieval World-Conception," which in religious and conservative circles, as the philosopher S. L. Frank tells us, "produced the impression of a bombshell."[17] The paper is basically Solovyov's variation on ideas outlined by Fedorov in his essay "What History Is."[18] But if the paper seemed too radical for the religious conservatives of the day, it did not seem radical enough to Fedorov. In a special critique of Solovyov's paper,[19] a critique almost as long as the paper itself, Fedorov presents a point-by-point account of what Solovyov failed to say. That Solovyov had defined Christianity as the task of resurrection, and that he had argued that the medieval world-conception had collapsed precisely because medieval Christianity had not understood and adopted that task, did not satisfy Fedorov. He laments that Solovyov said nothing about how that task was to be fulfilled. He blames what he calls Solovyov's "vagueness" about the means of resurrection on Solovyov's inability to understand the true implications of the task. But here Fedorov is clearly wrong. Solovyov did have a clear understanding of both the idea of resurrection and the means by which the resurrection would be achieved. But his understanding was altogether different from Fedorov's. Even in his first, enthusiastic letter to Fedorov, Solovyov had mentioned that "several of the underlying theoretical assumptions or suppositions" had to be discussed. In his second letter to Fedorov, in June or July of 1882, Solovyov touches directly on one of the major points on which he ultimately had to disagree with his "teacher and spiritual father."

> The task of resurrection not only as a process but even in the goal itself is something conditional. The simple, physical resurrection of the dead cannot, in its own self, be the goal. The resurrection of people in the same state in which they strive to devour each other—to resurrect man in a stage of cannibalism—would be both impossible and utterly undesirable. This means that the goal is not the simple resurrection of man in his personal organic structure but the resurrection of man in the form he ought to take, namely, in that state in which all his parts and separate units do not exclude and change each other. You, of course, perfectly agree with this.... We are all still children, and for this reason we need the child-guidance of external religion. Consequently, in salutary religion and in the church we have not only elements and a prototype of the resurrection and the future Kingdom of God but also a present (practical) path and actual means toward this end. Therefore, our task must have a religious, and not scientific, character, and it must rely on the believing masses and not on disputatious intellectuals. So there is a short explanation for you of the feelings that I was trying to express to you my last time in Moscow.
>
> Until we meet again, dear teacher. God keep you. Take more care for your physical health—the rest you have in surplus. Are you collecting your manuscripts? It would be good to have them ready for the printer by autumn.[20]

We note that even after pointing out the major difference (spiritual against scientific) that will eventually separate them, Solovyov here still speaks of "our" task. He believed that what they shared was more important than any minor points of disagreement. And even after the furor following the 1891 address to the Psychological Society, Solovyov continued to emphasize the centrality of the idea of resurrection. In an 1894 letter to Tolstoy, he wrote: "Our [i.e., Solovyov and Tolstoy's] entire disagreement comes down to one concrete point—Christ's resurrection."[21] But Solovyov's idea of resurrection by then had little in common with Fedorov's.

From the beginning, Solovyov viewed the resurrection as a spiritual task. He agreed with Fedorov that the resurrection would be real and personal, and was to be accomplished by human effort over a long period of time, perhaps as long as ten thousand years. But he completely rejects the technological side of Fedorov's project and believes that spiritual development through exercises and disciplines already available in the world's religions will lead to resurrection. In the letter to Tolstoy mentioned above, he continues:

> For man, immortality is the same as reason is for animals; the telos of the animal kingdom is the reasoning animal, i.e., man. The telos of humanity is the immortal one, i.e., Christ. As the animal world tends toward reason, so the human world tends toward immortality. If the struggle with chaos and death is the essence of the world process, whereby the side of light and spirit ever so slowly and gradually takes control, then resurrection, i.e., actual and decisive victory of a living being over death, is a necessary element and indeed the culmination of that process.

Solovyov compares the appearance of Christ, the "firstborn from the dead," to the first appearance of a living organism in the organic world, or the first human among orangutans. Victory over death is a "natural consequence of internal spiritual perfection." And a person in whom the spiritual principle has taken over all the lower functions cannot be overcome by death. "Spiritual power, having attained its full degree of perfection, inevitably spills, as it were, over the edge of subjective mental life, fastens onto physical life, transforms it, and finally spiritualizes it completely, unites it constantly with itself." And it is precisely this "image of complete spiritual perfection" that Solovyov finds in the Christ of the Gospels.[22]

For Fedorov, we recall, the long resurrection project is one in which children will resurrect their parents, who in turn will resurrect their parents, and so back to Adam and Eve. The family is the basic unit of life, and in the project each family will grow backward through time, merging with other families, until all humankind is, literally, one family. Brotherhood becomes co-sonship, sisterhood co-daughterhood. Universal brotherhood will be as obvious a given as existence.

Solovyov is much less specific about how the project will be conducted. Generally, instead of children resurrecting parents, he writes of a growing brotherhood based not on race, nationality, or family ties but on spiritual development. He seems to envision something like an Albigensian society of perfects—or a higher order of evolved Christians—mingling with the lay population like Madame Blavatsky's "Masters" of Theosophy, developing in the individual and in the population at large spiritual powers sufficient to overcome death

Fedorov in more than one article[23] attacks Solovyov for valuing individual immortality over resurrection of the ancestors. To live forever without resurrecting one's parents is, for Fedorov, eternal adolescence, everlasting orphanhood. But contrary to Fedorov's contention, Solovyov does not confuse immortality with resurrection; he merely states that the task of creating immortal spirits must precede any attempts to resurrect the dead, otherwise one would be bringing people back to life only to let them die again.

As Solovyov stated in the letter to Fedorov cited above, "the simple physical resurrection of the dead cannot, in its own self, be the goal." For Fedorov, resurrection of the ancestors will coincide with the creation of heaven on earth, and this indeed should be the goal of all human action. For Solovyov, resurrection is part of the greater task of "all-unity," a human and natural world wholly integrated and wholly infused with divine spirit. Resurrection is, for Solovyov, the ultimate demonstration of divine-human spiritual power, the ultimate victory of order over chaos and of love over discord.

In his last work, "A Short Story of the Antichrist," Solovyov parodies perhaps not Fedorov himself but a representative of the Fedorovian idea in Apollonius, "a man of genius, semi-Asiatic and semi-European," who

> marvelously combined a mastery of the most recent discoveries and technologies of Western science with a knowledge both practical and theoretical of all major tendencies in the traditional mysticism of the East. The results of this combination were amazing. Apollonius, for instance, had perfected the half-scientific and half-magical art of producing atmospheric electricity at will, so that it was said that he commanded fire down from heaven.[24]

This is actually not far from one of Fedorov's fantastic projects mentioned above, whereby enormous cones of some kind would be placed on earth in such a way that they would conduct electromagnetic force and allow men to steer Earth like a spaceship through the cosmos in search of particles of departed ancestors.

Instead of regulating nature, whether external or internal, Solovyov views the great human task as one of incarnating divine love on a universal scale. In one of his major works, *The Meaning of Love*, he develops the idea of a Christian androgyny that would embrace all humanity. In the present world, physical love exists in embryo, as a promise, a foretaste of a greater love that will embrace the entire world of the future. It is love, now embryonic but eventually becoming fully developed and mature, that will lead humanity to immortality. Already within itself physical love bears the death-defeating force, the seeds of life and immortality—our task is to realize in full what now exists only as an ideal in Plato and in potential in our everyday lives. Wholeness, "all-unity," in love means androgyny. The separation of sexes and sex roles is, for Solovyov, a most important aspect of the disintegration of humanity that was a major theme of Fedorov's—though Fedorov certainly did not call for androgyny as a solution. "The true human being," Solovyov writes, "in the fullness of its ideal personality, obviously cannot be merely a man or merely a woman, but must be a higher unity of the two. . . . To create the true human being as a free unity of the masculine and feminine elements, which preserve their formal separateness but overcome their essential disparity and disruption, is the direct task of love."[25] Further, in *The Meaning of Love*, he writes that we must have a part in the reinstatement of God in material humanity. We must

> tend its growth by our own conscious action. The passive receptivity of faith is enough to begin with, but it must be followed by active faith, moral endeavor, and effort in order to preserve, strengthen, and develop the gift of radiant and creative love and by means of it embody in oneself and in the other the image of God, forming out of two limited and mortal beings one absolute and immortal personality.

Idealization of the beloved should not lead merely to admiration of the other but, through active faith, imagination, and creativity, should lead to the transformation of reality to match the ideal image of the other. For Solovyov, love is a powerful, creative force, allowing us to transform everyday reality to correspond to a reality that is higher. "In the feeling of love, in accordance with its essential meaning, we affirm the absolute significance of another personality, and through it, of our own. . . . The inevitability of death and the emptiness of our life are incompatible with the emphatic affirmation of one's own and another's personality contained in the feeling of love."

Sexual love, which will not be a part of Fedorov's ideal future, will play an important role in Solovyov's universal resurrection. "It is self-evident that so long as man reproduces himself like an animal, he also dies like an animal. But it is equally evident that mere abstention from the act of procreation does not in any way save one from death: persons who have preserved their virginity die, and so do eunuchs, and neither enjoy even particular longevity." Sexual union becomes in Solovyov a step toward the more perfect union of androgynous wholeness. Physical union is a striving toward spiritual union. Eventually that striving will lead humanity, now suffering from sexual division into male and female, to consciously develop both the masculine and feminine principles now inherent but undeveloped, and in this way to eventually attain wholeness of personality. "Only the whole man can be immortal. And if physiological union cannot reinstate the wholeness of the human being, it means that this false union must be replaced by a true union and certainly not by abstention from all union, i.e., not by a striving to retain in status quo the divided, disintegrated, and consequently mortal human nature." Carnal love, now an embodiment of the principle of division, disintegration, and death, is, nevertheless, a step beyond abstemious solitude toward something higher. The true spiritual love toward which we must direct our evolution will not be a weak imitation of present physical love, "not a feeble imitation and anticipation of death, but triumph over death, not the separation of the immortal from the mortal, of the eternal from the temporal, but the transformation of the mortal into the immortal, the reception of the temporal into eternity. False spirituality is the negation of the flesh, true spirituality is its regeneration, salvation, and resurrection."[26]

Solovyov, then, presents his "resurrection by love" in contrast to Fedorov's technological resurrection. At the same time, he is contrasting his idea of incarnating the spiritual with the Neoplatonic idea of separating the spiritual from the physical. Like Fedorov, Solovyov utterly rejects any notion of a disembodied spiritual paradise. All-unity must include matter as well as spirit. Human wholeness must include the masculine and feminine principles balanced in every individual. In divine love, in creation, God established his relationship to the other. So when we act in God's image, we must activate our relationship to the other. Love, then, is Solovyov's solution to the problems of isolation, dividedness, fragmentation, emptiness, and death. Not

Neoplatonic withdrawal, then, but Christian love, the embracing of matter by spirit, is the essence of the illumination that Solovyov received from Sophia in the desert in 1875 and that informs so much of his subsequent writings.

"Impenetrability, i.e., mutual exclusion of one another's true being" is, in Solovyov, the basis of false existence. For him, "true life means living in another as in oneself or finding in another positive and absolute completion of one's own being." True life has always had sexual, conjugal love for its foundation and pattern. But a transformation of sexual love to a higher plane first requires a transformation of the entire external environment. Individual life must be wholly integrated into social and cosmic life. The perfect relationship of the one and the many, the part and the whole, the individual and society, the body and spirit, must be what Solovyov calls "a living syzygic relation. Not to submit to one's social environment and not to dominate it, but to be in loving interaction with it . . . that is the relation of the true human personality, not only to its immediate social environment and to its nation but to humanity as a whole." Solovyov envisions a gradual spreading of syzygic, interpenetrating relationships and a gradual diminution of separation and impenetrability. And here his idea comes as close as it ever will to Fedorov's idea of the end of divisiveness and the coming of all-unity. Like Fedorov, but without specifying a scientific-technological aspect of the task, Solovyov projects his own vision of eternal universal immortality: in order that separation and impenetrability should be "absolutely abolished altogether, and all individuals, both past and present, should finally become eternal, the process of integration must transcend the limits of social or strictly human life and include the cosmic sphere from which it started. . . . In this sense it is essential to change man's relation to nature. He must enter with it too into the same relation of syzygic unity which determines his true life in the personal and social sphere."[27]

Even though Solovyov includes the ancestors, the past, and the cosmos in his idea of syzygic love, Fedorov still takes him to task for treating the resurrection project as a mystical philosophical and religious idea instead of emphasizing immediate practical tasks to be undertaken. A syzygy is not an agenda for action. But Solovyov did indeed spend several years in a futile attempt to bring about a first practical step toward the spiritual unification of humanity—his efforts toward a reconciliation of the Catholic and Orthodox churches. Fedorov, we recall, wrote that after finding no positive response to the resurrection project among the students at St. Petersburg University, Solovyov "in the next year became a Catholic." And indeed, Solovyov's attempts to establish dialogue with Bishop Strossmayer and other Catholic high officials have unfortunately been interpreted by many Russian critics as a renunciation of Orthodoxy and an embracing of its Western rival, and a question that biographers long debated was whether Solovyov died a Catholic renegade or an Orthodox Russian reconciled with the true faith. In Solovyov's view, he was a true Orthodox believer all his life, and there could be no inconsistency between his Orthodoxy and his ecumenism. The unity of Eastern and Western Christians would serve as an important first step toward the unity of all humanity, which he assumed should be the goal of all Christian thought and activity. The Church, for Solovyov, even in its broken, fallen form, represented the feminine, earthly body of the principle of divinity, and must be reinfused with spirit—not further fragmented or abandoned. Wholeness and inclusiveness were Solovyov's principles, and this part of his thought, along with his idea that neither submission nor dominance but syzygy should define our relationship to nature, all might make Solovyov's comprehensive worldview more acceptable than Fedorov's to many readers today.

A very important, but often overlooked, part of Solovyov's writings is his work as a poet.[28] He began to write nonjuvenile poetry as a very young boy, but his most significant poems date from the mid 1870s, when he was in his early twenties, and continue into 1900, the last year of his life. Throughout his poetry, the self-image he projects is not so much the standard one of a lover seeking his beloved, but rather that of a male friend waiting for Sophia, his female friend and benefactress, to appear. He is on this shore; she is from elsewhere, beyond (Russian *nezdeshnaya*, "not here"), known by flower petals and other tokens, by memories of her from other places, other times, other lives. He speaks as a mortal poet, an ascetic devotee, gifted with clairvoyance and a view that penetrates the world of matter. She is a Queen, a Goddess, an Empress, Tsaritsa, the Eternal Feminine; in a few poems she is Isis, Eurydice, Beatrice, a resplendent seven-crowned figure in an icon—but most of all, Sophia, in both her aspects as Wisdom of God and as Soul of the World, Third Person of the Trinity. Within Solovyov's system, Sophia could be interpreted as his own unrealized feminine half: real, intuited, sensed for brief moments, but not yet fully materialized and present. Solovyov calls to her, and speaks to us, in a voice unique for its combination of earnest, lofty sincerity and modest self-deprecation. The slightly humorous, self-satirizing tone he uses when discussing the very subjects he cherishes most appears partly from a natural modesty, partly from a desire not to sound preachy or pedantic, and partly as a gesture of self-defense, out of a fear that the ideas dearest to him might seem ridiculous to others. But humor also sometimes seems to be used in its Gnostic function as "luminous substance," one of the passions that created the material world, the laughter of the Christos at the moment of the crucifixion.

A constant theme running from the very early poems through the very late ones is the sense of awe in the presence of unseen but clearly felt presences from another world. Often this is a benign presence, but sometimes it is a malignant presence: demons, monstrous entities, rents in the sky, underwater movements, underground fires. Another frequent theme is the mystical union, the syzygy, such as the esoteric wedding of the lily and the rose in "Song of the Ophite," or the marriage of azure and gold in his invocations to Sophia. In his poems, generally, he works into vivid and often memorable images the universe of unseen realities that he treats discursively in his philosophical works.

Like Fedorov, Solovyov was a lifelong ascetic bachelor. His many female acquaintances, friends, and followers included the widow of the poet Alexei Tolstoy, who supported his occult interests, and at whose estate he lived as a guest for some months most years, and the mysterious Anna Schmidt, whom Solovyov met only once, in the last year of his life, but who pestered him at length with letters and manuscripts claiming that she was the earthly embodiment of Sophia and that Solovyov was an incarnation of Christ. In photographs taken from his last years, Solovyov does have the look of an exhausted, infirm, perhaps even haunted prophet, one who though not yet even fifty had lived too long and seen too much. The poet Andrei Biely described him at this time: "His enormous, fascinating grey eyes, his bent back, the long, weak arms, his beautiful head with grey, ruffled strands of hair; his large mouth with protruding lip, his furrowed face. . . . A giant with powerless arms, long legs, a small body, inspired eyes . . . a powerless child with a lion's mane."[29] He spent his last days, very ill, at the home of his close friend and follower Prince Sergei Trubetskoy. The morning after his arrival,

> he told Troubetskoi that in the night he had had a dream in which he saw quite clearly Li Hung Chang, the Chinese statesman, who spoke to him in classical Greek, telling him that soon he would die. He was distracted, but made many jokes, though his memory was already weak and he couldn't recall where he had left his baggage upon arriving in Moscow. Later his things were discovered in the restaurant of the Slavyansky Bazaar.[30]

Solovyov's influence on the younger generation of major symbolist poets, especially on Andrei Biely and Alexander Blok, has often been treated.[31] He gave them their major themes: the higher reality beyond our everyday world, the poet as seer, the symbol as a portal between worlds. His influence on the generation of Russian thinkers and theologians of what has been called the Russian Religious Renaissance of the first half of the twentieth century was equally significant.[32] To them he bequeathed the doctrine of sophiology, the centrality of the eternal feminine in Christian spirituality. Fedorov's influence on these thinkers, in part direct and in part filtered through Solovyov, is also important but less frequently discussed. For, like Solovyov himself, such religious philosophers as Bulgakov, Florensky, and Berdyaev are well known for ideas and themes that are not necessarily Fedorovian or Cosmist. But also as with Solovyov, Fedorovian themes and Cosmist concerns occupy a sufficiently important position in their writings to justify including them in our discussion of major Cosmists.

## Sergei Nikolaevich Bulgakov (1871–1944)

Born into a family of six generations of priests in the town of Livny, in Orlov Province, deep in central Russia, Sergei Bulgakov had a troubled childhood: his father and two brothers died from drink, and his mother understandably suffered from emotional disturbances connected with these and other family illnesses and losses. Like Solovyov earlier, at about age thirteen young Bulgakov rebelled from his strict, religious upbringing and early seminary education. In his autobiography he wrote: "I gave up the positions of faith without defending them. . . . I accepted nihilism without a struggle."[33] At Moscow University he studied political economy, and in his first published works proved himself a brilliant Marxist analyst of socioeconomic systems. Early on, he was an active member of the Social Democratic Party and a close acquaintance of leading socialist activists and thinkers both in Russia and in Germany. But even as he was writing and lecturing from a Marxist perspective, gaining a wide reputation as a Marxist political thinker, he began to question the fundamental premises of Marxism, and in 1903 published *From Marxism to Idealism*. The "Damascus moment" in his conversion came in Dresden, where one day he stood silently for hours before Raphael's *Sistine Madonna*, the same painting that had transfixed Dostoevsky a generation before and that had inspired his declaration "Beauty will save the world!" Bulgakov, too, would later, in a major philosophical work, *The Unfading Light*, assign to art and beauty a major role in the salvation of the world. Bulgakov's illumination, however, did not lead him to reject economics, but rather led him to transform it from a Marxist to a Fedorovian-Solovyovian Christian discipline, from social to spiritual science. In the years that followed, he became not only a religious thinker but an ordained priest, and in 1922, with Nikolai Berdyaev, Nikolai Lossky, Ivan Ilyin, S. L. Frank, Lev Karsavin, and more than 160 other leading Russian intellectuals, he was exiled on one of the special "philosopher's ships" arranged by high Soviet officials for the exile of undesirable intellectuals, and he was never allowed to return to Russia. First going to Constantinople, then to Prague, he eventually settled in Paris where he served as dean of Saint Sergius Theological Institute until the end of his life. His prolific theological and sophiological writings, which had led to his expulsion from the officially atheistic Soviet Union, also led to charges of heresy and the threat of excommunication from the Orthodox Church. Partly political and partly doctrinal, the charges that Bulgakov had attempted to introduce a heretical fourth hypostasis to the Holy Trinity were eventually refuted sufficiently to allow him to remain dean at the institute. Among Orthodox theologians, his doctrines remain highly controversial, but as Father Alexander Schmemann wrote of Bulgakov: "Whatever the ultimate fate of his Sophiology, he himself will remain as a great and creative thinker who has contributed more than many others toward the direction and the ethos of modern Orthodox theology."[34] And today it is not only Orthodox theologians who find Bulgakov a compelling and relevant thinker. As Charles McDaniel has written, in a recent article on resolving conflicts between Islamic and Western cultures:

> Much has been written of the perceived "clash" between Islamic and western civilisations and of the need for reconciliation. . . . Sergei Bulgakov left a rich repository of economic thought that philosophically bridges a gap between the rationality of western market economies and the transcendent awareness of Islamic social structures. Bulgakov's philosophy of economy embraces ideas of freedom even as it recognises the need for "guidance" and the essential nature of economic relationships to the preservation of community. By engaging Bulgakov's economic ideas, westerners can better understand the apprehensions of intellectuals in traditional cultures concerning globalisation and the reticence of many Muslims to embrace it.[35]

And as another sign of growing interest in Bulgakov beyond Russia, Rowan Williams, the archbishop of Canterbury, has found Bulgakov's thought sufficiently relevant to today's Western spirituality to have edited a collection of his translated writings.[36]

Bulgakov's first major work, and the one that best illustrates his Cosmist views, is *The Philosophy of Economy* (*Filosofiia khoziaistva*, 1912), in which the Russian word for "economy" suggests with its root the ideas of "husbandry," "landlordship," "proprietorship," "management," "householding"—Bulgakov essentially extends the meaning of economy to taking good care of the universe, and his title could be translated *The Philosophy of Responsible Ownership*.

Like Fedorov, Bulgakov sees present nature as material necessity, a force of disintegration and death, and the human task is to take ownership, free life from material necessity, and overcome nature and death. "The struggle against the antagonistic forces of nature for the purpose of defending, affirming, and broadening life, with the aim of conquering and taming these forces, becoming their master or proprietor, is in fact what—in the broadest and most preliminary fashion—we call economy."[37] Bulgakov's philosophy of economy, then, is in many ways an attractive, eloquent, lucid, systematic, and more modern and realistic version of Fedorov's "common task." Like Solovyov, he sidesteps Fedorov's technological projects, but goes farther than Solovyov in applying the Fedorovian-Cosmist schematic to the world of social, political, and economic realities. Far from a "dismal science," economics for Bulgakov becomes the sacred, priestly care of all that God has entrusted to us.

Bulgakov finds that both the communist and capitalist economic systems objectify and depersonalize humanity and reduce individuals to mere producers and consumers of objects more valuable than themselves. Both systems deal only with the external man, typical man, man subject to the mechanisms of market and historical necessity. But for Bulgakov, real life is internal life, personhood, organic life free from "thingness" and mechanism. "We can say that the entire world-historical process proceeds from the contradiction between mechanism, or thingness, and organism, or life, and from nature's effort to transcend mechanism—the principle of necessity—within itself in order to transform itself into an organism—the principle of cosmic freedom, the victory of life, or panzoism." But nature cannot accomplish this liberation on its own—humanity must step in.

> Thus economy is the struggle of humanity with the elemental forces of nature with the aim of protecting and widening life, conquering and humanizing nature, transforming it into a potential human organism.

The economic process can therefore be described as follows: it expresses the striving to transform dead material, acting in accordance with mechanical necessity, into a living body with its organic coherence; in the end, the aim of this process can be defined as the transformation of the entire cosmic mechanism into a potential or actual organism, the transcension of necessity through freedom, mechanism through organism, causality through intentionality—that is, as the humanization of nature.[38]

Bulgakov would replace current theoretical and existing economic systems with a "sophic economy," in which the "world soul" rather than world matter, the internal rather than the external life of humanity, the unseen rather than the tangible, would be the primary field of operation. Bulgakov extends the meanings of basic economic terms: wealth becomes cultural and spiritual as well as material riches; labor becomes the production of culture and the creation of immaterial value as well as industry and agriculture. Consumption becomes the human internalization and spiritualization of the cosmos. Labor is good for man in that it allows one to get out of the prison of self, to overcome separateness. "The capacity for labor is one of the characteristics of a living being; it expresses the flame and sharpness of life. Only he lives fully who is capable of labor and who actually engages in labor."[39]

The interrelatedness of everything in the universe, physical and spiritual, means that economic activity is cosmic in scope. "Every living organism, as a body, as organized material, is inextricably connected with the universe as a whole, for the universe is a system of mutually connected and mutually penetrating forces, and one cannot disturb so much as a grain of sand, destroy so much as an atom, without, to one or another degree, disturbing the entire universe."[40] This inextricable connectedness, this holistic relationship, extends beyond the familiar world and beyond this present life. "There is a certain cosmological karma of essences. The unity of the universe, the physical communism of being, means that, physically, everything finds itself in everything else, every atom is connected with the entire universe; or if we compare the universe to an organism, we can say that everything enters into the makeup of the world body."[41] This is Bulgakov's variation on Fedorov's idea that all matter throughout the universe contains the particles of our ancestors.

For the universe is characterized not only by a general correspondence, a continuity and connectedness of the world of physical matter, but also by a certain relation between living, or organized, matter and nonliving, or dead, matter, or, in other words, between organic bodies and inanimate matter. . . . And the general relation between the two fields is that the kingdom of life constantly intrudes on the kingdom of nonlife, seizes and carries away cold, lifeless matter with its warm tentacles, and transforms it into living material, organizes dead matter into a living body.

Bulgakov's concept of the relationship between life and death is perhaps more profound, and certainly more mystical, than Fedorov's: "Life is death, and death is life, such is the formula of this identity. In more complete and developed form it would be expressed thus: life passes into a state of lifelessness, or death, that is new or transcendent to it, while the lifeless, or dead, is raised into a different, higher state of life that is also transcendent to it."[42]

Bulgakov asks: which is dominant, life or death? Is life a part of death, or is death a part of life? "And what is more real, more primordial, more substantial: life or death, the living or the dead principle? . . . Following the ancients (Plato and particularly Plotinus), Boehme and Baader, Schelling and Vladimir Soloviev, I consider this monism of life, panzoism, in contrast to the monism of death, or the panfantism of the materialists, to be the single metaphysical hypothesis capable of resolving this difficulty." For Bulgakov, closer on this point to Fedorov than to Solovyov, the body is essential to life, and a bodiless existence is unthinkable. A body is matter in organized form, and it is only through bodies, an organization of organs, that life overcomes dead matter. "Through the body, thanks to the connectedness of the universe, life in its various manifestations penetrates into the entire cosmos. The cosmos is in this sense the potential body of a living being, an organism in potential. This potential, of course, may never be realized, or may be realized only in part. It exists in a dual sense."[43]

The idea of potential here is important. The cosmos as it exists is not yet an organism, but human labor can—but not necessarily will—make it so. So like both Fedorov and Solovyov, Bulgakov assigns humanity a crucial, active role in the transformation of dead matter into living organism. The difference is primarily one of emphasis, and Bulgakov's emphasis is on the potential for sophic healing of the world's body. Fedorov's emphasis was on the deficiency of everything existing and on the duty to resurrect, the task of transforming, the universal obligation, an all or nothing proposition with dire consequences if we fail. Solovyov's emphasis was more on the desirability than on the absolute necessity of deification and godmanhood, a yearning for a world as it could be rather than a work order for the world as it ought to be. Bulgakov, closer to Solovyov, but with subtle differences, does not so much yearn as patiently anticipate that sophic economy will eventually achieve the humanization of nature, the spiritualization of matter, and the resurrection of the dead.

Consumption brings the entire universe into ourselves: "Our bodily organs are like doors and windows into the universe, and all that enters us through these doors and windows becomes the object of our sensual perception and, in the process, becomes in a sense part of our body." From the microscopic to the macroscopic, everything apparently dark and lifeless can be understood as an extension of our body—"All that is accessible to our cognition and that somehow affects our sensuality and thus enters the illuminated sphere of life, all of this, that is, potentially the entire universe, can become our body, its external, peripheral extension." Lifeless things become part of life by our consumption of them into our body. Thus the entire universe, apparently mechanical and lifeless, can become an organism through our act of realizing it to be an extension of our body.[44]

For Bulgakov, the process of consumption represents "ontological communication" with the world and is the basis of all life processes. "Life is in this sense the capacity to consume the world, whereas death is an exodus out of this world, the loss of capacity to communicate with it; finally, resurrection is a return into the world with a restoration of this capacity, though to an infinitely expanded degree."[45]

That we are already on the way to humanizing the universe is evident in the simple, everyday act of taking a meal. Where Fedorov saw the eating of particles of our ancestors as a form of cannibalism that could only be atoned for by resurrecting them, Bulgakov sees ingestion as part of the solution instead of a problem. "The boundary between living and nonliving is actually removed in food. Food is natural communion—partaking of the flesh of the world. When I take in food, I am eating world matter in general, and, in so doing, I truly and in reality find the world within me and myself in the world, I become part of it. . . . Food in this sense uncovers our essential metaphysical unity with the world."[46] Incarnation, then—the literal taking into the body—in Bulgakov, becomes not only a theological doctrine but a practical everyday activity.

The taking of food erases the difference between subject and object, and our act of incarnating the world parallels God's act in becoming man. "Even God had to become incarnate in the world in order to act on it from within, as an inner-worldly resurrective force. 'And the Word was made flesh.'"[47] God the Word, the Logos, moved from outside the world to inside the world in order to bring new life to the world and save it.

Holy Communion, for Bulgakov, enacts the potential of immortality.

> If food is a means of communion with the flesh of the world, regardless
> of its shape and quantity, then partaking of Christ's flesh and blood in
> the form of bread and wine is communion with the flesh of the Son of
> God, the divinized flesh of the world, which can also be conceived
> only dynamically. And as food maintains mortal life, so the Eucharistic
> meal means to partake of immortal life, in which death is conquered
> once and for all, and the deathlike impenetrability of matter is
> overcome.[48]

Consumption, then, has not only an economic and metaphysical dimension
but a sacred dimension as well. The sacrament of bread and wine, "the food of
immortality," serves as a transcendent promise of what our ordinary everyday
meals, properly understood, could lead us to.

Labor is "the living connection between the subject and object, the bridge
leading the I into the world of realities and irrevocably connecting him to this
world."[49] For Bulgakov, the "non-I" is really the "not yet I," and what is dead is
"not yet living." The labor to actualize the potential may take a long time, but
the opportunity already exists.

> As a consequence of the general connectedness of nature, the unity of
> the cosmos, we must speak of the accessibility or obedience of nature
> generally to man. Although man remains immeasurably far from pos-
> session of nature, this path is open to him. Nature is the passive, recep-
> tive, feminine principle; man is the active, male, conscious principle.
> Thus nature, with its reigning blind intellect of instinct, becomes con-
> scious of itself and acquires vision only in man. Nature becomes hu-
> manized; it is capable of becoming man's peripheral body, submitting
> to his consciousness and realizing itself in him.[50]

The Cosmist idea of active evolution becomes in Bulgakov a function of
human labor. Through labor, humanity introduces a new, cosmogonic,
world-creating force equivalent to natural force. God originally created the
world with Adam—humanity—at the center, "and what unfolds in time and
constitutes the content of history merely recreates the inner connection and
interrelation of the world's elements that was destroyed by the original sin."[51]

Bulgakov's man, then, is not a creator, but a re-creator, and nature as an
active force, *natura naturans*, which in the present world is hidden and

suppressed by its phenomena and products, *natura naturata*, realizes itself in man.

> Man slowly and gradually freeing himself from slavery to things, the products of the *natura naturata*, removes the deathly shroud from nature and apprehends its creative forces. . . . In economy, in the conscious re-creation of nature, we can see a certain adumbration and anticipation of that liberation of the *natura naturans* from the fetters of the *natura naturata* . . . from the imprisonment of thingness, from that heavy numbness in whose somnolence it dreams of its liberation.[52]

Humanity is capable of transforming the world, but how do we know that this transformation will be for the better? If the universe is fluid, if even life and death are interconnected, if the most basic boundaries can be redrawn or erased, what will ensure that the magic we work will be good magic?

Bulgakov writes:

> Since man obviously is not all-powerful, he cannot create from nothing but must draw on the existing world in re-creating his new, artificial world, the world of culture. He can imprint his ideas on the created world, experiment with it, and find in it the answers to his questions; in economic activity, the new world of culture takes shape. But where does he find the images, the model ideas on which to base his creative activity?[53]

His answer is, of course, Sophia:

> Humanity is and always remains the unifying center of the world in the eternal harmony and beauty of the cosmos created by God. The empirical world is immersed in "process," in time and space, in history, and as such is imperfect and disharmonious; yet, like humanity itself, it is never wholly separated from a higher metaphysical reality, from the divine Sophia that ever soars above the world, illuminating it through reason, through beauty, through . . . economy and culture.

Solovyov's Sophia seems to have been more of an ideal, serving as guide and inspiration to a higher life. Bulgakov's Sophia seems to be a more active presence and force, an ally in the human task of realizing the sacred cosmic potential within the given universe of actuality.

The world as cosmos and the empirical world, Sophia and humanity, maintain a living interaction, like a plant's nourishment through its roots. Sophia, partaking of the cosmic activity of the Logos, endows the world with divine forces, raises it from chaos to cosmos. Nature always perceives her reflection in man, just as man, despite his faults, always perceives his own reflection in Sophia. Through her he takes in and reflects in nature the wise rays of the divine Logos; through him nature becomes sophic.[54]

"Sophic" then, as a term for cosmic interconnectedness and interpenetration, is Bulgakov's equivalent of Solovyov's "syzygic."

To recreate nature, we need models, images, icons. By attuning ourselves to models given to us by Sophia, we will reshape the world for the better. If we try to take matters into our own hands and attempt independent choice of other models, outside Sophia, all we can do is shape "a shadowy, satanic world alongside the given, created one."[55] The illusion that one can create something from and by oneself is a form of hubris that can only result in bad art, bad science, and further degradation of the natural and cultural environment.

As many commentators have noted, Bulgakov, like Solovyov, nowhere exactly defines what he means by Sophia. She is in various passages the eternal feminine, the earth mother, the world soul, the earthly manifestation of the trinity, the substratum underlying human economic activity. Bulgakov describes Sophia's many functions, but does not try to pin her down to a single, consistent definition. As he explains, Sophia cannot be understood through science, nor through any examination of the phenomena of this world. Sophia can only be known to us through revelation.

> Truth reveals itself in miraculous, intuitive ways independent of scientific cognition. This revelation can take on different forms: religious, as myths and symbols; philosophical, as the brilliant intuitions of philosophical geniuses; artistic, as works of art, through which (according to Schelling's definition) the infinite shines through the finite. Sophia reveals itself, finally, in the mysteries of personal religious life. Whoever has once experienced the inexpressible knows about this, and whoever has not is incapable of understanding it.

For Bulgakov, Christ is the only way, truth, and life, and one who partakes of life in Christ, the Truth, "becomes a living member of the divine Sophia, the body of Christ, his church, and in so doing apprehends the sophic world—for us merely an ideal—a living reality. He becomes transparent and sophic; Sophia—that sun which shines and warms us while remaining invisible— emerges from the clouds and openly stands in the middle of the sky."[56]

Here then we see the depths, but also the down-to-earth quality, of Bulgakov's mysticism. Although at the time a philosopher and a social scientist, he first attained his knowledge of Sophia not by reading or debating or conducting a survey but by standing before Raphael's Madonna, not trying to analyze the painting, but absorbing it, opening himself to a great artist's intuition of higher reality. He came to understand Solovyov through Raphael. To use his terms, he consumed the Madonna: she became part of Bulgakov, and Bulgakov became part of her. Raphael's great vision became an extension of his body and life, and he became an extension of Raphael's vision. In art and deeds, then, is where Bulgakov finds truth, not in spiritual abstractions but in worldly embodiments of the spirit. Bulgakov's Sophia is not an idea, not a concept, but an active presence sensed by those open to revelation.

Another defining feature of Bulgakov's thought that we see here is the honor he pays to the priest's day-to-day work in the world, and to the church as the living, earthly body of God's word. Probably more than any of the other Cosmist thinkers, Bulgakov valued and actively participated in the corpus of the world. As Bernice Glatzer Rosenthal has shown in a perceptive article, Bulgakov "regarded Sophia as a living link between God, man, and nature,"[57] with emphasis on the living. He was not an ascetic or in any way removed from the everyday business of living in the world. He was happily married and a devoted father, active in state and church politics; he was an able administrator and, especially in his second major book, *The Unfading Light* (*Svet neverchenii*, 1917), exalted the feminine principle, human intimacy, and matrimonial sex. His emphasis is on "spiritual corporeality," and, as Rosenthal notes, he "envisioned the entire world as 'one corporeality and one body.'" Rosenthal cites a remarkable passage from *The Unfading Light*:

Great mother, grey earth! In you we are born, you feed us, we touch you with our feet, to you we return. Children of the earth love their mother, kiss her, wipe her tears, because they are her flesh and blood. For nothing perishes in her; she preserves everything in herself, the silent memory of the world that gives life and fruit to all. He who does not love the earth, does not feel her maternity, is a slave and an alien, a pitiful rebel against the mother, a fiend of nonexistence. . . . You silently preserve in yourself all the fullness and all the beauty of creation.[58]

Where Fedorov's ideal was virginity, and Solovyov's was androgyny, Bulgakov believes in holy matrimony, with emphasis on the "holy." His church is the Bride of the Lamb, and earthly human relationships are reflections of that higher one. "Male and female He created them"—Bulgakov accepts traditional gender roles of active masculinity and passive femininity, but as Rosenthal observes, he generally exalts the feminine over the masculine.

> In effect he was invoking Mother Russia against the German Fatherland, and "feminine" qualities against "masculine" ones—love rather than force, mediation rather than conflict, and selflessness rather than self-assertion, aggressiveness, and war. The abstract rationalism he hated is conventionally linked with a "masculine" style of thought, and war has always been a "masculine" affair. Orthodoxy, he pointed out, stresses motherhood and the glory of the earth. The world rests in the bosom of God as a child in the womb of its mother. His dead son was resting in Mother Earth.[59]

In "The Holy Grail" (*Sviatyi graal*)[60], a poetic exegesis of John 19:34, the passage about the piercing of Jesus's body by the spear of Longinus and the flow of blood and water from the wound, Bulgakov further develops the idea of Christ's bond with the world. For Bulgakov, the Grail legend, in which Joseph of Arimathea collected the blood and water from the wound in the same chalice that had been used in the Last Supper and took the chalice to Glastonbury in England, where it became the object of Arthurian quests, a symbol of holiness and spiritual beauty intermittently visible only to the purist knights—the Arthurian legend has as its origin and inner meaning Christ's gift of himself to the world. The Grail is the world, the earth, into which flowed the "living corporeality that was separated out from the spirit-abandoned body of Christ on the cross."[61] Bulgakov further notes that in Orthodox iconography, the blood from Christ's wounds falls into the earth and quickens the skull of Adam buried under the cross on Golgotha.

> Out of the side of the old Adam was created woman, who tempted him to fall. But the wound delivered to humankind from Adam's side is healed by the spear wound in Jesus' side. The blood and water that flowed into the world abide in the world. They sanctify this world as the pledge of its future transfiguration.... And the whole world is the chalice of the Holy Grail. The Holy Grail is inaccessible to veneration;

in its holiness it is hidden in the world from the world. However, it exists in the world as an invisible power, and it becomes visible, appears to pure hearts who are worthy of its appearance.[62]

In one of the first assessments of Fedorov's thought by a major thinker,[63] Bulgakov finds his emphasis on universal kinship and on Christianity as an active faith to be among the highest achievements of Russian thought. But like Solovyov, he rejects the technological side of Fedorov's project, considering it the apotheosis of economic materialism. He argues that Fedorov's active Christianity overemphasizes the potential of humanity by itself and slights the active presence of God in the world. For Bulgakov, Fedorov lacks appreciation of the mystery of God's relationship to humanity and the world. Bulgakov accepts that so long as we remain human in this world, much remains and will remain unknowable, whereas Fedorov believes that we all can and must eventually know all. Bulgakov says that Fedorov does not clearly understand—or at least never clearly states—what life is and what death is, and ignores the reality, intuited by all Christian mystics, that a person's life already extends beyond the body's death. This world, as Bulgakov apprehends it, suffused with sophic presence and activity, already contains the potential of its redemption, and divine-human cooperation—with emphasis on the divine—can eventually realize that potential. As an active priest, Bulgakov emphasizes the symbols, sacraments, and daily pastoral care, which, in his view, can perform magic beyond any scientific technology.

Bulgakov's contribution to Cosmist thought is to emphasize the active aspects of Christian Orthodoxy as it already is, and not as it must transform itself to become. In Bulgakov, the liturgy of transformation, properly understood, happens within the existing church, and the existing world is the body in and through which Sophia is manifest. We are the owners and managers of the cosmos, responsible under divine guidance for its survival and growth. In Bulgakov's economy, we need to apply more care and understanding than radical redirection. We do not need to build or purchase a new universe but to take better care of the one we already own.

## *Pavel Aleksandrovich Florensky (1882–1937)*

Although many of the Russian Cosmists were polymaths, probably no one deserves to be called "the Russian Leonardo" more than Pavel Florensky, whose wide-ranging, seminal contributions to mathematics, physics, electrodynamics, folkloristics, philology, marine botany, art history and theory,

earth science, philosophy, theology, and esotericism were all part of his lifelong quest for a comprehensive worldview, uniting science, religion, and art;
reason and faith; Orthodox tradition and futuristic thaumaturgy. Of Florensky, Sergei Bulgakov, friend and soul mate, forever paired with him in a
famous dual portrait by Mikhail Nestorov, wrote: "Of all the contemporaries
whom I was fated to meet over the course of my long life, he was the greatest."[64] And the composer, musicologist, and scholar of mysticism Leonid
Sabaneev would add: "Florensky was one of those persons in my life who
made the deepest impression on me, owing to the intensity and profundity of
his intellect, which amounted to unquestionable genius despite his propen-
sity to paradox and contradictions. He was a man quite unlike any other."[65] A
North American branch of the Russian Orthodox Church has even listed
him as a martyr and saint. But, as we shall see later in this chapter, for other
sides of his life and thought Florensky has been labeled a Neanderthal in a
cowl, an apologist for the black hundreds, a twentieth-century Savonarola,[66]
and has recently even been branded a forerunner of Adolf Hitler and the most
vehement Nazi racists.[67]

Contradictions, antinomies, and paradoxes pulse through Florensky's life
and thought. Born in an obscure railway town in Azerbaijan, schooled in Tif-
lis three years after Ioseb Dzhugashvili, who would change his name to Stalin,
no one, Bulgakov tells us, loved Russia more yet was less of a Russian nationalist than Florensky, who, knowing exactly what he was in for, stayed to suffer
imprisonment, labor camps, and eventual execution rather than seek comfort
and probable fame in emigration. His father was Russian, a railway engineer,
interested in all sciences, well read in European literature, neither religious
nor antireligious but tolerant and glad to include religious holidays as an
important part of family culture. Florensky's paternal grandfather was a
doctor, descended from a long line of priests, but like many of his generation
of similar background, a militant 1860s positivist, socialist, and atheist. Florensky's mother was the thoroughly Russified daughter of a prominent but, in
the words of biographer Avril Pyman, "decadent, effeminate"[68] Armenian
trader of fine wools and silks. In St. Petersburg, where she met Florensky's
father, she used the Russian version of her surname, Saparova, instead of
Saparian, and after marriage was known as Olga rather than by her Armenian
name, Salome. She loved European art, music, and poetry, and had little to no
interest in things Armenian, somewhat to Florensky's later disappointment
when he attempted to learn more about the Armenian half of his ethnic heritage. Despite Florensky's thoroughly Russian cultural background, some acquaintances, such as Sabaneev, remarked on his "Asiatic" appearance and

"oriental" cast of mind. Bulgakov thought that he looked somehow un-Russian, more ancient Greek or Egyptian. The Symbolist poet, novelist, and memoirist Andrei Biely, under whose father, the mathematician Nikolai Bugaev, Florensky studied at Moscow University, wrote, "Florensky should be drawn in Egyptian outline; at his feet I would put a crocodile!"[69]

In ethnicity, in culture, in intellectual interests—in every way imaginable—Florensky was a walking example of unified contraries. The one image that perhaps best illustrates his natural complexity is of him standing in a classroom after the 1917 revolution, probably beside a bust of Lenin, lecturing on theoretical and practical technicalities of electrification to young workers and Bolshevik officials, while still wearing his white priest's cassock. His religious piety, his devotion to medieval Russian traditions and values, and his dedication to Soviet scientific, social, and technological projects were all equally genuine. As Bulgakov explains, he was a citizen of both Athens and Jerusalem. He was indifferent to politics and inwardly free of all forms of external government. Ready to serve God and Russia however and wherever he could, whether as monk or married priest, whether in the monastic village of Sergiev Posad or in Siberia, whether before or after October 1917, his focus seems to have been three-quarters on eternity, one-quarter on the present moment.

In 1900, during his first year at the University of Moscow, he wrote to his mother: "For me mathematics is the key to a world view."[70] And in his third year of study, his approach to mathematics and the worldview he found in it had become so well developed that a later scholar would write:

Arithmology is P. A. Florensky's philosophical method and pervades his entire oeuvre. In the narrow sense of the word, arithmology is the theory of discontinuous functions. In the wider sense—it is the idea of discontinuity, an integral factor, according to [Florensky's] judgment, of a whole new way of looking at the world which was then in process of formation, which was just coming into being to replace various types of analytical ways of thinking based on the concept of the continuum.[71]

Eventually, this mathematical concept of "discontinuity" would be extended to any number of nonmathematical applications, and Lobachevsky's non-Euclidian geometry would become a model for a worldview based on revolutionary premises and radically untraditional logic. Florensky believed that the mathematics of continuity formed the basis for the nineteenth-century determinism and materialism that new thought needed to overcome. The mathematics of discontinuity could now serve as a foundation for alternatives to the deterministic materialism that dominated all fields of thought and culture. The logic of discontinuity allows Florensky to argue that instead of accepting that "truth" is either something or its negation, A or (−A), "truth" must instead be considered both something and its negation, A + (−A). The thing and its contradiction, the thing and its opposite, the thing and its "other"—all join as part of one truth that is greater than either. So in Florensky's "discontinuous" worldview, one thing does not counter or replace its opposite but joins with it, neither part losing its identity, to form something higher and greater.

The cosmos, for Florensky, is united and whole in a way that is beyond our comprehension: we cannot grasp the unified wholeness but only seize upon individual strands of the whole truth, and therefore cannot assume that because one thing is certainly true, then its negation, opposite, or contradiction must be untrue. Florensky's view looks away from a mechanical world order, forward toward our fluid, mysterious universe of matter and antimatter, waves that are also particles, and subatomic whatnots that are simultaneously there and not there. And Florensky applies this concept of "discontinuity" to everything he writes about: icons, ethnic customs, or electrons.

Some of Florensky's strongest critics[72] have, possibly, misunderstood his intentions, have assumed that because he wore a priest's cassock while lecturing to workers, he was protesting the Revolution and rejecting the Soviet order, or because he worked for Soviet institutions he had abandoned his religious calling—that because he was taking a clear stand for A, he must obviously be taking an equally clear stand against (−A). His critics have argued that his discovery and endorsement of certain higher truths in the Ptolemaic worldview must mean that he rejected the Copernican; his love for everything about medieval Russia must mean that he despised everything about the Italian Renaissance; that he valued the reverse perspective of Russian icons means that he must have found Raphael's work ugly, without form or soul, *bezobraznyi*. But it is likely that his intention was less to denigrate or reject the realities and values of the present time than, while abiding the given world, to rediscover and revive higher truths and values that had been forgotten or were being neglected. Complete truth equals A + (−A), and Florensky's role was to demonstrate to those who knew only the truth of A that (−A) also could be true. So to a neo-Kantian intellectual world, in which human reason is autonomous and truth does not determine consciousness but rather consciousness determines truth, Florensky exalted Plato's magical, religious world of "more real" verities. And in the face of an aesthetic dogma that places the beginnings of "realistic" art in the Italian Renaissance, Florensky points out the "higher realism" of the great Russian icon painters, who not naively but knowingly and deliberately use "reverse perspective" with planes and angles, allowing the Savior's eyes and nose to point toward the viewer while the neck and chin turn slightly sideways, to depict the world from a higher, wider, rounder godlike point of view rather than from the individual artist's narrow, temporally and spatially limited viewing angle. Whereas a well-painted Renaissance portrait gives us an image (Russian *obraz*) of our physical reality from a limited individualistic, "illusory" perspective, a well-painted icon, when viewed by the right person (a sensitive believer) in the right setting (an irregular, round cornered Russian church interior, with the sight and aroma of drifting incense, dimly lit by flickering candles, accompanied by the slow, choreographed movements of priests in folded, rich, flowing vestments) allows the viewer to behold something like Plato's world of ideal forms.[73] Here we recall that Vladimir Solovyov, in his poem "Three Meetings," and Alexander Blok, in his "Beautiful Lady" poems, set their epiphanies of a higher, Platonic, sacred reality in church atmospheres very similar to those described by Florensky. Florensky tells us that when viewed in a museum under bright, cold light, an icon closes its window to higher reality. In pointing this out, Florensky is not so much suggesting that we should stop supporting and visiting museums, but rather that there is more to reality than we can experience even in the best institutions of our modern secular culture. Moreover, as he argues in this essay and elsewhere, anything removed from its living environment loses much of its value and meaning. We can try to abstract truth from experience; we can read books about, for example, a higher reality; but we can truly know it only by experiencing it whole, in life, embracing the living discontinuities, irrationalities, and contradictions.

Like Fedorov before him, Florensky rejected the doctrine of "progress" and believed that as much was lost as gained as Russia followed in the wake of European transitions from medieval to Renaissance to Enlightenment to industrial societies. As Michael Hagemeister points out,[74] the Middle Ages, for Florensky, represented principles of objectivism as opposed to subjectivism, collectivism as opposed to individualism, wholeness as opposed to atomization, synthetic as opposed to analytic vision, constructive as opposed to self-destructive ideals. Florensky sometimes openly described himself as a medieval thinker and a man with medieval preferences. But that he highlighted what he considered the strengths of the medieval and the weaknesses of the Renaissance and post-Renaissance worldviews does not mean that he saw a black-and-white history of no weaknesses in the medieval view and no positive features in later periods. His view of history was not so much one of linear decline leading to fall as of general characteristics that submerge for a time and then resurface, never taking the exact same form, but reappearing with recognizable similarities. To some degree, Florensky believed that the Communist future could possibly (but not necessarily) lead to a revival of medieval objectivism, collectivism, and constructive vision, and a turning from the illusory individualism and self-destructive atomization that had characterized prerevolutionary modernity. As his acquaintance Leonid Sabaneev saw it: "He seemed to look upon the Bolsheviks from some mystical height, as a necessary link in the historical process."[75] His medievalism was neither a nostalgic yearning for the past nor a total rejection of the present, but a nuanced, guardedly hopeful vision of a revival of certain characteristics, with a difference, in the future.

Florensky's brilliant start as a mathematician,[76] making him at an early age a leading figure in a movement subsequently recognized as a major revolutionary force in the history of international mathematics, could have led to a productive and distinguished academic career. But like Solovyov before him, Florensky turned to the study of theology, not abandoning science for religion but, joining A to (−A), adding profound immersion in Orthodox spirituality to his previous precocious accomplishments in mathematics and natural science. After passing his master's examination at the Moscow Academy of Theology, he accepted a position there as lecturer in philosophy and in 1914 published his dissertation and best known work, *The Pillar and Ground of the Truth*,[77] a brilliant, if eccentric, or as Berdyaev would later label it, "stylized" collection of twelve "letters" to an unidentified "meek and radiant friend" that has become a classic of Russian spiritual literature. One of the major ideas developed in the letters is that of "consubstantiality," which Florensky treats as a Christian, antinomian alternative to modern secular, materialistic rationalism. That three can be one is a rational and material absurdity, but a higher, spiritual truth, exemplifying an epistemology that "is not only a gnoseological but also an ontological act, not only ideal but also real. Knowing is a real going of the knower out of himself, or (what is the same thing) a real going of what is known into the knower, a real unification of the knower and what is known. That is the fundamental and characteristic proposition of Russian and, in general, of all Eastern philosophy."[78] Thus "knowing," in Florensky, is, like "consumption" in Bulgakov, an act of love, earthly and heavenly, a going out of oneself and a taking into oneself of an other. This is the moral dimension of Florensky's epistemology, the importance that he assigns to the idea of "friendship."

In his own life, Florensky, who, as Bulgakov once remarked, was in his personal life "as solitary as Mt. Elbrus,"[79] intended to live as a monk but was advised by his religious superior to marry instead and become a priest in the world. His previous intellectual and spiritual intimacies had all been with males, giving rise to suspicions then and now of homosexual inclinations, and those close to him were astonished to learn of his sudden decision to marry. As longtime friend Vladimir Ern wrote to his own wife on September 2, 1910:

Pavlusha has got married. I called in on him as dusk was falling, we embraced and without a word he showed me his ring. I was thunderstruck, but he called out "Anna" and introduced us. Vasen'ka [Vasili, Anna's brother, a friend of Florensky's from the Theological Academy,] appeared, we sat down to tea, everything so easy and simple, and I sat there in amazement, trying to take in the fait accompli. She behaves affectionately to [Vasili] and calls him "Thou." I look at her face: his sister! It's three days since she arrived from Riazan and when they were wed I don't know. Pavlusha is quiet, calm and merry, natural and tender with his wife without any sign of being in love, as though they'd been living together for 20 years. And so—it's happened! But all my fears are dispersed. Nothing tragic. Everything very simple and good. The old, complex Pavel has died down and it seems he took this step without forcing himself. There will be children to whom they will be devoted and there will be one more close-knit family in Russia. She is very like Lilya [one of Florensky's sisters], not pretty at all, but obviously unassuming, good-natured, simple and perhaps very beautiful in soul.[80]

The marriage, making up in love for what it lacked in romance, did indeed turn out to be a happy one. For the rest of his life, Florensky remained a devoted husband and father, sending whenever possible playful, loving, reassuring messages to every member of the family through the worst times of his exile and imprisonment. Florensky's natural inclinations may have led toward a kind of figurative levitation, up and away from everyday earthly realia and into a world of Platonic realiora. His role as married priest provided, among other things, ballast, allowing him to embrace both Anna and Divine Sophia, to dwell simultaneously in visible and invisible worlds.

As early as 1904, through his friend, the son of his mathematics professor, the poet who wrote under the name Andrei Biely (real name Boris Bugaev), Florensky had entered the elite circles that created Russia's Silver Age of culture. He knew the writers, artists, musicians, and thinkers, attended the salons and discussion groups, and contributed poems, reviews, and scholarly, philosophical, and theological essays to the journals that defined the epoch. Here, as always, he was soon a leading figure, a master theorist of the avant-garde, formulating in mathematical, philosophical, and theological terms the revolutions that were taking place in all the arts, from traditional to experimental forms and from realist to symbolist themes and images, from Newtonian to Einsteinian, from earth-centered to Cosmist views of the world. With Dmitri Merezhkovsky, Zinaida Gippius, Andrei Biely, Vyacheslav Ivanov, Alexander Scriabin, and others, he was at the forefront of the Godseekers, Prometheans, New Argonauts, and eventually the Makovets, groups with different names and members, but all looking to discover or create a new unity of all art, science, and spirituality.

As Biely would write, one of the tasks that his generation of artists and thinkers set for themselves was to update and apply to the circumstances of the new century the nineteenth-century ideas of Vladimir Solovyov and Nikolai Fedorov.[81] One of Florensky's major contributions to this effort was his attempt to establish a legitimate role in Orthodox theology for the worship of Divine Sophia. Bulgakov acknowledged Florensky's writings as a major influence on his own developing sophiology. And Florensky's creative discourses on the early fathers and features of the Orthodox tradition, particularly the exaltation of the feminine principle, helped Silver Age intellectuals discover new depths in rituals and artifacts previously ignored or dismissed. In letter 10, "Sophia," of *The Pillar and Ground of the Truth*, Florensky explores concepts and images of Sophia from before Christianity, through Christian doctrine and iconography, up through the writings of Vladimir Solovyov, and concludes:

> Sophia, the true Creation or creation in the Truth, is a preliminary hint of the transfigured, spiritualized world as the manifestation, imperceptible for others, of the heavenly in the earthly. This revelation occurs in the personal, sincere love of two, in friendship, when to the loving one is given—in a preliminary way, without ascesis—the power to overcome his self-identity, to remove the boundaries of his I, to transcend himself, and to acquire his own I in the I of another, a Friend. Friendship, as the mysterious birth of *Thou*, is the environment in which the revelation of the Truth begins.[82]

Sophia, then, as we experience her, is our hint of the heavenly in the earthly. This is our perception and experience of the "world soul." And for

Florensky, we cannot really know Sophia, the soul of the world, rationally or by means of definitions and concepts, but only through living experience, through friendship and love. It is through our souls, not through our minds, that we can grasp Sophia, the soul of the world, and the holistic truth that she represents. Solitude cannot lead to truth, for Florensky. Only through a friend, an other, can we enter the cosmos and be entered by the cosmos.

As in his writings on Sophia, so in his writings on other topics Florensky's real interest and focus is on the windows between two worlds. In "Iconostasis," he writes of the icon, and the saint's face as windows, objects in our world that allow hints and previsions of another world. And in an essay titled "The Word as Magic" (*Magichnost' slova*),[83] he defines the word as an intermediary between the inner and outer world, as "an amphibian," living both here and there, a thread between this world and that. Before we are able to speak, the word is only inside our heads, and as soon as we can speak we no longer have control over it. Paradoxically, then, while we have power over the word, it does not, strictly speaking, exist, and when it emerges from us and does exist, we no longer have power over it, as in the wise folk saying: "A word is a sparrow: let it go, you can't catch it." And like Fedorov before him, Florensky suggests that the folk knowledge behind this saying shows more wisdom than all previous learned scientific discourses on the subject. The magic in the word (like the magic in icons) is due to its moving in two directions: in the first place from the speaker out into the world, and in the second place from something in the outer world entering the listener's inner world. "To put it another way, life is metamorphosed by means of the word, and by the word life acquires spirit. Or to put it yet another way, the word is magical and the word is mystical. To consider the word as magic means to understand just how and why by the word we can act upon the world. And to consider just how and why the word is mystical means to clarify for oneself the doctrine according to which the word is the reality it signifies."[84]

In the world of everyday material reality, the signifier and the signified are not identical. The word "shoe" is not a shoe. But in the higher world of ultimate all-unity, according to Florensky, the signifier and the signified are mystically joined. The seed and energy of the thing can mystically inhere in the word for that thing. In ancient Egyptian religion, and in the ancient Hebrew Kabbalah, God and the name of God are one. In yogic practice a god's name repeated as a mantra mystically joins one to the god named. And in Name Worship (*Imiaslavie*), an early Russian Orthodox heresy that was resurfacing in Florensky's day, the name of God, when pronounced in the hesychastic Jesus Prayer, itself attained a kind of divine status, and the believer uttering

"Lord Jesus Christ, Son of God, have mercy on me, a sinner" mystically experiences the actual presence of God. The simple formula for Name Worship was "The Name of God is itself God." Florensky envisioned a mathematical basis for this mystical belief. As Loren Graham explains: "When a mathematician created a set by naming it, he was giving birth to a new mathematical being. The naming of sets was a mathematical act, just as the naming of God was a religious one, according to the Name Worshippers."[85] Mathematics, then, for Florensky, is creation, and mathematical symbols, like words, are more than counters for realities, but can act upon and create realities. Pythagoras and Saint John the Evangelist represent, for Florensky, revealers of the sacred magical power of the signifier, as number and as Logos. In linear history Athens and Jerusalem may represent differences, but in eternal ultimate reality, they are one.

Florensky was apparently never able to turn down a request for a preface, or introduction, or contribution to any book or collection of essays being edited by an ally or acquaintance. Even though he was reluctant to get involved in what he knew would be a political and theological controversy, which eventually resulted in riots, anathemas, and troops and gunships threatening heretical monks,[86] Florensky's contribution to the Name Worship dispute came about in part because he was sympathetic to the practice, but mainly because his friend Mikhail Novoselov had asked him to lend his name and support to a venerable monk who was under attack for having attempted an unscholarly defense of a practice that Florensky had a scholarly, intellectual interest in. Florensky's editorial revisions and erudite introduction to the publication simply fanned the fires of a controversy that he hoped to put out. In the wake of the controversy, he wrote: "It is unbearably painful to me that *Imiaslavie*—an ancient, sacred mystery of the Church—has been dragged out into the market place and tossed from hand to hand by people who have no right to so much as touch it and who, by their whole make-up, are incapable of understanding it."[87] The attacks on him that accompanied the 1913–1915 controversy over Name Worship convinced Florensky that the Orthodox Church of his day was too much driven by political considerations, too deeply mired in the material world of the early twentieth century, too willing to knuckle under to government pressure, and would not be a force for good in the political changes he could see coming.

But if his writings on *Imiaslavie* damaged his relationship with the Orthodox Church of his day, another controversy would more severely injure his future international reputation. In 1911, Menachem Mendel Beilis, a Jewish artisan, was falsely accused of the murder of Andrei Iushchensky, a thirteen

year old Christian boy. Rumors of ritual blood sacrifice quickly spread with
the charge, and a polarizing clamor of extreme anti-Semitic and philo-Semitic
accusations ensued. During the trial one of the experts for the defense, Professor Danil Khvolson, defended not only Beilis but all Jews, present and past,
modern and ancient, from accusations of blood sacrifice. Florensky, perhaps
naively thinking that he could inject a disinterested scholarly opinion on the
matter, anonymously published an article in a collection edited by his friend
Vasily Rozanov under the ominous title "Sense of Sight and Smell in the Jews'
Attitude to Blood," arguing that the ancient Hebrews, like nearly all ancient
peoples, did indeed practice human sacrifice, and that, as he had suggested in
an earlier essay on the Slavophile Khomiakov, the Christian sacrament of
Eucharist, the symbolic eating and drinking of Christ's body and blood,
reflects an antecedent Hebrew ritual of periodically eating the flesh and
drinking the blood of a human sacrificial victim as an offering to God in
atonement for the community's collective sins. And though he offered no
opinion on the specific case of Beilis, who was indeed innocent and eventually acquitted, Florensky suggested that it was entirely possible that this
ancient ritual could, perhaps in isolated instances, still be practiced somewhere, perhaps even in Russia, even as late as the twentieth century. Other
mysterious rituals and customs from ancient times had survived into the present, so why not instances of human sacrifice? And, while on the subject, he
could not decline to provide an introduction, signed only with a Greek initial, to Novoselov's collection of articles *Israel in the Past, Present, and Future*,
and exchanged a series of letters with Rozanov on the subject of Jews and
blood, in which he used his mathematical skills to determine how much Jewish blood, and, with that blood, Jewish character traits, would remain after so
many generations of dilution through intermarriage.[88] As Hermann Goltz
points out, in his defense of Florensky's character,[89] in his personal life and in
his letters, with the exception of those to Rozanov, Florensky shows no signs
of anti-Semitism. His interest in the questions of blood rites, ancient rituals,
genealogy, and ethnic characteristics were, Goltz argues, scholarly and intellectual. As a person of mixed ethnic heritage himself, his attitude toward
people of any background, ethnicity, or religion was one of love, never hatred.
But, Goltz's defense aside, if Florensky thought that as a scientist he could
emerge unscathed from a controversy so marked by label slinging from all
sides, he was naively mistaken. As Avril Pyman notes: "Blood sacrifice and the
importance of genealogy were all very well when Florensky was writing about
the Christian churches and his beloved Slavophiles, but his interest in such
things took on a very different complexion when he ventured to write about

the Jews."[90] His writings on blood and the Jews have done little harm to his growing reputation as a "native" Russian thinker, but may well prevent his being unanimously acclaimed—as some Russians have proposed—as one of the great European minds of the twentieth century.

For a short time, Florensky was able to serve as priest in a village some distance from his residence in Sergiev Posad, and with the coming of war in 1914 he served briefly as a chaplain on a hospital train for the wounded. But the press of teaching, administrative, and editorial duties—not to mention responsibilities as head of a growing extended family, and his extremely prolific output as a writer and scholar—forced him to give up trying to maintain the social dimension of his spiritual activity. As Bulgakov tells us, Florensky's priesthood became more one of sacramental duties than of pastoral care. And after the February and October Revolutions of 1917, he first had to diminish and finally curtail his regular activities as a priest. As a highly regarded mathematician and scientist, he was a recognized, valuable national asset during the early years of the Soviet Union. He served on a large number of scientific and educational boards and commissions, lectured on all of the many subjects he was qualified to speak on, wrote hundreds of technical papers, led research expeditions, edited and contributed more than 140 entries to a great encyclopedia of technology, and took on any additional assignment he was offered in order to support his growing family. Reading a chronological list of his activities and publications[91] for the period 1910–1930 can only make one wonder how he ever found time to eat, sleep, and breathe.

The artist Lev Zhegin (1892–1969), who worked with Florensky in the new arts movement "Makovets," tells of an incident in the early years after the revolution:

> In 1919 L. Trotsky was serving as head of Glavelektro. Making an inspection of the facility, while in a laboratory in the basement, Trotsky noticed Florensky, who was wearing his usual white cassock.
>
> "And that's who?"
>
> "Professor Florensky."
>
> "Ah, Florensky, I know!"
>
> He walked up to him and invited him to join a conference of engineers.
>
> "Only, maybe, not in that outfit."
>
> Florensky replied that he would not remove his priestly garment and would not appear in street clothes.
>
> "Okay, you can't. Then do it in that outfit!"

At the conference, Florensky gave a paper. When he came into the meeting room you could hear some ignorant remarks: "A priest in the room!" Florensky's paper was, as always, pithy and brilliant in delivery. He finished to great applause.[92]

In 1922, when Bulgakov, Berdyaev, and more than two hundred other intellectuals out of step with the Soviet government were loaded onto one of the so-called philosopher's ships and sent into permanent exile, Florensky stayed in Russia. As Bulgakov would write in his obituary, Florensky was in no way a Russian nationalist but was a thoroughly native, patriotic (*otechestvennyi*) Russian thinker and accepted inevitable persecution in the homeland rather than material comfort but spiritual misery elsewhere. His first arrest came in 1928, ostensibly on account of his earlier work for the Commission for Preservation of Art and Antiquities in the Trinity Saint Sergius Monastery. Accused of being part of a Church-sponsored, counterrevolutionary, monarchist plot, Florensky confessed and took all responsibility upon himself rather than inform on any others, and was exiled to Nizhni Novgorod, where he served only two months, thanks to the intervention of E. P. Peshkova (Maxim Gorky's wife) and other sympathetic science and technology officials. Permitted to return to a position as director of science materials, he continued to publish scientific and technical articles and to write unpublishable chapters toward a great projected but never completed philosophical work, "On the Watersheds of Thought."[93]

Early in the 1920s Lenin famously declared that "Communism equals Soviet power plus the electrification of the entire country."[94] Lenin, Trotsky, and Stalin supplied the power; Florensky provided major assistance with electrification. But this was only a part of Florensky's Promethean, Fedorovian, Cosmist endeavor to bring about a new world in which every aspect of human life would be transfigured. In the arts, he was a central figure in the Makovets movement, in which, as we shall see in chapter 11, one of the other founders, Vasily Chekrygin, undertook an artistic realization of Fedorov's resurrection and planetary colonization project. And in a 1919 article titled "Organoprojection,"[95] Florensky discusses the projection of artificial organs, continuations of our bodies, to extend human capabilities throughout the cosmos. Projected organs and body parts can operate and act on the world beyond the limits of our present physical bodies. "Magic, in that circumstance, could be defined as the art of altering the limit of the body with respect to its customary location."[96] Many of our present organs are only partly developed, far below the abilities and capacities that our imaginations can project for them.

By a combination of flesh and machinery we can extend our organs to reach as far as we can imagine, and operations now considered magical can become routine. As we shall see later in this study, recent Russian immortalist concepts of future humans as living machines echo Florensky's ideas of organ projection.

A further example of the Cosmist dimension of Florensky's thought and activity is evident in his letter of September 21, 1929, to the eminent scientist and Cosmist thinker Vladimir Vernadsky concerning the idea of the biosphere's becoming a noosphere, or planet of thought. Citing both classical Greek and Christian texts, Florensky outlines his theory, both panpsychist and Fedorovian, that spirit inheres in all matter,

> that the individual mark . . . of a person, like a stamp and an imprint, lies on the soul and on the body, so that the elements of the body, although scattered, can again be identified by their correspondence to the imprint, the *sfraga* [Gk. "seal"], the stamp, as belonging to the soul. In such manner a spiritual force always remains in the particles of the body, its registration, no matter where those particles are scattered and mixed with other matter.

And he suggests that interpenetrating the biosphere, or perhaps lying over it, is what he would call the "pneumatosphere," a sphere of spirit and culture intimately related to, affecting and affected by, the rest of the biosphere. At the present time, he concludes, it may still be "premature to speak of the pneumatosphere as a subject for scientific investigation; perhaps such a question should not even be set down in writing. But the impossibility of a personal conversation has compelled me to express this thought in a letter."[97]

Although this was a private letter, Florensky's published writings and essays that could only be kept "in the drawer" contained ideas that would prove to be as heretical within Soviet culture as the "pneumatosphere." One of the charges against him when he was arrested again in 1933 was that he had argued that the mathematical basis for Einstein's theory of relativity provided Kabbalistic proof of the existence of God. The other, and main, charge was that he had acted "as ideologist for a monarchist-fascist conspiracy preparing to invite and cooperate with a German take-over of the Soviet Union, supported by monks, priests, and 'Soviets without Bolsheviks.'"[98] Again he confessed to the trumped-up charges, and even wrote and signed the *Presumed Organization of the Future State*, a supposed manifesto and plan for the postcoup government. He was sentenced to ten years of hard labor, which he began to serve in far eastern Siberia, near the Chinese border, and later continued in the notorious far northern camp Solovki. During imprisonment, he was allowed one brief visit from his family, was allowed to correspond with them for the first years, and was able to continue his scientific work, conducting experiments and publishing papers on permafrost and ice formations in Siberia, and on iodine and seaweed properties and harvesting in Solovki. For a long time first no information then false information was released about his death, but after the fall of the Soviet Union, research into Soviet intelligence files found that he was tried and sentenced to death in November and executed near Leningrad on December 8, 1937.

Although the charges against him were false in detail and the punishment was unjust, Soviet officials were correct in judging that Florensky's loyalties were not to the existing government. But neither were they to the existing world. He was a man who happened to be dwelling in this world but was not of it, part ancient, part medieval, part modern and even postmodern man, a resident of more than a single dimension in time. Even his earliest acquaintances, who bore him no ill will, recognized his "otherness." Rafail Solovyov, a young nephew of Vladimir Solovyov, once remarked to Leonid Sabaneev that Florensky "looks as if he had already lived a thousand years."[99] And Sabaneev, himself a scholar of esoteric doctrines, noted:

> He lived in his own closed, ascetic, intensely intellectual world and in the world of his secret "spiritual exercises." He never talked about it, and when I questioned him he would give some evasive answer or none at all. Yet I had good reason to assume that he at times engaged in Yogic exercises and was well acquainted with Hindu mysticism. In his tastes and psychological attitudes he seemed close to the early medieval Gnostics (Origen, Basilides, and others), much closer probably than to pure and naïve Orthodoxy."[100]

Whatever esoteric knowledge or powers he may have sought, however, were not directed toward personal, Faustian ends. With Fedorov and other Cosmists, his interest was in the transformation of the world. In the end, he was like the man in Plato's myth who has seen the sun and breathed the fresh air, but then returns to the cave to enlighten those who have never left, fully aware of how he will be received, ready to endure the fate that awaits him.

## Nikolai Aleksandrovich Berdyaev (1874–1948)

Berdyaev begins one of his most important books, *The Meaning of the Creative Act*, with a characteristically bold statement: "The human spirit is in prison. Prison is what I call this world, the given world of necessity. 'This world' is not the cosmos; it is a non-cosmic condition of divisions and enmity, the atomization and falling apart of the living monads of the cosmic hierarchy."[101] Although he denied that he was a Platonic thinker, Berdyaev consistently views the visible, mundane world of our necessary daily life as essentially unreal, inauthentic, unfit for free human habitation. The real, authentic, free world is the invisible but imaginable cosmos which is our divinely human Christian task to create. This is a very different idea of Christianity from, for example, Bulgakov's idea that this world is the Holy Grail into which Christ's blood flowed, and it is precisely this given world which, in "sophic economy," we should endeavor to manage and carefully tend, but not attempt to co-create.

Rebellion, freedom, and creativity are Berdyaev's most important themes. In rebellion he reworks Nietzsche, in freedom Dostoevsky, and in creativity Fedorov, three of the thinkers whose portraits were most prominently displayed in his study at Clamart in France.[102] As he was the best known of Russia's twentieth-century religious thinkers, often discussed as a major existentialist, Berdyaev's emphases on rebellion and freedom have frequently been noted.[103] In this chapter, we shall emphasize his Fedorovian concept of creativity as a Christian task, not to try to label him a total Fedorovian Cosmist (he resisted all labels) or to deny his contributions to other tendencies of thought (he refused to admit that he belonged to any philosophical or intellectual "school") but to indicate that in addition to all else he accomplished, he contributed significantly to the Cosmist worldview.

Born into the upper but not uppermost Russian social class, with French, Polish, and Tatar roots, and descended from military and administrative dignitaries—no priests—Berdyaev simultaneously embodied, enjoyed, and rebelled against everything aristocratic in Russia, adored "the Russian people" whenever he encountered a particular specimen, and loathed the bourgeoisie and the commonplace world it represented. Like Florensky in his white cassock, Berdyaev addressed boisterous revolutionary gatherings in his best counterrevolutionary attire: elegantly tailored suits, long manicured fingernails, silk handkerchief, perfectly trimmed beard, pince-nez, and expensive French scent. Initially a Marxist, eventually a Christian, and once wealthy but later indigent, he remained a revolutionary and, even when he could no longer afford it, a dandy. As a young man he loved to visit the palatial estates of his aristocratic relatives, enjoy their rich food, wines, and cigars, and scandalize everyone present with his energetic radicalism. As a student, he was a very slow, mediocre learner, unable to memorize lines of poetry or arithmetic tables, but a precocious early reader of Dostoevsky, Tolstoy, Kant, and Hegel, unable to score above one on a twelve-point scale for catechism, but able to astonish his tutors and instructors with the maturity and complexity of his analyses of dense discursive texts. As both a writer and speaker, he was a brilliant polemicist, finding that he could best formulate and articulate his own views in opposition or contrast to the views of others. Even late in life, his friend and biographer Donald Lowrie tells us, Berdyaev would offer only a minimal and dull response if asked a direct question, but if an idea of his was challenged, whether by a naive young student or a famous visiting intellectual, he would come alive, eyes flashing, and launch into a brilliant monologue, no matter what the question. The contradictory character he ascribes to the Russian soul, cited at the beginning of this study, was essentially a self-analysis of his own mind. Throughout his life, he would get carried away in argument, shout, point, turn abstract concepts into personal attacks, insult and offend his very best friends, and expel invited distinguished visitors from his house. Over the decades, in Russia before and after 1917, and in emigration in Berlin and Paris, he was at one time friendly or closely associated with nearly every major intellectual of the period, but of all these acquaintances other than family, only two—Andrei Biely and Lev Shestov—escaped the inevitable break in relations and resulting cold shoulder, possibly because Biely returned to the Soviet Union, and Shestov died too soon for relations with Berdyaev to deteriorate. With a few once-close friends, such as Bulgakov, no decisive break occurred, but though they lived in relative proximity, they simply no longer sought each other's company.

Several times in his various writings, Berdyaev cites "The Angel," an 1831 poem written by Lermontov when he was seventeen. In Dimitri Obolensky's excellent plain prose translation:

An angel was flying through the midnight sky, and softly he sang; and the moon, and the stars, and the clouds in a throng hearkened to that holy song. He sang of the bliss of innocent spirits in the shade of the gardens of paradise; he sang of the great God, and his praise was unfeigned. In his arms he carried a young soul, destined for the world of sorrow and tears; and the sound of his song stayed, wordless but alive, in the young soul. And for a long time it languished in the world, filled with a wonderful longing, and earth's tedious songs could not replace for it the heavenly sounds.[104]

Like the soul borne into this world by the angel, Berdyaev longed for another, paradisiacal world remembered in celestial song and could never be satisfied with the tedious sounds of this world. But Berdyaev goes a step beyond Lermontov's poem, moving from passive yearning to active eschatology, urging the creation of a new paradise not only as an expression of human freedom and creativity but because God needs us to complete the work he began.

Berdyaev's idea of rebellion manifested itself biographically in his turning first against his aristocratic background to embrace Marxism, then against Marxism to embrace Christianity, and then, finally, against existing Christianity to embrace a future active Christian life based on freedom and creativity. Before the revolution he rebelled against the monarchy, after against Bolshevism, and in emigration against anti-Bolshevism. Essentially, Berdyaev's stance was of lifelong rebellion against the given world of perceived necessity, a constant process of freeing his mind from whatever set of ideas would currently fix and constrain it. Whatever exists must be transformed, re-created by man to fulfill God's intent. His biographer tells us that as a homeowner Berdyaev could neither replace a blown fuse nor build a new fire in the stove.[105] But as a philosopher, he finds that no task is beyond man's creative ability. If the whole universe needs a new fuse, someone will be able to come along and do it. Berdyaev acknowledges that in spirit, though not in specific details, he is closer to Fedorov's active, forceful, masculine Christianity than to the various sophiologies of Solovyov, Bulgakov, and Florensky.

According to Berdyaev, human history could be divided into three epochs: the epoch of the Law, represented by the Old Testament; the epoch of Redemption, represented by the New Testament, which fulfilled the Old; and the epoch of Creativity, which would fulfill both the preceding epochs. This division is similar to, but differs in emphasis from, Dmitri Merezhkovsky's and Zinaida Gippius's idea, so influential among the Russian symbolists, of three ages and three testaments: the prehistoric age of the Father, the historic age of the Son, and the coming age of the Holy Spirit. Though Berdyaev for some time not only attended but presided over the gatherings at the Merezhkovsky-Gippius home, he was not a Trinitarian, and in his writings, unless criticizing Christian dogma, avoids the subject. For Berdyaev, the epoch of Creativity would not arrive on its own from above, would not be a gift of grace from Sophia or the Holy Spirit, but would develop when rebellious humanity, following Christ, begins to exercise its freedom from necessity and re-create itself and the universe.

Unlike Fedorov, with his specific project of resurrection, or Solovyov, with his prescription for godmanhood, or Bulgakov, with his plan of sophic economy, Berdyaev proposes no specific course of action. Sometimes citing the poet Tiutchev's line "A thought expressed is a lie," Berdyaev deliberately refuses to lay out a plan for action or a specific guide to how a free humanity should exercise its freedom, for he believed that any philosophical roadmap proposed would limit rather than encourage freedom. He did not want his thoughts ever to harden into a new dogma, a new closed system, or any intellectual equivalent of death. Whenever he speaks of the epoch of Creativity, he remains deliberately vague. "In its essence, creativity is painful and tragic. The purpose of the creative impulse is the attainment of another life, another world, an ascent into being." But the tragedy of creativity today is that the result of the creative impulse in this world now is not new life but culture, and all works of culture, being static, subject to preservation but not to change, are dead. "The dawn of the creative religious epoch also means a most profound crisis in man's creativity. The creative act will create new being rather than values of differentiated culture; in the creative act life will not be quenched. Creativity will continue creation; it will reveal the resemblance of human nature to the Creator. . . . Literature ceases to be only literature; it would be new being. . . . Art is transformed into theurgy, philosophy into theosophy, society into theocracy."[106]

Berdyaev strongly seconds Marx's and Fedorov's insistence that the time of philosophy as reflection has passed and the time for philosophy as action has come.

> For creative philosophy, truth is not a passive reflection of something: truth is rather activity in giving meaning to something. . . . The creative epoch and creative philosophy are characterized by a new and different gnosseology which throws light on the relative and partial truth of the old gnosseology, under the law. This new and different gnosseology is based entirely upon the idea of man as a microcosm and the centre of the universe. The microcosm, in its creative and dynamic relationship to the macrocosm, knows no fatal separation, no opposition. Man is a relative and an image of the cosmos, not because he is a fraction of the cosmos but because he is himself a whole cosmos and of one structure with the cosmos. . . . Man the microcosm is able to express himself dynamically in the macrocosm,

he has the power to create being, to change culture into being. . . . True creativeness is theurgy, God-activity, activity together with God. . . . We face the problem of Christian being rather than Christian culture, the problem of transforming culture into being, science and art into a new heaven and a new earth.[107]

Along with Marx, Nietzsche, Dostoevsky, and Fedorov, Jacob Boehme was a major source of inspiration for Berdyaev. Early in life, through his elder brother, Berdyaev was introduced to occult literature and mystical thought. As he wrote in his autobiography, *Homo mysticus* prevailed in him over *Homo religiosus*. "I believe in the existence of a universal mystical experience and a universal spirituality which cannot be described in terms of confessional differences. . . . There is more depth and insight in the Gnostic and 'esoteric' type of mysticism than in that which has received the official sanction of the church and is not suspected of heterodoxy."[108] But as with drink, so with intellectual intoxicants, no matter how deeply he drank, of Kantism, Marxism, Nietzscheism, Tolstoyism, Fedorovism, occultism, Theosophy, or Anthroposophy, he "succeeded . . . in remaining sober among the intoxicated."[109]

Berdyaev faulted Florensky for being devoted to occultism, but to Bulgakov, Berdyaev's philosophy of creativity seemed "demonic, titanic, humanistic, and nearly akin to anti-Christ."[110] This criticism is similar to the criticisms of Fedorov's works, which had recently been published. Both Fedorov and Berdyaev were accused of usurping God's powers and assigning them to mankind, of interpreting "Thy kingdom come" not as a promise to be awaited but as something to be created. As Berdyaev insists: "It is imperative to bear in mind that human creativity is not a claim or a right on the part of man, but God's claim on and call to man. God awaits man's creative act, which is the response to the creative act of God. . . . Man awaits the birth of God in himself, and God awaits the birth of man in himself."[111]

Berdyaev's chief criticism of Fedorov is that the "common task" of resurrecting the dead seems directed more nearly to restoring the past than creating the future, recreating detail for detail exactly what was instead of creating a new humanity and a new world. He agrees with Fedorov that death can and must be overcome. "I am not prone to the fear of death, as, for instance, Tolstoy was, but I have felt intense pain at the thought of death and a burning desire to restore to life all who have died."[112] But "to restore to life" means for Berdyaev not necessarily a bodily resurrection but something more like a completion of an individual's potential spiritual personality. "Created beings do not create beings—these are created only by God. Personality is created in

God before all worlds. And every attempt on the part of created beings to create being leads only to the production of an automat, a dead mechanism. Such an attempt is always demonic—it is black magic."[113] Adam's Fall and the world of necessity have imprisoned and condemned to death the individual's spiritual personality. Creativity for Berdyaev means restoring vitality to the individual's spiritual personality.

> Freedom and creativity tell us that man is not only a natural but a su-pernatural being. And this means that man is not only a physical being and not only a psychic being, in the natural meaning of the word. Man is a free, supernatural spirit, a microcosm. . . . Freedom is the power to create out of nothing, the power of the spirit to create out of itself and not out of the world of nature. Freedom is one's positive expression and assertion is creativity. Free energy, i.e. creative energy, is substan-tially inherent in man. But man's substantiality is not a closed circle of energy within which everything is spiritually determined. In man's very substantiality there are bottomless well-springs. Creative energy is increasing energy, not energy which merely rearranges itself."[114]

Berdyaev admits that he sometimes seems to contradict himself. And indeed, we find him arguing in one place that everything existing must be elimi-nated and in another that wellsprings within the existing world can supply energy for the world's renewal. If we eliminate everything, do we eliminate the wellsprings? And if so, where does the renewal come from? In the course of his writings, the theme of self-renewal generally prevails over the earlier anarchis-tic calls for total elimination. And in his life, the idea that the true Russian spirit of Christian collectivism (*sobornost*) would renew itself from within the prison of Bolshevism led him to break decisively with former friends and asso-ciates in emigration who called for an armed invasion of the Soviet Union, believing that the Russian spirit could only be saved from outside.

Unlike Florensky, Berdyaev had no scientific or technical skills that could be put to temporary use in building the new Soviet society. Thanks to Lunach-arsky, the former aristocrat and later Bolshevik commissar; the science fiction writing revolutionary Bogdanov; and a few other high Bolshevik officials with roots in, and some slight lingering respect for, the values of the prerevo-lutionary high culture, Berdyaev and others were permitted to continue to speak and write freely for a few years. In his autobiography, Berdyaev even describes being called from his prison cell in the middle of the night to be interrogated by a Cheka official in a military uniform wearing a red star. He had fair hair, a thin, pointed beard and dull grey and somewhat melancholic eyes. His appearance and manner suggested good breeding and gentleness. He asked me to sit down and said: "My name is Dzerzhinsky." This, then, was the notorious head of the political police, believed to have much blood on his hands, at whose name all Russia trembled with horror.

Before Dzerzhinsky could begin the interrogation, Berdyaev took the initiative:

> I said to Dzerzhinsky: "Please bear in mind that my dignity as a thinker and writer demands that I should speak frankly and plainly." To this Dzerzhinsky replied: "That is what we expect of you." I then proceeded with my attack and spoke for more than half an hour, giving reasons for my religious, philosophical and moral opposition to communism, while stressing that I was not concerned with party politics. Dzerzhinsky listened very attentively, from time to time interposing a short remark.

After Berdyaev had finished his "attack," Dzerzhinsky asked several questions and offered a few comments, first about Berdyaev's views, then about other people. Berdyaev willingly elaborated on his views, but refused to inform on other people. At the end of the session, Dzerzhinsky said he was free to go but could not leave Moscow without permission, then turned to an associate and added: "It is late and there are plenty of bandits about; would it not be possible to take Mr. Berdyaev home by car?" No car was available, but a Red Guardsman did take "Mr."—not "Comrade"—Berdyaev and his luggage home on a motor bike.[115]

But his relative freedom did not last long. He had been in and out of prisons, both Tsarist and Soviet, many times, but because of his reputation and connections, he had never had to serve a complete sentence. In 1922, Berdyaev, Bulgakov, and some two hundred other intellectuals were judged incorrigible. A year earlier, Nikolai Gumilev, a major poet with prerevolutionary views and sentiments, but who had been trying to work within the new system, was executed on trumped-up charges of armed conspiracy—a fate that could easily have befallen Berdyaev and the others. Instead they were boarded onto one of three "philosophers' ships" and expelled from the Soviet Union for life.

For Berdyaev, life in emigration, first in Germany then in France, gave only the illusion of freedom. He had not wished to leave Russia but was not given a choice. In Germany, earlier exiles from Russia assumed that Berdyaev and the other new arrivals would turn out to be Soviet agents. And Berdyaev, who unlike most of his fellow émigrés believed that the wellsprings of Christian renewal still were to be found within rather than outside Communist Russia, encouraged Western recognition of the Soviet Union, met with Soviet officials whom he still regarded as fellow Russians even though they served in the "anti-Russian" government, and in so doing made fresh enemies at every turn. The experience of living through two revolutions, civil war, prison, expulsion, hostility in emigration, and the ultimate horrors of World War II seemed only to intensify the urgency of Berdyaev's call for rebellion, freedom, and creativity. Near the end of his life he wrote that, while his later books may have been more mature and nuanced in their formulations, the themes from *The Meaning of the Creative Act*, his first major book, remained at the core of his life's work and thought. He had never shared the sophiological outlook of Solovyov, Bulgakov, and Florensky, but he did have his own version of love as androgyny. He writes:

> But I have never indulged in what is known as the cult of eternal womanhood, so dear to many of my contemporaries in early twentieth-century Russia, when "fair ladies" in Dantesque or Goethean guise were so highly popular. I even suspected in myself positive dislike of "the feminine", although I was never indifferent to it. I felt particularly inclined towards medieval romanticism as expressed by the troubadours of Provence, who were the first to bear witness to the greatness and nobility of love-eros. But the introduction of eroticism into religion and into man's relation to God was quite foreign to me. Rather, I was attracted by Jacob Boehme's conception of the androgyn, who marks the ascendancy of integral human nature over sexual differentiation."[116]

For Berdyaev, sex, reproduction, and family life stand in the way of personal freedom and creativity.

> Sex pertains to the genus and love to the personality. . . . I could not help seeing in child-bearing something hostile to personality, something that is evidence of the dissolution of personality. The genus may evoke pity, but it cannot inspire love-eros. The latter is ultimately

incompatible with family life, which is of the genus. Love betokens a victory of personality over genus and sex, which are devoid of uniqueness and individuality. Love-eros must and does prevail over sex. When love is strong it has a depth which reaches out to infinity: sex, on the contrary, carries within itself the sting of finitude; it fails tragically to attain fullness, and is doomed to remain an isolated, separate sphere of fallen nature. It is this desperate character of sex which is in a measure responsible for the horror of atomization characteristic of modern man. But man must fight against the autonomy of sex.[117]

Part of this idea goes back through the late period Tolstoy of *The Kreutzer Sonata* to Fedorov, who believed that the sex drive represents a malignant natural force in need of human regulation. In the project of resurrection, there would be no sexual relations, no childbirth or need for reproduction. Contrary to Berdyaev, Fedorov understood the idea of love to represent an expression not of personality but of family feeling, relatedness, brotherhood, *rodstvo*. On a biographical level, Berdyaev's hostility to the idea of family and genus may be in part a rebellion against his own privileged background, an assertion of personal freedom from an upbringing which he considered to be based on social injustice. In a similar manner, Fedorov's idealization of family and *rod* may in part stem from his early sense of being excluded from full family membership. Where Fedorov's most intimate friendships were almost exclusively (Nekrasova being the exception) with males, Berdyaev tells us that he always felt closer to, and was better understood by, women. Despite a sometimes violent nervous tick that frightened new acquaintances, he was considered to be a handsome man, attractive to women, and as a young man, he tells us, and others agree, he was always in love. But his love affairs, and later his marriage, were all apparently what the Russians sometimes called "immaculate," "sinless"—we would probably say "platonic." Berdyaev, his wife Lydia, and in widowhood his wife's sister Eugenia, lived together as if three loving, but strong willed, independent siblings: arguing, joking, encouraging, and supporting one another through decades of change, hardship, and sometimes joy.

One of the problems Berdyaev raises in *The Meaning of the Creative Act* is how creativity relates to sanctity. He recalls that Pushkin, Russia's greatest creative genius, and Seraphim of Sarov, Russia's greatest saint, lived at the same time in the beginning of the nineteenth century, but essentially lived in different worlds, did not know each other, and never had contact of any kind.

Two equally noble majesties of holiness and of genius—they are incomparable, impossible of measurement by one standard—it is as though they belonged to two different sorts of beings. The Russian soul may be equally proud of Pushkin's genius and of the saintliness of Seraphim. And it would be equally impoverished if either Pushkin or St. Seraphim should be taken away from it. And here I pose the question: For the destiny of Russia, for the destiny of the world, for the purpose of God's providence, would it have been better if in the Russia of the early nineteenth century there had lived not the great St. Seraphim and the great genius Pushkin, but two Seraphims—two saints—St. Seraphim in the Tambov Government and St. Seraphim in Pskov?

Berdyaev notes that Pushkin's religious frailty, his worldliness, sinfulness, and imperfection are all part of his genial creativity, and that if he had been a saint he would never have written the works that so resonate in the soul of Russia and humanity. Strict churchly logic would argue that Pushkin's worldliness renders his creations worthless for redemption and for the world's salvation. And if personal purification is the only goal, as "in Yoga, in Christian asceticism, in Tolstoyism, in occultism," then that spiritual way must be hostile to Pushkinian creativity. But Berdyaev proposes a broader spiritual way. "In the creative ecstasy of the genius is there not perhaps another kind of sainthood before God, another type of religious action, equal in value to the canonical sainthood? I deeply believe that before God the genius of Pushkin, who in the eyes of men seemed to lose his own soul, is equal to the sainthood of Seraphim, who was busy saving his. The way of genius is another type of religious way, equal in value and equal in dignity with the way of the saint."[118]

Before Berdyaev, other Russian thinkers had wrestled with this problem. In the middle of the nineteenth century, Gogol, tormented that he could only entertain and not save the souls of his readers, had turned against his own genius, burning his manuscripts and renouncing all his published works. Dostoevsky agonized over the relationship between aesthetics and Christian morality, and could not be satisfied at having dramatized great tragic heroes and confrontations, but again and again, in Prince Myshkin, Alyosha Karamazov, and Father Zossima, attempted to create a literary icon of "the perfectly good, Christlike man." In his last public appearance, he was still trying to unite literature and faith by depicting Pushkin as Russia's iconic spiritual prophet. And Tolstoy, like Gogol, late in life turned against his own genius and attempted to transform himself from a great writer into a religious teacher.

All three of these literary geniuses at one time in their lives considered saintliness to be something higher than creative genius: creativity is not in itself a valid separate way, but must either give way to or somehow be fused with spirituality. Their view reflects the nineteenth-century Russian impulse to seek social or spiritual utility in art. Berdyaev's bold assertion that creativity and sanctity should be considered separate but equal religious ways reflects a Russian twentieth-century impulse: a Promethean, theurgic energy that characterized the early decades of the century. It is in this context that the scientific dimensions of Russian Cosmism can best be understood.

## 9

## *The Scientific Cosmists*

AS WE HAVE seen, the religious Cosmists did share a thematic thread that linked them to Fedorov and to each other. But when the term "Cosmist" is mentioned, Solovyov, Bulgakov, Florensky, and Berdyaev are not the first names that come to mind. The names that do immediately come to mind are the scientific thinkers, especially Tsiolkovsky, Vernadsky, Chizhevsky, and Kuprevich. In this chapter we shall consider what these specialists from various disciplines have in common with Fedorov and with each other, and how they differ.

### *Konstantin Edouardovich Tsiolkovsky (1857–1935)*

In the 1870s, while working in the library, Fedorov often went out of his way to serve a special group of ragged young scholars whom he liked to call his "stipendiates." One of these was Konstantin Tsiolkovsky, then a sixteen-year-old raw youth who had arrived in Moscow from a provincial village in 1873 with no money, no friends, and only a minimal education. Nearly deaf from a childhood bout with scarlet fever, solitary, a daydreamer, caring little about appearance or conventions, the teenager was already on his way to becoming the "Kaluga eccentric" (*kaluzhkii chudak*), that would eventually become his nickname. As he later described himself:

> I often became shy and behaved awkwardly among other children my age, and among people in general. My deafness, due to my scarlet fever, compelled me however to read and daydream endlessly. I felt isolated, even humiliated as an outcast from society. This caused me to withdraw deep within myself, to pursue great goals so as to deserve the approval and respect of others and not be despised by my peers.[1]

His mother died when he was a child; his father, a forest worker, was away from home much of the time, and the village school could do little for a deaf and extraordinarily gifted child. So he had come to Moscow to learn, and in Fedorov he found his ideal teacher. He later told an interviewer how they first became acquainted.

> It happened on one of my first visits. I dropped in and here's what I saw: a dozen or so people, mostly students, were crowding around the librarian. I was shy. I stood there waiting for the librarian to get free. I had time to look him over: a bald head, around it white curls sprinkled with gray, coal-black eyebrows and surprisingly young eyes. He looked about fifty, but he had youthful movements—quick and sharp.
>
> When the last student had left, the librarian noticed me and motioned for me to come to him. Apparently I looked nervous, because he smiled encouragingly. If you could only have seen his smile! It changed him and brightened him up at once. It was so affable and open, the way a father smiles at a son, or one brother at another. But this was the first time he had seen me. I was immediately filled with affection for him, and, having forgotten my earlier shyness, walked up to him. He cheerfully asked:
>
> "What do you want to read?"
>
> "Give me, if you can, *The History of the Peasant War*."
>
> "That book is forbidden."
>
> "Please speak a little louder—I don't hear well."
>
> "The book is for-bid-den!"
>
> The words sounded so harsh, as if to say: "See here now, with the kinds of readers we have—give out forbidden books indeed!" But his eyes were merry and smiling. Still, I hadn't been around people much and didn't know what to say. He went off somewhere, quickly returned, and handed me a book. I asked:
>
> "What's this?"
>
> "*The History of the Peasant War*."
>
> "But isn't this book forbidden?"
>
> "Take it!"[2]

Tsiolkovsky tells us that he was soon visiting Fedorov every day, and joined an "enchanted" group of young people, led by a certain "Volodya" (probably Vladimir Kozhevnikov), under Fedorov's spell. Each day, Fedorov brought the young scientist a fresh stack of books and often spent hours with him discussing his studies. And once, noticing that Tsiolkovsky's coat was too light for the cold weather, Fedorov said: "Let's go to the store and get you a new overcoat—I suddenly have some spare money." Tsiolkovsky tells us: "The library was my university." He adds: "Understanding my inclination toward mathematics, physics, and, in part, chemistry, he selected literature for me and directed my self-education. He taught me to use the catalogue, to draw up a conspectus, and to extract from books what was foremost and basic. It is no exaggeration to say that for me he took the place of university professors, with whom I had no association."[3]

Oddly enough, however, in the interview, Tsiolkovsky says that he and Fedorov never discussed the idea of space travel. Instead, he wrote:

> It seems to me that the first seeds of the idea were cast by the famous fantasy writer Jules Verne; he awakened my mind in this direction. Then the longings arose followed by mental activities, which of course would have led to nothing had they not encountered the aid of science. What is more, I have the feeling—probably erroneous—that the principal ideas and love for an eternal striving outwards to the sun, to a release from the chains of gravitation, were almost inborn in my case. At any rate, I have a perfect recollection that my favorite dream from the earliest years of childhood, even before books, was a nebulous consciousness of a medium without gravity, where motion in all directions would be perfectly free and where one would feel better than a bird in the air. Where these desires came from I cannot understand even to this day; there weren't any fairy tales of this nature, yet I dimly believed and felt and desired precisely this medium without the encumbrances of gravitation.[4]

But, according to Peterson, as early as 1864 Fedorov had incorporated the idea of space travel into his resurrection project. How strange, then, that between 1873 and 1876, two of the few people in Russia who were able to take the idea of space travel seriously met almost every day and discussed ideas of all kinds but supposedly did not once touch on the subject that set them apart from almost all their contemporaries. Yet when asked directly if they had discussed space travel, Tsiolkovsky answered:

> No. And I very much regret it. How could this have happened? At that time I had youthful dreams about exploring interplanetary space, and tormented myself looking for a path to the stars, but didn't meet even one like-minded person. In the person of Fedorov, fate had sent me a person who thought, as I did, that people would certainly master the

cosmos. But by an irony of that same fate, I absolutely didn't know about Fedorov's views. We had many discussions on various topics, but somehow we avoided space. Probably our difference in age accounted for this. He apparently found that conversations about space with me would have been premature.[5]

But the literary critic and memoirist Viktor Shklovsky, who apparently asked Tsiolkovsky the same question, has written just the opposite. Both in his memoirs *Once Upon a Time*, and in an article on cosmonautics for *Literaturnaia Gazeta*, Shklovsky tells us, in his characteristically aphoristic way, that it was Fedorov who first encouraged Tsiolkovsky to develop his serious interest in space travel.

> There once was a man named Fedorov, a philosopher, respected by Lev Tolstoy. He said that mankind would soon find the earth too crowded. And he said this in the last century. He's the one who was Tsiolkovsky's teacher.
>
> Tsiolkovsky was deaf. He was deaf and he was studying in school. He was sitting in the then Chertkov Library, over books of mathematics. The old man Fedorov walked up behind him and started speaking. The mathematician didn't turn around—he was deaf. Then Fedorov wrote on paper: "I'm going to do mathematics with you, and you'll help mankind build rockets so that we will finally be able to know more than the earth and so we can see our earth." People need a distant view, because only those people who are thinking about the future are real and present.[6]

But whether he did or did not discuss space travel with Fedorov, Tsiolkovsky returned to his village to prepare for the qualifying examination for science teachers while dreaming of interplanetary travel. He passed the exam in 1879 and began to teach in the town of Borovsk, where Fedorov had taught some twenty years before, in the Kaluga region, not far from where Tsiolkovsky had grown up. And in that year of his first teaching experience, he began to make notebook sketches for rocket boats, rocket wagons, and rocket-powered spaceships. Initially, inspired, as he said, by Fedorov's almost exact contemporary Jules Verne, he wrote narratives about traveling beyond earth by rocket ship, exploring and colonizing first the solar system and then the entire cosmos. But what distinguished Tsiolkovsky's imagination from that of any of his contemporaries is that after writing fantasy narratives and drawing rough pencil sketches, he developed the mathematical formulas that would make the realization of some of his fantasies possible. Over the years, while still teaching school and working after hours in a homemade attic laboratory, he built a series of large wooden model rockets, dirigibles, aerostats, wind tunnels, centrifuges, and primitive space vehicles, and wrote the papers that would eventually lay the foundation for the 1957 launching of Sputnik 1, the world's first artificial satellite. As a Soviet historian of science wrote:

> The works of Tsiolkovsky contain in embryo nearly all the scientific-technical attainments of the Soviet Union in the exploration of space. With amazing accuracy he determined the path, stage by stage, of the development of engineering facilities for the solution of this problem. It is quite natural therefore that with each new development in this field we recall Tsiolkovsky as the scientist who foresaw in one way or another the outcome of these events.[7]

And the American literary scholar and intellectual historian Michael Holquist concisely summarizes the international import of Tsiolkovsky's accomplishments:

> Tsiolkovsky was the first to do most of the things necessary to make, launch, and sustain life inside rockets as we now know them. The list of his original contributions is overwhelming: he developed aerodynamic test methods for rigid air frames; he solved the problem of rocket flight in a uniform field of gravitation; he calculated the amount of fuel needed to overcome the earth's gravitational pull; he invented gyroscopic stabilization of rocket ships in space; and he discovered a method for cooling the combustion chamber with ingredients of the fuel itself (a method still widely used in most jet engines).[8]

In his autobiography, Tsiolkovsky would complain, not entirely accurately, that his groundbreaking papers were largely ignored by the Tsarist scientific establishment, and that it was only in Soviet times that his work was recognized. His earliest papers were published in respectable journals as early as 1898, and as a result he was awarded a modest government stipend for research and experiments between 1899 and 1903. Indeed, many of his most important discoveries were made during Tsarist times, between 1890 and 1917, but it was only after the revolution that his work gained national, and later international, recognition. He complained in a diary that "if a more famous scientist in Imperial Russia, such as Dmitri Mendeleev, had published these ideas on rocketry, they might have been transferred abroad and translated into French or German much earlier."[9] It is probably true that his curriculum vitae—as a self-educated eccentric school teacher working with wooden models in a homemade laboratory in Kaluga—did not qualify him to rank among the leading scientists of Imperial Russia, but his great accomplishments from humble beginnings made him an ideal model of the new Soviet intellectual worker, a democratic rocket scientist, a genius emerged from the proletariat.

Through the 1920s and 1930s, the powerful Soviet propaganda machine turned the Kaluga eccentric, planning interplanetary expeditions while riding his bicycle along village dirt paths, into a national hero—so much so, in fact, that in post-Soviet times a moderate backlash has occurred, and a few critics have gone out of their way to try to prove him a mythologized mediocrity whose discoveries are overrated. Tsiolkovsky's reputation reached a peak on May Day 1935, when he was invited to address the nation by radio during the grand annual parade. Due to ill health, he could not attend the ceremony in person, but a speech he recorded in his Kaluga laboratory was broadcast over all nine Soviet time zones and from speakers atop the Lenin Mausoleum in Red Square, with Stalin leading the applause. But as biographer James T. Andrews has shown, the exploitation was mutual, and Tsiolkovsky played the Soviet system as skillfully as it played him.

> Even though the Bolsheviks and Stalin used Tsiolkovskii for their own propaganda, he was also an agent of his own destiny. Much like other scientists, he worked the system for his own benefit as a conscious actor constructing his own identity locally, nationally, and internationally. He also used the Soviet bureaucracy, popular publishers, and the Soviet press to popularize his ideas on space flight and rocketry. He therefore understood, as his own publicist, so to speak, how to manipulate a variety of venues to popularize his futuristic visions of human space travel.[10]

His great accomplishment as a scientist was not only to quantify the dream of space travel through mathematical equations but to actively promote and popularize the idea of flight beyond earth, to inspire an enthusiasm for rocket science among young people and even school children throughout the Soviet Union. He provided a kindly, grandfatherly, down-to-earth image for an otherwise daunting field of study.

He popularized space exploration primarily by publishing, in addition to his technical papers, a number of long and short science fiction pieces which, although not always impressive from a literary standpoint, drew many future Russian rocket scientists into the field. Generations of young readers were thrilled by the narratives of brave international teams of scientists—often a German, French, Chinese, and American scientist, led by a Russian—blasting off from earth to explore and colonize the cosmos. Among those young readers who grew up to be outstanding scientists were members of the team that launched Sputnik 1 in 1957, the cosmonaut and first man in space Yuri Gagarin, and the Cosmist heliobiologist Alexander Chizhevsky, whose ideas we shall discuss later in this study.

But it is not only rocket scientists who are interested in Tsiolkovsky. From early in his career until late in life, he speculated profusely about man's relationship to the cosmos. Some of these speculations found their way into his science fiction narratives, others were published in tiny editions as discursive pamphlets or tracts, but most remained unpublished during his lifetime, and have only begun to emerge since the collapse of the Soviet Union. As a result of these speculations, many of them Gnostic or theosophical in orientation, Tsiolkovsky has become something of a New Age cult figure in Russia, and his home and museum in Kaluga have become a destination for esoteric as well as scientific pilgrims.

One of his central ideas has to do with the presence of life and spirit in all matter. He writes: "I am not only a materialist but also a panpsychist, recognizing the sensitivity of the entire Universe. I consider this characteristic inseparable from matter. Everything is alive, but with the condition that we consider living only that which possesses a sufficiently strong sense of feeling. Since everything that is matter can, under favorable circumstances, convert to an organic state, then we can conditionally say that inorganic matter is in embryo (potentially) living . . ."[11]

An idea at the heart of most of his nontechnical writings is that of the "atom spirit" (*atom-dukh*) inherent in every particle of matter in the cosmos, recalling Fedorov's idea of all matter as the dust of ancestors. Tsiolkovsky's view of the cosmos is that it is teleological, rationally organized, and hierarchical—lower life forms, consisting mainly of matter in which spirit is dormant, evolve into higher ones, in which the spirit is awakened and more dominant, and eventually as we approach perfection we will outgrow our material envelopes and join the rays of cosmic energy that constitute something like the pleroma of the Gnostics. The dark side of Tsiolkovsky's ideal of self-perfecting humanity is that it requires the elimination, the "weeding out," of those of us who are in some way defective.[12] Unlike Fedorov, whose future resurrection society must include absolutely everyone, Tsiolkovsky's future perfect society is highly selective—losers of any kind will not make the cut. In articles titled "Grief and Genius" (*Gore i genii*) and "The Genius Among the People" (*Genii sredi liudei*), Tsiolkovsky offers his variation on Plato's idea of the philosopher-king, suggesting that scientific geniuses and inventors should occupy the key positions in future government, and that the many nations of the world should become a single cosmic political system governed by the most advanced and therefore most nearly perfect specimens of humanity.

Like Fedorov and many esoteric writers before him, Tsiolkovsky considered the macrocosm and microcosm to be structured upon the same organic principles, and the perfection of the inner man and the outer world to be mutually interdependent. All the planets in our solar system, and, indeed, all material bodies and gaseous clouds in the cosmos, contain life in one form or another and in one stage of development or another. Asteroids and moons, for example, may contain only the dormant seeds or embryonic forms of life, while other planets in or beyond our galaxy may be inhabited by life forms far more advanced than ours, life beyond the physical stage. Our earth, Tsiolkovsky proposed, could merely represent one of the more primitive, earlier steps in the self-perfecting development of life. We, however, are made of the same "atom spirits" as the "ethereal beings," existing beyond our dimensions of recognized reality, so eventually, led by geniuses, we may attain the stages of life traditionally ascribed to mahatmas, angels, demiurges, and other higher beings. Already, Tsiolkovsky believed, these higher beings are in communication with us, reading our thoughts and sending us messages through celestial symbols which most of us do not even perceive, much less understand. A genius is one who comprehends and channels these messages from higher beings into earthly projects, the poet who hears the muses, the inspired inventor who turns a dreamed universal symbol into a useful object.

Tsiolkovsky's version of metempsychosis proposes that our living atom spirit does not expire when our body dies but continues, perhaps after a dormant interval, in some other physical or nonphysical fresh being. "We always have lived and always will live, but each time in a new form, and, it goes without saying, with no memory of what came before."[13] He writes that when most people hear this idea, they are unhappy. They immediately wish their new life to be a continuation of the previous one, to live again, even if in some other realm or on some other plane, with the family and friends they previously knew. Tsiolkovsky uses the analogy of a happy dream, to which we wish after awakening to return and continue. But just as each new happy dream in a night can be different, without reference to the previous ones, so each fresh life of our atom spirit will begin as a clean slate. "In dying one says farewell forever to one's circumstances. After all, they are in the brain, but the brain is decomposing. New circumstances will arise when the atom spirit finds itself in another brain. That new brain will provide circumstances, but different ones, having no connection to the previous ones."[14]

The ends and beginnings of atoms, of individuals, and of civilizations mirror the larger, longer processes of cosmic ends and beginnings, the death and birth of planets, suns, and galaxies—while life itself, both macrocosmic and microcosmic, continues forever. In an article written near the end of his life, he summarizes his philosophy:

A. Integral life is distributed throughout the universe.

B. The most advanced development of life is not to be found on earth.

C. The mind and might of the leading planets are guiding the Universe into a state of perfection. To put it succinctly, integral life, with minor exceptions, is mature, and therefore powerful and beautiful.

D. This life for every being seems uninterrupted, since nonbeing is not experienced.

E. Throughout the cosmos extend social organizations governed by a "president" of varying merit. One is higher than another, and in this way there is no fixed limit to personal or individual development. If every mature member of the cosmos is lofty beyond our understanding, then isn't the "president" of the first, second, tenth, or hundredth rank also incomprehensible?

F. The endlessness of past time compels us to propose the existence of still additional series of independent worlds of a lower order separated by eternities. These worlds, as they become complex, have left as residue a part of their matter and a part of their animal life in a primitive state.

From this is apparent the endless complexity of the manifestations of the cosmos, which, of course, we are not able to grasp in full measure, since it is even higher than we can imagine. According to how much the mind expands, knowledge may increase and reveal to it a Universe that is greater and greater.[15]

Even to an admiring reader, Tsiolkovsky's grand vision of an ever perfecting cosmos may sound less inspiring today than it did when written, given that the process of perfecting would require not simply a Fedorovian elimination of a resurrected person's individual imperfections but the elimination of imperfect individuals themselves. Tsiolkovsky does not, of course, offer formulas or detailed plans for how those standing in the way of cosmic "cleansing" would be eliminated, but his leaving such details to future scientific geniuses may be less than universally reassuring.

Nevertheless, for his combination of esoteric imagination and hard science, and by virtue of his image as a largely unpretentious self-made genius, Tsiolkovsky has become a leading icon of Russian Cosmism. Since 1967, the Tsiolkovsky State Museum of the History of Cosmonautics in Kaluga has conducted ongoing research and sponsored frequent conferences and seminars exploring all sides of its namesake's work and influence. Yuri Gagarin himself laid the cornerstone for the museum. A typical conference with participants from Russia, Europe, Asia, Africa, and the Americas now hosts at least twelve sections, which focus on such topics as Tsiolkovsky's scientific legacy, the history of rocketry and astronautics, technical problems of rocketry and spacecraft, the mechanics of spaceflight, issues of space medicine and biology, aviation and aerostations, astronautics and philosophy, Tsiolkovsky's philosophy, Tsiolkovsky and scientific prognosis, Tsiolkovsky and issues of space vehicle production, Tsiolkovsky and issues of cosmonauts' professional activity, Tsiolkovsky and education, Tsiolkovsky and the economics of astronautics. The papers presented at these conferences and later archived online are usually illuminating and of high academic quality. Under the rubric of "Tsiolkovsky's philosophy," recent papers that have been particularly useful for the writing of this study include works on such topics as: "The Concept of Life in Tsiolkovsky's Metaphysics," "Gnostic Ideas in Tsiolkovsky," "The Idea of Social Structure in Solovyov and Tsiolkovsky," "Giordano Bruno and Tsiolkovsky," "Tsiolkovsky's Noospheric Hierarchy," "Tsiolkovsky's Philosophy and the Teachings of the Roerikhs," "Tsiolkovsky on the Coevolution of Microworlds and Megaworlds," and "The Problem of Tsiolkovsky's Concept of the Atom Spirit."[16]

Tsiolkovsky's Kaluga, then, has become a mecca for Cosmist research as well as for New Age pilgrimages. In most of the conferences, articles, and books that contribute to the thriving academic industry of Cosmist studies in Russia—whether in Moscow, St. Petersburg, Krasnoyarsk, or Kaluga—Tsiolkovsky and Fedorov are considered two of the three central figures. The third, to whose thought we shall now turn, is Vladimir Vernadsky.

# *Vladimir Ivanovich Vernadsky (1863–1945)*

Of the major Cosmists, Vladimir Vernadsky is the most thoroughly academic, in the best sense of that term. He inherited and passed on to the next generation his family's tradition of intellectual achievement. His father, Ivan, was an actively liberal professor of political economy and journal editor in Russia and the Ukraine, his son George a professor of history first in Russia, then in Czechoslovakia, and finally at Yale. Vladimir himself, while still a schoolboy, translated academic papers for his father's journal, and began to publish his own scholarly works during his first years of university study. Growing up in a highly educated, cultured family environment, he read Darwin in English at age seventeen, Humboldt in German the following year, lectured and published in French at the Sorbonne, and eventually could read at least fifteen languages, including ancient Greek, Latin, and the major modern Slavic, Romance, and Germanic languages. From his earliest school years, he led extracurricular discussion groups, read widely in history, philosophy, and world literature, and in the course of his long life founded and directed new scientific disciplines and institutions in Russia and the Ukraine, both in Tsarist and Soviet times.

Though still not a household name in the West, he is considered by learned Russians to rank with the very greatest figures in the history of Western science. The editors of the volume *Vernadskii: Pro et Contra* write: "As time passes, Vernadsky's contribution to world science should by rights take an equal place with the legacy of such giants of the natural sciences as Newton, Darwin, and Einstein."[17] Other twentieth-century Russian intellectuals have been equally laudatory. For example, in reply to a questionnaire for an academic science journal, the internationally honored literary critic and intellectual historian Dmitri Likhachev wrote: "V. I. Vernadsky, in my judgment, is the greatest scientist and thinker of the twentieth century, the pride of Russian science."[18]

Throughout his life and career, Vernadsky stood for intellectual freedom and integrity against all contrary pressures, whether from Tsarist or Soviet sources. He stood for continuity rather than breaks with tradition, and for the highest rather than broadest intellectual and cultural standards. An exemplary liberal, and for a while a prominent member of the Constitutional Democratic (Kadet) Party, he made no secret of his opposition to both Tsarist and Soviet repressive policies. Through the worst purges of the Stalinist era, he continued to write, both in private memoranda to Communist officials and in published scientific papers, criticisms not only of classical Marxist but also contemporary Soviet tendencies affecting the natural sciences. A moderate among radicals of every tendency, he was arrested briefly but spared the harshest punishments, and was allowed to continue his scientific research primarily because his work in many fields, including atomic energy, was valuable to economic and military development; his patriotism was unquestionable; and his consistent philosophical opposition to classic dialectical materialism could be dismissed by ideological watchdogs as eccentric, harmless, mystical eyewash from an earlier era. Officially ignored as a thinker but respected as an experimental scientist through the Soviet era, he has been venerated since the fall of the USSR both as a creative scientific genius and as a thinker who prominently lived an honorable life through difficult times. Boldness, creativity, profundity—and most of all, integrity—marked his entire career.

As a scientist he is chiefly noted for his concept of the surface of the earth as a biosphere evolving into a noosphere (from the Greek *nous*, "mind"), a sheath of life increasingly infused with and directed by the human mind. Vernadsky, of course, was not the first or only thinker to emphasize the human intellect's contribution to our planet's development. Even before Darwin in 1859, the Yale geologist James D. Dana, often cited by Vernadsky and later Cosmists, had developed the idea of "cephalization," the evolution of living matter in a single, headward direction. And another American geologist cited by Vernadsky, J. Le Conte, had written about the "psychozoic era." Closer to Vernadsky's time, the Russian A. P. Pavlov was writing about the "anthroposphere"; P. A. Florensky, as we have noted, advanced the concept of a "pneumatosphere"; and Vernadsky's pupil A. E. Fersman wrote of the emerging "technosphere." Even the terms "biosphere" and "noosphere" were not coined by Vernadsky: "biosphere" was used earlier by the Austrian geologist Eduard Seuss, and "noosphere" first appeared in publications by Vernadsky's French colleagues Teilhard de Chardin and Édouard Le Roy, who had probably developed their concepts while attending Vernadsky's Sorbonne lectures. But it was Vernadsky who presented the fullest elaboration of these concepts in a body of scientific and philosophical speculations that remain central to Russian Cosmist thought today.

As the historian of Russian science Kendall Bailes has noted,[19] so much of Vernadsky's thought has now been accepted as axiomatic in natural science that it is difficult to appreciate how fresh and bold his ideas seemed when initially published. He was one of the first scientists to emphasize that the exchange of matter leads to a basic unity of the planet, its human inhabitants, and the cosmos. He demonstrated the role of living matter—humans, animals, and plants—in the transfer of solar energy into mineral matter, showing that life not only evolves from hard mineral matter but in the process of disintegrating over eons contributes to the creation of new matter. Vernadsky believed (wrongly, according to most subsequent scientific opinion) that there has never been a time in the history of the universe when the earth has been devoid of life. What we term inert matter, he argued, actually contains within itself the makings of life, even if in almost negligible quantities. Vernadsky rejects any separation of matter from spirit, but defines all present life as "living matter," and holds that all presently nonliving matter shares with all life a fundamental unity that includes the potential to change from inert to living matter and from living matter back to inert, from being presently alive to being alive formerly and once more alive in the future—a twentieth-century scientific analog to Pythagorean metempsychosis.

Human beings, to Vernadsky, were "first and foremost inhabitants of the planet, one component in a cycle of physical and chemical interactions and transmutations, and as such they possessed an obligation to think and act for the good of the planet as well as for their own personal comfort and well being."[20] We are, in a very deep sense, related to all on our planet—to animals, vegetables, and minerals, as well as to other human beings, and as the rational component of the biosphere, we have a responsibility, literally, to all.

Vernadsky was not religious in any conventional sense, but he was a deeply spiritual thinker, well read in the literature of the world's religions, and in Eastern and Western philosophy. One of his closest lifelong friends was the noted Orientalist and specialist in Hindu thought and culture Sergei Oldenburg, with whom Vernadsky exchanged many long letters on fundamental questions of life and belief. Vernadsky recognized that a unified view of nature, the idea of the interconnectedness of all, has for millennia been at the heart of much religious and philosophical speculation, and so at the deepest level he found no conflict between scientific and spiritual views of the world. He noted that of all the world's religions he had studied, the one he felt closest to would be the ancient Greek hylozoistic pantheism of Thales, Anaximenes, and Heraclitus, which finds life to some degree present in all matter. Vernadsky looked at life and at humanity's role in life from the perspective of a geologist, taking the long view, seeing over eons of interchange and transformation "the migration of atoms and their particles within living matter and between living and inert matter."[21]

Living and writing through a period when science often had to conform to political ideology—the worst example being the Lysenko affair, in which politically correct, "anti-Fascist" research into seed grains led to disastrous harvests, many deaths, and the crippling of biological science for decades in the USSR—Vernadsky courageously spoke out for the independence of scientific investigation from all external political, religious, philosophical, and cultural constraints. For Vernadsky, of all intellectual activities in history, science alone could show definite, proven progress over time, and is humanity's one irrefutable, universal body of knowledge. While other disciplines moved this way or that, back and forth and sideways, cycling and recycling, only science demonstrably advanced. And only science could be understood and applied universally, beyond all differences in language, religion, politics, and culture. At the time Vernadsky was writing, overarching Marxist deterministic economic theory was supposed to be superior to all other intellectual disciplines—every idea and every human action was assumed to be economic and class-based at root. Vernadsky insisted on the superiority of scientific knowledge, arrived at by empirical scientific methods. Free science, more than any other intellectual activity, could bring genuine benefit to human beings. As inhabitants first and foremost of the cosmos and the planet, human beings owe allegiance to the biosphere more than to any nation, ethnic entity, economic class, or system.

And writing further against the grain of his times, Vernadsky insisted that outstanding individual minds contributed more of value to all humanity than any mass movements. Vernadsky drew upon, and cited in his works, advances contributed by individual scientists from many countries, including works by Germans when at that very moment Russia was at war with Germany. Though basically apolitical and internationalist in outlook, he was more drawn to socialist than to capitalist values, and as conditions grew more severe, he made a conscious decision to stay in Russia rather than emigrate with his son and family, who went first to Czechoslovakia then to America. He saw himself as a patriotic Russian, loyal more to his people's cultural traditions than to the present government, and at the same time, as a scientist working within a universal tradition that had begun thousands of years before and would continue thousands of years after him, one person, who happened to be Russian, contributing to the worldwide, even cosmic evolution of knowledge.

For Vernadsky the biosphere represents the planet's sheath of "living matter," and the noosphere represents the biosphere's emerging sheath of "thinking matter." Scientific knowledge is "noospheric matter," and is emerging as a force that over time will have as much influence on the planet as life did with the emergence of the biosphere. In Vernadsky, all the natural sciences—physics, chemistry, biology, geology—are interconnected and interrelated, and all are evolving together, hence the new compound terms such as "biogeochemistry" for the fields of research that Vernadsky founded. Unlike Fedorov and some of the other Cosmist thinkers, Vernadsky did not consider the development of the noosphere to be a task that humanity could choose or fail to choose to undertake, but rather that the noosphere proceeds from the biosphere as a natural cosmic evolutionary process, an inevitable development in which human reason gradually expands, fully obedient to, rather than in opposition to, the laws of nature.

In Vernadsky's thought, life, along with matter and energy, is an eternal constant in the cosmos. Through many transformations and exchanges of form, life has always been and will always be. Among the new concepts and terms that Vernadsky introduced to science are the "ubiquity of life," the "pressure of life," the "thickening of life," and the "speed of life." Present in thin or thick, fast or slowly interchanging concentrations throughout the cosmos, living matter exerts a pressure on inert matter at the atomic and subatomic level, particles are exchanged, thin concentrations of living matter—so thin in inert matter as to be almost nonexistent—thicken under the pressure from exchanges with living matter, the speed of exchange increases, and in this way life as we know it emerges from matter that appears—but never entirely is—lifeless.

As a scientific description of a cosmic unity that some religions and philosophies also posit, and which Alexander Chizhevsky would develop further, Vernadsky writes that the biosphere develops on earth not only from planetary sources but from solar and other cosmic forces beyond earth:

> Cosmic forces outside in large measure shape the face of the earth, and as a result, the biosphere differs hypothetically from the other parts of the planet. . . . We can gain insight into the biosphere only by considering the obvious bond that unites it to the entire cosmic mechanisms. . . . The biosphere may be regarded as a region of transformers that convert cosmic radiation into active energy in electrical, chemical, mechanical, thermal, and other forms. Radiations from all stars enter the biosphere, but we catch and perceive only an insignificant part of the total: this comes almost exclusively from the sun.[22]

Biogenic migrations from beyond earth contribute to the formation of earth's atmosphere and play "an integral role in the formation of the mineral deposits in the earth's crust."[23] Vernadsky, concurring with a strong tradition of

Russian thought, holds that man is not, as he sometimes wrongly believes, a free and independent creature, separate from and above the kingdom of nature:

> In the intensity, complexity, and depth of modern life, man forgets in a practical sense that he himself and all humanity, from which he may not be separated, is inescapably linked with the biosphere. . . . In reality no one living organism finds itself in a free circumstance on Earth. All these organisms are constantly and inextricably linked—first of all in their food and breathing—with the material-energy environment around them. Outside of it they cannot exist under natural conditions.[24]

For Vernadsky, science proves the organic, cosmic wholeness that mystical poets and spiritual thinkers have traditionally intuited.

Vernadsky foresaw the positive and negative potential in the development of atomic power. In an essay, "A Few Words about the Noosphere," written in 1944, in time of war near the end of his life, Vernadsky recognizes that with the splitting of the atom a decisive moment would arrive both in the course of the war and in the course of human history. "In the geological history of the biosphere, a great future lies open to mankind, if he will accept it and will not use his reasoning powers and his labor for self-destruction."[25]

During and just after World War I, Vernadsky had considered the Bolshevik Revolution, with its glorification of the uneducated masses and denigration of the cultivated individual, an unnatural phenomenon. Now, at the height of World War II, he considers the racist ideology of German National Socialism to be equally unnatural and antiscientific.

> A geological evolutionary process is responsible for the biological unity and equality of all peoples—Homo sapiens and his geological ancestors Sinanthropus and others, whose descendants of the white, red, yellow, and black races—in whatever variations among them all— have developed ceaselessly in innumerable generations. Such is the law of nature. All races mix among themselves and produce fruitful progeny. In historical confrontations, for example in war of such scale as the present one, in the last analysis the victor will be the one who follows this law. One cannot act with impunity against the principle of the unity of all peoples, as one cannot act against a law of nature.[26]

And just as World War I brought both a violent end to the old social order and inevitable change to the biosphere, this war will coincide with a new, inevitable era for Earth—the emergence of the noosphere, which, despite all peril associated with the war, Vernadsky views with a degree of optimism.

> The noosphere is a new geological phenomenon on our planet. In it for the first time mankind becomes a major geological force. Mankind can and must transform his habitat by his labor and thought, transform it radically in comparison to its previous state. Before mankind wider and wider creative possibilities are opening. And perhaps my grand-child's generation will glimpse their flourishing. . . . The noosphere is the latest of many stages of biological evolution in geological history— the stage of our days. The course of this process is only beginning to become clear to us from the study of the geological past in certain of its aspects.[27]

It is sometimes pointed out that Vernadsky's concept of the noosphere is in some ways similar to the Theosophical and Anthroposophical idea of *akasha*, the Sanskrit term for "aether," a fifth element beyond fire, air, earth, and water, a nonmaterial realm in which all human thoughts and memories are recorded, constantly updated, and preserved. In theosophical literature, advanced adepts may read the akashic record clairvoyantly, or during the out-of-body experience of astral travel. Noted clairvoyants who have reported for the rest of us their readings from the akashic record include the British theosophist Charles W. Leadbeater; the founder of Anthroposophy, Rudolf Steiner; and the American seer Edgar Cayce. A major difference between the two ideas is that *akasha* is assumed to have existed from time immemorial, whereas we are just now in the process of creating the noosphere.

Vernadsky recounts that two billion years ago, plants containing calcium emerged from the world of minerals, and then five hundred million years ago animals with calcium skeletons began to emerge. This development of calcium within living matter was, Vernadsky believes, one of the major stages in the geological history of the biosphere. Although the dates he assigns to some events might now be questioned, Vernadsky argues that the appearance of green forests seventy to one hundred and ten million years ago was another major stage in evolution, analogous to today's emergence of the noosphere. In these forests, human beings appeared fifteen to twenty million years ago. Now, as a new geological stage is appearing, just in the most perilous of times, what is "important for us is the fact that the ideals of our democracy move in unison with the elemental geological process, with the laws of nature, with responsibility for the noosphere. . . . Therefore it is possible to view our future confidently. It is in our hands. We will not let it fall."[28] Though certainly not a political activist, Vernadsky did believe that moderately socialistic democratic ideas were, like scientific knowledge, part of noospheric content and would guide humanity and the biosphere in gradual but inevitable evolution in accordance with the laws of nature.

Like Fedorov, Vernadsky was convinced that one of the steps in man's eventual evolution would take him through an autotrophic stage. The depletion of resources in the biosphere will not permit humanity to continue to live as it now lives, and at some point in the future, humanity will have to change itself radically or perish in a much degraded biosphere. The solution is through a science much advanced over today's, involving the ability to alter the physical and chemical makeup of the human constitution so that humans can be transformed from heterotrophic to autotrophic beings, subsisting, as some plants and bacteria now do, on air and sunlight instead of on other living matter.

> As soon as it can be discovered, the direct synthesis of food, without the intermediary of organic substances, will in a radical manner alter the future of mankind. . . . Discoveries of this synthetic process are awaited, and great consequences for life will not be slow in coming. . . . It is now difficult, perhaps even impossible, for us to imagine the geological consequences of this event; but it is evident that this will be a crowning achievement of paleontological evolution, and will not be an act of free human will but a manifestation of a natural process. Human reason by this means would not only accomplish a new great social achievement but would introduce into the mechanism of the biosphere a great new geological phenomenon. . . . In the last analysis, the future of mankind will always in large measure be created by mankind himself. The creation of a new, autotrophic existence will give him the possibility so far lacking to fulfill his age-old spiritual yearnings; it will in reality open before him the path to a better life.[29]

Honored in his own day as a brilliant experimental scientist, Vernadsky has in recent years, with the publication of many manuscripts kept in the drawer during Soviet times, gained iconic status as a scientific thinker, a pioneer environmentalist, and a model of integrity, dignity, and rectitude consistently exhibited in a time and place where such qualities in prominent individuals were in short supply. He is a figure revered in Cosmist studies in Russia today, and one hopes he might eventually be equally honored elsewhere.

# *Alexander Leonidovich Chizhevsky (1897–1964)*

Like many of the other Russian Cosmists, Alexander Chizhevsky[30] began life as a child prodigy, sickly but extraordinarily bright, talented, and sensitive, privately educated at his family's country estate. Both as a child and as an adult, he was noted not only for his many-sided interests and talents, but also for an exceptional sensitivity to the physical, social, and spiritual environment—he was said to have a heightened ability to anticipate changes in the weather, unseen vibrations, fluctuations in the natural and social atmosphere. In his autobiography, he speaks of a constant lifelong sensation of fever, a burning, as if of an inner sun, which he directed outward in a never-ending passion to learn and absorb all. His life's work, perhaps not accidentally, would be the study of solar and other cosmic influences on human behavior.

Alexander's father, Leonid Chizhevsky, was a well-educated military officer from an old aristocratic family. His mother died young, but the aunt and grandmother who took over his upbringing encouraged his precocity in music, poetry, and painting, activities which he continued through life. Alexander's father, very devoted to his young wife, did not remarry after her death but dedicated all his energies outside military matters to his only son's education, providing him from a very early age with his own miniature laboratory for experiments in physics and chemistry. Every year until he was ten, the family took young Alexander abroad, to the milder climates of France and Italy, where his health improved, he learned new languages, and he gained a broader, sunnier perspective on life. Later, with friends, he undertook archeological investigations in Greece and Egypt, and for some years studied painting at the academy in Paris under an instructor said to be a follower of Edgar Degas. In World War I, he served with his father's regiment in Galicia, was awarded a George Cross for bravery, and after a serious wound accepted a discharge to resume his studies.

Surprisingly, perhaps, for a future (though unsuccessful) Nobel nominee in chemistry, Chizhevsky's first academic degree was in the humanities; his master's thesis was titled "Eighteenth-Century Russian Lyric Poetry"; and his first teaching position was on the faculty of the history and philology department at Moscow University. But while teaching subjects in the humanities, he also audited courses on statistics at the business school and on chemistry, physics, biology, and astronomy in the department of natural sciences. He would eventually publish a collection of poems praised by literary contemporaries, and would produce hundreds of accomplished impressionist oil paintings, watercolors, and pastels, but the works that would earn him an international reputation, like

Florensky, as another " Da Vinci of the twentieth century," were his discoveries in aeroionization, heliobiology, and hemodynamics.

His discoveries in aeroionization, which led to effective air-purification devices, such as the so-called Chizhevsky Chandelier, and in hemodynamics, which shed new light on the cycling of blood through living bodies, some first published in French, others in Russian, fell within the limits of acceptable Soviet science and earned Chizhevsky high national and international honors. But his other important work, in heliobiology, demonstrating the effects of solar pulsations on human life, aroused great controversy and provoked accusations of mysticism, occultism, and general irrationality. Eventually, during the Stalinist terror, these accusations led to his arrest as an "Enemy Under the Mask of a Scientist," resulting in sixteen years in prison camps and exile, from 1942 until his rehabilitation in 1958. During imprisonment, despite special punishment for refusing to wear a large prison number on his back and for objecting to being addressed in the familiar second person singular, he still painted, wrote poetry, and, with whatever means he could find, continued to conduct scientific research. At one point, realizing that they had an internationally famous biologist in their hands, prison authorities dragged Chizhevsky barely alive from a punishment cell to see if he could help stop a cholera epidemic that was sweeping the camp—which, with bleaching powder and other crude remedies at hand, he managed to do. As a reward, he was allowed to set up a minimal laboratory in the prison clinic, in which, using only a borrowed microscope and glass capillaries, he conducted groundbreaking investigations into the movement of blood that would later, after his rehabilitation, win public accolades from the president of the Academy of Sciences of the USSR.

He first outlined his thoughts about the influence of solar and other cosmic forces upon human behavior and history in his 1918 doctoral dissertation, "Analysis of Periodicity in the Worldwide Process," which was published a few years later as "Physical Factors of the Historical Process."[31] Here, as throughout his scientific publications, Chizhevsky writes as a confirmed determinist. He finds that all human psychical activity—indeed, all that we think of as the sphere of intellect, culture, and history—consists, essentially of physico-chemical neurological interactions, and lies in the domain of ordinary natural phenomena. Further, as natural phenomena, all intellectual and social activities are affected by interactions with their natural surroundings, including powerful geophysical and cosmic forces. As human beings, with only five senses and other limitations, even when aided by mechanical devices, we are aware of only a very small fraction of the innumerable rays, waves, particles, forces, and bundles of energy that constantly bombard our planet and us, forces from both within our solar system and beyond not only our solar system but even our galaxy. According to Chizhevsky, these waves and particles of energy come at us in regular, measurable patterns of periodicity, in cycles and rhythms of which we may not be conscious, but which lend order, rhythm, and cycles of periodicity to our lives. In an image that Chizhevsky likes to repeat, our blood flows with the "veins of the cosmos," and our heart beats with "the pulse of the cosmos." The extent to which Chizhevsky discovered cosmic influences on human events understandably struck the ideological watchdogs for Soviet science as blatant heresy. The proposition that it was not only great Comrades Lenin and Stalin, the working classes, and historical necessity but also sunspots and invisible cosmic rays that brought on the Great October Revolution makes it a wonder that Chizhevsky remained free until 1942.

It is no accident that in his almost mystical—if deterministic—sense of a living cosmos, Chizhevsky sounds more than a bit like Tsiolkovsky. For just as in the 1870s Fedorov served as mentor to the sixteen-year-old Tsiolkovsky, so in 1914 Tsiolkovsky began to serve as mentor to the seventeen-year-old Chizhevsky. In 1913 Chizhevsky's father was assigned to head an artillery regiment in Kaluga, where young Alexander, continuing to experiment in his miniature laboratory, soon made the acquaintance of his fellow town genius, the Kaluga eccentric. In a memoir written near the end of his life, Chizhevsky reminisced:

> In my heart, Konstantin Edouardovich occupies a special place: we spent a great deal of time together. I remember his enormous erudition in the most diverse fields of science and his exceptional breadth as a human being; he often expressed thoughts absolutely out of the ordinary and unexpected, about the cosmos, about the future of mankind, thoughts about which you couldn't read or hear anywhere else.... Yes, and association with him brought radical changes to my understanding of the world. With the aid of specific examples he led me to think about the need for great changes in mathematics and physics, so vital for scientific work in the natural sciences.... Good advice from Konstantin Edouardovich was of great use to me at that time.[32]

Early commentators on Chizhevsky's thought tended to view him primarily as a disciple and younger colleague of Tsiolkovsky. But while they share many assumptions and conclusions, they also display significant differences.

Tsiolkovsky provided needed public support from a well-established figure for an early, heavily criticized publication by Chizhevsky, and in return Chizhevsky, after establishing an international reputation of his own, contributed a preface to one of Tsiolkovsky's major books on rocketry. But Chizhevsky had little to contribute to Tsiolkovsky's emphasis on how we can affect the cosmos, and neither Tsiolkovsky nor any of the other Cosmists shared Chizhevsky's emphasis on how the cosmos affects us. In contrast to all the other Cosmists, who highlight the active role human beings take in universal processes, including human evolution, Chizhevsky explores humanity's passive role as a receiver of cosmic influences and as a subject of cosmic laws of nature.

In general, Chizhevsky's work can be seen as an attempt to discover and define a single governing principle for the entire cosmos, an early twentieth-century Russian equivalent to Ken Wilbur's "Theory of Everything" or Stephen Hawking's "M Theory."[33] For Chizhevsky, the principle behind everything, including human culture and history, is electronicity, the power of electrons to attract, combine, and form larger units of matter and energy. Gravity, magnetism, space-time, and matter-energy are all, fundamentally, electronic phenomena. The sun's influence on the biosphere, including on human behavior, is a matter of the transfer of electrons. In the twentieth century, Chizhevsky argues, physics, chemistry, and astronomy have begun to coalesce into a single "science of matter," and the social sciences and the humanities have begun coalescing into a different "science of human culture." Chizhevsky believes that the great scientific task for him and others now is to unite the "science of matter" and the "science of human culture" into a single science of everything, the examination and quantification of the one principle that governs all living and nonliving phenomena in the cosmos. The discovery that patterns of solar activity—sun storms, sunspots, etc.—coincide with patterns of mass human behavior—wars, revolutions, epidemics, etc.—represents, for Chizhevsky, a large first step toward uniting the two separate great branches of knowledge.

Chizhevsky also believed that the study of cosmic energy patterns could have useful, predictive value. Knowing that a period of mass human excitability is approaching might allow wise leaders to direct that excitability into productive rather than destructive channels, into grand constructive projects and mass movements for the benefit of humanity—modern equivalents to pyramid building—instead of riots and wars. His studies in aeroionization led directly to purer air in factories and poultry barns, resulting in more productive workers, whether clothed or feathered. He hoped that someday applications from his work in heliobiology would prove equally useful to Soviet society and humanity in general.

A convenient summary of his basic idea accompanied his 1922 work "Physical Factors of the Historical Process." He tells us that since 1915 he has engaged in research "to investigate whether or not there existed a correlation between the more important phenomena of nature and events in the social-historical life of mankind." In "Physical Factors" he presents his findings on the connection between sunspot activity and both human mass behavior and the "universal historical process." The "facts" he presents here are, he says, "based upon statistics gathered by me while submitting to a minute scrutiny the history of all the peoples and states known to science, beginning with the V century B.C. and ending with the present day."

A problem that immediately comes to mind is how anyone can direct "minute scrutiny" toward "all the peoples and states known to science" from ancient times to the present. In the first place, science still knows almost nothing except the names of most peoples and states of remote eras, and even what is assumed to be known can change from generation to generation. Earlier science, for example, portrayed the Mayans as wise, happy, nonviolent, agrarian predecessors of the bloodthirsty Aztecs—until later scientists discovered all the horrible evidence of Mayan atrocities. And how do we scrutinize the Toltecs and Zapotecs? Or the many important peoples and states described by Herodotus—the Sarmatians, Massagetae, Alans, Medes, and the like—who today knows any more about them than the colorful but questionable information provided by a writer known as both "the father of history" and "the father of lies?" Or the many biblical kingdoms, like the Amalekites, Jebusites, Moabites, Edomites, Ammonites, and their successors—all we know is their names and that they were enemies of ancient Israel. And in the case of more recent peoples and states, about which information is plentiful, the more minute the scrutiny, the messier the picture gets, and the more difficult an event or movement becomes to classify and quantify. For example, would the French Revolution be classified a peak of mass liberation or, as Fedorov argued, a trough of irresponsibility? Nuanced historiography can deal with such questions, but can graphs and charts?

Chizhevsky writes: "As soon as the sun-spot activity approaches its maximum, the number of important mass historical events, taken as a whole, increases, approaching its maximum during the sun-spot maximum and decreasing to its minimum during the epochs of the sun-spot minimum." Again, this presents some difficulties, especially in deciding what constitutes a "mass historical event" in ancient times. Would the Peloponnesian War qualify as a mass event, or was it a local skirmish largely ignored in China, Ethiopia, Peru, and everywhere else outside the Aegean basin? Are "mass historical events" confined to those peoples fortunate enough to have lived in a time and place of good chroniclers, decipherable languages, and durable surfaces to write on? In ancient Africa, who knows what unrecorded "mass historical events" may have occurred from time to time? And in well-recorded modern times, if during a given year of maximum or minimum sunspot activity, peace and plenty prevail here while violent uprisings are taking place there, which one do we put on the chart?

Chizhevsky continues: "In each century the rise of the synchronic universal military and political activity on the whole of the Earth's territory is observed exactly 9 times. This circumstance enables us to reckon that a cycle of universal human activity embraces 11 years (in the arithmetical mean)." Again we have the same questions: what counts and what does not count as "universal military and political activity"? What about wars, violent uprisings, and vicious suppressions of political activity in times and places where such things go unrecorded? In earlier centuries, if only four or five such rises in excitability have made it into the literary records, what events do we add to get to nine? And more recently, how do we interpret our data if more than nine surges of political and military activity are recorded in one century, especially if surges nine, ten, and eleven seem almost equally powerful? And what do we say when some of the most important surges occur in years with minimal solar activity? And what if we know the century, or perhaps even the decade in which something important happened, but not the exact year? We know, for example, that the Great Mogul movement into India occurred over the course of the sixteenth century, but even if we say it began under Babur between 1519 and 1530, how can we determine whether the "maximum excitability" for this movement did or did not occur during the solar eruption of 1528?

Chizhevsky divides each eleven-year cycle occurring nine times each century into four parts or periods: (1) minimum of excitability, 3 years; (2) growth of excitability, 2 years; (3) maximum of excitability, 3 years; (4) decline of excitability, 3 years. He finds from statistical analysis that the number of historical events in the mean in each cycle falls into a pattern, at least for the five hundred years from the fifteenth through the twentieth centuries—for this point, he does not pretend to have sufficient data for earlier centuries. In period 1 (minimum), 5 percent of the century's important historical events; period 2 (growth), 20 percent; 3 (maximum), 60 percent; 4 (decline), 15 percent. From all his data, he derives what he calls a law of the historical process: "The course of the universal historical process is composed of an uninterrupted row of cycles, occupying a period equaling in the arithmetical mean 11 years and synchronizing in the degree of its military-political activity with the sun-spot activity." And he attributes certain "historo-psychological peculiarities" to each cycle. In the middle points of each cycle, provided economic, political, or military conditions are ripe, the "mass activity of humanity all over the surface of the earth" reaches maximum tension, manifesting itself in "psychomotric pandemics: revolutions, insurrections, expeditions, migrations, etc., creating new formations in the existence of separate states and new historical epochs in the life of humanity." In these middle periods, majorities tend to exert power.

At the extreme ends of every cycle, "the tension of the all-human military-political activity falls to the minimum, ceding the way to creative activity and is accompanied by a general decrease of military or political enthusiasm, by peace and peaceful creative work in the sphere of state organizations, international relations, science and art, with a pronounced tendency towards absolutism in the governing powers and a disintegration of the masses."

Thus, in Chizhevsky's theory, it is during periods of maximum solar activity every century that new political and religious doctrines appear; heresies, religious riots, and pilgrimages spread; great social, military, religious leaders, and reformists arise; corporations, associations, unions, leagues, sects, and powerful companies form; and, frequently enough to be included, pathological epidemics and natural disasters coincide with maximum solar activity. Chizhevsky, if not all who encounter his theory, can confidently conclude: "Thus the existence of a dependence between the sun-spot activity and the behavior of humanity should be considered established."

He calls the new science "historiometry," and supports his narrative with a number of charts and graphs, all now available on the internet,[34] in which the peaks and valleys of solar and human activity turn out to be almost too nearly identical. The problem, as suggested above, lies in what data Chizhevsky selects for his definition of "universal human military-political activity." As a general theory, it does seem plausible that cosmic forces of which we are only partly aware influence both individual and mass activities in ways we do not yet understand. For thousands of years, many human traditions, with the exception of our relatively recent rationalist tradition, have accepted such influences as self-evident. For me, the problem with "historiometry" lies more in the details than in the general thrust, more in the effort to offer quantitative proof instead of a nuanced narrative. The data that Chizhevsky would need for a convincing proof of his argument does not and will not ever exist. Who can now say exactly when the Mongol expansions under Genghis Khan—a mass political-military movement if there ever was one—displayed their peak of excitability? How universal is the "universal process"? The moving spotlight of history is too narrow in scope to illuminate all the dark places and times when important activities may have occurred, and too dim to adequately illuminate even those times and places it hovers over.

If we look at our own recent past and recall events with which we may be most familiar, we can see that Chizhevsky's theory scores some hits on periods of maximum solar activity, but is less impressive on the minimums. Solar cycle 20, in NASA's table of cycles from 1755 to the present, for example, began in 1964, reached its maximum in 1968, and ended in 1976.[35] This period very conveniently coincides with the crescendo and diminuendo of the nearly worldwide mass activism that we think of as "the sixties." The early buildup, with new hair, new clothing, new music, and peaceful civil rights marches, culminating in a peak of "excitability" in 1967–1969 with the "summer of love," the Six Day War, the Biafran War, the Chinese Cultural Revolution, the Prague Spring and the invasion that crushed it, the Tet Offensive, violent youth protests in Paris and Chicago, the assassinations of Robert F. Kennedy and Martin Luther King, the Manson murders, the moon landing, and so many other important events that the year 1968 (extended a bit on each side) has been labeled "the year that changed everything."[36]

Other cycles, such as solar cycle 23, beginning in 1996, ending in 2008, and reaching its maximum in 2000, offer the theory mixed success. Although on July 14, 2000, a powerful solar flare caused a major geomagnetic storm nicknamed "the Bastille Day event," the year 2000 was relatively calm, and did not experience any of the doomsday events predicted for the coming of the new millennium. The major event that occurred within the three-year middle period of maximum excitability was, of course, the terrorist attack of September 11, 2001. This, however, was more a trigger for subsequent mass political-military activity than an instance of mass action itself.

Cycle 24, which started in 2008 and is peaking in 2011, has already, in the so-called Arab Spring, displayed obvious examples of the "psychomotoric pandemics" that Chizhevsky finds characteristic of the middles of cycles. If it continues as it has started, the cycle of historic eruptions now peaking in 2011 could match the one that peaked in 1968.

In examples such as cycle 20 and cycle 24, when parallels between solar and human activity are found to occur, it would seem that Chizhevsky's theory may have something to it. But too many great events occur without sunspot activity, and too many periods of maximum sunspot activity are not accompanied by major historical events to make the theory much more than interesting, imaginative speculation. Much more work would need to be done to make Chizhevsky's detailed theory more credible than those derived from close readings of the Book of Revelation, the predictions of Nostradamus, or forecasts from the Mayan Codex.

During his career, Chizhevsky was at times accused of trying to take human knowledge back to a prescientific state, for attempting to replace chemistry with alchemy, astronomy with astrology. Chizhevsky strongly denied these allegations, but added that he did respect and did wish to restore to modern science not the actual practices of alchemy and astrology but the intuition underlying those prescientific efforts, that in some very profound and mysterious but eventually definable way we and all matter in the cosmos are one, and that through exchanges of energies and matter, via particles and rays, transformations between elements, cosmic and ours, can result. And he was always careful to point out that he was not arguing that solar eruptions cause wars and revolutions, or that periods of solar calm cause peace and goodwill on earth, but that solar and cosmic energies do contribute to and perhaps even trigger events that other factors have been leading toward. He certainly did not solve all the problems he posed, and "historiometry" has not become a mainstream science, but Chizhevsky paid with sixteen years of his life in prison for his efforts to establish a direction and an agenda that at least a few scientists in Russia, in research and conferences in Kaluga, if not elsewhere, have, with amendments and cautions, begun to follow.[37]

## *Vasily Feofilovich Kuprevich (1897–1969)*

The future great botanist, naturalist, and proponent of unlimited longevity Vasily Kuprevich[38] was born in Klenniki, a village in the Smilavichy region of what is now Belarus. In order to support his four children, Vasily's father, Feofil, moved the family to the eastern Belarus town of Orsha, where he took a position as forester on the estate of a certain Count Lubinsky. There, in the forests and fields of the estate, young Vasily developed his lifelong love of nature, surprising grownups with his ability to remember the names and healing properties of so many of the plants in the vicinity. He began his education at the local *zemstvo* school for peasant and working class children, at age sixteen went to Petersburg for naval cadet school, then underwent two years of officer training, after which he served in the Baltic on the destroyer "Samson" until he was wounded and demobilized in 1918.

Kuprevich served as a village schoolteacher for some years, studied science on his own, and began to publish papers based on his independent research. In 1931 he graduated from the People's Institute for Advanced Training in Moscow, an institution specifically set up to encourage and develop talent from the working classes, and in 1934 he took a position at the Byelorussian Academy of Sciences Institute for the Biological Sciences. In 1938 he became head of one of the laboratories of the Academy of Sciences Botanical Institute in Leningrad, and from 1949 to 1952 served as director of the institute itself. In 1952 he returned to Byelorussia to serve as president of the Byelorussian Academy of Sciences, a position he occupied until his death in 1969.

As a gifted and not terribly controversial botanist, he made important contributions to the understanding of processes of photosynthesis. He proved the possibility of heterotrophic nutrition of higher plants under natural conditions, and demonstrated the possibility of using the activity of certain enzymes as an indicator of biological activity in soil. He produced definitive taxonomic studies of fungi and catalogues of mushrooms, and investigated the healing properties of plants. Later in his career, he turned to the more controversial study of aging in plants, animals, and humans, and essentially introduced the science of gerontology to the USSR. For his scientific accomplishments in established fields, he won drawers full of awards and medals, and today laboratories, institutes, and streets bear his name throughout Belarus. As a Cosmist thinker, he has become best known since the end of the USSR for his pioneering contributions to the field of scientific immortalism, for his Fedorovian contention that death is not necessary, and that someday relatively soon, perhaps within the twenty-first century, science will discover the means to prolong life indefinitely.

Kuprevich updates Fedorov to hold that death is not permanently inherent in nature, but is a temporary adaptation to facilitate the process of evolution—old forms of life must die so that new forms may arise. But with the development of the noosphere, humanity has evolved to the point that death is no longer needed for future evolution—human reason, not biological necessity, will shape the future of humanity. The great obstacle to overcoming death is not physical but intellectual and emotional—we now simply assume that the elimination of death is one of those things that cannot be done. But, Kuprevich reminds us, major scientific and technological advances have previously nearly always belonged to the category "cannot be done." Like Fedorov before him, Kuprevich contends that the first step to indefinite longevity must be a change in attitude and orientation, that scientists and other leading intellectuals must rediscover a truth long contained in myth, legend, and popular religion, that people can live a very long time, that even Methuselah's nine hundred years need not be an ultimate limit.

Death is against human nature. People embodied the dream of eternal
life in myths about the immortal gods. Probably man intuitively understood that ages of ongoing evolution would be wasted if one could live
only 50–70 years. The church promised man immortality up there, in
heaven. Then philosophers convinced him that to live means to be dying
all the time, and the dream of a very long life—that's metaphysics![39]

Kuprevich's investigations into the process of aging in plants proved to his
satisfaction that in nature there is no permanently fixed human lifespan, no
prohibition against extreme longevity, no reason why we cannot live as long
as the universe itself. As Kuprevich puts it: "Having invented death, nature
should also show us how to combat it."[40]

A basic mechanism in life, Kuprevich submits, is the ability of an organism
to repair and renew itself. In humans, this ability continues through much of
life in some parts of the body (e.g., fingernails, skin, liver), but not for the body
as a whole. The task for science is to discover why this happens and how the
process of self-renewal can be universalized and extended indefinitely.
"Organisms lost the ability to renew 'worn out' cells not because in their nature
they are unable to reproduce without limit. This ability was simply lost as a
result of natural selection, and the life of a hypothetically immortal individual
then shortened a span whose length was no longer of use to the species."[41]

In his researches, Kuprevich found fossils of poplar trees from the Creta-
ceous period that were practically indistinguishable from those of the present
day, meaning that for over seventy to eighty million years, from generation to
generation, an individual poplar had passed on traces of its ancestors. Kuprevich notes that there are also individual specimens of certain woody plants that
have reached an age of ten to twelve thousand years.

> We are talking about a span of life over the course of which mountains
> have collapsed, rivers have changed course or disappeared, civilizations
> have risen and fallen, the climate of large regions has changed more
> than once, and the configuration of continents has changed. Mean-
> while, a thing, an individual, has continued to live, spreading around
> its offspring, increasing its own mass. . . . There is nothing in the world
> of material structure that can compare in hardiness and durability with
> a protoplast, the bearer of life.[42]

In the animal kingdom, the span of life has evolved to its present length
simply to accommodate the individual's need to reproduce itself and to

nurture offspring to the point where they can survive on their own. Once the time required for the continuation of the genetic line has been reached, the individual begins its sudden or gradual decline toward death. As humans, we inherited from our ancestral primates a lifespan that meets biological requirements—but we differ from the rest of nature by being more than biological creatures. Like Fedorov, Kuprevich believes that our intellectual, emotional, and social evolution marks us for a special purpose in the cosmos, and that through our noospheric endeavors we may free ourselves from our inherited biological limitations. Kuprevich says that he does not necessarily give credence to legends of ancient, even prehistoric animals still alive today in various lakes (and lochs) around the world, but he finds nothing in nature that would absolutely preclude the survival into our time of an animal from a previous geological age.[43] Kuprevich does not endorse the existence of Nessies, Yetis, or other cryptozoological phenomena, but neither does he reject them out of hand. Here, like other Cosmists, he urges readers to keep an open mind and accept that some truth may yet be found in disciplines and investigations thoroughly rejected by mainstream science.

Kuprevich suggests that the campaign against death cannot simply be waged by medical science—which might postpone an individual's death for a few years or even decades—but should be waged through genetics, by isolating and eliminating the genes that mark us for aging and death. He suggests that in our search for the "elixir of immortality" we should look not just to myth and legend but to nature itself. One leading theory of aging holds that decline and death result from some genetic defect that leads to a failure in the cells' process of self-renewal. But, Kuprevich tells us, geneticists have found that in certain cases a father and a mother with genetic defects produce an embryo without those defects, showing that nature through its processes of reproduction is sometimes able to eliminate a defective genetic element. "It is possible that similar paths can be found to eliminate the defects that occur in the elements of cells in the process of self-renewal." The task for future gerontology is to discover what aging—human old age—actually is. "If it is a disease, then it can be cured. If it is programmed in a gene, then the program needs to be changed."[44]

A major problem, Kuprevich emphasizes, is in the way biology is taught and conducted today. He reminds us, and particularly his Soviet readers, that Marx left us a great principle: question everything. In the realm of science, it is from time to time essential to question absolutely everything—particularly everything that is universally considered to be natural and obvious. If we accepted what seemed most natural, obvious, and evident to all eyes, we would still believe that the sun goes around the earth every day. He suggests that the same is now true of the "natural and obvious fact" that we may live, on average, approximately seventy years, and then we must die.

Like most other Cosmists before him, Kuprevich was accused during his lifetime of abandoning genuine science for pseudoscience—in his case, attempting to revive the medieval alchemical search for some "fountain of youth" or "elixir of life." But like Vernadsky, Tsiolkovsky, and Chizhevsky before him, Kuprevich refused to allow his scientific researches to be limited to directions his predecessors and contemporaries had already established as safe to follow. As one of the best models for scientific Cosmism, he let imagination and intuition prompt—but not misdirect—his empirical investigations.

Today in Russia, Krupevich's works are most frequently cited by scientists working in the immortalist branch of Cosmism. In communication with Western researchers in transhumanism and cryonics, the Russian immortalists define their field as

> a philosophical tendency which includes within itself: (1) through natural science the investigation of the possibility of the radical extension of human life until the attainment of physical immortality; (2) a search for optimal socioeconomic models for the organization of a society consisting of immortal individuals; (3) a worldview for people who want to be physically immortal, and who believe that it is achievable by scientific means and that immortality is a boon to mankind.[45]

The immortalist movement today attempts to offer a deliberate synthesis of biological and sociological research. In previous times, evolution was viewed primarily as a biological phenomenon, dominated by the "striving" for survival by means of reproduction, and the preconscious psyche primarily served the aims of reproduction. With the emergence of the noosphere, immortalists contend, other factors begin to dominate, paving the way for *Homo immortalis*: "Evolution of the psyche led to the emergence of consciousness, which allows the psyche to model itself, allows it to become conscious of itself, so that in addition to the purposes of reproduction there arises an awareness of the existence of the self-worth of the individual consciousness and its carrier, and as a consequence—a striving for immortality."[46]

For the immortalists the best use of the mind is in the imagining of ideal, immortal worlds, and the best society is that which tries to embody those ideal, immortal worlds. Freedom, for the immortalists, includes freedom from time, attaining a state in which time no longer dictates our actions—practical immortality.

With these and other ideas, today's Russian scientific immortalists and other Cosmists extend concepts from Fedorov, Tsiolkovsky, Vernadsky, Chizhevsky, and especially Krupevich to address twenty-first-century scientific concerns. As we shall see in the next chapter, Cosmist ideas have also had a significant impact on certain general facets of Russian cultural life.

# *10*

# *Promethean Theurgy*

RUSSIAN COSMISM CONTRIBUTED to and benefited from a general ethos prevalent in the first decades of the twentieth century, which George L. Kline has termed "Promethean theurgy."[1] The ideas, that philosophy should be a form of action, not simply reflection, from Marx, and from Nietzsche, that with the death of God, humanity must create its own destiny, lent philosophical underpinnings to wave after wave of fresh creative energy in all the Russian arts, sciences, and social and political culture. Since leading intellectual historians and others have explored this topic in considerable depth and detail,[2] the purpose of this chapter will be merely to sketch in review some of the major themes, each interwoven with all the others, that characterize both the general Promethean theurgical ethos and the Cosmist tendency in Russian thought.

## *Life Creation*

As Ezra Pound famously observed, artists are "the antennae of the race." In Russia, the Symbolist poets and artists were among the first to record the shift in attitude toward nature and life from one of observation, interpretation, and depiction to one of active, Promethean creation. The poet Vyacheslav Ivanov (1866–1949), a leading theorist of the movement, stated: "Symbolism never was and never wanted to be merely art. . . . Art is not the creation of images [or icons] but the creation of life."[3] Art must go beyond its traditional task of representation, and must discover, and even create, new lives and new realities. The émigré poet Vladislav Khodasevich further noted:

> Symbolism did not want to be merely an artistic school, a literary movement. It continually strove to become a life-creating method, and in this was its most profound, perhaps unembodiable truth. Its entire history was in essence spent in yearning after that truth. It was a series of attempts, at times truly heroic, to find a fusion of life and art, as it were, the philosopher's stone of art.[4]

*Zhiznetvorchestvo*, the Russian term for "life creation," attempted a new answer to the eternal Russian "accursed" question of the relationship between art and life—framed earlier, in the radical 1860s, as a matter of which was more important, Shakespeare or boots. To the earlier generation of radicals, the correct answer was clearly boots, but through *zhiznetvorchestvo* the Symbolists hoped to establish that art and life were not opposed, but, when properly understood, became one.

But what did the Symbolists actually understand by "creating life"? As rhetoric it sounded grand, ambitious, elevating the artistic process to a godlike act. But in practice, *zhiznetvorchestvo* sometimes meant little more than projecting an aesthetic (or in some instances simply arty) persona and trying to live up to the role. For the enthusiastic young Symbolists of the early years of the century, the perfect example of *zhiznetvorchestvo* was the symbolically ideal—but in daily life unhappy—marriage of Aleksandr Blok and Liubov Mendeleeva. Blok not only was considered Russia's greatest poet since Pushkin but also looked like a divine Russian Apollo who spoke and recited in profound oracular tones. Mendeleeva, whose first name meant "love," was not only the daughter of the best known Russian scientist of the early century but was also pretty enough to pass for a living embodiment of *Prekrasnaia Dama*, the "Beautiful Lady" of Blok's then-best-known cycle of poems. Their marriage was not simply to be a joining of two attractive young mortals but a union of Art and Science, Poetry and Love, the Dark Handsome Knight and the Beautiful Lady, the Divine Male Apollonian Spirit and the Eternal Feminine Russian Sophia, the creation of a magnificent whole new life beyond the quotidian tedium embodied in the Russian word *byt*, "humdrum daily existence." A complicating factor was that Blok's close friend and fellow poet Andrei Biely, no doubt "altruistically" attempting to lend triangular stability to the marriage, inserted himself into the relationship, severely testing Oscar Wilde's dictum that in marriage three is company and two is none. Unfortunately, the ideal couple turned trio proved to be "human, all too human," and as a consequence "soon, too soon" split.

As Irina Paperno observes, such episodes as the Blok-Mendeleeva-Biely relationship "were self-conscious in a way suggesting deliberate aesthetic organization of behavior. In semiotic terms, the artist's life was treated as a text, constructed and 'read' by a method similar to that used in art."[5] Not surprisingly, treating life semiotically, as a text, was not a satisfactory solution to everyday domestic problems for Blok, Mendeleeva, Biely, or for another notorious *zhiznetvorchestvo* triangle involving the poets Valery Briusov, Nina Petrovskaia, and, again, as familiar third party, Andrei Biely. To cite once more Khodasevich, one of whose special talents was to pour cold water on Silver Age enthusiasms:

> They attempted to transform art into real life and real life into art. The events of life were never experienced as merely and solely life's events; instead, because of the lack of clarity and the instability of the boundary lines that outlined reality for these people, the events of life immediately became a part of the internal world, a piece of creation. Conversely, something written by any member of the circle became real, an event of life for all. In this manner, both life and literature were created, as it were, by joint, sometimes hostile, but still united, forces of all who found themselves in this extraordinary life, in this "symbolist dimension." This was, it seems, a true instance of collective creation.

And a bit later Khodasevich adds: "The history of the Symbolists turned into a history of ruined lives."[6]

## Cultural Immortalism

Immortalism, a search for some form of eternal life not merely in an azure afterworld but here on the dark, moist Russian earth, emerged as another major theme in the general Promethean ethos. As mentioned earlier, in his "Reminiscences of Blok," Andrei Biely noted that the generation of poets who emerged in the early years of the twentieth century in Russia viewed as one of their chief tasks "the problem of combining Vladimir Solovyov and Fedorov with the philosophy of Russian social thought (with Lavov and with Herzen)."[7] For Biely, this meant the fusing of resurrection with reform, the sacred task with social-democratic process. As Irene Masing-Delic has demonstrated in her study of the salvation myth in Russian literature, *Abolishing Death*, the initially poetic theme of immortalism, inspired in large part by the writings of Fedorov and Solovyov, spread beyond literature, metamorphosing with many twists and turns into strange new forms of thought and action well into the Soviet period. From Blok's poem "The Twelve," in which a dozen marauding armed revolutionaries turn out to be led by Jesus Christ, bearing the Red banner, impervious to bullets, through Mayakovsky's versified drumbeats on the theme of a deathless Soviet future, through the preservation of Lenin's body and the slogan "Lenin Lived, Lenin Lives, Lenin Will Live," on through Stalin's grandiose reconstruction schemes in which the apparent loss of so many lives was made acceptable by the assurance that Soviet science would someday resurrect the victims, immortalism stretches even into the 1960s children's song so popular among American students of the Russian language perhaps not only because of its uplifting sentiments but also because it was so extremely easy to remember: *Pust' vsegda budet solntse,* "May there always be sunshine, may there always be blue skies, may there always be Mama, may there always be me!"

During this period, revolutionary immortality, to be achieved by future human labor and science, was judged to be superior to the traditional, unverifiable "myth" of religious immortality that could be "known" only by faith. Revolutionary immortality meant that individuals would die, but The People for whom the individual died would live on forever, and through inevitable progress in science and labor, The People of the future would eventually restore life to the sacrificed individuals—Fedorov's idea, stripped of its religious and monarchical dimensions. If Christ was the firstborn of the mythical resurrection, Lenin, waiting in his glass coffin, would be the first resurrected by science. In a seminal essay on Soviet immortalism, Peter Wiles cites one after another high Soviet official, such as Leonid Krasin, who publicly endorsed the idea of scientific immortalism. He also describes various scientific attempts to extend the human life span, including one Dr. Voronov's practice of grafting tissue from ape testicles onto humans in hopes of extending not only life but virility as well, a treatment undergone by (among other international celebrities) the aging W. B. Yeats. Another example of immortalism noted by Wiles is the practice on the part of perfectly atheistic Soviet citizens of toasting their dead comrades as if they were still present, in the manner of the old Slavic Radunitsa festival, in which the dead ancestors were supposed to reappear for the feast celebrated in their memory.[8] Soviet immortalism exhibits, then, a longstanding Russian fascination, perhaps even obsession, with the idea that we should not—must not—die. This idea is at the heart of Fedorov's philosophy and continues through the Promethean theurgy of the early Soviet period, extending even into the twenty-first century, making immortalism one of the most productive branches of today's Cosmist research.

## God Building

In spiritual culture, the prerevoltionary movement of antimaterialist "god seekers" (*bogoiskateli*), who gathered around the writer Dmitri Merezhkovsky and his wife, the poet Zinaida Gippius, led to and was eventually superseded by the "god builders" (*bogostroiteli*), a group of Marxist intellectuals and future

Soviet officials, including Alexander Bogdanov, Anatoly Lunacharsky, Leonid Krasin, and Maxim Gorky, who recognized and attempted to redirect the religious character and spiritual energy of the Russian Revolution. During the early decades of the twentieth century, leading intellectuals in every field were trying to apply the idea of creating a "New Adam" for a "New Eden" to every possible situation and context. Thinkers from many ideological orientations were discovering new dimensions of reality—in non-Euclidean mathematics, subatomic physics, depth psychology, structural linguistics, non-European anthropology, Ouspenskian metaphysics—and proposing new plans for reestablishing paradise, whether here on earth or on other eventually reachable "*planity*" somewhere in the physical universe. The Wagnerian impulse to unite all the arts into a single great pageant found early twentieth-century Russian expression in the 1916 production of "Victory Over the Sun," a much derided but recently revived Futurist-Suprematist-Cosmist opera for which the Futurist poet Aleksei Kruchonykh contributed the libretto, Mikhail Matyushin composed the music, Kasimir Malevich designed the sets, and Velimir Khlebnikov composed the *zaumnyi* ("beyond rational") prologue. Another attempt at universal synthesis and control over nature was Scriabin's unfinished *Mysterium*, to be set in the Himalayas and to unite smell and touch with music—no audience, all participants—in a seven-day performance leading to a cosmic crescendo, signaling the end of the present human race and the beginning of a next, Blavatskian, higher race of superhumans. Music thus synthesizes all the arts and becomes a catalyst for evolution.

Not only on stage but throughout the new Soviet Union, nature was to be tamed and trained to serve humanity. A radical, and notorious, example was Belomorkanal, Stalin's 1931–1933 White Sea Canal project, in which some 100,000 political and other prisoners were forced to dig a 140-mile canal using no modern machinery and under extremely severe conditions and, in the process, "reforge" themselves, metamorphosing, by means of this new social alchemy, from "enemies of the people" into solid, productive Soviet citizens. Between eight and nine thousand died while "reforging," and many more were injured or weakened, never to regain their health. A delegation of 120 leading Soviet literary figures, including Gorky, Viktor Shklovsky, Boris Pilnyak, Alexei Tolstoy, and Mikhail Zoshchenko, were treated to a Potemkin tour of the project, and praised it as a model for radically transforming both environmental and human nature. As Irene Masing-Delic observes, the literary elite found that "the *Belomor* laborers, it could be argued, far from being penalized, were actually being immortalized."[9]

One source for the generally atheistic god-building tendency was the traditional importance assigned to incarnation and deification in Russian Orthodox doctrine. God became man so that man could become God. In an essay on Solovyov, Richard Gustafson explains that in the incarnation, as Solovyov understands it, "all nature is drawn and strives toward man, while the whole history of humankind is directed toward the Godman." And further: "Deification does not mean union with the Absolute or the attainment of absolute perfection, but the acquisition of immortality, bliss, and a super-human fullness and intensity of life often coupled with a transformation of the natural cosmos itself."[10] The god builders, while themselves no longer Orthodox believers, emerged from a profoundly Orthodox culture in which they all at one time had been immersed. In god building as it developed in Soviet times, in which all traditional notions of God are considered outdated, the incarnation is a relic, no longer a necessary condition for the deification of man: the Promethean man-god updates and displaces Solovyov's godman.

## *Reaiming the Arrows of Eros*

Another aspect of Prometheanism, again traced in part back to Fedorov and Solovyov, was the effort to redirect erotic energy, including the surprisingly common practice among intellectuals of attempting to overcome nature in themselves by practicing "chaste" (celibate) marriage.[11] We have already mentioned this practice in reference to Berdyaev, but Blok and Mendeleeva, and Biely and his first wife Asya Turgeneva were also said to have enjoyed this kind of relationship. But the married couple most openly celibate were Merezhkovsky and Gippius, who lived together as Platonic soul mates for more than fifty years, apparently never spending a day apart or a conjugal night together. Both considered themselves complete, androgynous persons in an immortal harmonious relationship beyond any duty of or need for procreation. In her diary, Gippius recorded that on the evening after their wedding, for which they had worn simple gray street clothes, they quietly read, had dinner, and then departed peacefully into their separate bedrooms. For years after their wedding, Gippius continued to wear her hair in a single braid, traditionally the symbol of virginity. Another who chose celibacy in marriage was Alexander K. Gorsky, a devoted follower of Fedorov who, writing under various pseudonyms, applied Fedorovian ideas to intellectual tendencies of the 1920s and 1930s. We shall discuss his ideas in more detail later, but for now may note only that he vigorously applied Fedorov's idea of regulation of nature to Freud's concept of eros, and believed that in the New Eden, the New

Adam and New Eve would get it right this time, eschewing the apple, opting for obedience over self-will, sublimation over procreation.

As Olga Matich observes, the practice of married celibacy was just one of several tendencies in the Promethean attempt to restructure nature by experimenting with alternatives to traditional procreative love and marriage. "The ultimate goal of the men and women at the turn of the century was a total transformation of life resulting in earthly immortality.... Love played a seminal role in these utopian projects. For Solov'ev love was even more powerful than art in that it had real-life potential to bring about the actual end of history and transform material reality." Following Solovyov, Fedorov, and Chernyshevsky's ideal couple in his didactic novel *What Is to Be Done*, the new men and women of the period "were driven by the eschatological impulse toward rebirth or resurrection, not procreation. Premised on the continuous cycle of birth and death, procreation was rejected; hence the common preoccupation with abstinence in the here and now and with conquering death by a higher form of love that rechanneled erotic energy away from the biological drive to reproduce." In their search for something higher, the Symbolists offered a variety of erotic practices as alternatives to the traditional family. Among them were "Platonic love for a soul twin, Dionysian eros, new versions of the romantic triangle, homoerotic love, narcissism, and romantic love for an unattainable object. These models were frequently intertwined, reflecting the eclectic, syncretic spirit of the time."[12]

Vyacheslav Ivanov, a leading spirit in the Symbolist movement, seems to have been a figure around whom these models and others intertwined, exhibiting a sometimes Platonic, sometimes frenzied Dionysian relationship with his wife, Lydia Zinovieva-Annibal; sacred incest with Lydia's daughter, Vera; combined sensualist voyeurism and narcissism with the young poet Sergei Gorodetsky; and homosexual relations with younger Symbolists such as Mikhail Kuzmin. For his part, in his novel *Wings*, Kuzmin projected a shining new world of free eroticism for bold fellow Argonauts:

We are Hellenes, lovers of the beautiful, the bacchants of the coming day. Like the visions of Tannhauser in Venus' Grotto, like the inspired revelations of Klinger and Thoma, somewhere lies our ancient kingdom, full of sunlight and freedom, of beautiful and courageous people, and thither we sail, my Argonauts, over many a sea, through mist and darkness. And in things yet unheard we shall descry ancient roots, in glittering visions yet unseen we shall know our own dear land![13]

Alternatives to traditional marriage and family life easily carried over from the Symbolists to early Soviet intellectuals: Lenin and Nadezhda Krupskaia were married but for most of their life together probably not physically intimate; Gorky and Maria Andreeva, on the other hand, who caused a great scandal by traveling together to America, were assumed to be intimate but were not married. Through the late 1920s, traditional attitudes toward love and family were considered to be—at least among many leading intellectuals—holdovers from a dying bourgeois world. Androgyny was often upheld as an ideal solution to the complex problem of sexual oppression, in which bourgeois society forced men into the unwanted role of oppressor and women into the inescapable role of the oppressed. Alexandra Kollontai, among others, proposed free love as the relationship appropriate to the new socialist people in the new socialist society. Children should be raised by the collective rather than by the biological family, and nostalgia for traditional family behavior and values should be discarded as degrading to both men and women. A look at the biographies of major early Soviet figures finds hardly any in what might be regarded as a traditional marital relationship. Even Lenin and Krupskaia, who stayed together for life, temporarily made room in their relationship for at least one of Lenin's infatuations, the vivacious French revolutionary Inessa Armand.

With a tradition of rulers as notorious for unapologetic promiscuity as Ivan the Terrible, Peter the Great, and Catherine the Great, puritanism has not been the powerful recurrent force in Russian culture that it has perhaps been in Britain and North America. In the turbulent early years of Soviet power, a rare individual like Feliks Dzerzhinsky, the first head of the Soviet secret police, may have served as a model for extreme personal asceticism in a position of leadership. But many others who led the struggle against remnants of prerevolutionary bourgeois morality were probably more like Gleb Boky, the head of the OGPU (predecessor of the KGB) cryptology section, who regularly and quite openly invited his fellow high officials and their assistants, male and female, to recreational outings for "children of the sun"—nude bathing parties that ended as wild drunken orgies.[14] If in the history of Russia, scandalous sexual behavior has ever toppled any powerful figure, the event does not come readily to mind. Flexibility and a tolerant shrug greet practices in Russia that might inspire headlines, resignations, lawsuits, or even criminal charges elsewhere. The varieties of erotic experience prevalent during the period of Promethean theurgy may have seemed more experimental to outsiders than to the Russians.

## *Technological Utopianism*

Another strand of Promethean theurgy worth mentioning in connection with Cosmism is its technological utopianism, for which the artistic "antennae" were not the Symbolists but the post-Symbolist and anti-Symbolist poets: Acmeists (Gumilev, Akhmatova, Mandelstam), Futurists (Mayakovsky, Khlebnikov), Imaginists (Esenin), and Biocosmists (Ogienko, a.k.a. "Svyatogor"). Neither the seer, with his head in the clouds, nor the peasant, with his eyes on the ground, but the urban proletarian worker, master of nature by means of machines and tools, was to be the post-Symbolist New Man. Acmeist poets, who grew out of Symbolist reading and discussion circles in Vyacheslav Ivanov's Petersburg "tower," now organized themselves into what they called a craftsman's "guild" and later a worker's "shop" (*tsek*). For the rising generation, scientific and technical education was to replace bourgeois humanistic studies. Even formerly humanistic disciplines, such as aesthetics and literary criticism, became, through the emergence of Formalism, technological in orientation, emphasizing the artist's tools, devices, and techniques, rather than the broad themes, continuities with the past, and relevance to life and society emphasized by previous generations of critics. Futurists in all the arts—especially the new arts of photography and cinema—took as their subjects cities, architecture, machines, and people at work, man over nature, rather than man as part of, or subject to, nature.

A major example of the technological utopian tendency was Alexander Bogdanov, a prerevolutionary rival outmaneuvered by Lenin in the struggle for control of the Bolshevik party, and later along with Gorky and Lunacharsky a leader in the god-building movement mentioned in the previous section. In addition to his sociopolitical activity, Bogdanov was a physician, an experimental scientist, a seminal opposition thinker, and a science fiction writer. *Red Star*, his 1908 novel about a Russian scientist-philosopher–social activist who travels to Mars in the company of a Martian disguised as an Earthling, presents the Red Planet as site of an ideal society, harmonious, communist, and sexually egalitarian, which the Russian hopes to import for the benefit of Earth. On Mars, the Russian discovers that the Martian guide he thought was male turns out to be female, and the complicated love story that follows is interspersed with descriptions of the social and technological wonders of Mars, as well as intrigues, including mortal combat against a brilliant but heartless villain intent on colonizing Earth. Though primarily of historical interest now, *Red Star* in its own time was considered an important literary work, and Bogdanov followed its success with a shorter work,

"Engineer Menni," a 1913 prequel describing how communism was established on Mars. Bogdanov continued his theme in "A Martian Stranded on Earth," a poem that appeared to be an introduction to a sequel to *Red Star*.

As a scientist, Bogdanov experimented with blood transfusions as a means of rejuvenation, and found that he indeed looked and felt much younger as a result of the transfusions he had performed on himself. But like his fictitious predecessor from half a century before, Turgenev's Bazarov, who contended in *Fathers and Sons* that nature was not a temple but a laboratory, Bogdanov died as a result of his own medical experiment, probably from injecting himself with blood of an incompatible type.

Bogdanov's major philosophical work was *Tektology*, a three-volume collection of essays that defined a new comprehensive science, a way of organizing knowledge now regarded as a precursor of systems analysis and cybernetics. Nature, in Bogdanov's view, is essentially an organization of complexes of phenomena, and the human task is to be master of that organization. *Ovladenie* ("mastery," "control") is the key concept throughout Bogdanov's thought. In Bernice Rosenthal's concise summary,

> Bogdanov tried to create a monistic metascience of nature and society that would unite "the most disparate phenomena" in the organic and inorganic worlds—a planned global organization of things, people, and ideas in one well-structured system. . . . Bogdanov wanted to replace chaos with cosmos, to bring order and harmony into a strife-torn world. On one level, Tektology was an attempt to realize Marx's concept of a single science of man. On another level, it was a technological version of the symbolist project of "life-creation."[15]

The emphasis on technology as a means to achieve an ideal society echoes Fedorov's "Common Task," but largely ignores Fedorov's insistence that religious and spiritual development must accompany technological advance. Without significant spiritual development, Fedorov feared, technological progress alone could only lead to a mechanical hell. Another difference is that even though Bogdanov sends his character to Mars, all his concerns remain focused on Earth. Bogdanov's interest is in earthly society, not the total cosmos of which our planet is a part. Despite futuristic intentions, Bogdanov's universe is not Copernican but Ptolemaic. Like Bogdanov, Fedorov and the scientific Cosmists Vernadsky, Tsiolkovsky, and Chizhevsky all viewed science as vital to our survival, but unlike Bogdanov they project our survival as inhabitants and even potential masters of more of the universe than one small planet.

## Occultism

*Civilization cannot evolve further until "the occult" is taken for granted on the same level as atomic energy.*
—COLIN WILSON, *The Occult: A History*

The last tendency we shall mention here in connection with the Promethean ethos of the first decades of the twentieth century is occultism, which was seamlessly interwoven with all the tendencies previously discussed: life creation, immortalism, god building, redirected eroticism, and technological utopianism. As Maria Carlson has written about Silver Age Russia:

> Occultism, in a bewildering variety of forms, was a popular intellectual fashion of the period. Most educated readers had at least a nodding acquaintance with spiritualism and Theosophy, but there was also Rosicrucianism, Freemasonry, Martinism, Hermeticism, as well as manifestations of "common" or "boulevard" mysticism, such as somnambulism, chiromancy, Tarot, phrenology, mesmerism, astrology, fortune-telling, and dream interpretation. In the cities, people attended public and private séances, demonstrations of hypnotism, and lectures by famous Indian yogis. . . . For creative, innovative individuals like Bielyi, Aleksandr Scriabin, Konstantin Balmont, Max Voloshin, Nikolai Roerich, Vasily (Wassily) Kandinsky, occult philosophy was a lifetime pursuit that impinged on all aspects of their personal, spiritual, and creative lives. To ignore this dimension in their work is like trying to understand medieval art without a knowledge of Christianity.[16]

Although each of the forms of occultism listed above by Carlson has its own special emphasis and orientation, they all have enough in common that a consideration of some of the major ideas central to Theosophy may be relevant to most of the others as well. The worldwide movement known today as Theosophy (from the Greek "divine wisdom") was founded by Helena Petrovna Blavatskaia (Madame Blavatsky, or HPB) in New York in 1875, but like most other esoteric societies it defines itself as a revival of timeless wisdom known in ancient Mesopotamia, Egypt, India, and Greece, or perhaps even earlier, in vanished Atlantis. Guardians of that ancient wisdom, called in Theosophy the Mahatmas, a highly evolved brotherhood of spiritually advanced Masters, are believed to still reside in small, hidden communities in inaccessible places in or near the Himalayas. Sometimes these Masters leave their communities to travel about the world, either in astral bodies or incognito in physical bodies, delivering the brotherhood's instructions for the benefit of all humanity to a few chosen worthy recipients, who in turn are then able to pass along this timeless wisdom to a wider public in the idiom of their place and time.

The wisdom to be communicated is of two kinds: exoteric, presented in books, popular media, and open meetings for the general public, and esoteric, communicated only orally, one on one, to the initiated adept worthy to receive and retain the secret teachings. Outside Theosophy, this tendency toward esotericism can be seen in the use of code words and images, understood merely in a mundane sense by the uninitiated but recognizable as keys to higher meaning by those in the know. As an example, Andrei Biely's use of colors in *St. Petersburg* may seem merely vivid description to most readers but have higher, Anthroposophical significance to those familiar with the theories of Rudolf Steiner, as do the paintings of Kandinsky and the compositions of Scriabin.

In Theosophy, the fundamental exoteric, public teaching consists of the "Three Objects": first, to form a nucleus of the universal brotherhood of humanity, without distinctions of race, creed, sex, caste, or color; second, to encourage the comparative study of religion, philosophy, and science; and third, to investigate unexplained laws of nature and the powers latent in humanity. The esoteric teachings, which HPB communicated to a group of her closest followers, and which are apparently still presented and studied in special groups today, are said to deal with special techniques for spiritual advancement and deep penetration into the mysteries presented in *The Secret Doctrine*, HPB's multivolume masterpiece, readily available but largely impenetrable to the unaided lay reader.

In the wider society, all branches of the socialist movement shared the First Object of Theosophy, viewing themselves as a vanguard of universal human brotherhood. A growing awareness of and interest in the diverse religions of the Siberian and Central Asian parts of the Russian empire, marked especially by the 1913 opening of a Buddhist temple by the Buryat lama Agvan Dorjiev in St. Petersburg, and the movement on the part of intellectuals away from dogmatic Orthodoxy toward more creative versions of Christianity, such as variations on Solovyov's Sophiology and the Merezhkovsky-Gippius proclamation of a "Third Testament," parallels Theosophy's Second Object, a comparative approach to religion, philosophy, and science. The Third Object, exploration of unexplained laws and latent powers, was reflected everywhere in the wider culture, from Rasputin's role as mystical healer in the

Tsarist court, to the popularity of presentations by Gurdjieff and Ouspensky, to the laboratory experiments of paranormal abilities and activities conducted by Gleb Boky's section of the early Soviet secret police,[17] and the many varied investigations into psychic phenomena reported in the 1970s bestseller by Sheila Ostrander and Lynn Schroeder, *Psychic Discoveries Behind the Iron Curtain*.[18]

Evolution, in Theosophical literature, was not a one-way Darwinian progress from simple to more complex organisms and species but an up-and-down and roundabout process, starting with eons of descent of spirit into matter, and now entering the early stages of a reascent of matter upward again into spirit. Present humanity is not the most advanced in history—vanished races of humanity, Atlantean and Lemurian, were physically, mentally, and spiritually superior to present humans. The Himalayan Masters retain traces of the qualities lost by humanity in general, and these traces now serve as guides for the future evolution of humanity.

The prelude to *The Secret Doctrine* is in the form of "The Stanzas of Dzyan," said by HPB to be "the records of a people unknown to ethnology" which were discovered in manuscript form in a cave connected to a Tibetan monastery, "written in a tongue absent from the nomenclature of languages and dialects with which philology is acquainted."[19] Since the language of the stanzas was unknown, HPB apparently was able to translate them only by an occult method of telepathic "precipitation" from a higher Master. Commentators who have not only read but understood the stanzas report that they contain the germ of the entire Secret Doctrine. Maria Carlson characterizes *The Secret Doctrine* as a whole as

> eclectic, syncretic, dogmatic, strongly pantheistic, and heavily laced with exotic Buddhist thought and vocabulary and not a few false analogies. Combining bits and pieces of Neoplatonism, Brahminism, Buddhism, Kabbalism, Gnosticism, Rosicrucianism, Hermeticism, and other occult doctrines past and present in an occasionally undiscriminating philosophical *mélange*, Blavatsky was trying to create a "scientific" religion, a modern gnosis, based on absolute *knowledge* of things spiritual rather than on *faith*. It was an attempt to bridge the perceived abyss between science and religion, between reason and faith.[20]

The elitist, antipositivist, *zaumnyi* ("beyond rational") character of Theosophy and the other forms of occultism resonated powerfully with many Silver Age Russian intellectuals. The world and mindset characterized by Dostoevsky's

Underground Man as "twice two makes four" belonged to the previous age of realism and rationalism, inadequate to quantify the new realities. "Twice two makes five," irrational perhaps but stated in the form of a rational proposition, was an equation better suited to new times. Even writers and thinkers whose reputations were for antimystical, anti-Theosophical views of the world sometimes succumbed to the attractions of the occult.[21] The Acmeist poet and theoretician Nikolai Gumilev, for example, famously rejected the Symbolist poets' "fraternization with mysticism, then Theosophy, then occultism," but many of his own best poems, such as "Sixth Sense," "The Forest," "The Serpent," "The Muzhik," "Memory," and others, especially in his most highly regarded collections, *Bonfire* (*Koster*) and *Pillar of Fire* (*Ognennyi stolp*), are full of past lives, supernatural beings, uncanny transformations, paranormal abilities and events. And in the early Soviet Union, even prominent officials, nominally atheists and materialists, exhibited keen interest in studies normally associated with the occult. Maxim Gorky, for example, endorsed the neurologist and "Father of Objective Psychology" Vladimir Bekhterev's experiments in thought transference.[22] From the 1920s through the 1970s, Soviet scientists in special laboratories were conducting parapsychology experiments involving humans and animals, eyeless sight, and energy bodies, and using Kirlian photography to record the auras of humans, animals, and plants.[23] The filmmaker Sergei Eisenstein (1898–1948) was a Rosicrucian initiate who gathered around himself a "Gnostic circle" of adepts prominent in the history of Soviet film and visual arts.[24] According to Dmitri Shostakovich, Stalin, who devoted no small amount of energy to attempting to root out every trace of "superstition"—his term for religion—was himself an extremely superstitious man.[25] And Marc Bennetts, a *Guardian* and online journalist who is writing a book about Russia's obsession with the occult, tells us: "Aside from widespread, albeit whispered, rumors that Stalin was an occult adept himself, the 1930s saw speculation that the dictator made use of the unearthly powers of one Natalya Lvova, 'a third generation witch.' Shakeups in the top ranks of the Party, which usually meant a trip to the Gulag for the unfortunate official, were said by terrified Muscovites to be the result of Stalin and Lvova's black magic Kremlin sessions."[26]

Much has been written about occult researches and activities during the Third Reich in Germany, but the Soviets, apparently, also developed their own equivalent of the Nazi Ahnenerbe, the search for ancestral Aryan roots and ancient occult artifacts. The Russian equivalent was centered on the mysterious "Red Merlin," Alexander Barchenko, a medical school dropout, writer of occult adventure stories, and follower of the French esotericist Alexandre Saint-Yves d'Alveydre, popularizer of the legend of Agartha, a subterranean paradise hidden in a network of caves somewhere in Central Asia. Barchenko persuaded the OGPU secret police section head, Gleb Boky, to sponsor paranormal research in government laboratories and to undertake a mission to Central Asia in search of the magical kingdom of Shambhala, where powerful secret knowledge was hidden that could win the world for the Bolshevik cause. The expedition failed in its attempts to enter Tibet, but with secret police sponsorship, Barchenko continued to explore other remote areas in search of esoteric knowledge: the Kola Peninsula, in search of remnants of an ancient civilization said to have known the secret of splitting the atom; the Altai region, to investigate the ability of shamanic drumming to induce altered states of consciousness; the Crimean Peninsula, to study the secret meaning of Sufi teachings and practices; and Kostroma in central Russia, where members of the Old Believer sect set legends of Belovodie (Beautiful White Water), their hidden dreamland.[27]

In his testimony before the 1937 tribunal that would sentence him to death, Gleb Boky described Barchenko's idea:

> According to Barchenko, in ancient times there existed a culturally advanced society that later perished as a result of a geological catastrophe. This was a communist society, and it existed in a more advanced social (communist) and materially technical form than ours. The remnants of this society, as Barchenko told us, still exist in remote mountain areas at the intersection of India, Tibet, Kashgar, and Afghanistan. This ancient science accumulated all scientific and technical knowledge, representing a synthesis of all branches of science. The existence of this ancient society is a secret carefully guarded by its members. Barchenko called himself a follower of this ancient society, stressing that he was initiated into it by messengers of its religio-political center.[28]

As described by Boky, Barchenko's idea owes much not only to Saint-Yves d'Alveydre, but also to Madame Blavatsky, and, though he was probably unaware of it, to Fedorov's idea of the Pamir region as a prehistoric paradise in need of restoration. After the collapse of the Soviet Union, as we shall see later in this study, similar ideas resurfaced, this time about Arktos, the hypothetical original arctic homeland of the Indo-European peoples. Groups of investigators who called themselves Hyperboreans, some of whom were also Cosmists or at least published in Cosmist publications, set off on far-northern expeditions to search for confirmation of their theory.

Although the examples of Promethean theurgy outlined above do not exhibit all the qualities earlier defined as "Cosmist," they do indicate the broadly shared rich and dynamic intellectual and cultural background from which the Cosmist movement emerged and back into which it fed. In the next section we shall consider the ideas and activities of several followers of Fedorov—Iona Brikhnichev, Alexander Gorsky, Nikolai Setnitsky, Valerian Muravyov, and Vasily Chekrygin—whose works helped to turn Fedorovism into the broader movement of Cosmism.

## *II*

# *Fedorov's Twentieth-Century Followers*

RUSSIAN COSMISM DID not quite emerge full-blown from the head of Nikolai Fedorovich Fedorov. As much as it owes to him, it would not have emerged without the assiduous devotion of two extraordinary disciples: the educator, law clerk, and later circuit court judge Nikolai Peterson, and the philosopher, poet, and scholar of eastern religions Vladimir Kozhevnikov.

### *Nikolai Pavlovich Peterson (1844–1919) and Vladimir Aleksandrovich Kozhevnikov (1852–1917)*

Peterson was born in Penza Province in central Russia, attended the local gymnasium and institute for nobility, and in 1861 entered Moscow University as a student of history and philology, from which he was almost immediately forced to withdraw for lack of means.[1] In 1862, at age seventeen, he became the youngest of the applicants chosen to teach at Tolstoy's experimental school for peasant children at Yasnaya Polyana, and before the academic year ended, he was appointed secrétary of the house pedagogical journal. After a year at Tolstoy's school, Peterson returned to Moscow University, this time as a student of medicine. While there, apparently devoting more attention to political activism than to medical studies, he became involved with a group of radicals led by Dmitri Karakozov, who in 1866 would attempt to assassinate Tsar Alexander II. Leaving the university without finishing his degree in 1864, Peterson took a position as teacher of geography and arithmetic in the village of Bogorodsk, where, as we have seen, he met Fedorov, abandoned political radicalism, and became Fedorov's lifelong friend, disciple, and scribe. While teaching in Bogorodsk, Peterson and Fedorov met every day for walks, simple meals, and long discussions. One special memory for Peterson was an Easter week when he joined Fedorov for his annual walk from Bogorodsk to Moscow, twenty-one miles, hearing from a distance all the city's church bells gradually ringing louder as they approached.

In 1865, at his next position, in Bronnitsa, Peterson began to apply some of Fedorov's ideas, an attempt to begin the "common task," by organizing a museum of local history and devising civic, agricultural, and ecological projects that allowed his pupils and their families to work together at putting newly acquired book knowledge into action. Just as these activities were beginning to have positive results, Peterson, as noted in chapter 6, was arrested and sentenced to six months in prison for his former association with the Karakozov terrorist group. After his release, in 1867, Peterson took a position as assistant to the librarian of the Chertkov Library in Moscow, where among other duties he transcribed materials for P. I. Bartenev's *Russkii Arkhiv*, the foremost Russian monthly "thick" journal for history and documents. Another of his library duties was to assist with proof corrections for an edition of Tolstoy's *War and Peace*.

In 1869 Peterson began to work in the Russian district court system and recommended Fedorov for the position he was leaving at the library. For the rest of his life, Peterson served the judicial system in various capacities and in various locations, first serving as a court clerk in a village near where he had grown up, then moving on to the nearby town of Mokshan, where he served as a judge, then as district judge for the southeastern market city of Voronezh, and finally as judge for the district courts of Ashkhabad, in today's Turkmenistan, then in Verny (now Almaty) in Kazakhstan, ending back in central Russia as judge in Zaraisk, Moscow District. During all this time, he kept in close touch with Fedorov, both in person and through correspondence. Nearly every year, Fedorov would spend his vacation with Peterson and his growing family, wherever they happened to live, and during these times together Fedorov would dictate the long and short essays that would eventually find their way into *The Philosophy of the Common Task*. It was, as we have seen, through one of the early dictated manuscripts that Peterson introduced Fedorov's ideas first to Dostoevsky, then to Tolstoy. And it was through Peterson's connections in Ashkhabad, where he was a leading citizen and founding member of the local archeological society, that Fedorov's ideas were first presented to a puzzled and largely antagonistic public. This initial public exposure, which Fedorov considered a debacle, affected Fedorov deeply, and made him even more reluctant to present "the common task" to anyone beyond his narrow circle of friends and followers. Fedorov seems to have held Peterson partly responsible for the Ashkhabad disaster, and in the last few years of his life he began to distance himself from his first follower. After Fedorov's death in 1903, Peterson, devotion never flagging, undertook the monumental job of editing and publishing *The Philosophy of the Common Task* in collaboration with his fellow disciple Vladimir Kozhevnikov, and until his death in 1919, the promotion of Fedorov's book and ideas remained his principal task.

Fedorov's other close friend and follower, Vladimir Kozhevnikov,[2] was born into a prominent family in the town of Kozlov in Tambov Province. Between 1868 and 1872, he audited courses as an external, nondegree student at Moscow University, and in 1872, at age twenty-two, attracted favorable attention from leading intellectuals with his first scholarly publication, "The Moral and Intellectual Development of Roman Society in the Second Century A.D." In the late 1870s, he began a multivolume study of the process of secularization from the Italian Renaissance through the nineteenth century, thirty parts of which were apparently drafted before his death, but the work was never published, and the manuscript perished with the rest of the Kozhevnikov archive in the 1930s. Though he did not have a university degree, Kozhevnikov, like many of the Cosmist thinkers, was an independent scholar of great erudition. He had command of at least eight languages and was a man of profound culture, in whom, in the words of one of his contemporaries, there "dwelt an entire academy of sciences and arts." He published over twenty books on religion and philosophy, the best known of which were: *The Philosophy of Feeling and Faith* (*Filosofiia chuvstva i very*, 1897), and *Buddhism in Comparison with Christianity* (*Buddizm v sravnenii s khristinstvom*, 2 vols., 1916). Fedorov often cited Kozhevnikov's poems and scholarly insights; Zenkovsky, in his standard *History of Russian Philosophy*, gives favorable mention to Kozhevnikov's philosophical work; and Solovyov, Florensky, Bulgakov, and other leading religious thinkers respected Kozhevnikov as both a philosopher and a man.

Kozhevnikov met Fedorov in 1875 and was probably the "Volodya" mentioned by Tsiolkovsky as the leader of the late 1870s circle of young people who gathered around Fedorov in the library. Where Peterson worked to present Fedorov's dictated writings to eminent contemporaries like Dostoevsky, Tolstoy, and Solovyov, Kozhevnikov absorbed Fedorov's ideas and, like Solovyov, incorporated Fedorovian themes into his own original philosophical and religious works. And while Peterson lived and worked in far-flung regions of the Russian Empire, Kozhevnikov, staying in Moscow, was able to maintain close direct contact with Fedorov, contributed significantly to some of Fedorov's writings, and in frequent letters during the last fifteen years of Fedorov's life kept Peterson informed of their friend's fluctuating state of health and mind. From these letters, the difficulties that both Kozhevnikov and Peterson experienced in working with Fedorov become clear. Fedorov did and did not want to publish his writings. He sincerely believed that his project could redirect the world from its disastrous course, but at the same time feared that, if presented prematurely to the general public, the project would provoke such a storm of ridicule that it might never again be seriously considered. Nevertheless, in 1894, with the persuasion and help of Peterson and Kozhevnikov, Fedorov submitted to the censors an essay contrasting his "philosophy of action" with Tolstoy's "philosophy of inaction." The plan was to issue the essay as an anonymous brochure, and in order to limit and control its circulation, the question was whether to make it too expensive for a wide public to buy or issue it "not for sale" and distribute it without charge to a closely selected readership. Fedorov chose the latter course, but when the censors prohibited publication of the essay, Fedorov was at once unsurprised yet deeply wounded. In the aftermath, he apparently blamed Kozhevnikov for having persuaded him to attempt publication, rebuked him both for offering to pay for the printing of the brochure and for having sent him some medicines when he was ill, and threatened to break off all relations with his Moscow friend. And, as Kozhevnikov generously notes in another letter, breaking off all relations with his dearest friends was not a rare event in Fedorov's later years. Both in 1894 and between 1900 and 1902, he did the same with Peterson, apparently also in a dispute over publication, worrying (correctly) that Peterson, a sometimes overzealous enthusiast, was too eager to present his own incomplete and sometimes incorrect versions of Fedorov's ideas, and fearing (also correctly) that upon his death Peterson was planning to publish all of Fedorov's writings. At one point, to prevent premature and inaccurate presentation of "the common task," Fedorov burned "a great many" of his own writings.[3] But Kozhevnikov and Peterson loved Fedorov too much to be alienated by these brief flare-ups. His single-minded intensity, difficult as it made friendship with him, was one of his most endearing characteristics. Kozhevnikov was present at Fedorov's death, and his letter to Alexander Gorsky written shortly afterwards provides a touching and memorable description of their friend's last thoughts and hours.[4]

During his lifetime Fedorov published nothing under his own name and so very little pseudonymously and anonymously that while his erudition, character, and eccentricities were known to many library patrons, his ideas were known to only a few of his contemporaries. Some, like Tsiolkovsky and the Bartenev publishing family, learned of his philosophy directly, in dialogue, and others, including Dostoevsky, Tolstoy, and Solovyov, through Peterson's privately circulated manuscript. Tolstoy and Solovyov were able to see Fedorov's ideas reflected in his life, while Dostoevsky admired Fedorov's thoughts on paper alone, without ever meeting him or even learning his name.

After Fedorov's death in December 1903, Kozhevnikov and Peterson undertook the task of gathering, deciphering, editing, and publishing at their own expense *The Philosophy of the Common Task*, a massive, two-volume, 1,200-page miscellany of long and short essays, newspaper articles, "letters to the editor," finished and unfinished works, drafts, fragments, variations on arguments developed more fully elsewhere, responses to books read, polemics with dead philosophers, and inspired jottings. The work as a whole reads like an unfinished first draft, a frequently eloquent but unsystematic call for action, a series of fresh attempts to develop a single enormous idea from different starting points.[5] The two volumes, published in 1906 and 1913, which Kozhevnikov and Peterson distributed gratis to libraries, academic institutions, and interested individuals, though printed in editions of only 480 copies, soon began to have an impact. Each of the two editors also published personal accounts of Fedorov and his ideas, Kozhevnikov serially in 1904–1906, and in a monograph of 1908,[6] and Peterson in a monograph of 1912.[7] The editors made certain that influential reviewers received copies, resulting in important critical analyses by Bulgakov (1912), Golovanenko (1913–1915), Berdyaev (1915), and others, all of which soon helped to make Fedorov's idea and project an important part of the overall Promethean ethos that characterized the period. While not themselves Cosmist thinkers, Peterson and Kozhevnikov brought to light the ideas that would provide the basis and stimulation for all subsequent Cosmist speculation. This was the first wave of posthumous Fedorovism. As we shall next see, a second wave of Fedorovism, sometimes directly and other times indirectly connected to both the scientific and spiritual Cosmists discussed previously in this study, would follow in the 1920s and be suppressed by the end of the 1930s. And as we shall see at the conclusion of this study, the third wave of Fedorovism, which fully identifies itself with Cosmism, began in the last years of Soviet rule, and continues as an intellectual and cultural movement still growing today.

## Svyatogor and the Biocosmists

Not representative of the Fedorovist-Cosmist main tendency, but a notable, if weird, outgrowth was the short-lived "Biocosmist" movement, led by the anarchistic activist and poet, the self-described "Rooster of Revolution," Alexander F. Agienko, who wrote and performed publicity stunts under the ancient Slavic name "Svyatogor."[8] The writer and critic Boris Agapov described him as:

a little man . . . in a cheap tweed jacket, high top boots with holes in them, wearing riding breeches, who in front of his wildly blinking eyes would spread all ten fingers and wave them back and forth as if searching for the right words. On every occasion and at every opportunity he would declare that for humanity the time had come to inhabit outer space and to bring life to all the planets. Only therein lay poetry—all the rest was bullshit. And for that reason he called himself a Biocosmist.[9]

As one of the first to present semi-Fedorovian, semi-Cosmist ideas to a post-revolutionary audience, Svyatogor did not always create a winning impression of the tendency. Berdyaev describes a debate in which he and an unnamed Biocosmist, most likely the Rooster of Revolution, participated a few years after the October Revolution.

> A number of Tolstoyans, followers of Nikolai Fyodorov, professing a mixture of Fyodorov's ideas and anarchistic communism, some straightforward anarchists and communists also took part in the debate. As I entered the crowded hall, I had an almost physical sensation of terrific tension in the air. The crowd contained a great many Red Army men, sailors and workers. The whole atmosphere was significant of the elemental forces behind the Revolution, exalting in the downfall of intolerable restraints, wanton, unbridled, ruthless, and frank to the point of naked shamelessness. One worker read a paper on the Gospel, in which he affirmed as scientifically proved that the Mother of God was a prostitute and Jesus Christ the illegitimate son of a Roman soldier—a statement which was greeted with wild applause from the audience. He also dwelt incessantly on the "contradictions" and "inconsistencies" in the Gospels. He was followed by a Tolstoyan who made a sharp attack on the church. A follower of Fyodorov, who described himself as a "biocosmist," produced, in what sounded like unprintable slang, some incredible hotch-potch of science, Gnosticism, and the Gospels. He finished by proclaiming that, since the maximum social programme had already been put into practice, "the cosmic resurrection of the dead" will occur any moment. This statement provoked an uproar of laughter in the audience.[10]

The Biocosmists made news for about two years, in 1920–1922, and included, in addition to Svyatogor, such now forgotten figures as Pavel Ivanitsky,

Nikolai Degtyarev, V. Zikeev, and others—perhaps twenty-six members in all. They had a presence in both Moscow and St. Petersburg, published the journal *Immortality* (*Bessmertie*), rallied under the slogan "Immortalism and Interplanetarianism," and issued a manifesto declaring two fundamental human rights: "the right to exist forever, and the right to unimpeded movement throughout interplanetary space."[11] They viewed the struggle against nature and death as a logical continuation of the revolution's struggle against bourgeois culture, and, as Berdyaev's debating opponent had proclaimed, the victory over the bourgeoisie meant that the victory over nature and death would inevitably follow.

The Biocosmists departed from Fedorov in their rejection of all that smacked of Orthodoxy and monarchy, and in their emphasis on the creative individual rather than the all-embracing community. As one of the group's declarations stated: "Biocosmism is a new ideology, for which the cornerstone principle is the concept of personhood [*lichnost'*], growing in power and creativity to establish itself in immortality and in the cosmos. As real and essential rights of personhood, we consider the right to existence (immortality, resurrection, rejuvenation) and to freedom of movement throughout the cosmos."[12]

In contrast to the concept of "brotherhood," so important in Fedorov's thought, Svyatogor proposes the concept of "companionship" (*soratnichestvo*), which seems to him a more active, creative mutual relationship than brotherhood, which he finds static, entirely subject to nature, and uncreative. Furthermore, as a revolutionary, not an archivist-utopian as he considers Fedorov to have been, Svyatogor places restoration of life to the "dust of the fathers" at the bottom, not the top, of his to-do list. Svyatogor also wants to eliminate all "religious-Platonic dualism" and derides "all the absurdity of Fedorov's attempt to save Tsarism and Orthodoxy."[13]

What Svyatogor and the Biocosmists did take from Fedorov was the insistence that death is not inevitable, and that by our own efforts we can make individual human life limitless in both time and space. By accepting and further developing the immortalist element in Fedorov's thought, and at the same time rejecting the religious and political traditionalism, Svyatogor and the Biocosmists anticipated not the Cosmist tendency as a whole, which still treats science and religion as parts of a holistic unity, but the transhumanist, cryogenic, cyborgianist, and other branches of technological immortalism that have emerged both in Russia and internationally in recent decades. These latter groups customarily grant Fedorov a tip of the hat but do not attempt to defend or follow him.

## New Wine and the Universal Task

In 1912, a small group of Fedorovian religious thinkers and activists gathered in Moscow under the leadership of a former priest and later poet, publicist, and Communist functionary, Iona Brikhnichev, and the previously mentioned former seminarian Alexander Gorsky, to publish a short-lived journal, *New Wine* (*Novoe vino*), featuring poems, essays, and testimonials reflecting Fedorov's ideas. This was followed in 1914 by a miscellany published by the same Fedorovians, now based in Odessa, under the title *The Universal Task, Issue 1* (*Vselenskoe delo, vypusk 1*). Although Brikhnichev and Gorsky had been discussing the idea of such a miscellany for about two years, the collection itself does not reflect careful planning or good editorial judgment. Propagandistic poems and exhortations urging the victory of immortal life over death, similar in quality and style to the literature of revolution urging the proletariat to smite the bourgeoisie, were interspersed with exegetical essays on holy scripture, scientific works on anabiosis and the effects of cold temperature on certain organisms, and responses solicited from various writers on their concepts of death and resurrection. The eclectic nature of the selections coupled with inconsistent editorial standards helped to doom the project from the start. Peterson and Kozhevnikov both declined the editors' invitation to contribute to the miscellany, fearing that it would turn out to be a vulgarization of Fedorov's ideas. To make matters worse, the scheduled publication date was December 1913, but production problems delayed the printing until the spring of 1914, coinciding almost exactly with the outbreak of World War I. The printers, who happened to be citizens of Germany and Austro-Hungary, were arrested, the presses were shut down, and all paper and printed materials were confiscated. The editors somehow managed to get a few dozen copies of their miscellany, which they distributed to a very few libraries and individuals. A bibliographic rarity, only a small handful of copies of the original *The Universal Task, Issue 1* are known to exist today.[14]

Brikhnichev, the primary editor of both *New Wine* and *The Universal Task, Issue 1*, was born and grew up in Georgia, and attended the same seminary, and at approximately the same time, as both Florensky and the future Stalin, then still Ioseb Dzhughashvili. Brikhnichev was a leader of "Golgothan Christianity,"[15] a movement focused on suffering and emphasizing the need for radical communal action to redeem the fallen world. In 1906 Brikhnichev was editor of a Tbilisi weekly Christian newspaper, "Arise, Sleeper!" (*Vstan', spiashchii!*), and in 1907 was defrocked for political agitation. In the aftermath of the 1905 revolution, he worked closely with a group of Moscow religious "Third Testament" thinkers and seekers, including Vladimir Ern, Valentin Sventsisky, Pavel Florensky, Dmitry Merezhkovsky, and Zinaida Gippius. He was one of the organizers in 1910 of the important religious journal *New Land* (*Novaia zemlia*), and after it was banned he collaborated with Gorsky, from whom he apparently first learned of Fedorov, to launch the Fedorovian journal mentioned above, *New Wine*. In 1913 he was expelled from Moscow and settled in Odessa, where he and Gorsky put together the doomed *Universal Task, Issue 1*.

After the 1917 October Revolution, Brikhnichev endorsed Soviet power and joined the Communist Party, sincerely believing that the new Communist government would mean the realization of a selfless, truly Christian, Fedorovian society. He served in a number of Soviet institutions: the Central Commission to Aid the Hungry, the All-Russian Commission to End Illiteracy, the Georgian Commission for Popular Enlightenment—and though a former priest, he even served on the editorial board of the major Soviet antireligious journal, *The Atheist* (*Bezbozhnik*). For as long as he was allowed, he continued to be a propagandist for Fedorovian ideas that were at least arguably compatible with Soviet policy, such as universal literacy, the unity of thought and action, and the deficiencies of the existing Orthodox Church. In a book published in 1931, *The Book in the Lives of Great People* (*Kniga v zhizni velikikh liudei*), Brikhnichev was one of the first in an official Soviet publication of the Stalinist era actually to mention Fedorov's name in print. He died in a Moscow retirement home in 1968, one of the few outspoken followers of Fedorov to have survived the terrors and hardships imposed by his former Georgian schoolmate Dzhughashvili-Stalin.

## *Alexander Konstantinovich Gorsky (1886–1943) and Nikolai Alexandrovich Setnitsky (1888–1937)*

The two major figures in the second wave of twentieth-century Fedorovism, assisting its transition to Cosmism, were Alexander Gorsky, who published under the pseudonyms "A. Gornostaev" and "A. Ostramirov," and Nikolai Setnitsky, who published many works under his own name as well as others anonymously and pseudonymously.

As mentioned in the previous chapter, Gorsky was a leading proponent of the Fedorovian—and not only Fedorovian—idea of "chaste" marriage, in which husband and wife would abstain from sexual relations but otherwise share total love and devotion. As Gorsky points out, Fedorov anticipated Freud's insights into the power of the erotic instinct, the control over which would represent a significant stage in the evolution to a higher level of humanity, from "pornocracy" to "psychocracy." In the present stage, men and women are prisoners of sex: defined when young largely by their potential as sexual partners, when old largely by their offspring, their sexual productions. In Gorsky's new society, the new bodies which we shall create will be androgynous, and eros will become a transformed, regulated version of the sex drive, a force for spiritual and cultural rather than merely physical creation.

Gorsky was born into a priest's family, attended church school, religious academy, and seminary at the Holy Trinity monastery, upon graduation from which, as one of the brightest in his class, he was offered a highly desirable clerical post in the capital, St. Petersburg. But he turned this down to follow instead, as Svetlana Semenova has suggested,[16] the path of Dostoevsky's Alyosha Karamazov, "the monk in the world." He studied for a year at Moscow University, then settled in Odessa, where he taught at a religious academy and church school. He published poems and essays in the journal *New Wine*, then collaborated with Brikhnichev to edit and publish the ill-fated Fedorovian miscellany *The Universal Task, Issue 1*. In 1918 he met Setnitsky at a literary gathering and introduced him to Fedorov's thought, thus beginning their twenty years of close friendship and collaboration. In the early 1920s, back in Moscow, Gorsky and Setnitsky wrote articles for a weekly journal on the rational, scientific method to organize labor, and then together anonymously issued a very strange pamphlet, *Smertobozhnichestvo* ("The apotheosis of death"), a militant demand for the total transformation of society toward Fedorovian goals, ending with a grim series of anathemas upon all who have ignored or rejected "the common task."

Gorsky's friend and collaborator Setnitsky grew up in a civil-service family, attended a classical grammar school, and initially studied oriental languages, then law, at St. Petersburg University. Like others in the Cosmist tendency, Setnitsky was interested in all branches of knowledge, and in addition to his major subjects in the humanities took courses in physics and mathematics. Later, while working primarily as an economist and statistician, he would publish articles and books on a very wide range of topics, applying Fedorov's ideas to all facets of twentieth-century society and culture, always following Fedorov's example in looking for the higher goal, the ultimate ideal toward which any activity pointed, condemning those that pointed toward death and exalting those that pointed toward new eternal life. In 1925, Setnitsky moved to Harbin, China, where he spent the next ten years working in the Economic Office of the Chinese-Eastern Railway and teaching as a member of the legal faculty of the technical institute. Harbin at that time enjoyed the unusual advantage of being a city with a strong Russian cultural presence but not under Soviet control, and thus was a center in which many Russian émigrés temporarily resided or through which they passed on their way to new homelands. Setnitsky was able to use Harbin as a base from which to publish Fedorovian materials that could not be published in Soviet Russia. In 1928, he published a second edition of sections of the first volume of *The Philosophy of the Common Task*, accompanied by a substantial (if in places inaccurate) biographical work on Fedorov by Gorsky, writing as "A. Ostromirov." Other books and booklets written by Gorsky and Setnitsky under various pseudonyms analyzed Fedorov's influence on Dostoevsky, Tolstoy, and Solovyov, and related "the common task" to major twentieth-century Russian and international intellectual and cultural developments.[17] It is in Gorsky's and Setnitsky's application and extension, rather than the simple elucidation, of Fedorov's ideas that we see the beginnings of the transition from strict Fedorovism to its broader outgrowth and upgrade, Cosmism.

Where Gorsky was especially interested in the psychological implications of Fedorov's ideas, Setnitsky focused more on the socioeconomic mandates of "the common task." In his book *On the Ultimate Ideal* (*O konechnom ideale*), Setnitsky considers current Soviet willingness to use but unwillingness to credit certain of Fedorov's ideas.

> In this connection there are many instances of proposed and realized Fedorovian ideas, though his name, as painted always in strongly religious colors, is not mentioned and even the idea and connection of these projects with Fedorov's conceptions is not recognized. Thus, a clear example in this area is the receptivity on the part of Soviet policy makers to the direction Fedorov initiated on the struggle against drought. Recent [1931] actions and government declarations in this area appear copied whole from the pages of *The Philosophy of the Common Task*. And one could also say the same concerning the latest projects for the exploitation of the water routes of the USSR, concerning exploration and development of the Russian and Siberian far north, concerning the construction and direction of railways, concerning irrigation in Turkestan, etc.[18]

In 1934, through printers in Riga, at that time in independent Latvia, Set-nitsky published *The Universal Task, Issue 2*, which included valuable obituaries of Peterson and Kozhevnikov, bibliographies, and materials that Peterson and Kozhevnikov had intended to include in their never published third volume of *The Philosophy of the Common Task*. And in several successive issues of *Izvestiia Iuridicheskogo Fakul'teta v Gorode Kharbine* (Proceedings of the Department of Law in the city of Harbin), Setnitsky published essays and articles on Fedoro-vian themes, many of which later appeared as separate brochures. Setnitsky also sent Fedorovian materials to Berdyaev and other leading émigré writers and publishers, resulting in excerpts from Fedorov's writings and commentary on them in leading émigré religious and Eurasian-movement journals in Paris and Berlin.

From Harbin, Setnitsky carried on an extended correspondence with Maxim Gorky, who was not only a leading Soviet writer but also a major force in the Soviet publishing industry, concerning the possibility of an official So-viet edition of Fedorov's writings. Gorky had long been interested in Fedo-rov's ideas and, while dismissing his religious views, strongly admired his "activist" approach to all life's problems. In letters to receptive Soviet writers, such as Mikhail Prishvin and Olga Forsh, Gorky wrote about his interest in and agreement with some of Fedorov's ideas.[19] But the mid 1930s was not the right time to push for a Soviet edition of Fedorov. As Solzhenitsyn tells us, Fedorov had become one of the "non-persons" whose ideas were generally understood to be in disgrace.[20] Gorsky, who had been arrested in 1929, spent most of the 1930s in prison. Setnitsky, who returned to Russia from Harbin in 1935, was arrested and executed in 1937. And Maxim Gorky himself died under suspicious circumstances in 1936. By the end of the decade, while some of his uncredited projects were being implemented, Fedorov, his followers, and his ideas were still discussed privately but could not even be whispered about in public.

After his release from prison in 1937, Gorsky spent his exile in Kaluga, where Tsiolkovsky had died and Chizhevsky still lived. There, until his re-arrest and death in prison in 1943, he developed close ties with his "spiritual daughters," Setnitsky's daughters Olga and Elena, and their friend Ekaterina Krasheninnikova, young Fedorovian enthusiasts who hid and preserved the archives of both Setnitsky and Gorsky until they could be safely brought again into the light.

Setnitsky's youngest daughter, Elena Berkovskaia, who died in 1998, left a vivid reminiscence about her family's friendship with Gorsky and enthusiasm for Fedorov.[21] Setnitsky had earlier tried unsuccessfully to convert his wife and older daughter, Olga, to Fedorov's teachings, but when Gorsky arrived at their home in 1937 after ten years in prison camps, he was able to accomplish, largely by the force of his smile and personality, the conversions that his friend Setnitsky had not. After Setnitsky was arrested and (unknown to his family and friends) executed in 1937, Gorsky became "father, friend, teacher, and shepherd"[22] to the Setnitsky girls and their friend Katya Krasheninnikova.

> Alexander Konstantinovich was by nature a man of action. I would even say that he was a fiery agitator and promoter of N. F. Fedorov's ideas in the world. He wrote great works with the intent of restoring Fedorov's ideas to life. Yes, yes, precisely to life, in that most terrible time about which one speaks with fear and trembling. Alexander Konstantinovich and Puna [family nickname for Setnitsky] thought and hoped that our centralized form of government could and should use its powers to encourage developments in the fields of biology, medicine, and chemistry directed toward the prolongation of human life, the struggle against aging, and regulation of nature.[23]

Thinking, as others had, that Fedorov's teachings coincided perfectly with Soviet objectives, Setnitsky and Gorsky both at first, then Gorsky alone, sent letters to leading Soviet writers and officials, outlining Fedorov's ideas and asking for official help in propagating them. In 1942 Gorsky apparently even wrote a letter to Stalin thinking it might gain Setnitsky's release from the gulag, not realizing that his friend had long since been executed. After Gorsky's arrest, the Setnitsky daughters and their friends continued to write letters about Fedorov and his teachings to important figures in Soviet literature and culture, including Boris Pasternak, Ilya Ehrenburg, Vladimir Vernadsky, and Marina Tsvetaeva.[24] Going beyond letters, Setnitsky's daughters and friends managed to establish an ongoing personal relationship with Pasternak, and were present at an early private reading by him of the opening chapters of his most Fedorovian work, *Doctor Zhivago*.[25]

The transcripts of Gorsky's own interrogations in 1928–1929 and 1943 reveal an apostle who openly professed Fedorov's teachings, knowing they would lead to a death sentence. In the questioning from 1928 to 1929, he went into great detail about what was compatible and incompatible between Fedorov's project and Soviet policy. He spoke freely about his proselytizing efforts, his attempts to contact potentially interested thinkers and activists, and his disappointment at the indifferent or negative responses on the part of people from whom he had high hopes of agreement. In his responses to the interrogator's questions, he holds nothing back. Asked "Are you a mystic?" he replies frankly: "Yes, I'm a mystic, but I think that mysticism ought to lead to a path of great scientific progress; I am an advocate of Fedorov's teachings."[26] His tone in all these responses is candid, even helpful, as though he still believed that he could be both a Fedorovian and a loyal Soviet citizen. His confession reveals a conviction shared by other Cosmists that mysticism and science were not incompatible. He sincerely believed that in confessing commitment to the "common task," he was confessing to an acceptable variation of official ideology, not to a criminal heresy. But in 1943 he knew otherwise, and both the interrogator's questions and Gorsky's responses contain none of the earlier comradely spirit.

QUESTION: You are accused of counterrevolutionary espionage activity against the Soviet government. Stop denying and begin a frank account of your treacherous activities.

ANSWER: I accepted the revolution and Soviet power because they contained that which moved humanity forward, toward realization of the dream of controlling all the forces of nature, right up to the complete liquidation of nature's idiocies—death and dying. But in actuality I see the same petty bourgeois submission to nature and absence of the struggle for the realization of ideals and dreams and I can't reconcile myself to it.

QUESTION: Don't hide under flowery phrases, are you an enemy of Soviet power—do you openly admit it?

ANSWER: I have never been an enemy of Soviet power, but I had a suspicious and sometimes negative attitude toward certain representatives of that power, for example, toward Bukharin, Yagoda, Zinoviev [three high Soviet officials executed after notorious show trials for anti-Soviet behavior] and the like.

QUESTION: You continue to avoid a direct answer about your counterrevolutionary activities. Have courage, tell yourself A: to talk, and B: not to be evasive.

ANSWER: I refuse to testify.

QUESTION: Why?

ANSWER: If you wish, I can say directly: I don't want to give evidence because I am an enemy of Soviet power, was, am, and will remain so. My convictions have not developed accidentally, and I am not at an age to change them, therefore I do not wish to testify to you. Decide the question regarding me and don't drag out the investigation.

QUESTION: You have to tell us in concrete terms about your counterrevolutionary activities.

ANSWER: I refuse to give any testimony for the previously indicated reason.

QUESTION: That you are an enemy of Soviet power—that is known. As proof of this, we can submit the impudent declaration you have just made. But this declaration is insufficient because it does not present a detailed account of your treacherous espionage activities and says nothing about your counterrevolutionary connections. Therefore the investigation insists upon full and open testimony.

ANSWER: I have already said that I refuse to give any kind of testimony.

QUESTION: This position of yours is incorrect. We insist on continuing the testimony.

ANSWER: I will not be giving testimony. Interrogation ended 11 May 1943, 5:00.[27]

In addition to having propagated the teachings of Fedorov, Gorsky had helped to keep the local church open and the cemetery functioning through the German occupation of Kaluga, which to his interrogators meant collaboration with the enemy. He was found guilty of all charges and executed on June 2, 1943.

In Gorsky and Setnitsky we find extraordinary energy and courage, if not the intellectual originality that we find in Tsiolkovsky, Vernadsky, Berdyaev, Florensky, and the other major Cosmists. Their efforts were directed toward proving the continuing relevance of Fedorov's grand project, the insistence that Fedorov was a thinker for the future rather than a relic of the past. They were, in the best sense, presenters rather than innovators, propagandists rather than objective scholars. In their view, Dostoevsky, Tolstoy, and Solovyov owed their best ideas to Fedorov. And in the twentieth century, the discoveries of the greatest new geniuses—Einstein, Freud, Bohr, and the rest—had largely been anticipated by the obscure nineteenth-century Moscow librarian. Gorsky and Setnitsky's main contribution to the Cosmist movement was that through their republication of Fedorov, their own writings, their personal contacts, and their persistent letters, they continued to bring Fedorov's ideas to the attention of major creative thinkers who would take Fedorov's ideas further than he, even with his powerful imagination, was able to extend them. Thus they contributed enormously to the transition from strict Fedorovism to Cosmism, a movement that would extend and at the same time depart from Fedorov's "common task."

## *Valerian Nikolaevich Muravyov (1885–1932)*

Another Fedorovian and genuine Cosmist who tried to continue to work within the Soviet system, and who went considerably farther beyond Fedorov than his friends Setnitsky and Gorsky, was Valerian Muravyov, a philosopher, poet, diplomat, and descendent of a long line of distinguished public servants. Well traveled and educated in Western European schools, Muravyov, despite his initial monarchist and anti-Bolshevist leanings, became useful to the Soviet government in its early struggles, mainly because of his acknowledged brilliant intellect, his fluency in several languages, a background that immediately earned the trust and respect of outsiders, and—though this later became a handicap—a close acquaintanceship with Leon Trotsky. Like many young intellectuals from the upper nobility, Muravyov quickly abandoned his anti-Bolshevist prejudices and became an enthusiastic supporter of the revolution. As he discovered only too soon, however, his idea of revolution and the revolution that actually emerged were only distantly related.

Muravyov, as much an esotericist as a Marxist, wanted a total alchemical transformation of the individual and the cosmos. He wrote much but was able to publish very little during his lifetime: an essay on Russian spirituality and intellectual history, "The Roar of the Tribe" (*Rev plemeni*), for the important 1918 collection of dissident essays on the revolution, *De Profundis* (*Iz glubiny*), and an essay on "Universal Productive Mathematics" (*Vseobshchaia proizvoditel'naia matematika*) in the 1934 Fedorovian miscellany *The Universal Task, Issue 2*. While working on projects for various Soviet government institutions, he wrote and published at his own expense a remarkable little book, his masterpiece, called *Control over Time* (*Ovladenie vremenem*),[28] in which, without mentioning Fedorov, he proposes a "common task" for restructuring the human being, uniting all humanity, and overcoming death—all by means of controlling time, Muravyov's version of Fedorov's regulation of nature.

In his introduction to *Control over Time*, Muravyov writes that, parallel to, but different from, the mathematical discoveries of Einstein, he wishes to investigate the question of time not theoretically but practically, and not in a laboratory but in history and society, based on the Russian revolution's experience in the total organization of society. Einstein's theories, then, become the basis for a new sociology. For Muravyov, the revolution was, among other things, a vast experiment in directing and steering the masses in a planned, predetermined direction toward a specific goal, an experiment in the scientific organization of labor. "The problem of mastering time is none other than the further deepening of the problem of the scientific organization of labor, especially that part of the science that relates to the utilization of time . . . utilization which passes into the control over time."[29] Using Fedorov's terminology without mentioning his name, Muravyov writes that the problem of time is the problem of human control over the world's "blind, inert forces."

Einstein's theory of relativity suggests that there are multiple time frames, which Muravyov calls simply "multiple times," each associated with a known system and therefore different and relative. At the same time, recent experiments in biological rejuvenation, specifically Bogdanov's experiments in rejuvenation through blood transfusion, suggested to Muravyov that in limited circumstances and within limited boundaries, time becomes reversible. Multiplicity and reversibility of time, then, become two qualities that lead, at least in principle, though not yet completely in daily reality, to human control over time. For time, he argues, is nothing but change and movement, and movement and change are functions of multiplicity (*mnozhestvo*), in the sense that in changing, one thing becomes another thing, and a unit becomes a series. "The key to overcoming time, thus, lies in our ability to manage multiple things."[30]

In terms of history and society, Muravyov's example of managing multiplicity is in the recognition of the potential importance of the human collective, and in the search for methods to organize and extend the collective to achieve rational goals for humanity. In Muravyov's view, to be effective, both subject and object, director and directed, must be multiple—thus the collective, and not the isolated great individual, is the effective shaper and director of humanity. Control over time will come, then, not from a lone inventor sitting in a time machine, as in the story by H. G. Wells, but from a collective—eventually all humanity—joined in a common task to rearrange the order of things in sets of multiples. Muravyov gives, as a simple laboratory example of controlling time, the procedure of combining hydrogen and oxygen to form water, then separating the elements back into hydrogen and oxygen, then combining them once more into water, which Muravyov describes as a limited form of time reversal and resurrection. The task of collective intelligence and effort is to deepen and broaden these limited forms of simple rearrangement of elements into the rearrangement of complex sets of multiples that would lead to the resurrection and rejuvenation of human beings.

Following the Pythagoreans, Muravyov holds that all things are, in essence, numbers, and that even human beings are basically multiple sets of numbers—extremely complex sets designated by extremely complex formulas, to be sure, but nevertheless numbers, quantifiable and therefore eventually replicable. Like everything else in the cosmos, we are multiples, and the many things that constitute us can be rearranged and reordered. So control over time means also control over ourselves, individually and collectively. For as individuals we exist only in relation to others, and therefore only as parts of a greater collective. And that collective exists as part of an even greater collective, and so on, in greater and greater collectives, until each individual is connected to every other individual, and to every thing living and not living, past, present, and future. In this way, each individual person is part of the entire cosmos and related to every particle in both the microcosm and the macrocosm.

Muravyov asks us to imagine two lines extending from our individuality: one extending back into what we think of as the past, and the other extending forward into what we consider the future. These two lines connect us to all that has been and will be, the difference being that what we consider the past is given to us and what we consider the future is what we shall make, the project whose goal now exists in our mind as something thought or imagined but which with effort we can attempt to realize and transform into a fact, a given, moving it on the imaginary line from the prospective future to the realized past. Our position, then, is the midpoint between the world of given facts and the world of projects. Another form of control over time, then, is the ability to choose what will and what will not move from what we consider to be the future into what we consider to be the past. As Muravyov argues: "In mathematics, one can change the sign to reverse the process. In philosophy such reversibility is possible for any sequence of events in which the cause would become the purpose or the purpose would become the cause. And if we can *ad libitum* install such a sequence, we thus control time."[31]

As his version of the idea of multiples times, Muravyov emphasizes two kinds of time: inner time, which represents freedom, and external time, which represents necessity. To a degree, we already control inner time. In a race, for example, a runner speaks of his or her time, different in duration but the same in space and goal or purpose as another runner's time. External time is clock and calendar time, independent of our goals and efforts. We can change, repeat, or reverse inner time, but not external time.

> But if we consider my own movements, which I may take and repeat, this is change under my control. If we made a clock and calendar to correspond to my movements, rather than to the sun's, it would not simply be gradual and unidirectional, but would have to include retreats, repetitions, and restarts. In other words, they would show instances of

the redirection and resumption of time. Also, if I completed a job twice as fast as another person, it would show that I made a time different from the one he made. I can write a word or not write—in this framework I have the power, but the power I have is only relative, because I am isolating the movement from the world of determinism, which governs it.[32]

Again, this is a partial, limited form of control over time, and the task of the collective is to extend and deepen this limited control to a scope much greater and more significant, eventually to control over time throughout the cosmos.

Consciousness is the key: if we take a system of entirely unconscious elements, time and motion are wholly necessary and determined. This is blind action and change subject entirely to external laws. This is like a subject in a dictatorship. Everything becomes different when consciousness is present. Here control over time is possible. Collective consciousness, obtained when consensus is present in the system, is the guide that must shape and direct the blind force of necessity, overcoming both time and death. In Fedorov, this guidance was to be provided by a task force of the learned. In Muravyov, Councils (Soviets) of scientists and scholars are to be the guiding force for the common task in science; Arts Councils and Economic Councils are to lead the tasks for other systems. A Supreme Council is to be the Council of Councils, the Soviet of Soviets. The proper task for scientists is the creation of a genetically new humanity; for artists the creation of works that will inspire the collectives to pursue their tasks energetically; and for economists the task is to create a new organization of labor. For Muravyov, medieval European art serves as an example of a movement in which all architecture, literature, music, and visual creation were united in service to a single worldview and a single task of salvation. What is needed is not a regression to that worldview but similar unity, intensity, and energy directed toward a new worldview appropriate to our epoch with its emphasis on collective identity and action. Medieval art projected a symbolic victory—the new art must project and embody a real victory over time and death.

Mystics and spiritual visionaries of all ages have envisioned a unity between man and the cosmos, but until now, Muravyov observes, that unity has been merely symbolic, transitory, and usually attained by individual spiritual effort, such as prayer and meditation. But individual victories are illusory. "The goal of unity with the cosmos, which a dreaming mind thinks to attain by means of direct individual association with the all-one, which is supposed to provide some kind of eternal existence, is in fact attained by other means, through collective historical action."[33] Time can be overcome only by regulating it, that is, only within time, in the historical process of collective action. In this action there is created that which the dreaming meditator dreams of.

Muravyov, like other Russian thinkers with a totalitarian cast of mind, believes that the best society, like the best bus tour, is the one most totally organized, the one with the least possibility of accidental discovery or spontaneous development. Our goal should be the total organization of culture, with carefully planned goals to fulfill and carefully devised incentives to ensure that the goals are realized. Organization of culture begins with control of knowledge, which for Muravyov, as for many Russian thinkers, is of much higher priority than freedom of enquiry. Philosophy should be theory realizing itself in activity. Consciousness means primarily "to be conscious that every present action is connected to every past and future action, mine and everyone's—if everyone acted with that consciousness, the common task and overcoming of time would be possible."[34] Muravyov cites the American pragmatist philosophers John Dewey and William James as sources for his ideas on time, but the great difference is that the pragmatists, especially James, emphasize the individual variations in what "works"—i.e., it is acceptable that what works for me may not work for you—whereas for Muravyov, and Russians in general, what "works" must work for all.

Individual creativity is not a positive goal for Muravyov's ideal society. He submits that art and culture today are not truly free, but are representative of a worldview dictated by commercial and other powerful interests. According to Muravyov, today's art is degenerate and needs to be reborn. Originality is an illusion—one person or one group rearranges given materials to accord with his or her personal interests or even character defects, and if that rearrangement is particularly attractive or well promoted and therefore commercially successful, everyone else follows. Instead of being directed by commerce and random personal preferences and disorders, Muravyov argues, culture should be collectively organized to bring about a desired collective result, namely, the transformation of humanity, the control over time, and the defeat of death. Muravyov takes the Masonic, Rosicrucian view that art and architecture should build human character as well as construct images and edifices. He envisions a future architecture represented by new versions of ziggurats, pyramids, onion domes, and New York–style skyscrapers with huge antennas beaming energy outward toward, and receiving it inward from, the cosmos.[35]

An important part of control over time is control over the process of human reproduction.

> Genetics has as its main goal to create the most perfect of creatures known to us—people. . . . Besides the general fact of creation, the birth of people in this age from mating of the two sexes, through a woman, is a fact unimportant, casual and temporary; there was a time in the history of life when our ancestors—some primitive animals or plants— were produced by direct division. There will be a time when perhaps the birth process will be streamlined and moved to the laboratory.

> In time, people will create not merely things but living things, and not merely living but conscious and rational things. We must create a population of su-permen, "not in the sense of Nietzsche's 'Blond Beast,' but in the sense of a future perfect and powerful creature, with a cosmic perspective and cosmic power. . . . The creation of a human being is a real overcoming of time in the sense of confirming the constancy of individuality against the corrosive force of time."[36]

Like Fedorov, Muravyov belongs to the very long and broad tradition of Russian thought that places the interests of the collective above the interests of the individual, or that defines the individual's interest as realizable only through the collective. What he calls "cosmocratic government" has as its task to mold humans psychologically and socially—as science molds them geneti-cally. Cosmocracy should create a single all-human, all-world culture, in which people would not be chaotically at liberty to pursue their own egotis-tical ends but would all be part of a single task. Industry presently creates objects not for overcoming time but for passing time. People now consider not how to overcome time and eternalize life but how to kill time, how to spend the time remaining until the hour of death. This is the basis of all pre-sent culture. The synthesis of the person (*litso*) and the collective (*kollektiv*) in Muravyov is "instrumentality," in which the individual owns his own tools and does his own work, but as an instrument of a broader, higher, all-human cause. "I" can be free and fulfilled only as part of the greater "we." (For the antithesis within a Russian context, see Dostoevsky's *Notes from Underground* or Zamiatin's anti-utopian novel *We.*) But Muravyov, as a twentieth-century thinker writing in times of revolution and civil war, goes beyond Fedorov, to say that in the event of recalcitrance or opposition, coercion is in order. He writes that agreement is always and everywhere considered to be useful, beau-tiful, and good, while discord, or strife (*rozn'*) is held to be ugly, bad, even evil. Discord and only discord stands as a possible obstacle to control over time. For control to happen, it must be total, and to be total everyone must partic-ipate. So what is to be done with those who refuse to participate?

In the end, the only obstacle to control over time is strife, manifested in unenlightened beings by hostile separation, for enlightened beings as confusion of their efforts, and sometimes open mutual struggle. In reality, no one is either wholly enlightened or unenlightened, but mixed, so those who are more conscious of their being part of multiplicity (collective consciousness) should be active and lead those less conscious. . . . The neutralization of the malevolent activity of strife, salvation from the annihilating flow of certain elements, the partial victory over time . . . is attained by the submission of the blind elements to the higher ones, by means of a dictatorship of the latter. . . . Ideally, but only with all participating in the common task, agreement would be total and voluntary. But unconscious strife impedes the common task; therefore what can be accomplished with the help of the unenlightened is very limited. The task is to transform the unenlightened into the enlightened. Coercion may be used against those who create obstacles to the common task.[37]

So here we have the unintended philosophical link between Fedorov's "common task" and the coercive policies conducted in Soviet times, which theoretically were for the good of all but in practice meant the liquidation or death by deprivation of millions of people, including Muravyov.

In a posthumously published autobiographical sketch (included in a 1998 reprint of *Ovladenie vremenem*), Muravyov writes that he had passed through stages of interest in religion, religious heresies, Pythagoreanism, Neoplatonism, Freemasonry, Theosophy, and the ideas of the Illuminati before finding his real calling: working through Soviet agencies for the betterment of the people. Despite this apparently sincere declaration, and despite (or perhaps because of) his close relationship with Trotsky, he was arrested as an enemy of the people in 1929, and sent to work in a meteorological station in the far north, where he died of typhus in 1931 or 1932.

## Vasily Nikolaevich Chekrygin (1897–1922)

As we noted in our look at Prometheanism, many twentieth-century Russian artists and writers, major and minor, worked Fedorovian or Cosmist themes into their compositions. Among prominent visual artists Kazimir Malevich, Wassily Kandinsky, and Pavel Filonov; in music Alexander Scriabin; and in literature Alexander Blok, Andrei Biely, Vladimir Mayakovsky, Sergei Esenin,

Anna Akhmatova, Marina Tsvetaeva, Andrei Platonov, Nikolai Zabolotsky, and Boris Pasternak have all exhibited, to one degree or another, Fedorovian and Cosmist concerns.[38] But the figure in all the arts whose works most clearly reflect Fedorovian and Cosmist themes is the now relatively obscure visual artist Vasily Chekrygin. All the others listed above can be—and have been— understood and appreciated on grounds independent of any reference to Fedorov and Cosmism. But not Chekrygin. Knowledge of Fedorov and the Cosmists may add to our understanding of all the others, but without knowledge of Fedorov and the Cosmists, Chekrygin cannot be understood at all.

Chekrygin, who either fell or threw himself under a train at age twenty-five, was considered to be one of the brightest and most promising of the many talented Russian artists who came of age during the years of revolution. At age thirteen he performed "brilliantly," according to one commentator, on the examination for the Academy of Painting, Sculpture, and Architecture, where he became a Levitan fellow.[39] One of his fellow student artists at the academy was the poet Vladimir Mayakovsky, and at age sixteen Chekrygin was chosen to illustrate *I (Ia)*, Mayakovsky's first book of poems. Like the English Romantic poet-artist William Blake, Chekrygin interwove the hand-written texts and illustrations into a unique lithographic synthesis of verbal and visual art. An early representative of the Russian avant-garde, both as a theorist and as a practicing artist, Chekrygin became acquainted with Fedorov's teachings around 1920, an influence that gradually changed the focus and direction of his art. No longer sharing his Futurist friends' desire to "heave overboard from the ship of modernity" the great works of the past, Chekrygin "turned his gaze toward the past, studied Egyptian art, antiquity, the Renaissance, and Old Russian icons, and concluded that it was necessary to strengthen ties with traditions of the past and make an attentive study of old art."[40] He turned from earlier cubist, semiabstract, and nonrepresentational creations to heroic, semirealistic images from the past and present: the seventeenth-century Cossack rebel Stenka Razin, figures from more recent uprisings, scenes from the Bolshevik Revolution, all elevated to superhuman scale, icons for transformation to a new world. Fully developed, his new Cosmist aesthetic led him to undertake, as his intended masterpiece, a project of frescoes intended for a proposed future equivalent of the Sistine Chapel—a Cathedral of the Museum of Resurrecting—illustrating the actual resurrecting of the dead and the flight of the newly resurrected bodies upward toward their new abodes in the cosmos.

With Pavel Florensky, the poet Velimir Khlebnikov, and others, Chekrygin took a leading role in the Makovets movement, a union of spiritually but

also futuristically inclined artists and thinkers, named for the hill upon which
Saint Sergius laid the foundations for the Holy Trinity Monastery. It was
through Makovets and especially through his discussions and sometimes dis-
agreements there with Florensky[41] that Chekrygin confirmed his views on the
purpose of art. Like the Biocosmists, Chekrygin advocated an art that would
transform man and the world, but unlike the Biocosmists, who held that no
god was necessary for the transformation, Chekrygin, now a devout if not
traditionally orthodox believer, saw this transformation as a task for a new,
active Christianity. With Florensky, he understood the Divine Liturgy, with
its flickering lights, aromas of incense, colors of icons and costumes, sculptures, and poetic solo and choral musical cadences within curved walls and
under curved domes, to be a synthesis of all the arts, greater than anything
conceived by Wagner, Nietzsche, or Scriabin. But where Florensky believed
that the liturgy as traditionally performed in the Orthodox Church represented that synthesis, Chekrygin argued for the more Fedorovian idea of liturgy outside the walls of the church (*vnekhramovaia liturgiia*). And like
Fedorov, by liturgy outside the walls of the church, Chekrygin meant the literal, physical reconstruction of man and the restoration of life to the dead. As
within the church the liturgy celebrates the mystical transformation of bread
and wine into the body and blood of Christ, so outside the church walls the
liturgy should begin the real transformation of the dust of ancestors into
living bodies. For Chekrygin, as for Fedorov, the simple belief that the dead
go to heaven is reinterpreted to mean that the resurrected ancestors will go
out into space to populate, and "inspirit," the currently uninhabited, soulless
regions of the universe.

For Chekrygin, art should not merely represent life in the world but
should become the creative means to save the world. With Fedorov, he
believes that while intellectually, abstractly, we may recognize that we live
in a Copernican universe in which the earth orbits the sun, emotionally and
in every other way we still live in a Ptolemaic universe in which the sun
circles the earth every day—and art must guide our emotional as well as
intellectual transition into the Copernican worldview. "All art of the Ptolemaic worldview, i.e., contemplative—cubism, suprematism, naturalism,
and Tatlinism—is one and the same unnecessary creation of an illusion (a
likeness of what is being lived and what has been lived). Genuine art does
not submit to the law of the fall of bodies, gravitation, it is not doomed to
death and destruction. Genuine art saves the falling world from death,
builds it."[42] The highest creation, the greatest product of all art, is humanity
itself.

Man is the synthesis of the truest living arts, but man is imperfect, needs support, and is condemned to death. *Man is a museum* (not only of natural history), for in that case he would be passive and dead, but instead he is an active agent, he is master of reason, nature's reason is in him (according to the researches of the positivists), in accordance with the law of association, memory. *What is subjectively remembrance will objectively become the activity of resurrecting*, what is subjectively oblivion *objectively is death*; what is subjectively the preservation of connections (association) objectively is *consciousness of kinship*.[43]

Chekrygin's fullest statement of his Cosmist worldview in literary form is a longish prose poem, "On the Cathedral of the Museum of Resurrecting," written in rhythmical cadences, reminiscent of Ecclesiastes and the Psalms. It begins: "I, who have lived in pain and trouble, write this book, and believe that the days will come when its lofty plan will become the task of man."[44] After several sections, in which he presents images of the chaos and ruin prevalent throughout the history of the world, he announces "The Uprising" (*Vosstanie*): "Your body is of stars. In infinity a brightly burning star once broke out of its inert course and moved toward a beckoning star, and on its loving path scattered its fiery seeds and, still cherishing, fled, toward perfection, but with the death of the stars, with universal discord, with the dying of the world, there came into being—you."[45] The newly created being is not an animal, not subject to nature only, but a rational being who assumes an upright posture, the Fedorovian triumph of the vertical over the horizontal, the first step toward control over nature and eventual victory over death. In poetic prose, Chekrygin then gradually takes his reader step by step through the Fedorovian tasks of "Transformation of the World (Regulation of the Cosmic Process)," "Resurrecting the Dead Fathers (Eucharist Beyond the Church Walls)," and "Ascension and Construction (Copernican Architecture)." He ends with a prayer that goes a small step beyond Fedorov, specifically including mothers and daughters in the resurrecting process along with the fathers and sons.

At his death, Chekrygin left some 1,500 works, many of them charcoal sketches toward his grand, unfinished project of frescoes for the never-begun Cathedral of the Museum of Resurrecting. The sketches are of figures and scenes from both the present falling world and the projected world of the resurrection: mostly nude prodigal sons and prodigal daughters feasting over the graves of their ancestors, scenes from the world of empty pleasure, discord, and death, then shadowy figures, both male and female, with confused and sometimes frightened expressions, being caught up in the whirlwind of revolution and resurrection. The figures at the bottom of the whirlwinds, those just beginning to be resurrected, are heavier, fleshier, and sometimes disfigured, while those higher up are lighter and more nearly transparent.

Chekrygin, then, attempted to devote his artistic gift to visualizing the actual Fedorovian process of resurrecting the ancestors and the Cosmist vision of resettling them in other parts of the universe. He attempts at least an artistic solution to such problems as how the bodies will look, and how they will differ from earthly bodies. But as both Fedorov and Chekrygin repeated time and again, projection by the aesthetic imagination, while a necessary first step, is precisely that—just a first step. To go beyond that first step, science must be joined to spirituality and art. In the next chapter, as we look at Cosmism in post-Soviet Russia, we shall see that some scientists have indeed gone beyond those first steps.

# Cosmism and Its Offshoots Today

DURING THE SOVIET period, as we have seen, the major religious Cosmists either worked in exile, such as Berdyaev and Bulgakov, or were restricted, suppressed, and eventually liquidated, as were Florensky, Gorsky, Setnitsky, and Muravyov. The scientific Cosmists—Tsiolkovsky, Vernadsky, Chizhevsky, and Kuprevich—were honored for their work in fields that did not contradict the tenets of dialectical materialism, but were attacked in official publications for their Cosmist speculations, which went beyond orthodox materialism, and which either had to be kept "in the drawer," expressed in private communications, or circulated through unofficial channels. With the lessening and eventual end of Soviet restrictions in the 1980s, hidden works from earlier periods began to come out, and along with other formerly suppressed activities and forms of expression, new waves of Cosmist research and speculation began to flourish.

## The N. F. Fedorov Museum-Library

The central institution for the study and propagation of Russian Cosmism today is the N. F. Fedorov Museum-Library housed in the Central Children's Library on Profsoiuznaia Street in Moscow. The idea for a special museum devoted to Fedorov and his intellectual heirs developed through a seminar on Fedorov in the 1980s directed by the philosopher and literary scholar Svetlana Semenova, who has been writing about Fedorov's ideas since the 1970s. Her cautious, early studies emphasized Fedorov's faith in advanced science and technology, and downplayed the religious and political sides of his thought. In 1982 she edited the first official Soviet edition of Fedorov's writings, a one-volume selection of his major essays, revealing the entire range of his thought. Biographical and analytical works followed—all of which generated controversies, polemics, denunciations, and, at the same time, a growing respect for Fedorov's contribution to Russian intellectual history, his stature as a "native," "fatherland" (*otechestvennyi*) thinker. In 1988 Semenova and others convened the first "Fedorovian Readings" (*Fedorovskie chteniia*), a now more or less annual conference for the presentation of papers on Fedorov and related topics by Russian and international scholars. In *The Common Task* (*Obshchee delo*), the 1990 publication of selected papers from that first conference, the lead papers were grouped under the heading "Fedorov's Teaching and Russian Cosmism," thus establishing a definitive connection between the man and the movement. The next two collections of "Fedorovian Readings" were titled *Russkii Kosmizm* (Russian Cosmism) Parts 1 and 2, and contained articles on Cosmism in general as well as articles on Fedorov and other figures in the tendency. Since 1990, then, "Fedorovian Readings" could just as well be called "Cosmist Readings," since every collection has contained several articles on Cosmism, with or without reference to Fedorov.

The Fedorov Museum-Library itself was officially chartered in 1993, and has since been directed with unflagging devotion and energy by Semenova's daughter, Anastasia Gacheva. Together, Semonova and Gacheva have edited Fedorov's collected works in four volumes plus a supplement, including materials not published in the 1906–1913 edition, all illuminated by extensive notes and commentary. In addition, each has published important individual works on Fedorov and related thinkers and writers, and together they have edited two valuable collections of previously difficult-to-locate biographical materials, analyses, criticism, and documents under the title *N. F. Fedorov: Pro et Contra*. Among other activities of the Museum-Library, Gacheva and Semonova conduct frequent seminars, sponsor conferences, and organize many kinds of educational programs and publications related to Fedorov and the Cosmists. The Museum-Library has also created a very useful Web site through which weekly sponsored events are announced, and from which Fedorov's collected works and many other related texts and Cosmist materials can be downloaded free of charge.[1] The Museum-Library collaborates with filmmakers on videos, provides learning materials for schools, displays works of art, organizes celebrations of important anniversaries, and conducts excursions to sites in and around Moscow, reflecting a selfless, enthusiastic round-the-clock commitment on the part of Gacheva and Semonova to Fedorov's idea that in the "common task" the museum-library-temple-school-laboratory should be a center for restorative activity and not merely a repository for artifacts.

A major event in establishing Cosmism as a field for study was Gacheva and Semenova's previously cited 1993 publication, *Russkii kosmizm: Antologiia filosofskoi mysli* (Russian Cosmism: An anthology of philosophical thought), the collection that defined who the Cosmists were and what shared themes made them a movement. Before the anthology, the religious thinkers Berdyaev, Bulgakov, and Florensky were not generally considered to belong to the same tendency of thought as the scientists Tsiolkovsky, Vernadsky, Chizhevsky, and others. But in their selection of texts, their introduction to the anthology, and their prefatory comments and notes on the individual thinkers, Gacheva and Semenova present a persuasive argument that despite differences, the shared theme of "active evolution" allows these seventeen thinkers[2] to be considered together as participants in a common intellectual tendency, the major constituents of the Cosmist canon. Those in the group who lived into the twentieth century shared at least an initial interest in Fedorov's "project" and endorsed at least the activist spirit of his "common task." And except for the two most devoted Fedorovians, Gorsky and Setnitsky, all the others significantly departed from, or at least modified, Fedorov's main ideas. As creative thinkers, they were stimulated and challenged by Fedorov and took what they could from him, and then each went off in his own direction to do the work that defined him as an original thinker. The differences between Fedorov and his successors are at least as interesting and important as the similarities. And the selections of works chosen by Gacheva and Semenova allow readers to see both what the other Cosmist thinkers shared with Fedorov and where they departed.

By now, hundreds of academic papers have been published in the "Fedorovian Readings" series, analyzing Cosmist and Fedorovian ideas both in themselves and in their relation to other Russian and international philosophical tendencies. A few titles from these conferences will give an idea of the range and breadth of recent scholarship: "Russian Cosmism and the Restoration of Humanistic Traditions in Science and Society," "Cosmism as a Paradigm of the Noospheric-Ecological View and the New Political Thinking," "The Cosmization of Scientific-Technological Progress and the New Political Thinking," "The Principle of Autotrophy for Humanity and Cosmic Ecology," "Toward a Peaceful Development of the Cosmos," "A Noospheric Assessment of Global Problems," "On the Cosmological Understanding of the Nature of Man in Ancient Greece and its Significance for Our Time," "The Search for Extraterrestrial Civilizations: Gnoseological Difficulties," "The Autoevolution of Homo Sapiens: Contemporary Aspects of the Hypothesis," "Cosmic Psychology," "From Egocentrism to a Systemic Worldview," "The Cosmization of Worldview as a Theoretical Step Toward the Noosphere," "When Marxist Matteriocracy Turns Into Psychocracy," "Globalization and the Noosphere."

These and other similar papers published after conferences are merely the tip of the iceberg. Panels, round tables, commemorations, video presentations, and displays supplement the individual papers delivered. Participants include academics in the humanities, natural sciences, and social sciences from Russian and international institutes and universities, independent scholars, writers, artists, journalists, and government officials—and at the sessions I have attended, all the seats have usually been filled. Cosponsors with the Fedorov Museum-Library are the Russian National Library (where Fedorov worked when it was the Rumiantsev Museum), the Russian Academy of Sciences, the Gorky Institute of World Literature, and the Philosophy Department of the University of Moscow. The proceedings of these conferences are considered important enough to have been reported in major Russian newspapers and journals and broadcast on television—all indicating the degree to which Fedorov and the Cosmists have been accepted into the historical mainstream of Russian intellectual culture.

In addition to sponsoring scholarly conferences and publications for intellectuals, the Fedorov Museum-Library works to integrate Fedorovian and Cosmist ideas into the general popular culture of post-Soviet Russia. Following the Russian tradition of celebrating many anniversaries and holidays, whether on the church, cultural, or political calendar, the Fedorov Museum-Library lets no date relevant to Cosmism pass without an announcement on the Web site, an interview in the media, or some kind of event open to the public. The Fedorov Web site's announcements for April 2011 list Berdyaev's memorial, Vernadsky's birthday, the beginning of Galileo's trial, the granting of a charter for the Russian Museum, Astronomy Day, the inauguration of Runet (the Russian internet system), the restoration of Moscow as the national capital, international Writer's Day—all dates of special significance, but of secondary importance to the two major Cosmist celebrations of the month: Easter and the fiftieth anniversary of Yuri Gagarin's pioneering flight into the cosmos. In Cosmist terms, these two celebrations are related: spiritual and scientific commemorations of human victory over gravity and death.

In addition to Semenova and Gacheva, other people regularly associated with the Fedorov Museum-Library carry on their own independent Cosmist projects. Independent researcher Valery Borisov, for example, has tracked down every house, apartment, or closet that Fedorov occupied during his nearly forty years in Moscow, and will gladly conduct visitors to as many of these places as they wish to see. Borisov, who in his rust-colored leather jacket, Australian outback hat, and bare-chested open shirt even (or especially) in freezing winter blasts, stands out in any Moscow crowd, has defied all bureaucratic, hooliganistic, and other organized and unorganized opposition, to create a unique Cosmist garden in a courtyard of the large Moscow housing block where he lives. Not only flowers but leaves, limbs, rocks, and other natural objects are arranged symbolically to represent microcosmic-macrocosmic harmony and the human ability to transform an ugly patch of the urban environment into a small paradise. Videos, newspapers, and magazines have publicized Valery's garden, perhaps encouraging others to undertake similar projects. And other creative minds and hands have been at work. As we have noted, Fedorov never allowed himself to be photographed or painted during his lifetime, but his portrait is now often seen in various illustrations, plaques, sculptures, magazines, and newspapers, and even on the lapel pins (*znachki*) that Russians of all ages like to wear. Working together, then, and through others, Semenova and Gacheva have campaigned to win both academic and popular respect for Fedorov and the Cosmists, and to make the Fedorov Museum-Library an active center for the "common task" in Moscow.

## *The Tsiolkovsky Museum and Chizhevsky Center*

Beyond Moscow, Cosmist centers in St. Petersburg, Voronezh, Kiev, Astana, and elsewhere carry on similar activities on a smaller scale, but the center outside Moscow that seems most active is the Konstantin E. Tsiolkovsky Museum for the History of Cosmonautics and the adjoining A. L. Chizhevsky Center in the small city of Kaluga. Annual conferences there, like the ones in Moscow, touch on every aspect of Cosmism, but with an emphasis on Cosmism in relation to Tsiolkovsky and cosmonautics rather than Fedorov and the task of resurrecting the ancestors. Typically conferences focus on such topics as the study of Tsiolkovsky's scientific heritage, problems of rocketry and space technology, space flight mechanics, problems of space medicine, biology in aviation and aeronautics, Tsiolkovsky and philosophical problems of space exploration, Tsiolkovsky and scientific forecasting, Tsiolkovsky and the problems of space industry, Tsiolkovsky and the problems of cosmonaut's activity, Tsiolkovsky and the problems of education.[3] While the Tsiolkovsky Museum conferences emphasize cosmonautics, Tsiolkovsky's great-grandson Sergei Samburov, who also lives in Kaluga, is the individual now most responsible for the propagation of Tsiolkovsky's philosophical and Cosmist speculations. It is thanks to Samburov's efforts that works unpublished during Tsiolkovsky's lifetime are now coming to light and we can begin to see what a strange and distant future the "Kaluga eccentric" envisioned. Tsiolkovsky, along with Vernadsky, Chizhevsky, and Kuprevich, is still considered to have been a major figure in what is now termed "classical" scientific Cosmism. We shall now turn to the "new" scientific Cosmism that has emerged since the end of the Soviet period.

## ISRICA—Institute for Scientific Research in Cosmic Anthropoecology

Since the early 1990s, in Novosibirsk, Siberia, under the aegis of the Russian Academy of Sciences, the Institute for Scientific Research in Cosmic Anthropoecology (ISRICA) has been conducting experiments on esoteric aspects of human perception of time and space, specifically investigating telepathic communications not only between human subjects but also between human subjects and inanimate objects and between human subjects on earth and unidentified forces in the cosmos. Alexander Trofimov, the current director, and Vlail Kaznacheev, the senior scientist, base their experiments in part on Vernadsky's theory of the noosphere, but mainly on research conducted during the Soviet period by the brilliant but extremely controversial astrophysicist Nikolai Kozyrev.[4]

Both as a very promising young scientist who published his first paper at age seventeen and as an elder, honored statesman of Soviet science, Kozyrev made important discoveries about the properties of the moon, Venus, and other bodies in our solar system. He won international medals and awards, and an asteroid and moon crater are named for him. In 1936, however, denounced by a disgruntled graduate assistant, Kozyrev was arrested and sentenced to ten years in the gulag for counterrevolutionary activity. During his imprisonment, he apparently associated with inmates who were Siberian shamans, and he began to see connections between his work as a scientist and their spiritual activities. Observing the night sky from the prison camp in remote Siberia, he sensed that the stars were alive and communicating among themselves and—somehow—also communicating with him.

On his release from prison in 1946, Kozyrev's research took new directions, and his investigations into the nature of time and causality, enormously controversial then, have provided theoretical bases for today's experiments at ISRICA. Time, according to Kozyrev's theory, is a spiraling movement of energy, "torsion waves," pervasive throughout the cosmos. This spiraling energy manifests itself in phenomena as disparate as the spiral of the nautilus shell and the location of the heart on the left side of the human body. Kozyrev's theory reinstates the aether as a fluid medium of energy underlying everything in the universe—a western scientific equivalent of chi, *prana*, *akasha*, and other concepts borrowed by Western esotericists from non-Western sources. Kozyrev and the ISRICA scientists posit that in the remote past all living entities in the cosmos shared, through the aether, a common consciousness and were in constant telepathic communication regardless of physical location or distance. In today's world, only certain mystics and shamans retain this ability to communicate telepathically at will, but the potential exists for all humans to recover this lost ability.[5]

In ISRICA experiments, Kaznacheev and Trofimov have discovered that the weaker the surrounding magnetic field, the stronger the sense of oneness with the cosmos and the greater the likelihood of telepathic communication. With this in mind, they have devised the "Kozyrev Mirror," a lined cylinder in which a resting or meditating subject can experience something like a shamanic cosmic consciousness and can perhaps communicate telepathically not only with other remote human subjects but also with seemingly inanimate objects, including distant planets and stars. In addition to expanding human consciousness, the Kozyrev Mirror has been used to treat physical and psychological disorders and to modify the chemical composition of animate and inanimate objects. Susan Richards, a British writer who participated in a Kozyrev Mirror session, gives a vivid account of her experience:

> What happened next takes me to the very edge of the sayable. After lying in the dark for a while, my heart started leaping about like a cricket in a box. Then everything went calm and the images began. A dark column seemed to rise out of my forehead. I found myself standing in a deep, dark canyon. This canyon came and went, alternating with a spiral. When that faded away, a brightly colored fairground carousel appeared. There were people riding the whirling wooden trains, cars, and animals. It was a merry scene, at least to start with. But even as I watched, something started going wrong. The movement of the carousel became chaotic, alarming. The painted wooden animals and engines were slipping. The center was not holding; it was falling apart.
>
> Then this sequence faded and I found myself back at the bottom of that great dark spiral, which in turn evolved back into a crevasse. Black rocks rose up on either side and there was light streaming down on me. I basked in that light. This, this I wanted never to end. But eventually this image faded, too. I lay not knowing where my body finished and the world outside began. Everything around me seemed to be spun out of light. The rhythm of my breathing seemed to have changed. It was as if I was learning to breathe for the first time, learning to support this lightness of being through the way I breathed.[6]

Without smoking, swallowing, injecting, or otherwise ingesting any kind of chemical substance, Susan Richards has described the fluidity of boundaries, the oneness with surroundings, and the waves of warm light that characterize many classic accounts, from Samuel Taylor Coleridge to Aldous Huxley and Carlos Castaneda, of experience—both benign and scary—with hallucinogenic drugs. Special in her account, though, is the sense of spirals, which would seem to indicate a genuine connection between the subject's experience of being whirled by something and Kozyrev's theory of what it is we are whirled by. Susan Richards seems to have been a very sensitive subject, as well as a writer exceptionally able to find words and images to articulate her experiences at "the very edge of the sayable." Others who have tried the same experiment, like the filmmaker George Carey,[7] have either felt nothing or had a mostly negative or incommunicable experience. But just as Cosmism in Kaluga now stands for research into the exploration of outer space, Cosmism in ISRICA emphasizes the exploration of inner space. Like the Kaluga Cosmists Tsiolkovsky and Chizhevsky, the ISRICA Cosmists believe that waves of energy from distant stars created life on earth. But ISRICA's research suggests that we do not have to leave our planet, or even Siberia, to experience life and communicate with living entities throughout the cosmos.

## Lev Nikolaevich Gumilev (1912–1992) and Neo-Eurasianism

Although himself neither a Fedorovian nor a Cosmist, Lev Gumilev[8] was a polymath thinker whose works reflect some of Fedorov's ideas and are frequently cited by recent Cosmist thinkers and scholars. The only son of two of the greatest Russian poets of the twentieth century, Nikolai Gumilev and Anna Akhmatova, Lev Gumilev was a writer of profound erudition and equally profound creativity and imagination. Too broad in his interests and expertise to be pigeonholed into a single academic category, Gumilev wrote as a general humanist whose major investigations were into ethnic identity, mass human migration, and the rise and fall of the civilizations, hordes, and tribes of the Eurasian continent. Like other prominent unorthodox thinkers of the period, he spent his middle years, 1938–1956, in one of Stalin's concentration camps—the first half of his sentence, he would later say, for being the son of his father, and the second half for being the son of his mother, both major dissident intellectuals, the father executed and the mother persecuted for anti-Soviet behavior.

After release from prison, Gumilev worked at the Hermitage and took special interest in the great museum's collections of Scythian and Central Asian artifacts. He took part in archeological expeditions to the Caucasus and the Central Asian steppes, learned the languages of various Mongol and Turkic peoples of the steppe regions, and wrote his first books on nomadic migrations, the quest for the imaginary kingdom of Prester John, the ancient Turks, and the steppe as a major factor in Russian history. Whether consciously or unconsciously, Gumilev's ideas of the importance of the steppe and Central Asia to Russian culture and history reflect Fedorov's ideas about Russia's virtues as a land-cultivating Eurasian continental power in opposition to the insular and peninsular land-seeking powers in history, such as Greece and Rome in ancient times and Britain and Japan in the present. In Fedorov, geography is a major factor in ethnic and national character; Gumilev develops these ideas further, presenting the migrations of Central Asian peoples as the main event in both European and Asian history. Geography—in Eurasia, the steppe—is a dominant factor in the emergence of any ethnos or people.

To explain the rise and fall of tribes, kingdoms, and ethnic groups, Gumilev introduces the concept of "passionarity," the intensity of a given group's ethnic identity and vitality, the energy in its will to power. Like some of the Cosmists, Gumilev views passionarity as, in part, energy derived at least indirectly from solar and other extraterrestrial sources. For example, solar winds and rays influence the growth of grass in the steppe, and the abundance or insufficiency of grazing grass influences the stationary or migratory behavior patterns of the steppe peoples and contributes to the intensity of their identification with ethnic values and traditions, whether warlike or peaceful, nomadic or sedentary. In the modern world, Gumilev believed that Western Europe was low and sinking further in passionarity, while in the Turkic and Arab Muslim peoples passionarity was significantly higher and still rising. Russia's future as an international power lay not in emulating the Western European and Atlantic powers with their diminishing passionarity but instead in gathering and uniting the passionarity of the steppe peoples in the east.

Fedorov viewed Russian culture as a continuation of ancient Aryan Iran, a combination of Eastern and Western principles, struggling against a hostile natural environment, wary of Greco-Roman power to the west and Turan to the east. Similarly, Gumilev views Russia as an absorber and continuation of the great steppe powers of ancient Eurasia, different from and stronger than both Western Europe and eastern Asia. For Gumilev, the Mongol invasion by Genghis Khan was not a curse but a blessing for Russia, saving the entire Eurasian heartland from the aggressive clutches of the Catholic West, then represented by Poland and the Baltic Teutonic Knights. Under the khans, Russian Orthodox spirituality was tolerated and allowed to mature, whereas medieval Orthodox spirituality would have been crushed under the heels of the Teutonic Knights, and the Eurasian heartland would eventually have become simply an extended version of the European spiritual and political battleground of Catholics versus Protestants.

Gumilev's views have been a major influence on the neo-Eurasian cultural and political movements prominent since the breakup of the Soviet Union.[9] And although he seldom mentions Fedorov, Gumilev renews themes from the earlier "classical" Eurasian movement among émigré Russians in Berlin and Paris during the 1920s and 1930s, a movement which featured such thinkers as the philosopher Prince Nikolai Trubetskoy, the literary historian Prince D. S. Mirsky, the historian George Vernadsky, the political activist P. N. Savitsky, the Fedorovian K. Chkheidze, and Marina Tsvetaeva's husband, Sergei Efron. These Evraziitsi, as they called themselves, openly acknowledged their debt to Fedorov, debated in their journals whether Marx or Fedorov presented the better model for future Russian development, and concluded that Marx might offer the best plan for the twentieth century, but Fedorov would best serve the twenty-first century and beyond. Gumilev draws some of his ideas from these earlier Evraziitsi, but especially in his major work, *Ethnogenesis and the Biosphere of Earth*,[10] also draws upon some of the Cosmists, including Vernadsky's ideas of the biosphere and noosphere, and Chizhevsky's ideas of the influence of variations in waves of solar energy on human history. In recent times, Gumilev's theories have proved especially useful to Russian neonationalists, neo-Eurasianists and others with an anti-Western, anti-Atlanticist political bias,[11] the most prominent of whom is the ideologist Alexander Dugin—and, some might add, Vladimir Putin.

In addition to Gumilev, Fedorov too has been viewed as a source not only for Russian neonationalist thought but also for the renewed Russian admiration for Stalin. Edmund Griffiths, in a recent *Times Literary Supplement* essay, suggests that Alexander Prokhanov and other recent literary "patriots" have adopted a Gnostic worldview in which all outer, exoteric phenomena contain hidden esoteric significance, and—surprisingly—the esoteric core of Stalinism turns out to be Fedorovism. According to Prokhanov, "Communism is not an enormous patchwork quilt for all humanity to sleep under. It is not a machine that yields an infinite quantity of goods. It is not an 'honor board' with photographs of shock workers. It is the defeat of death. The whole pathos of Soviet futurology and Soviet technocratic thought was directed at creating an 'elixir of immortality'."[12]

As the early Fedorovians of the first decades of the twentieth century looked forward with hope, so Prokhanov and other neonationalist and post-Soviet Communist intellectuals today look back with nostalgia on the idea that Soviet rule meant the adoption of Fedorov's "common task." As Griffiths writes: "Part of the attraction of Prokhanov's esoteric Fyodorovism, undoubtedly, is that it preserves the orientation toward the 'radiant future' so characteristic of Soviet thinking."[13] For the neonationalists, the possibility of that "radiant future," the potential restoration of Eden, came crashing down in 1991. For them, as Putin has repeatedly stated, the demise of the Soviet Union was the greatest disaster of the twentieth century. Griffiths goes on to point out that, true to the Gnostic pattern, in every collapse of an Eden, a serpent is found to be involved. In current Russian neo-nationalist political theater, the Jews, the Chechens, and the Atlanticists are often cast as the serpent. Fedorov and the Cosmists (Florensky perhaps the exception) do not generally share current neonationalist tendencies toward anti-Semitism, but they do (except Solovyov) generally share the anti-Western, anti-Atlanticist views inherited from the Russian Slavophile tradition.

An interesting feature of Prokhanov's attempt to link Stalinism to Fedorovism is that it shows the degree to which Fedorovism is now accepted as a positive model for the "native" (*otechestvennaia*) tradition of Russian thought. Stalin may have ordered the murder of millions, but he is justified because secretly he was a Fedorovian. A thinker whose name could not be mentioned in public is now used to support the rehabilitation of the one who made his name unmentionable. But as we shall see next, this is not the only strange use to which the ideas of Fedorov and the Cosmists have recently been put.

## *The Hyperboreans*

Along with Gumilev, another prominent unorthodox scholar with at least some direct connection to the Cosmist movement is Valery Demin, a proponent of a Russian version of the "Arktos" theory, designating the Hyperborean extreme north as the original homeland of the Indo-Europeans, and perhaps all other peoples. Demin's 1997 Moscow University doctoral dissertation was titled "Philosophical Principles of Russian Cosmism," and he is the author of more than twenty books and one hundred shorter works, including essays in Cosmist collections, about the peoples, legends, history, and prehistory of the far north. He has conducted meteorological research and led archeological expeditions in the Russian arctic, and is a leading spokesman for the Hyperborean offshoot of today's Russian Cosmist movement.

Basing their theories on the writings of Herodotus, Pliny, Ptolemy, and other ancient authorities, and supported by modern research including Fedorov's speculations on the origins of civilization in the Pamir Mountains, and Bal Gangadhar Tilak's writings on the far northern origins of the Vedas,[14] Demin and the Hyperboreans argue that the arctic, which had a much milder climate some 40,000 years ago, was a kind of northern Shambhala, or perhaps a prototype for Plato's Atlantis; in any case, the original homeland of a happy, healthy people who lived far beyond present life spans.

In Fedorov's theory, the invisible Mount Meru, the universal axis of Indian mythology, rises above the North Pole, and the Pamir Mountains in Central Asia represent an earthly manifestation of that cosmic center. Fedorov found that in local legends, Adam's bones were said to be buried in the Pamirs, so the Pamirs stand for the grave of all humanity, the buried original ancestral dust in need of resurrection, a former paradise that is now an uninhabitable wasteland in need of restoration. For Fedorov, the Pamirs in history have been the earth's center of repulsion, from which the original Indo-Europeans and later the Mongol and other nomadic hordes fled, bringing death and destruction to their settled neighbors.[15]

Demin essentially changes the earthly manifestation of Mount Meru from Fedorov's Pamirs to Hyperborea, citing petroglyphs, fossil evidence, linguistic keys, shifts in polar magnetism, legends of unsetting suns and unrelieved darkness, and other data to argue that the original Indians, Aryans, Cretans, and other cultural forebears all migrated south from Hyperborea.[16] In Demin's version, the golden age, featured in the legends of nearly all peoples, actually took place in the arctic. A great cataclysm, possibly caused by abrupt changes in solar or stellar energy, best known to us as the Biblical flood, variants of which are also recorded in the legends of nearly all the world's peoples, drove Hyperborean survivors to settle elsewhere and to bring with them their history, symbols, skills, and language. Originally one people, one culture, and one language, the Hyperboreans over time split and dispersed into the many peoples, languages, and cultures we know today. The shared features of many peoples, religions, and cultures separated by significant distance—for example pyramids in Egypt, Mesoamerica, and perhaps in Bosnia—are relics from Hyperborea. For Demin and his followers, Russians and other Europeans should no longer think of themselves as "out of Africa" but "down from Hyperborea."

In recent years, at midsummer and on other astrologically significant occasions, groups of Russians who might be described as Hyperborean reenactors, have gathered for neo-pagan ceremonies in the far north—perhaps

Russian equivalents of the neodruidic ceremonies at Stonehenge. On one of the Web sites devoted to Hyperboreanism,[17] Demin attributes to the ancient Hyperboreans some thirty qualities which he deems positive, ranging from happy disposition to blond hair and vegetarian diet. The photos of the neo-Hyperboreans—mostly of radiant young women in diaphanous white gowns and with flowers in their hair—would suggest that the reenactors are carefully selected to illustrate every one of those thirty positive qualities. Like other Cosmists, the Hyperboreans look toward a restoration of a lost golden age: one people, one language, one culture, all good, all healthy, all youthful again and forever. As Demin's list of thirty qualities emphasizes, there were no evil, ugly, or unhealthy people in ancient Hyperborea, and presumably there will be no defective individuals or groups in the New Hyperborea to be created. In his vision of Hyperborea, past and future, Demin is content to project only the most positive images and does not attempt to explain how all that is negative in us and in the world will be eliminated.

## *Scientific Immortalism*

One of the most active branches of today's Russian Cosmist movement is scientific immortalism, which, with different personnel, different localities, and perhaps slightly different emphases, also operates as transhumanism, cryonicism, scientific anabiosis, and perhaps other names as well. Essentially, all these terms represent the search for a technological, physical, material solution to the problem of death, with little or no recognition of possible spiritual realities. Though they participate in Cosmist conferences, publish in Cosmist collections of papers, and often cite Fedorov, Tsiolkovsky, and Vernadsky as predecessors, Russian scientific immortalists generally have more in common with international movements of similar orientation than with the traditional Russian Cosmist mixture of mystery, technology, and spirituality. They participate in international symposia, sometimes teach or lecture abroad, and invite European and American colleagues to contribute to their colloquia and group publications. In their writings Russian scientific immortalists are as likely to cite the Swedish transhumanist Nick Bostrom or the American futurologist Ray Kurzweil as Fedorov or Vernadsky. Everything, in their view, even thoughts of love and memories of childhood, can ultimately be understood as matter and energy, chemical and electronic impulses and interchanges. Mind is nothing but operations of the physical brain. When our body dies, our life is over. Scientific immortalists would not endorse Walt Whitman's assertion that we are not contained between our hat and boots.

A major figure in this branch of Cosmism is Igor Vishev, who at age fourteen suffered a totally and permanently blinding chemical accident, but who with great courage and energy has engaged in a lifelong pursuit of learning, first as a student at Moscow State University and eventually as a professor of philosophy at the Chelyabinsk Polytechnic Institute. He has led a very active personal and professional life; is married, with two children and three grandchildren; enjoys skiing, skating, playing chess; travels to international scientific and philosophical conferences; and has authored the seminal works in the field he has named "*immortalogiia.*"[18]

Vishev writes that from the earliest known work of literature, the Sumerian epic of Gilgamesh, all human intellectual and spiritual history has essentially been a search for a means to attain real personal immortality. The history of views of immortality shows several gradual transitions: from religious pessimism to religious optimism, then to scientific pessimism, and from there to scientific optimism, leading now toward actual resolution of the problem of the possibility of attaining personal immortality.

His view of the state of the science is that in the second quarter of the twenty-first century, the fundamental theoretical problems of unlimited life extension will be solved, and in the second half of the century unlimited longevity will actually be achieved. He proposes that there are already some people alive today who will never die.

In his essay "From Postmortalism to Immortology and Homo Immortalis," Vishev writes:

> The radical prolongation of human life must pass, it would appear, through three stages: the gerontological, when the period of old age is prolonged; the juvenological, when the period of youth is prolonged; and the immortological, as a result of which practical human immortality will be achieved. The attitude taken in such researches should be scientifically based optimism, for amidst possibilities the pessimist will stubbornly seek out difficulty, whereas amidst difficulties the optimist persistently seeks and finds possibility.[19]

Like Fedorov and other Cosmists, then, Vishev suggests that a major step toward immortality must involve a redirection of attitude, from a general sense of "can't be done" to a confident "can do."

Another prominent immortalist today is Danila Medvedev, who—at least in filmed and televised interviews—is in no way lacking in "can do" confidence. He contends that since the breakup of the Soviet Union, Russian confidence in scientific solutions to environmental and other problems has drastically diminished. Fears of global warming, economic collapse, and nuclear and environmental disasters have led to a widespread Russian distrust of science and technology. The problem, Medvedev suggests, is one of education—Russians no longer study science as eagerly as they did in the Soviet period, and therefore Russians do not understand what science and technology can do for the world. But the new sciences of transhumanism and immortalism are a step in the right direction.

> Transhumanists readily accept radical changes, such as curing the aging problem, creating artificial intelligence or uploading the human consciousness into a computer. Their position results from a clear understanding of the opportunities that science and technology provide and from a willingness to reconsider philosophical and cultural norms in view of the changes in the environment.[20]

Education in the principles and goals of transhumanism, then, is the answer to Russia's problem of lack of confidence in science. Appearing youthful and fit, well dressed, and speaking in articulate, rapid fire, complete sentences in Russian or English, Medvedev shines in panel discussions and personally exudes the confidence in the future that he says his countrymen currently lack.

In "Mind Upgrade,"[21] a video presentation at a 2004 philosophical conference in Helsinki, Medvedev, then twenty-four, speaking in extremely articulate English, and using all the most recent technological terminology, outlines a plan for "cognitive enhancement" that will allow us to overcome our current human limitations and become not merely superhuman but transhuman. We cannot upgrade the world until we have upgraded ourselves. To get from A to B, he says, we must learn to view our brains as software and ourselves as programmers, redesigning our cognitive circuits to eliminate errors or cognitive biases caused by our obsolete apparatus. Eventually, as our brain functions become more nearly mechanical and therefore perfect (!), we will be able to program our futures for practical self-directed evolution. Someday, perhaps centuries from now, we will be able to upload all our thoughts, memories, and sensations into advanced versions of today's microchips. Immortality will be endless preservation in a cosmic data bank. Man and machine will be one with the cosmos.

As a blogger, Medvedev keeps readers informed of his latest interests and inspirations. In a blog entry from May 2007, he writes that if or when he attains superintelligence,

> there is no single human value that I expect to keep. Books are of no use to superintelligence. Love and sex are something many of us already want to get rid of, a dark vestige of our evolutionary past. Games are inferior forms of Monte-Carlo simulations and evolutionary algorithms. Work will no longer be needed, thought alone would accomplish everything I might ever need. And the food I would need would be measured in ergs, not in calories.[22]

Here as elsewhere, the point of view Medvedev writes from would seem to be that of one who has already evolved beyond normal humanity but who is still willing to help and encourage those of us who have not gotten that far. In the future that Medvedev foresees, the difference between man and machine will be insignificant, but in reading and listening to him, one may get the clear impression that the more we are silicon and the less we are carbon, the more intelligent and therefore virtuous Medvedev believes we will be.

As director of a cryonics laboratory, Medvedev is in the business of freezing brains and even entire heads of people who wish to become immortal when adequate technology becomes available. In a 2011 documentary, "Knocking on Heaven's Door,"[23] aired as part of BBC 4's *Storyville* series, the British filmmaker George Carey and his producer Teresa Chervas visited Medvedev's laboratory and interviewed him about his work. Most striking about this sequence in the video is the location and appearance of the laboratory. This most futuristic of technologies was being practiced not in a shiny steel and glass science tower but in something that looked like a small farm chicken house, with a muddy unpaved pathway, various pieces of metal junk strewn here and there, and a preservation chamber that looked like a frosty ice cream vat, out of which, when opened, a foggy greenish cloud emerged. The contrast between the rhetoric, equally rapid, fluent, and brimming in confidence, whether in English or in Russian, about the inevitable future of transhuman immortality, and the ramshackle setting in which that rhetoric was uttered was enormous, but at the same time so characteristic of Russia, where world-shaking ideas have often stood out so starkly from their backgrounds: great novels from prison camps, rocket science from wooden huts, a vision of Holy Sophia from a desk in the reading room of the British Museum, cosmic projects from a humpback trunk doubling as a thinker's bed.

# Conclusions about the Russian Cosmists

*Magic was not the "science" of the past. It is the science of the future.*
—COLIN WILSON, *The Occult: A History*

One of Fedorov's favorite Bible passages was: "Truly, truly I say to you, he who believes in me will also do the works that I do; and greater works than those will he do, because I go to the Father" (John 14:12, RSV). Fedorov interpreted these words as Christ's charge to his true followers to match and outdo his own miraculous works, i.e., in terms of the "common task," to resurrect not only one Lazarus but all the dead ancestors. But perhaps in repeating this passage so often, Fedorov also intended that his own followers should meet and even go beyond the "projects" he was assigning. And this is what the Russian Cosmists have been attempting to do in the century since Fedorov's death. As noted throughout this study, the Cosmists have often developed positions divergent from and even opposed to Fedorov's, and have readily discarded aspects of Fedorov's teachings that they consider irrelevant, obsolete, unacceptable, or indefensible. But at the same time they have retained much. All the Cosmists have followed Fedorov's teaching that knowledge must be active, whether spiritual or scientific. All have subscribed to a sense of wholeness, a view that man and the cosmos are interrelated, that the individual and the community complete and fulfill each other, that life is in one way or another present throughout the cosmos, that whether called God or aether or some other term, a supreme source and support of life and energy is present throughout the cosmos, and that we and our planet are not alone. All the Cosmists share a sense that throughout the cosmos much more is unknown than known, the present state of knowledge is inadequate, and searching through the past to find knowledge applicable to the future we may find that currently disparaged and currently unimagined sciences—alternative sciences, the "parasciences," or "pseudosciences"—could assist or supplement what we need to know. Therefore, nothing should be dismissed simply because it has been ignored or rejected by the accepted wisdom of our time. All the Cosmists, no matter how learned, shared Fedorov's skepticism toward whatever was considered axiomatic to "the learned." All drew at least some of their ideas or inspirations from the "higher magic," sources usually labeled "esoteric" or "occult." All were also keenly aware of the "Russianness" of their ideas and activities. They sensed that their best work would not—and possibly could not—have been done elsewhere. Those who were forced to live in exile remained thoroughly Russian in orientation and attitude. Those who could not work freely in Russia nevertheless preferred to stay, facing the probability of a term in a remote prison camp, the possibility of a bullet in the back of the head.

As noted at several points in this study, *otechestvennyi*, "native," is an adjective often used today in reference to Cosmism and the Cosmists. Sympathetic scholars in Russia have gone to great lengths to emphasize that Cosmism is a Russian development, something of their own that Russians can take pride in, even if foreign philosophers and intellectuals ignore or disparage the movement. For these scholars, Cosmism is the answer to Chaadaev's question: what, of cultural and intellectual value, has Russia given to the world? An early reviewer of *The Philosophy of the Common Task* wrote that

> Fedorov is a unique, unaccountable, and incomparable phenomenon in the intellectual history of mankind. . . . The thousand-year existence of Russia has been justified by the birth and life of Fedorov. No one anywhere on earth can now reproach us for having failed to offer up to the ages a fruitful thought or a labor begun by genius. . . . In Fedorov in and of himself lies the atonement for all sins and crimes of the Russian people.[24]

Similar tributes to Vernadsky, Tsiolkovsky, Florensky, and other major Cosmists, hailing them as "thoroughly Russian" geniuses, regularly turn up in the secondary literature today. Its homegrown, native quality, then, is one of the most appealing features of Cosmism to Russians today, especially given what they view as constant, relentless criticism on the part of American and Western European intellectuals toward Russian traditions, values, and policies.

In history, Russians have long been accustomed to life under all-embracing ideologies and totalitarian systems. Cosmism is often seen as a positive, spiritually advanced alternative to the previous all-embracing ideology of Communism, a more comprehensive thousand-year plan to replace the five-year plans that didn't work. That Cosmism does not emphasize such current Western priorities as free elections, free press, minority rights, and political and cultural diversity does not seem to lessen its appeal in Russia. Traditionally, Russians have not participated actively in the processes of government. As Sergei Kara-Murza, a current political ideologist, has written: "Voting is an ancient ritual found in all forms of democracy, from clan democracy to modern liberal democracy. This ritual is only the conclusion of a process by which interests are reconciled and a decision is reached that satisfies all influential groups. In a parliament voting is a ritual that symbolizes *competition*, where victory goes to the strongest (even if only by one vote). In soviets . . . voting is a ritual of *agreement*. Here people try to achieve *unanimity*."[25]

Whether in Tsarist or Soviet times, governing has been for royals and driven political leaders, while ordinary citizens have sought and found fulfillment elsewhere: in religion, work, family life, science, literature, and other activities in a very rich national culture. Cosmism does not change this tendency. The major question—do you want to live or do you want to die?—is not really a matter for democratic decision. The plan has been determined—our role is to use all our intelligence and energy to fulfill it. Cosmist politics is not the politics of campaigning for every vote and determining that every vote is counted but the politics of unanimous voluntarism. And while not all Russians accept this version of political life, enough do accept it to make Cosmism a total worldview of growing influence.

Cosmists who have written about the history of Russian philosophy find that Cosmism offers the ultimate grand synthesis of all Russian thought: Slavophile and Westernizing, progressive and conservative, religious and scientific, mystical and realistic, utopian and pragmatic, national and universal. Critics of Cosmism have usually found fault with it for being one-sided, that side being the opposite of whatever set of beliefs the critic is writing from. In the Soviet period, dialectical materialists found the Cosmists irrational and mystical, and in the post-Soviet period critics have accused Cosmist thinkers of crypto-Stalinist totalitarianism. Religious critics have found Cosmism to be too technological, too materialistic, and too mechanistic, whereas scientific immortalists and other futuristic materialists have dismissed the spiritual dimensions of their predecessors as residue from the previous centuries.

The very Russian orientation that makes Cosmism attractive to so many Russian intellectuals is precisely what has made it of so little interest to many foreigners. Russians can appreciate, for example, Fedorov's glorification of autocracy even if they disagree with it, for a strong Russian dictator is at least "ours" and "for us," even if he is ruthless in his "native" beneficence. The current rising nostalgia for Stalin and unfading loathing for the West's friend Gorbachev illustrates this point. Even liberal agnostic Russians can understand why intelligent believers revere the Orthodox Church. But Western intellectuals may well find it difficult to believe that any profound, futuristic thinker could sincerely endorse, as Fedorov did, the ideals of "nationalism, Orthodoxy, and autocracy." Or that a great scientist like Tsiolkovsky could seriously find higher truths in the mumbo-jumbo of Madame Blavatsky's *Secret Doctrine*. Or how a genius like Florensky, a "Russian Leonardo da Vinci," could argue that the mathematics behind Einstein's theory of relativity proved the existence of God. Western readers who have not devoted their professional lives to the study of the paradoxes in Russian literature, culture, and thought might very well wonder if Cosmism isn't precisely what Mary Shelley was warning us about in *Frankenstein*, or what Evgeny Zamyatin, George Orwell, and Aldous Huxley depicted as dystopia in *We*, *1984*, and *Brave New World*. The Cosmists and their ideas may suit the Russians, but what relevance and value do they have for the rest of the world? We all know that our planet, our civilization, and especially our Western ways of life are ailing, but do the Cosmists propose cures that are even worse than the ailments? In the end, are they at best just brainy kooks, and at worst dangerous apologists for totalitarian ideals? Why take them seriously?

A first Western response might be that even though today's Russia no longer compels the attention it did when the USSR was considered the primary enemy of Western democracy, Russia is still a major power and an important potential partner in any future international attempt to create a better world order. The more we can all know about the traditional cultural and intellectual tendencies of this partner, the better, and the Cosmists present as clear and deep a look as any into the past, present, and possible future tendencies of what has traditionally been called "the Russian soul."

But there are more and better reasons to know about the Russian Cosmists than the need to understand an important neighbor and partner. We in the West can sometimes be too complacent about our intellectual, cultural, and political superiority, too eager to assume that the values that we consider characteristic of our Western democracies are—or should be—at least global if not universal, applicable to all our fellow residents of this planet, if not to our extraterrestrial neighbors as well. Positions taken by the Russian Cosmists can challenge us to reexamine some of these assumptions, and perhaps even offer a preview of positions that we may surprise ourselves by entertaining more seriously for ourselves in the future. For example, if degradation of the environment, economic instability, terrorist threat, or some other problem were to lead to a prolonged sense of crisis, it is conceivable that demands could arise for a far less democratic and much more authoritarian form of government to undertake necessary (if unpopular) policies that democratic institutions often debate but never seem to enact. For most of us, still looking back at the twentieth century, totalitarianism can only mean the repugnant policies of a Hitler or a Stalin, a Mao or a Pol Pot. But unlikely as it sounds, could there be such a thing as benign totalitarianism? Plato thought there could be, and many of the Cosmists would agree. For Fedorov, government "as it ought to be" would be an ideal Russian autocrat exercising total authority—spiritual, political, aesthetic, and economic—over the universal common task. For Solovyov and the religious Cosmists, the one to lead us all in every way should be the godman, the individual of supremely advanced spiritual development. For Berdyaev, we should all look to the great creative artist; for Vernadsky, Tsiolkovsky, and many of today's active Cosmists, leading scientists should be in charge of humanity's future. Unlikely as it may seem today, the liberal democratic model for future world governments may become less attractive than it is today, and the matter of who should have total or near total authority to govern an inevitable global union could become a pressing question in the future. The Russian Cosmists have at least provided a starting point for the negotiations.

Another idea whose time has not yet come outside Cosmist literature, but surely will, is the problem of overcoming death. The Cosmists challenge us to consider precisely what death is, whether it is simply a cessation of all our chemical and electronic activity, or something more, and whether its elimination is indeed possible, and, if so, desirable. As Socrates famously argued in the *Apology*, we do not know what death is; perhaps it is bad, perhaps neutral, perhaps even a good thing. We simply do not know, but to regard death as something evil to be feared and avoided at all costs is to pretend to know what we do not know—an act of hubris in Socrates' view. So should we direct all human intelligence and energy toward the elimination of death, when we do not know what death is? And if we do think we know what death is and agree that in the future death should be eliminated, can we go on to agree that past life should be restored to all our ancestors? If so, how far back should the resurrection go? Should we include Neanderthals? Great apes? Or back even further? And what is the life that we shall be trying to restore? Will it include present memories—and present problems? Or will we all be starting again with a clean slate? In thinking about the details of resurrection, we can quickly slip into absurdity, but the problems are serious. Not simply the technological but also the social, cultural, and moral aspects of the possible elimination of death and restoration of life are issues which the Cosmists today and others in the future will be addressing. The standard Cosmist answer to such questions and apparent absurdities is that sometime in the future we will know what today we do not know. This admirable faith in the inevitable evolution and growth of human knowledge is one of the features of Cosmism that other schools of thought might profitably borrow from.

Other important future discussions to which the Cosmists have already made significant contributions have to do with the possibility of uniting things that now appear disparate: religion, science, art, and magic; tradition and progress; various fields of knowledge and activity; diverse cultural traits—not to mention all the diametric oppositions and contradictions that Berdyaev lists as being united in the "Russian soul."[26] But we may ask: can and should the many be squeezed into one? Today we emphasize the value of diversity—biological, ethnic, cultural; the value of each individual particle, assuming that if each thrives, so will the whole. But when does diversity become disintegration? For example, as a problem of ethnic unity versus diversity, how can a country with a well-developed culture accommodate distinctly alien customs on a large scale and still preserve its own distinct culture? In the interests of diversity, should women be free to wear veils in a country like France, or wear miniskirts in a country like Saudi Arabia? And in biological diversity, how far should we go to protect the interests of many different species against the interests of the dominant one? Should we, for example, prevent construction of a public park in order to preserve the habitat of an endangered salamander? Generally, equality and biodiversity are not ultimate values for the Russian Cosmists. For the most part, the Cosmists take the position opposite ours, and assume that if the whole is orderly and harmonious, the individual particle will be secure and well. If conflict should arise between the interests of the individual particle and the interests of the whole, the Cosmists would almost unanimously (Berdyaev being the possible dissident) prefer the interests of the whole. Thus if beyond Russia, in the future global village, with every part wirelessly connected to every other part—if the common interest should happen to be considered more important and the particular, individual interest less important; if the drive to forge unity should happen to overcome the drive to preserve diversity—the Russian Cosmists again will have prepared a way.

Another contribution the Cosmists have made—but, again, not universally accepted—is their attempt to rediscover possible spiritual and scientific truths in certain discarded, premodern bodies of knowledge, such as astrology, alchemy, kabbalah, and other traditional occult or esoteric researches. The Russian Cosmists, of course, are not alone in reintroducing certain aspects of esoteric investigation to respectability—the writings of C. G. Jung being a prime example. But the degree to which the Russian Cosmists—particularly Fedorov, Solovyov, Florensky, Tsiolkovsky, and Chizhevsky—have attempted to transform esoteric sources into intellectually respectable (though still controversial) philosophy, theology, and science can be regarded as a significant contribution to at least the Western esoteric tradition, if not to Western thought as a whole.

As an academic subject, Western esotericism has in recent decades gained a substantial following, with programs at reputable institutions in the United States, the United Kingdom, the Netherlands, and other countries offering undergraduate majors and granting advanced degrees. Study of the Russian Cosmists, bridging the traditional gap between exoteric and esoteric knowledge, could be a valuable addition to the curriculum of these programs. Exchanges between Cosmist institutes in Russia and programs in Western esotericism in American and European universities could significantly benefit both sides. This is perhaps a narrow, academic contribution, but still one worth making.

Perhaps the most important contribution the Russian Cosmists have made to modern intellectual life, however, is to offer a centered, directed, positive vision in a largely uncentered, rudderless, negative time. In noting the differences between Russian Cosmism and various schools of Western thought today, several commentators[27] have argued that Cosmist optimism and Cosmist spiritual and scientific conviction are qualities much needed in today's global intellectual atmosphere. Fedorov, Berdyaev, Bulgakov, and Florensky all proposed their ideas in part as a saving alternative to a broken, ailing Western intellectual tradition. And today's Cosmists have reinforced their predecessors' intentions. Semenova in particular presents a vigorous critique of today's "ecosophists." Although the Russian Cosmists and various branches of the Western ecology movement share the view that military and industrial exploitation is rapidly destroying earth's natural environment, primarily in pursuit of the corrupt ideal of more wealth and comfort for some and more misery for others, the two tendencies differ dramatically in what can and should be done to correct the problem. In Semenova's view,

> ecosophists invite man to humbly accept the position of absolutely equal rights among all living beings (biocentrism, ecological egalitarianism), insist that man return to a sympathetic and humbling harmonic symbiosis of himself and all living and nonliving nature, and [ecosophists] are prepared to take to heart and all but give their noble voluntary blessing to the principle, suicidal for themselves, that the world, nature, and the biosphere could peacefully go about its business without man, that it could even flourish in his absence.[28]

The ecosophists, who in Semenova's view represent the best of a bad lot in today's Western intellectual tradition, not only accept human mortality as an unchangeable fact but even act from a tacit death wish. Assuming that any human attempt to regulate, direct, or—heaven forbid—improve nature could only result in disaster, the ecosophists, in Semenova's view, condemn humanity to remain in a stage of infancy and would prohibit humanity from evolving to maturity.

We are, in the Cosmist view, still in the early stages of human development. To be sure, we have come far from our first clumsy efforts to rise from a horizontal to a vertical orientation, but we still have much farther to go. In the course of our evolution, we have sometimes made mistakes, causing harm to ourselves and to our surroundings, and in our further evolution we shall no doubt make more mistakes. But the faith of the Cosmists is that we shall continue to get back on our feet, to grow and learn from our mistakes. As Fedorov wrote: "Philosophy must become the knowledge not only of what is but of what ought to be, that is, from the passive, speculative explanation of existence it must become an active project of what must be, the project of universal action."[29] The project that Fedorov envisioned will not be realized any time soon—Vladimir Solovyov suggested a time frame of perhaps ten thousand years or more. Valuable as they are as stimulants, starting points for further reflection and discussion, at this point it is still too early to judge whether any of the ideas Fedorov and the Cosmists proposed ever could or even ever should be realized. But if Kuprevich and some of the more optimistic recent Cosmists and immortalists are right on one point, some people alive today may still be around for the span Solovyov estimated, and will thus be in a better position than we are to render a final verdict.

# *Notes*

CHAPTER 1

Epigraph: Nicolas Berdyaev, *The Russian Idea*, trans. R. M. French (Boston: Beacon, 1962), 4.

1. At a November 2007 Moscow conference on Fedorov and Cosmism, for example, speakers and participants included the general director of the Russian State Library, the first secretary of the Embassy of the Republic of Kazakhstan, the director of the Gorky Institute of World Literature, the procurator and dean of the Philosophy Department of Moscow State University, the editor in chief of *Literaturnaia Gazeta*, the director of the Russian Foundation for Advanced Technology, and the editor in chief of the newspaper *Zavtra*, as well as members of the academies of arts and sciences and leading academics from major Russian, Ukrainian, and Eastern European universities.

2. George Vernadsky, *The Origins of Russia* (Oxford: Clarendon, 1959), 108–73.

3. Birgit Menzel, "The Occult Revival in Russia Today and Its Impact on Literature," *Harriman Review* 16, no. 1 (Spring 2007): 1–13, available online at http://www.harrimaninstitute.org/MEDIA/00786.pdf.

4. Antoine Faivre, *Access to Western Esotericism* (Abany: State University of New York Press, 1994).

5. Frances A. Yates, *The Rosicrucian Enlightenment* (Boston: Routledge & Kegan Paul, 1972).

6. Nicolas Berdyaev, *Dream and Reality: An Essay in Autobiography*, trans. Katharine Lampert (New York: Macmillan, 1951), 233.

7. S. G. Semenova and A. G. Gacheva, eds., *Russkii kosmizm: Antologiia filosofskoi mysli* (Moscow: Pedagogika-Press, 1993), 4.

8. Bernice Glatzer Rosenthal, ed., *The Occult in Russian and Soviet Culture* (Ithaca, NY: Cornell University Press, 1997), 185–86.

9. George M. Young, *Nikolai F. Fedorov: An Introduction* (Belmont, MA: Nordland, 1979), 168–80.

CHAPTER 2

1. Nikolai Fedorovich Fedorov, *Filosofiia obshchago dela: Stat'i, mysli, i pis'ma Niko-laia Fedorovicha Fedorova*, ed. V. A. Kozhevnikov and N. P. Peterson, 2 vols. (1906–1913; repr., Farnborough, UK: Gregg, 1970), 2:260; hereafter *FOD*.

2. *FOD*, 2:261.

3. Jeremy Gray, *Worlds Out of Nothing: A Course in the History of Geometry in the 19th Century* (Netherlands: Springer, 2007), 115.

4. Cited in Semenova and Gacheva, *Russkii kosmizm*, 5.

5. Dimitri Obolensky, ed., *The Penguin Book of Russian Poetry* (Baltimore: Penguin Books, 1962), 52–54.

6. Semenova and Gacheva, *Russkii kosmizm*, 34–48; works of Odoevsky available in Russian online at http://az.lib.ru/o/odoewskij_w_f/. For brief overview in English, see James H. Billington, *The Icon and the Axe: An Interpretive History of Russian Culture* (New York: Knopf, 1966), 318–20. See also V. F. Odoevsky, *Russian Nights*, trans. Olga Koshansky-Olienikov and Ralph E. Matlaw (Evanston, IL: Northwestern University Press, 1997).

7. Victor Terras, ed., *Handbook of Russian Literature* (New Haven, CT: Yale University Press, 1985), 498.

8. Semenova and Gacheva, *Russkii kosmizm*, 38.

9. Ibid., 49–63. Sukhovo-Kobylin's works in Russian available online at http://az.lib.ru/s/suhowokobylin_a_w/. See also A. V. Sukhovo-Kobylin, *Death of Tarelkin and Other Plays: The Trilogy of Alexander Sukhovo-Kobylin*, trans. and ed. Harold B. Segal (Amsterdam: Harwood, 1995).

10. Semenova and Gacheva, *Russkii kosmizm*, 62.

11. Ibid., 52.

12. Ibid., 54.

13. Ibid., 54.

14. Ibid., 58.

15. Ibid., 59.

16. Ibid., 61.


CHAPTER 3

1. V. V. Zenkovskii, *A History of Russian Philosophy*, trans. George L. Kline, 2 vols. (New York: Columbia University Press, 1953); Berdyaev, *Russian Idea*.

2. Berdyaev, *Dream and Reality*, 89.

3. Konstantin Petrovich Pobyedonostseff, *Reflections of a Russian Statesman*, trans. Robert Crozier Long (London: Grant Richards, 1898).

4. P. Chaadaev, "First Letter," in *Russian Philosophy*, ed. James M. Edie, James P. Scanlan, and Mary-Barbara Zeldin (Chicago: Quadrangle Books, 1965), 1:122–23.

5. P. Chaadaev, "Third Letter," in Edie, Scanlan, and Zeldin, *Russian Philosophy*, 1:125–29.

CHAPTER 4

1. Berdyaev, *Russian Idea*; see esp. chap. 9, 193–218.

2. Alexander Schmemann, *Holy Week: A Liturgical Explanation for the Days of Holy Week* (Tuckahoe, NY: St. Vladimir's Seminary Press, n.d., ca. 1960), 45.

3. *The Way of a Pilgrim, and The Pilgrim Continues His Way*, trans. R. M. French (1954; repr., San Francisco: Harper, 1991).

4. *The Philokalia*, trans. G. E. H. Palmer, Philip Sherrard, and Kallistos Ware (London: Faber & Faber, 1983).

5. A hagiography of St. Sergius is available online at http://www.st-sergius.org.

6. Available online at http://orthodoxinfo.com/praxis/wonderful.aspx.

7. Serge A. Zenkovsky, *Medieval Russia's Epics, Chronicles, and Tales*, rev. ed. (New York: Dutton, 1974), 323–33.

8. Eugene N. Trubetskoi, *Icons: Theology in Color*, trans. Gertrude Vakar (Tuckahoe, NY: St. Vladimir's Seminary Press, 1973).

9. For a detailed analysis of Russian veneration of *rod*, see George Vernadsky, *Origins*, 9–17.

10. A good online source for lore about the many shadowy inhabitants of Slavic pagan myth is Moist Mother Earth: http://www.winterscapes.com/slavic.htm.

11. Y. M. Sokolov, *Russian Folklore*, trans. Catherine Ruth Smith (New York: Macmillan, 1950).

CHAPTER 5

1. George Vernadsky, *Origins*, 110.

2. W. F. Ryan, *The Bathhouse at Midnight: An Historical Survey of Magic and Divination in Russia* (University Park: Pennsylvania State University Press, 1999), 13.

3. Ibid., 15.

4. George Vernadsky, *Origins*, 109.

5. Ibid., 17.

6. Ibid., 20.

7. Ibid., 22.

8. For more on Kuhlmann, see Wilhelm Schmidt-Biggemann, "Salvation through Philology: The Poetical Messianism of Quirinus Kuhlmann (1651–1689)," in *Toward the Millennium: Messianic Expectations from the Bible to Waco*, ed. Peter Schäfer and Mark R. Cohen (Leiden, the Netherlands: Brill, 1998), 259–98.

9. N. A Figurovski, "The Alchemist and Physician Arthur Dee (Artemii Ivanovich Dii): An Episode in the History of Chemistry and Medicine in Russia," *Ambix* 13, no. 1 (1965): 1; John H. Appleby, "Arthur Dee and Johannes Bánfi Hunyades: Further Information on their Alchemical and Professional Activities," *Ambix* 24, no. 2 (1977): 96–109, cited in Robert Collis, "Alchemical Interest at the Petrine Court," *Esoterica* 7 (2005): 54.

10. Ryan, *Bathhouse*, 36.

11. Ibid., 44.

12. Ibid., 71.

13. For a concise history of the extent of alchemical knowledge and practice in England, see Philip Ball, "Alchemical Culture and Poetry in Early Modern England," *Interdisciplinary Science Reviews* 31, no. 1 (2006): 77–92.

14. Cited in Collis, "Alchemical," 56.

15. Ibid., 57.

16. Ibid., 59.

17. Ibid., 61.

18. Ibid., 62.

19. Ibid.

20. Ibid., 64.

21. Ibid., 61.

22. Raffaella Faggionato, *A Rosicrucian Utopia in Eighteenth-Century Russia: The Masonic Circle of N. I. Novikov* (Dordrecht, the Netherlands: Springer, 2005).

23. Tatiana Artemyeva, "Utopian Spaces of Russian Masons in the Enlightenment," in *Freemasonry and Fraternalism in Eighteenth-Century Russia*, ed. Andreas Onnerfors and Robert Collis (Sheffield, UK: University of Sheffield, Centre for Research into Freemasonry and Fraternalism, 2009), 63–85.

24. N. A. Berdiaev, *Samopoznanie: Opyt filosofskoy avtobiografii*, 2nd ed. (Paris: YMCA-Press, 1983), 222.

25. Maria Carlson, *"No Religion Higher than Truth": A History of the Theosophical Movement in Russia, 1875–1922* (Princeton, NJ: Princeton University Press, 1993).

26. Elena F. Pisareva, *The Light of the Russian Soul: A Personal Memoir of Early Russian Theosophy*, trans. George M. Young, ed. John Algeo (Wheaton, IL: Quest Books, 2008).

CHAPTER 6

Epigraph: V. F. Lazurskii, "Dnevnik V. F. Lazurskogo," *Literaturnoe Nasledstvo* 38 (1939): 465–66. Lazursky lived with the Tolstoy family between 1894 and 1898 as tutor to the children.

1. Isaiah Berlin, *The Hedgehog and the Fox: An Essay on Tolstoy's View of History* (London: Weidenfeld & Nicolson, 1953). This chapter updates and re-presents material from my earlier study *Nikolai F. Fedorov: An Introduction* (Belmont, MA: Nordland, 1979). New biographical and other information that has emerged since 1979 allows several important factual corrections and revisions, but the general presentation and analysis of Fedorov's idea remains essentially the same.

2. N. F. Fedorov, *Sobranie sochinenii*, ed. A. G. Gacheva and S. G. Semenova (Moscow: Progress/Traditsiia, 1995–2000), 2:258 (hereafter *SOB*).

3. *SOB*, 2:171.

4. *FOD*, 1:330.

5. Ibid., 1:4.

6. O. V. Marchenko, "K istorii evropeiskogo Sokratizma: N. F. Fedorov," in *Sluzhitel' dukha vechnoi pamiati: Nikolai Fedorovich Fedorov; 180-letiiu so dnia rozhdenii; Sbornik nauchnykh statei* (Moscow: Pashkov Dom, 2010), 1:89–94.

7. Plato, "The Apology," in *The Dialogues of Plato*, trans. Benjamin Jowett (1937; repr., Chicago: Encyclopedia Britannica, 1965), 212.

8. This information was discovered only relatively recently by Moscow researcher Valery Borisov and corrects misinformation presented in all earlier accounts of Fedorov's biography. V. S. Borisov, "Kto zhe mat' Fedorova?" in *Obshchee delo: Sbornik dokladov predstavlennykh na i Vsesoiuznye Fedorovskie chteniia, G. Borovsk 14–15 Maia 1988 goda* (Moscow: Komitet Kosmonavtiki DOSAAF SSSR, 1990), 233–34.

9. Quoted in A. G. Gacheva and S. G. Semenova, eds., *N. F. Fedorov: Pro et Contra*, vol. 2 (St. Petersburg: Russkii Khristianskii Gumanitarnyi Institut, 2008), 244.

10. Erich Neumann, *The Origins and History of Consciousness*, trans. R. F. C. Hull (1954; repr., Princeton, NJ: Princeton University Press, 1995).

11. Quoted in V. A. Kozhevnikov, "Nikolai Fedorovich Fedorov: Opyt izlozheniia ego ucheniia po izdannym i neizdannym proizvedeniam, perepiske i lichnym besedam" [1908], reprinted in A. G. Gacheva and S. G. Semenova, eds., *N. F. Fedorov: Pro et Contra*, vol. 1 (St. Petersburg: Russkii Khristianskii Gumanitarnyi Institut, 2004), 285.

12. V. V. Bogdanov, "Delo o sluzhbe uchitelia geografii i istorii Lipetskogo uezdogo uchilishcha Nikolaia Fedorova 7 aprelia 1854–26 marta 1857 g," in *Sluzhitel' dukha vechnoi pamiati Nikolai Fedorovich Fedorov: 180-letiiu so dnia rozhdenii; Sbornik nauchnykh statei* (Moscow: Pashkov Dom, 2010), 2:274–76.

13. Fedorov, who was actually a year younger than Tolstoy, was invariably mistaken for being several years older.

14. N. P. Peterson, *N. F. Fedorov i ego kniga 'Filosofiia obshchego dela' v protivopolozhnost' ucheniiu L. N. Tolstogo . . . 'o neprotivlenii' i drugim ideiam nashego vremeni* (Verny, Russia: Tipografiia Semirechen, 1912), 88–89.

15. *SOB*, 4:15.

16. F. M. Dostoievsky, *The Diary of a Writer*, trans. Boris Brasol (New York: Scribner, 1949), 2:247–48.

17. Letter of March 24, 1878 (no. 620), in F. M. Dostoevskii, *Pis'ma*, ed. A. S. Dolinin, vol. 4 (Moscow: Gosudarstvennoe Izdatel'stvo, 1959), 9–10.

18. *FOD*, 1:339–442.

19. Ibid., 1:3–352.

20. W. Komarowitsch, "Der Vatermord und Fiodoroffs Lehre von der 'Fleischlichen Auferstehung,'" in *Die Urgestalt der Brüder Karamasoff: Dostojewskis Quellen, Entwürfe und Fragmente* (Munich: Piper, 1928), 3–58; R. Lord, "Dostoyevsky and N. F. Fyodorov," *Slavonic and East European Review* 40 (1962): 408–30; A. G. Gacheva, "Novye materially k istorii znakomstva Dostoevskogo s ideiami Fedorova," in Gacheva and Semenova, *Fedorov: Pro et contra*, 1:814–43.

21. Young, *Fedorov*, 37–52.

22. N. P. Peterson, "Pis'mo k izdateliu Russkogo Arkhiva: Po povodu otzyva F. M. Dostoevskogo o N. F. Fedorove," *Russkii Arkhiv* 6 (1904): 300–301.

23. I. A. Linnichenko, "Moi vstrechi s L'vom Tolstym," in Gacheva and Semenova, *Fedorov: Pro et contra*, 1:220–21.

24. Cited in A. K. Gornostaev, *Rai na zemle: K ideologii tvorchestva F. M. Dostoevskogo, F. M. Dostoevskii i N. F. Fedorov* (Harbin, China: n.p., 1929), 6.

25. N. N. Gusev, *Lev Nikolaevich Tolstoi: Mater'ialy k biografii s 1881 po 1885 god* (Moscow: Nauka, 1970), 64; Linnichenko, "Vstrechi," 317.

26. Lazurskii, "Dnevnik V. F. Lazurskogo," 466.

27. Valery Borisov, who leads Fedorov excursions in Moscow, has listed at least twenty addresses for Fedorov over the years. V. Borisov, "Adresa Fedorova," in *Filosofiia bessmertiia i voskresheniia*, ed. S. G. Semenova, A. G. Gacheva, and M. V. Skorokhodov (Moscow: Nasledie, 1996), 2:251–55.

28. A. G. Gacheva, "'Nepodvizhno lish' solntse liubvi' (N. F. Fedorov i E. S. Nekrasova)," in *Na poroge griadushchego: Pamiati Nikolaia Fedirovicha Fedorova (1829–1903)*, ed. A. G. Gacheva, M. M. Panfilov, and S. G. Semenova (Moscow: Pashkov Dom, 2004), 414–16.

29. In the summer of 1976 I came upon this previously unknown and unexpected polemic while conducting research in the library of the Academy of Sciences in Leningrad. For a detailed discussion of the series, see "Fedorov in Askhabad," published as appendix 2 in Young, *Fedorov*. For further, updated analysis and discussion, see S. G. Semenova, *Filosof budushchego veka* (Moscow: Pashkov Dom, 2004), 129–50.

30. Kozhevnikov, *Nikolai Fedorovich Fedorov*, 331.

31. Ibid.

32. L. O. Pasternak, "Iz zapisok Leonida Pasternaka," *Novyi Zhurnal* 77 (1964): 190–214.

CHAPTER 7

Epigraph: Cited in Roelof van den Broek, "Gnosticism and Hermetism in Antiquity: Two Roads to Salvation," in *Gnosis and Hermeticism from Antiquity to Modern Times*, ed. Roelof van den Broek and Wouter J. Hanegraaff (Albany: State University of New York Press, 1998), 12.

1. George M. Young, "Fedorov's Transformations of the Occult," in Rosenthal, *Occult*, 171–84; Michael Hagemeister, "Russian Cosmism in the 1920s and Today," in ibid., 185–202.

2. Faivre, *Access to Western Esotericism*, 10.

3. Ibid., 10–15.

4. *FOD*, 2:198–99.

5. Ibid., 2:273.

6. Ibid., 2:239–40.

7. Trubetskoi, *Icons*.

8. *FOD*, 2:52.

9. Ibid., 2:44.

10. Ibid., 2:202–3.

11. George Vernadsky, *Origins*, 117ff.

12. Quoted in Peter Kingsley, *Ancient Philosophy, Mystery, and Magic: Empedocles and Pythagorean Tradition* (Oxford: Clarendon, 1995), 218.

13. Mircea Eliade, *The Forge and the Crucible*, trans. Stephen Corrin (New York: Harper & Row, 1962), 158.

14. Ibid., 159.

15. *FOD*, 1:441.

16. S. N. Bulgakov, "Zagadochnyi myslitel' (N. F. Fedorov)," in Gacheva and Semenova, *Fedorov: Pro et contra* 1:392.

17. *FOD*, 1:19–20.

18. Mark Sedgwick, *Against the Modern World: Traditionalism and the Secret Intellectual History of the Twentieth Century* (Oxford: Oxford University Press, 2004).

19. *FOD*, 1:373.

20. Ibid., 1:375.

21. Ibid.

22. Ibid., 1:428.

23. Ibid.

24. Ibid., 1:95–96.

25. Ibid., 1:276–89.

26. Ibid., 1:283–84 and passim.

27. Cited in van den Broek, "Gnosticism and Hermetism in Antiquity," 12.

CHAPTER 8

Epigraph: S. L. Frank, "Introduction," in Vladimir Solovyov, *A Solovyov Anthology*, arr. S. L. Frank., trans. Natalie Duddington (New York: Scribner, 1950).

1. Paul Marshall Allen, *Vladimir Soloviev, Russian Mystic* (Blauvelt, NY: Steinerbooks, 1978), 47.

2. Cited in Zenkovskii, *History*, 2:474.

3. Allen, *Soloviev*, 89.

4. For complete translation and commentary on the poem, see George M. Young, "Vladimir Solovyov's Poems of Wisdom, Mystery, and Love," in *Esotericism, Art, and Imagination*, ed. Arthur Versluis, Lee Irwin, John Richards, and Melinda Weinstein (East Lansing: Michigan State University Press, 2008), 145–61.

5. Thanks to John Algeo of the Theosophical Society in America for pointing this out to me.

6. Vsevolod Solovyoff, *A Modern Priestess of Isis*, abr. and trans. Walter Leaf (London: Longmans, Green, 1895).

7. Allen, *Soloviev*, 119.

8. Berdyaev, *Russian Idea*, 167.

9. Dostoevsky's letter of March 24, 1878, no. 620, in Dostoevskii, *Pis'ma*, 4:9–10.

10. Semenova identifies this as a reference to a draft of Part 2 of the essay prepared by Fedorov and Peterson to send to Dostoevsky, later published as "Brotherhood." See Semenova, *Filosof*, 115.

11. Semenova, ibid., identifies this as an early condensed version of Part 3 and Part 4 of "Brotherhood."

12. *SOB*, 4:48.

13. In Solovyov's collected works, the letter is undated; from Fedorov's account (see preceding note), we know it was written January 12, 1882. Vladimir Sergeevich Solov'ev, *Pis'ma Vladimira Sergeevicha Solov'eva*, vol. 2 (St. Petersburg: n.p., 1910), 345.

14. E. N. Trubetskoi, *Mirosozertsanie Vl. S. Solov'eva* (Moscow: Put', 1913).

15. Cited in Semenova, *Filosof*, 118.

16. N. P. Peterson, "Polemika," *Voprosy Filosifii i Psikhologii* 118 (May–June 1913): 409.

17. Frank, "Introduction," in Solovyov, *Solovyov Anthology*, 24.

18. *FOD*, 1:128–247.

19. Ibid., 1:479–91.

20. Solov'ev, *Pis'ma Solov'eva*, 2:346–47.

21. Ibid., 3:38.

22. Ibid., 38–40.

23. Ibid., 1:418–21; 2:169–83 and passim.

24. Vladimir Sergeevich Solov'ev, *Sobranie sochinenii*, ed. S. M. Solov'ev and E. L. Radlov, vol. 10 (Brussels: Mysl', 1970), 213.

25. Solovyov, *Solovyov Anthology*, 164.

26. Edie, Scanlan, and Zeldin, *Russian Philosophy*, 3:92–94.

27. Ibid., 3:97, 98.

28. No volume of Solovyov's poetry is available yet in English. For selections in translation, see Allen, *Soloviev*; Young, "Solovyov's Poems"; and Vladimir Solovyov, *Divine Sophia: The Wisdom Writings of Vladimir Solovyov*, ed. Judith Deutsch Kornblatt (Ithaca, NY: Cornell University Press, 2009).

29. Cited in Allen, *Soloviev*, 322, 323.

30. Ibid., 327.

31. See especially Samuel D. Cioran, *Vladimir Solov'ev and the Knighthood of the Divine Sophia* (Waterloo, ON: Wilfrid Laurier University Press, 1977).

32. See especially Zenkovskii, *History*, 2:754–57, 873–75; and Nicolas Zernov, *The Russian Religious Renaissance of the Twentieth Century* (New York: Harper & Row, 1963).

33. Cited in Zenkovskii, *History*, 2:890.

34. Alexander Schmemann, *Ultimate Questions: An Anthology of Modern Russian Religious Thought* (New York: Holt, Rinehart & Winston, 1965), 298.

35. Charles McDaniel, "Sergei Bulgakov's 'Philosophy of Economy': A Resource for Economic Bridge-Building between Islam and the West," *Religion, State, and Society* 36, no. 4 (December 2008): 451–67.

36. Sergii Bulgakov, *Sergii Bulgakov: Towards a Russian Political Theology*, ed. Rowan Williams (Edinburgh: T & T Clark, 1999).

37. Sergei Bulgakov, *Philosophy of Economy: The World as Household*, trans. and ed. Catherine Evtuhov (New Haven, CT: Yale University Press, 2000), 72.

38. Ibid., 71, 72.

39. Ibid., 75.

40. Ibid., 95.

41. Ibid., 96.

42. Ibid., 96, 97.

43. Ibid., 98.

44. Ibid., 99, 100.

45. Ibid., 102.

46. Ibid., 103.

47. Ibid., 104.

48. Ibid., 104–5.

49. Ibid., 114.

50. Ibid., 120–21.

51. Ibid., 120–21.

52. Ibid., 122.

53. Ibid., 144.

54. Ibid., 144, 145.

55. Ibid., 146.

56. Ibid., 156.

57. Bernice Glatzer Rosenthal, "The Nature and Function of Sophia in Bulgakov's Pre-revolutionary Thought," in *Russian Religious Thought*, ed. Judith Deutsch Kornblatt and Richard F. Gustafson (Madison: University of Wisconsin Press, 1996), 155.

58. Ibid., 167.

59. Ibid., 167–68. And see Rosenthal's further discussion of Bulgakov's idea of masculine and feminine, 168–72.

60. First published in Put', 1932, repinted in Gacheva and Semenova, *N. F. Fedorov: Pro et Contra*, 1:419–23, available in English in Sergius Bulgakov, *The Holy Grail and the Eucharist*, trans. Boris Jakim (Hudson, NY: Lindisfarne Books, 1997).

61. Bulgakov, *Holy Grail*, 27.

62. Ibid., 33.

63. Bulgakov, "Zagadochnyi myslitel'," 1:391–99.

64. S. N. Bulgakov, "Sviashchennik o. Pavel Florenskii" [Obituary for Pavel Florensky], available online at Biblioteka "Vekhi," http://vehi.net/bulgakov/florensky.html.

65. Leonid Sabaneeff, "Pavel Florensky—Priest, Scientist, and Mystic" *Russian Review* 20, no. 4 (October 1961): 312–25.

66. Cited by Avril Pyman in her review of *Pavel Florenskii i simvolisty*, by E. V. Ivanova, *Slavic and East European Review* 83, no. 4 (2005): 740–42.

67. Michael Hagemeister, "'Novoe srednevekov'e' Pavla Florenskogo," *Zvezda* 11 (2006): 131–44, available online at Biblioteka "Vekhi," http://vehi.net/florensky/oflorenskom.html.

68. Avril Pyman, *Pavel Florensky: A Quiet Genius; The Tragic and Extraordinary Life of Russia's Unknown da Vinci* (New York: Continuum, 2010), 3.

69. Pyman, *Quiet Genius*, 37.

70. Ibid., 27.

71. S. M. Polovinkin, as cited in Pyman, *Quiet Genius*, 28.

72. For a summary and refutation of Soviet criticism of Florensky during his lifetime, see Hermann Goltz, "'He Backed the Logos to Defeat the Chaos': The Death of Pavel Florensky (1882–1937)," *Religion in Communist Lands* 18, no. 4 (1990): 343–55, available online at http://www.biblicalstudies.org.uk/pdf/rcl/18-4_343.pdf. For recent renewal of some of the same charges, see Hagemeister, "Novoe srednevekov'e."

73. See Florensky's 1922 essay "The Church Ritual as a Synthesis of the Arts," in *Pavel Florensky, Beyond Vision: Essays on the Perception of Art*, comp. and ed. Nicoletta Misler, trans. Wendy Salmond (Reaktion Books, London, 2002), 95–113.

74. Hagemeister, "Novoe srednevekov'e."

75. Sabaneeff, "Florensky," 316.

76. For the significance of Florensky's work in mathematics, see Loren Graham and Jean-Michel Kantor, "Russian Religious Mystics and French Rationalists: Mathematics, 1900–1930," *Bulletin of the American Academy of Arts and Sciences* 58, no. 3 (Spring 2005): 12–19.

77. P. A. Florenskii, *Stolp i utverzhdenie istiny: Opyt pravoslavnoi feoditsii v dvenadtsati pis'makh* (Moscow: n.p., 1914), published in English as Pavel Florensky, *The Pillar and Ground of the Truth*, trans. and annotated Boris Jakim (Princeton, NJ: Princeton University Press, 1997) (hereafter *PGT*).

78. *PGT*, 55.

79. Pyman, *Quiet Genius*, 147.

80. Ibid., 86.

81. Andrei Bielyi, "Vospominanie o Bloke," *Epoeia* 2 (September 1922): 119.

82. *PGT*, 283.

83. Available online at Biblioteka "Vekhi," http://vehi.net/florensky/vodorazd.

84. Ibid.

85. Graham and Kantor, "Russian Religious Mystics," 16.

86. See Pyman, *Quiet Genius*, 99–110 for details.

87. Ibid., 101.

88. For an unsparing critical account of this controversy, see Hagemeister, "Srednevekov'e." For a justification of Florensky's role, see Goltz, "He Backed the Logos." For a sympathetic critical account, see Pyman, *Quiet Genius*, 100–108.

89. Goltz, "He Backed the Logos."

90. Pyman, *Quiet Genius*, 104.

91. Ibid., 183–210.

92. L. F. Zhegin, "Vospominaniia o P. A. Florenskom." Available online at Biblioteka "Vekhi," http://vehi.net/florensky/zhegin.html.

93. Parts of this projected work have been published and are available online at Biblioteka "Vekhi," http://vehi.net/florensky/vodorazd.

94. Cited in Bernice Glatzer Rosenthal, *New Myth, New World: From Nietzsche to Stalinism* (University Park: Pennsylvania State University Press, 2002), 124.

95. Pavel Aleksandrovich Florenskii, "Organoproektsia," in Semenova and Gacheva, *Russkii kosmizm*, 149–62.

96. Ibid., 150–51.

97. Ibid., 164–65.

98. Pyman, *Quiet Genius*, 206.

99. Sabaneeff, "Florensky," 312.

100. Ibid., 313.

101. Nicolas Berdyaev, *The Meaning of the Creative Act*, trans. Donald A. Lowrie (New York: Collier Books, 1962), 11.

102. Donald A. Lowrie, *Rebellious Prophet: A Life of Nicolai Berdyaev* (New York: Harper, 1960), 180.

103. See, for example, Rosenthal, *New Myth*; and Matthew Spinka, *Nicolas Berdyaev: Captive of Freedom* (Philadelphia: Westminster, 1950).

104. In Obolensky, *Penguin Book of Russian Verse*, 154.

105. Lowrie, *Rebellious Prophet*, 26.

106. Berdyaev, *Meaning of the Creative Act*, 111–13.

107. Ibid., 117–18.

108. Berdyaev, *Dream and Reality*, 83.

109. Ibid., 148.

110. Ibid., 212.

111. Ibid., 208–9.

112. Ibid., 202.

113. Berdyaev, *Meaning of the Creative Act*, 132.

114. Ibid., 135, 136.

115. Berdyaev, *Dream and Reality*, 238, 239.

116. Ibid., 74, 75.

117. Ibid., 75.

118. Berdyaev, *Meaning of the Creative Act*, 159, 160.

### CHAPTER 9

1. Cited in James T. Andrews, *Red Cosmos: K. E. Tsiolkovskii, Grandfather of Soviet Rocketry* (College Station: Texas A & M University Press, 2009), 16.

2. Konstantin Altaiskii, "Moskovskaia iunost' Tsiolkovskogo," *Moskva* 9 (1966): 180.

3. Ibid., 181.

4. K. E. Tsiolkovsky, "Investigation of World Spaces by Reactive Vehicles (1911–1912)," in *K. E. Tsiolkovsky, Selected Works* (Moscow: Mir, 1968), 83–84.

5. Altaiskii, "Moskovskaia iunost' Tsiolkovskogo," 182.

6. Viktor Shklovskii, "Kosmonavtika ot A do Ia," *Literaturnaia Gazeta* April 7, 1971, 13.

7. V. N. Sokolsky and A. A. Blagonravov, "From the Editors," in Tsiolkovsky, *Selected Works*, 7.

8. Michael Holquist, "Konstantin Tsiolkovsky: Science Fiction and Philosophy in the History of Soviet Space Exploration," in *Intersections: Fantasy and Science Fiction*, ed. George E. Slusser and Eric S. Rabkin (Carbondale: Southern Illinois University Press, 1987), 78.

9. Andrews, *Red Cosmos*, 41.

10. Ibid., 10, 12.

11. From his self-published pamphlet "Universal Monism" [1925], excerpted in Semenova and Gacheva, *Russkii kosmizm*, 266.

12. For an essay emphasizing the dark side of Tsiolkovsky's philosophy, see Michael Hagemeister, "The Occult Roots of Soviet Space Travel" (paper presented at the conference "The Occult in Russia/Okkul'tizm v Rossii: Metaphysical Roots of Soviet Civilisation," March 11–13, 2007, Europäische Akademie Berlin).

13. Tsiolkovskii, "Kosmicheskaia filosofiia," in Semenova and Gacheva, *Russkii kosmizm*, 279.

14. Ibid., 277.

15. Ibid., 281.

16. For online versions of these and other conference papers from the Museum, see http://readings.gmik.ru/.

17. V. P. Vaznacheev and A. L. Ianshin, "V. I. Vernadskii v nastoiashchem i budushchem," in A. L. Ianshin, ed., *V. I. Vernadskii: Pro et Contra: Antologiia literatury o V. I. Vernadskom za sto let (1898–1998)* (St. Petersburg: Russkii Khristianskii Gumanitarnyi Institut, 2000), 476.

18. D. S. Likhachev, "Otvety na voprosy redaktsii zhurnala 'Nauka v SSSR,'" in Ianshin, *Vernadskii: Pro et Contra*, 96.

19. Kendall E. Bailes, *Science and Russian Culture in an Age of Revolutions: V. I. Vernadsky and His Scientific School, 1863–1945* (Bloomington: Indiana University Press, 1990).

20. Ibid., 181.

21. Ibid., 184.

22. V. I. Vernadsky, *Khimicheskoe stroenie biosfery Zemli i ee okruzhenii* (Moscow: n.p., 1965), quoted in ibid., 190.

23. Bailes, *Science and Russian Culture*, 191.

24. V. I. Vernadsky, "Zhivoe veschestvo" [Living matter], unpublished manuscript from 1916–1923, quoted in ibid., 197.

25. V. I. Vernadskii, "Neskol'ko slov o noosfere," in Semenova and Gacheva, *Russkii kosmizm*, 308.

26. Ibid., 308.

27. Ibid., 310.

28. Ibid., 310.

29. V. I. Vernadskii, "Avtotrofnost' chelovechestva," in Semenova and Gacheva, *Russkii kosmizm*, 301–3.

30. See Semenova and Gacheva, *Russkii kosmizm*, 312–27.

31. A. L. Tchijevsky, "Physical Factors of the Historical Process," *Cycles*, January 1971, 11–27, available online at http://cyclesresearchinstitute.org/cycles-history//chizhevsky1.pdf.

32. Aleksei Manakin and Liudmila Engelgardt, "Aleksandr Chizhevskii, Leonardo da Vinchi XX-ogo veka," *Nash Sovremennik* 11 (2002).

33. Ken Wilbur, *A Theory of Everything: An Integral Vision for Business, Politics, Science, and Spirituality* (Boston: Shambhala, 2000); Stephen Hawking and Leonard Mlodinow, *The Grand Design* (New York: Bantam, 2010).

34. The entire paper is available online at http://www.astrotheos.com/Page5.htm.

35. *Wikipedia*, s.v. "List of solar cycles," last modified April 13, 2010, http://en.wikipedia.org/wiki/List_of_solar_cycles.

36. Christopher Dickey, "1968: The Year that Changed Everything," *Newsweek*, November 10, 2007.

37. Dom-muzei A. L. Chizhevskogo, http://gmik.ru/chizhevsky.

38. "V. F. Kuprevich," in Semenova and Gacheva, *Russkii kosmizm*, 345–51.

39. V. F. Kuprevich, "Dolgoletie: Real'nost' mechty," *Literaturnaia Gazeta*, December 4, 1968, reprinted in Semenova and Gacheva, *Russkii kosmizm*, 348.

40. Semenova and Gacheva, *Russkii kosmizm*, 346.

41. Ibid., 346–47.

42. Ibid., 349.

43. Ibid., 349.

44. Ibid., 351.

45. M. V. Solov'ev, "Nauchnyi Immortalizm i Perspektiva Fizicheskogo Bessmertiia," http://www.evangelie.ru/forum.

46. Ibid.

CHAPTER 10

1. George L. Kline, *Religious and Anti-Religious Thought in Russia* (Chicago: University of Chicago Press, 1968).

2. See for example Billington, *The Icon and the Axe*, 473–518; and Rosenthal, *New Myth*, especially 27–112.

3. Cited in Rosenthal, *New Myth*, 48.

4. Cited in Irina Paperno, "Introduction," in *Creating Life: The Aesthetic Utopia of Russian Modernism*, ed. Irina Paperno and Joan Delaney Grossman (Stanford, CA: Stanford University Press, 1994), 1–2.

5. Ibid., 2.

6. Ibid., 2–3.

7. Bielyi, "Vospominanie o Bloke," 119.

8. Peter Wiles, "On Physical Immortality: Materialism and Transcendence," *Survey* 56 (1965): 125–43; 57 (1965): 142–61.

9. Irene Masing-Delic, *Abolishing Death: A Salvation Myth of Russian Twentieth-Century Literature* (Stanford, CA: Stanford University Press, 1992), 74.

10. Richard F. Gustafson, "Solov'ev's Doctrine of Salvation," in Kornblatt and Gustafson, *Russian Religious Thought*, 38.

11. For details see Olga Matich, "The Symbolist Meaning of Love: Theory and Practice," in Paperno and Grossman, *Creating Life*, 24–50.

12. Ibid., 25–26.

13. Cited in ibid., 38

14. See details in Andrei Znamenski, *Red Shambhala: Magic, Prophecy, and Geopolitics in the Heart of Asia* (Wheaton, IL: Quest Books, 2011), 69–101; and in Dmitri Alioshin, *Asian Odyssey* (New York: Holt, 1940).

15. Rosenthal, *New Myth*, 92–93.

16. Maria Carlson, "Fashionable Occultism: The Theosophical World of Silver Age Russia," *Quest: Journal of the Theosophical Society in America* 99 (Spring 2011): 51–52.

17. Znamenski, *Red Shambhala*, 82–88.

18. Sheila Ostrander and Lynn Schroeder, *Psychic Discoveries Behind the Iron Curtain* (Englewood Cliffs, NJ: Prentice-Hall, 1970).

19. H. P. Blavatsky, *The Secret Doctrine: The Synthesis of Science, Religion, and Philosophy*, Theosophical University Press Online Edition, http://www.theosociety.org/pasadena/sd/sd-hp.htm, 1:xxii, xxiii.

20. Carlson, "Fashionable Occultism," 54

21. For extensive analysis, see N. A. Bogomolov, "Russkaia literatura nachala XX veka i okkultizm: Issledovaniia i materialy," *Novoe Literaturnoe Obozrenie* (1999).

22. Mikhail Agursky, "Gorky and Theories of Thought Transference," in Rosenthal, *Occult*, 247–72.

23. Ostrander and Schroeder, *Psychic Discoveries*, 233–34.

24. Håkan Lövgren, "Sergei Eisenstein's Gnostic Circle," in Rosenthal, *Occult*, 273–97.

25. Dmitri Shostakovich, *Testimony: The Memoirs of Dmitri Shostakovich*, as told to Solomon Volkov, trans. Antonina W. Bouis (New York: Limelight, 1979), 187ff.

26. Marc Bennetts, "Deeper than Oil: One Nation Under a Spell," *RIA Novosti*, June 12, 2010, http://en.rian.ru/columnists/20101206/161649467.html.

27. Znamenski, *Red Shambhala*, 43–99.

28. Ibid., 88.

CHAPTER II

1. Gacheva and Semenova, *Fedorov: Pro et Contra*, 1:994–96.

2. Ibid., 1:980ff.

3. See letters from 1894 in *SOB*, 4:271–90, and the editors' commentary in *SOB*, sup., 410–15.

4. V. A. Kozhevnikov, "Iz pis'ma A. K. Gorskomu o poslednikh chasakh zhizni Fedorova," in Gacheva and Semenova, *Fedorov: Pro et Contra*, 1:113–14.

5. For more on Fedorov's literary style, see Young, *Fedorov*, 77–86.

6. Reprinted in Gacheva and Semenova, *Fedorov: Pro et contra*, 1:231–351.

7. Peterson, *N. F. Fedorov i ego kniga*.

8. For more information, see I. Vishev, "'Filosofiia obshchego dela' N. F. Fedorova i biokosmizm," in Semenova, Gacheva, and Skorokhodov, *Filisofiia bessmertiia i voskresheniia*, 1:179–86; and Michael Hagemeister, *Nikolaj Fedorov: Studien zu Leben, Werk und Wirkung* (Munich: Sagner, 1989), 300–317.

9. Cited in Hagemeister, *Nikolaj Fedorov*, 302.

10. Berdyaev, *Dream and Reality*, 256–57.

11. Asif A. Siddiqi, *The Red Rockets' Glare: Spaceflight and the Soviet Imagination, 1857–1957* (New York: Cambridge University Press, 2010), 107–8.

12. Vishev, "Filosofiia," 180.

13. Ibid., 183

14. For reprinted selections, see Gacheva and Semenova, *Fedorov: Pro et Contra*, vol. 2.

15. For details on Golgothan Christianity, see Simon Dixon, "Archimandrite Mikhail (Semenov) and Russian Christian Socialism" *Historical Journal* 51 (2008): 689–718.

16. Semenova and Gacheva, *Russkii kosmizm*, 212.

17. A. K. Gornostaev, *Pered litsem smerti: L. N. Tolstoii i N. F. Fedorov, 1828-1903-1910-1928* (Harbin, China: Eurasie, 1928); Gornostaev, *Rai na zemle*; N. A. Setnitskii, *Russkie mysliteli o Kitae (V. S. Solov'ev i N. F. Fedorov)* (Harbin, China: n.p., 1926);. Setnitskii, *Kapitalisticheskii stroi v izobrazhenii F. F. Fedorova* (Harbin, China: n.p., 1926).

18. N. A. Setnitskii, *O konechnom ideale* (Harbin, China: N. A Frenkel', 1926), 82–83.

19. M. Gor'kii, letter to S. Grigor'ev, March 15, 1926; letter to M. Prishvin, October 17, 1926; letter to O. Forsh, September 5, 1926; all in "Gor'kii i sovetskie pisateli: Neizdannaia perepiska," *Literaturnoe Nasledstvo* 19 (1963): 134–36, 335, 591.

20. Alexander Solzhenitsyn, *The Gulag Archipelago, 1918–1956: An Experiment in Literary Investigation*, trans. Thomas P. Whitney (New York: Harper & Row, 1974), 641.

21. E. N. Berkovskaia, "Sud'ba skreshen'ia," Vospominaniia [Fragments], in Gacheva and Semenova, *Fedorov: Pro et contra*, 2:582–99.

22. Ibid., 582.

23. Ibid., 584.

24. Reprinted from the Setnitsky archive in ibid 2:599–607.

25. Ibid., 2:598.

26. "Iz materialov sledstvennykh del A. K. Gorskogo 1927 i 1929 gg," in ibid., 2:558.

27. "Iz materialov sledstvennykh del A. K. Gorskogo 1943 g," in ibid., 2:608ff.

28. Valerian N. Murav'ev, *Ovladenie vremenem* (1928; repr., Moscow: ROSSPEN, 1998).

29. Ibid., 4.

30. Ibid., 8.

31. Ibid., 18.

32. Ibid., 30.

33. Ibid., 44.

34. Ibid., 53.

35. Ibid., 59.

36. Ibid., 60–61.

37. Ibid., 30–35.

38. S. G. Semenova, "Fedorov i russkaia literatura XX veka," in Semenova, *Filosof,* 519–53.

39. A. Saltykov, "Pervyi illustrator Maiakovskogo," *Tvorchestvo* 12 (1965): 15.

40. Ibid., 15.

41. L. F. Zhegin, "Vospominaniia o P. A. Florenskom," available online at Biblioteka "Vekhi," http://vehi.net/florensky/zhegin.html.

42. V. N. Chekrygin, letter to N. N. Punin, February 7, 1922, in Gacheva and Semenova, *Fedorov: Pro et Contra*, 2:490.

43. V. N. Chekrygin, netter to N. N. Punin, December 29, 1929, in ibid., 2:486.

44. V. N. Chekrygin, "O Sobore Voskreshaiushchego Muzeia," in ibid., 2:450.

45. Ibid., 2:464.


CHAPTER 12

1. Muzei-Biblioteka Nikolaia Fedorova, http://www.nffedorov.ru/.

2. The seventeen are: V. F. Odoevsky, A. V. Sukhovo-Kobylin, N. F. Fedorov, V. S. Solovyov, N. A. Umov, S. N. Bulgakov, P. A. Florensky, N. A. Berdyaev, V. N. Murav-vyov, A. K. Gorsky, N. A. Setnitsky, K. E. Tsiolkovsky, V. I. Vernadsky, A. L. Chizhevsky, N. G. Kholodny, V. F. Kuprevich, and A. K. Maneev.

3. The URL of the conference's Web site is: http://www.informatics.org/museum/readings.html.

4. See N. A. Kozyrev, "Possibility of Experimental Study of Properties of Time" (unpublished paper, 1967, available online at http://www.univer.omsk.su/omsk/Sci/Kozyrev/paper1a.txt). See also David Wilcock, "Chapter 01: The Breakthroughs of Dr. N. A. Kozyrev" (unpublished paper, available online at www.divinecosmos.com/index.php?option=com_content&;task=view&id=95&Itemid=36).

5. Wilcock, "Breakthroughs."

6. Susan Richards, *Lost and Found in Russia: Lives in a Post-Soviet Landscape* (New York: Other Press, 2010), 154.

7. George Carey, dir., "Knocking on Heaven's Door—Space Race," *Storyville*, first broadcast April 10, 2011.

8. For Gumilev's works and biography, see http://gumilevica.kulichki.net.

9. Galya Andreyeva Krasteva, "The Criticism towards the West and the Future of Russia-Eurasia: The Theory of Lev Gumilyov as a Source of the Modern Russian Neoeurasianism," *The Eurasian Politician*, July 11, 2003.

10. Lev N. Gumilev, *Etnogenez i biosfera zemli*, available online at http://gumilevica. kulichki.net/EBE/index.html.

11. Marlène Laruelle, *Russian Eurasianism: An Ideology of Empire*, trans. Mischa Gabowitsch (Baltimore: Johns Hopkins University Press, 2008).

12. Edmund Griffiths, "Stalin: The Second Coming: The New Russian 'Patriotism' and the Search for Hidden Truths," *Times Literary Supplement*, January 30, 2009, 14.

13. Griffiths, "Stalin," 18.

14. Bal Gangadhar Tilak, *The Arctic Home of the Veda* (Pune, India: Govind, 1903).

15. For more detail, see Young, *Fedorov*, 130ff.

16. Valery Demin, "N. F. Fedorov i Prarodina Tsivilizatsii," in Semenova, Gacheva, and Skorokhodov, *Filosofiia bessmertiia i voskresheniia*, 2:197–210. For the German version of the Arktos theory and its role in Nazi mythology, see Joscelyn Godwin, *Arktos: The Polar Myth in Science, Symbolism, and Nazi Survival* (Kempton, IL: Adventures Unlimited, 1996).

17. The URL is: http://www.hyperborea.ru.

18. Vishev's works include: *Radical Prolongation of People's Lives* (1988); *The Problem of Personal Immortality* (1990); *Immortality of Man: Is it Attainable?* (1990); *Problems of Immortality, Book 1: The Problem of Individual Immortality in the History of Russian Philosophical Thinking of the XIX–XX Centuries* (1993); *Homo Immortalis—Man Immortal* (1999); *The Problem of Immortal Man in Russian Philosophy: Persons and Ideas: Manual* (2 vols., 1999, 2000); *On the Way to Practical Immortality* (2002).

19. I. V. Vishev, "Ot Postmortologii k Immortologii i Gomo Immortalis," *Nauka i Tekhnologii* 23 (2003): 13–28.

20. D. A. Medvedev, "The Decisive Role of Science in the Development of Philosophical Ideas in 21st Century" (paper presented at the Sixth International Philosophical and Cultural Congress, October 29–November 2, 2003, St. Petersburg, Section 6: The Prospects of Transhumanism, or the Man in Search of Authenticity, available online at http://danila.spb.ru/papers/sciencerole/sciencerole_summary_ENG.html).

21. Danila Medvedev, "Mind Upgrade," Vimeo video, posted by "Danila Medvedev," October 2, 2009, http://vimeo.com/6863890.

22. Danila Medvedev, "Singularity," *Danila* (blog), May 17, 2007, http://livingtomorrow.blogspot.com/2007/05/singularity.html.

23. Carey, "Knocking on Heaven's Door."

24. A. L. Volynskii, "Voskresenie mertvykh," in Gacheva and Semenova, *Fedorov: Pro et contra*, 1:479ff.

25. Cited in Edmund Griffiths, "Why Do Some Russian 'Communists' Love the Tsar?," *National Identity in Russia from 1961: Traditions and Deterritorialisation Newsletter* 3 (May 2009): 4, available for download at http://www.mod-langs. ox.ac.uk/russian/nationalism/newsletter.htm.

26. Berdyaev, *Russian Idea*, 4.

27. N. N. Moiseev, " Russkii kosmizm i vosstanovlenie gumanisticheskikh traditsii v nauke i obshchestve," in *Obshchee Delo*, 7–20; Semenova, *Filosof budushchego veka*; S. V. Kornilov, "Proekt 'vseobshchevo dela' i preodolenie 'filosofii beznadezhnosti i otchaianiia,'" in *Na Poroge Griadshchego: Pamiati Nikolaia Fedorivicha Fedorova (1829–1903)*, ed. A. G. Gacheva, M. M. Panfilov, and S. G. Semenova (Moscow: Pashkov Dom, 2004), 128–37; V. F. Priakhin, "Uchenie N. F. Fedorova kak miro-vozzrencheskaia osnova protivostoianiia global'nym vyzovam sovremennosti," in ibid., 314–22

28. Semenova, *Filosof*, 558.

29. *FOD*, 1:447.

# Bibliography

Agursky, Michael. "An Occult Source of Socialist Realism: Gorky and Theories of Thought Transference." In Rosenthal, *Occult*, 247–72.

Alekseeva, V. E. "K voprosu o kontseptsii atoma-dukha K. E. Tsiolkovskogo." Nauchnye chteniia pamiati K. E. Tsiolkovskogo, sektsiia: "Kosmonavtika i obshchestvo: Filosofiia K. E. Tsiolkovskogo." GMIK im. K. E. Tsiolkovskogo, Kaluga, 2002.

Alioshin, Dmitri. *Asian Odyssey*. New York: Holt, 1940.

Allen, Paul Marshall. *Vladimir Soloviev, Russian Mystic*. Blauvelt, NY: Steinerbooks, 1978.

Altaiskii, Konstantin. "Moskovskaia iunost' Tsiolkovskogo." *Moskva* 9 (1966): 176–92.

Andrews, James T. *Red Cosmos: K. E. Tsiolkovakii, Grandfather of Soviet Rocketry*. College Station: Texas A & M University Press, 2009.

Appleby, John H. "Arthur Dee and Johannes Bánfi Hunyades: Further Information on their Alchemical and Professional Activities." *Ambix* 24, no. 2 (1977): 96–109.

Artemyeva, Tatiana. "Utopian Spaces of Russian Masons in the Enlightenment." In Onnerfors and Collis, *Freemasonry and Fraternalism*, 63–85.

Bailes, Kendall E. *Science and Russian Culture in an Age of Revolutions: V. I. Vernadsky and His Scientific School, 1863–1945*. Bloomington: Indiana University Press, 1990.

Ball, Philip. "Alchemical Culture and Poetry in Early Modern England." *Interdisciplinary Science Reviews* 31, no. 1 (2006): 77–92.

Belyi, Andrei. "Vospominanie o Bloke." *Epopeia* 2 (September 1922).

Berdiaev, N. A. "Priroda i svoboda: Kosmicheskoe prel'shchenie i rabstvo cheloveka u prirody." In Semenova and Gacheva, *Russkii kosmizm*, 179–85.

Berdiaev, N. A. "Religiia voskreseniia ('Filosofiia obshchego dela' N. F. Fedorova)" [1915]. In *N. Berdiaev o russkoi filosofii*, ed. B. V. Emel'ianov and A. I. Novikov, 2:51–95. Sverdlovsk, Russia: Izdatel'stvo Ural'skogo Universiteta, 1991.

Berdiaev, N. A. *Samopoznanie: Opyt filosofskoy avtobiografii*. 2nd ed. Paris: YMCA-Press, 1983.

Berdyaev, Nicolas. *The Destiny of Man*. Translated by Natalie Duddington. London: Geoffrey Bles, 1937.

Berdyaev, Nicolas. *Dream and Reality: An Essay in Autobiography*. Translated by Katharine Lampert. New York: Macmillan, 1951.

Berdyaev, Nicolas. *The Meaning of the Creative Act*. Translated by Donald A. Lowrie. New York: Collier Books, 1962.

Berdyaev, Nicolas. *The Meaning of History*. Translated by George Reavey. New York: Scribner, 1936.

Berdyaev, Nicolas. *The Russian Idea*. Translated by R. M. French. Boston: Beacon, 1962.

Berdyaev, Nicolas. *Slavery and Freedom*. Translated by R. M. French. New York: Scribner, 1944.

Berkovskaia, E. N. "Sud'ba skreshen'ia," Vospominaniia [Fragments]. In Gacheva and Semenova, *Fedorov: Pro et contra*, 2:582–99.

Berlin, Isaiah. *The Hedgehog and the Fox: An Essay on Tolstoy's View of History*. London: Weidenfeld & Nicolson, 1953.

Billington, James H. *The Icon and the Axe: An Interpretive History of Russian Culture*. New York: Knopf, 1966.

Billington, James H. *Russia in Search of Itself*. Washington, DC: Woodrow Wilson Center Press, 2004.

Blavatsky, H. P. *The Secret Doctrine: The Synthesis of Science, Religion, and Philosophy*. Theosophical University Press Online Edition, http://www.theosociety.org/pasadena/sd/sd-hp.htm.

Bogdanov, V. V. "Delo o sluzhbe uchitelia geografii i istorii Lipetskogo uezdogo uchilishcha Nilokaia Fedorova 7 aprelia 1854–26 marta 1857 g." In *Sluzhitel' dukha vechnoi pamiati Nikolai Fedorovich Fedorov: 180-letiiu so dnia rozhdenii; Sbornik nauchnykh statei*, 2:272–79. Moscow: Pashkov Dom, 2010.

Bogomolov, N. A. "Russkaia literature nachala XX veka i okkul'tizm: Issledovaniia i materialy." *Novoe literaturnoe obozrenie* (1999).

Borisov, V. S. "Adresa Fedorova." In Semenova, Gacheva, and Skorokhodov, *Filosofiia bessmerti voskresheniia*, 2:251–55.

Borisov, V. S. "Fedorovskie sady kak Edem voskresheniia: Landshaftnaia vizualizatsiia idei Filosofii Obshego Dela." In *Sluzhitel' dukha vechnoi pamiati Nikolai Fedorovich Fedorov: 180-letiiu so dnia rozhdenii; Sbornik nauchnykh statei*, 213–42. Moscow: Pashkov Dom, 2010.

Borisov, V. S. "Kto zhe mat' Fedorova?" In *Obshchee delo: Sbornik dokladov predstavlennykh na i Vsesoiuznye Fedorovskie chteniia, G. Borovsk 14–15 Maia 1988 goda*, 233–34. Moscow: Komitet Kosmonavtiki DOSAAF SSSR, 1990.

Briusov, V. Ia. *Sochineniia v dvukh tomakh*. Moscow: Khudozhestvennaia Literatura, 1987.

Bulgakov, S. N. "Dusha sotsializma." In Semenova and Gacheva, *Russkii kosmizm*, 141–46.

Bulgakov, S. N. "Sofiinost' khoziaistva." In Semenova and Gacheva, *Russkii kosmizm*, 131–41.

Bulgakov, S. N. "Svet nevechernii: Iz glavy 'Khoziastvo i teurgiia'" [1917]. In Gacheva and Semenova, *Fedorov: Pro et contra*, 1:400–413.

Bulgakov, S. N. "Sviashchennik o. Pavel Florenskii" [1939]. Available online at Biblioteka "Vekhi," http://vehi.net/bulgakov/florensky.html.

Bulgakov, S. N. "Sviatyi graal' (Opyt dogmaticheskoi ekzegezy In. XIX:34)" [1932]. In Gacheva and Semenova, *Fedorov: Pro et contra*, 1:419–23.

Bulgakov, S. N. "Zagadochnyi myslitel' (N. F. Fedorov)" [1908]. In Gacheva and Semenova, *Fedorov: Pro et contra*, 1:391–99.

Bulgakov, Sergei. *Philosophy of Economy: The World as Household*. Translated and edited by Catherine Evtuhov. New Haven, CT: Yale University Press, 2000.

Bulgakov, Sergii. *Sergii Bulgakov: Towards a Russian Political Theology*. Edited by Rowan Williams. Edinburgh: T & T Clark, 1999.

Bulgakov, Sergius. *The Holy Grail and the Eucharist*. Translated by Boris Jakim. Hudson, NY: Lindisfarne Books, 1997.

Carlson, Maria. "Fashionable Occultism: The Theosophical World of Silver Age Russia." *Quest: Journal of the Theosophical Society in America* 99 (Spring 2011): 50–57.

Carlson, Maria. "*No Religion Higher than Truth*": A History of the Theosophical Movement in Russia, 1875–1922. Princeton, NJ: Princeton University Press, 1993.

Cassedy, Steven. "P. A. Florensky and the Celebration of Matter." In Kornblatt and Gustafson, *Russian Religious Thought*, 95–111.

Chaadaev, P. I. "First Letter." In Edie, Scanlan, and Mary-Barbara Zeldin, *Russian Philosophy*, 1:122–23.

Chizhevskii, A. L. "Kolybel: Zhizni i pul'sy Vselennoi." In Semenova and Gacheva, *Russkii kosmizm*, 317–28.

Chudakov, A. P. "G. P. Georgievskii: 'L. N. Tolstoi i N. F. Fedorov: Iz lichnykhvospominanii' (Vstupitel'naia stat'ia)." In *Chetvertye Tynianovskie chteniia: Tezisy dokladov i materialy dlia obsuzhdeniia*. Riga, USSR: Zinatne, 1988.

Cioran, Samuel D. *Vladimir Solov'ev and the Knighthood of the Divine Sophia*. Waterloo, ON: Wilfrid Laurier University Press, 1977.

Collis, Robert. "Alchemical Interest at the Petrine Court." *Esoterica* 7 (2005): 52–77, available online at http://www.esoteric.msu.edu/VolumeVII/Russianalchemy.htm.

Collis, Robert. "Hewing the Rough Stone: Masonic Influence in Peter the Great's Russia, 1689–1725." In Onnerfors and Collis, *Freemasonry and Fraternalism*, 33–63. Audio available online at http://humbox.ac.uk/922/.

Demin, Valery. "N. F. Fedorov i Prarodina Tsivilizatsii." In Semenova, Gacheva, and Skorokhodov, *Filosofiia bessmertiia i voskresheniia*, 2:197–210.

Dixon, Simon. "Archimandrite Mikhail (Semenov) and Russian Christian Socialism." *Historical Journal* 51 (2008): 689–718.

Dostoevskii, F. M. *Pis'ma*. Edited by A. S. Dolinin. 4 vols. Moscow: Gosudarstvennoe Izdatel'stvo, 1928–1959.

Dostoievsky, F. M. *The Diary of a Writer*. Translated by Boris Brasol. 2 vols. New York: Scribner, 1949.

Edie, James M., James P. Scanlan, and Mary-Barbara Zeldin. *Russian Philosophy*. 3 vols. Chicago: Quadrangle Books, 1965.

Eliade, Mircea. *The Forge and the Crucible*. Translated by Stephen Corrin. New York: Harper & Row, 1962.

Faggionato, Raffaella. *A Rosicrucian Utopia in Eighteenth-Century Russia: The Masonic Circle of N. I. Novikov*. Dordrecht, the Netherlands: Springer, 2005.

Faivre, Antoine. *Access to Western Esotericism*. Albany: State University of New York Press, 1994.

Faivre, Antoine, and Wouter J. Hanegraaff, eds. *Western Esotericism and the Science of Religion*. Leuven, Belgium: Peeters, 1998.

Fedorov, N. F. "Letter to E. S. Nekrasova, April 6, 1880." In Fedorov, *SOB*, sup., 7.

Fedorov, N. F. *Sobranie sochinenii* [*SOB*]. Edited by A. G. Gacheva and S. G. Semenova. 4 vols. plus supplement. Moscow: Progress/Traditsiia, 1995–2000.

Fedorov, N. F. *What Was Man Created For? The Philosophy of the Common Task; Selected Works*. Translated and abridged by Elisabeth Koutaissoff and Marilyn Minto. London: Honeyglen, 1990.

Fedorov, Nikolai Fedorovich. *Filosofiia obshchago dela: Stat'i, mysli, i pis'ma Nikolaia Fedorovicha Fedorova* [*FOD*]. Edited by V. A. Kozhevnikov and N. P. Peterson. 2 vols. Farnborough, UK: Gregg, 1970. First printed 1906–1913.

Fedotov, G. P. *The Russian Religious Mind: Kievan Christianity, the Tenth to the Thirteenth Centuries*. New York: Harper Torchbooks, 1960. First published 1946 by Harper & Row.

Figurovski, N. A. "The Alchemist and Physician Arthur Dee (Artemii Ivanovich Dii): An Episode in the History of Chemistry and Medicine in Russia." *Ambix* 13 (1965): 35–51.

Florenskii, Pavel. *Izbrannye trudy po iskusstvu*. Moscow: Izobrazitel'noe Iskusstvo, 1995.

Florensky, Pavel. "The Church Ritual as a Synthesis of the Arts." In *Beyond Vision: Essays on the Perception of Art*, compiled and edited by Nicoletta Misler; translated by Wendy Salmond, 95–113. London: Reaktion Books, 2002.

Florensky, Pavel. *The Pillar and Ground of the Truth*. Translated and annotated by Boris Jakim. Princeton, NJ: Princeton University Press, 1997.

Florenskii, Pavel. *Vodorazdel* [excerpts]. Available online at Biblioteka "Vekhi," http://vehi.net/florensky/vodorazd.

Florenskii, Pavel Aleksandrovich. "Organoproektsiia." In Semenova and Gacheva, *Russkii kosmizm*, 149–62.

Florovskii, Georgii. *Puti russkogo bogosloviia*. 3d ed. Paris: YMCA-Press, 1983.

French, R. M., trans. *The Way of a Pilgrim, and The Pilgrim Continues His Way*. San Francisco: Harper, 1991; first printed 1954.

Fülöp-Miller, René. *The Mind and Face of Bolshevism: An Examination of Cultural Life in Soviet Russia*. Translated by F. S. Flint and D. F. Tait. New York: Putnam, 1929.

Gacheva, A. G. "'Filosofiia obshchego dela' N. F. Fedorova v dukhovnykh iskaniiakh russkogo zarubezh'ia." In *Filosofskii kontekst russkoi literatury 1920–1930-kh godov*, edited by A. G. Gacheva, O. A. Kaznina, and S. G. Semenova, 320–74. Moscow: IMLI RAN.

Gacheva, A. G. "'Nepodvizhno lish' solntse liubvi' (N. F. Fedorov i E. S. Nekrasova)." In Gacheva, Panfilov, and Semenova, *Na poroge griadushchego*, 414–16.

Gacheva, A. G. "Novye materially k istorii znakomstva Dostoevskogo s ideiami Fedorova." In Gacheva and Semenova, *Fedorov: Pro et contra*, 1:814–43.

Gacheva, A. G. "V. S. Solov'ev i N. F. Fedorov: Istoriia tvorcheskikh vzaimootnoshenii." In Gacheva and Semenova, *Fedorov: Pro et contra*, 1:844–936.

Gacheva, A. G., M. M. Panfilov, and S. G. Semenova, eds. *Na poroge griadushchego: Pamiati Nikolaia Fedorivicha Fedorova (1829–1903)*. Moscow: Pashkov Dom, 2004.

Gacheva, A. G., and S. G. Semenova, eds. *N. F. Fedorov: Pro et contra*. 2 vols. St. Petersburg: Russkii Khristianskii Gumanitarnyi Institut, 2004–2008.

Gavrilyuk, Paul L. "The Kenotic Theology of Sergius Bulgakov." *Scottish Journal of Theology* 58, no. 3 (2005): 251–69.

George, Leonard. "Iamblichus on the Esoteric Perception of Nature." In Versluis et al., *Esotericism, Religion, and Nature*.

Ginken, A. "Idealnyi bibliotekar': Nikolai Fedorovich Fedorov." *Bibliotekar'* 1 (1911): 13–26.

Gippius, Zinaida. *Zhivye litsa: Vospominaniia*. 2 vols. Tbilisi: Merani, 1991.

Godwin, Joscelyn. *Arktos: The Polar Myth in Science, Symbolism, and Nazi Survival*. Kempton, IL: Adventures Unlimited, 1996.

Godwin, Joscelyn, Christian Chanel, and John Patrick Deveney. *The Hermetic Brotherhood of Luxor: Initiatic and Historical Documents of an Order of Practical Occultism*. York Beach, ME: Samuel Weiser, 1995.

Golovanenko, S. "Proekt ili simvol? (O religioznom proektivisme N. F. Fedorova)." *Bogoslovskii Vestnik* 24, no. 6 (1915): S294–314.

Goltz, Hermann. "'He Backed the Logos to Defeat the Chaos': The Death of Pavel Florensky (1882–1937)." *Religion in Communist Lands* 18, no. 4 (1990): 343–55, available online at http://www.biblicalstudies.org.uk/pdf/rcl/18-4_343.pdf.

Gorodetzky, Nadejda. *The Humiliated Christ in Modern Russian Thought*. London: Society for Promoting Christian Knowledge, 1938.

Gor'kii, M. "Gor'kii i sovetskie pisateli: Neizdannaia perepiska." *Literaturnoe Nasledstvo* 19 (1963): 134–36, 335, 591.

Gornostaev, A. K. *Pered litsem smerti: L. N. Tolstoii i N. F. Fedorov, 1828-1903-1910-1928*. Harbin, China: Eurasie, 1928.

Gornostaev, A. K. *Rai na zemle: K ideologii tvorchestva F. M. Dostoevskogo, F. M. Dostoevskii i N. F. Fedorov*. Harbin, China: n.p., 1929.

Gorskii, A. K. "Nikolai Fedorovich Fedorov i sovremennost'." In Gacheva and Semenova, *Fedorov: Pro et contra*, 1:518–658.

Gorskii, A. K. "Organizatsiia mirovozdeistviia." In Semenova and Gacheva, *Russkii kosmizm*, 214–39.

Graham, Loren, and Jean-Michel Kantor. "Russian Religious Mystics and French Rationalists: Mathematics, 1900–1930." *Bulletin of the American Academy Arts and Sciences* 58, no. 3 (Spring 2005): 12–19.

Gray, Jeremy. *Worlds Out of Nothing: A Course in the History of Geometry in the 19th Century*. London: Springer, 2007.

Grechishkin, S. S., and A. V. Lavrov. "Andrei Belyi i N. F. Fedorov" [1979]. In *Simvolisty vblizi: Ocherki i publikatsii*. St. Petersburg: Skifiia/TALAS, 2004.

Griffiths, Edmund. "Why Do Some Russian 'Communists' Love the Tsar?" *National Identity in Russia from 1961: Traditions and Deterritorialisation Newsletter* 3 (May 2009): 2–5, available for download at http://www.mod-langs.ox.ac.uk/russian/nationalism/newsletter.htm.

Groys, Boris, and Michael Hagemeister, eds. *Die neue Menscheit: Biopolitische Utopien in Russland zu Beginn des 20. Jahrhunderts*. Frankfurt: Suhrkamp, 2005.

Gumilev, Lev N. *Etnogenesis i biosfera zemli*. Available online at http://gumilevica.kulichki.net/EBE/index.html.

Gumilev, Lev N. *Searches for an Imaginary Kingdom: The Legend of the Kingdom of Prester John*. Translated by R. E. F. Smith. Cambridge, UK: Cambridge University Press, 1987.

Gunther, Hans. "Mezhdu utopiei i pamiat'iu: Filosofiia obshchego dela N. Fedorova i ee retsetpsiia." In *Postsimvolizm kak iavlenie kul'tury: Materialy mezhdunarodnoi nauchnoi konferentsii*, vol. 3, edited by S. N. Broitman and I. A. Esaulov. Moscow: RGNF, RGGTJ, 2001.

Gusev, N. N. *Lev Nikolaevich Tolstoi: Mater'ialy k b iografii s 1881 po 1885 god*. Moscow: Nauka, 1970.

Gustafson, Richard F. "Solov'ev's Doctrine of Salvation." In Kornblatt and Gustafson, *Russian Religious Thought*, 31–48.

Hagemeister, Michael. *Nikolaj Fedorov: Studien zu Leben, Werk und Wirkung*. Munich: Sagner, 1989.

Hagemeister, Michael. "Novoe srednevekov'e Pavla Florenskogo." *Zvezda* 11 (2006): 131–44, available online at Biblioteka "Vekhi," http://vehi.net/florensky/oflorenskom.html.

Hagemeister, Michael. "The Occult Roots of Soviet Space Travel." Paper presented at the conference "The Occult in Russia/Okkul'tizm v Rossii. Metaphysical Roots of Soviet Civilisation," March 11–13, 2007, Europäische Akademie Berlin.

Hagemeister, Michael. "Russian Cosmism in the 1920s and Today." In Rosenthal, *Occult*, 185–202.

Hamburg, G. M., and Randall A. Poole. *A History of Russian Philosophy, 1830–1930: Faith, Reason, and the Defense of Human Dignity*. Cambridge, UK: Cambridge University Press, 2010.

Hanegraaff, Wouter J., and Jeffrey J. Kripal. *Hidden Intercourse: Eros and Sexuality in the History of Western Esotericism*. Leiden, the Netherlands: Brill, 2008.

Hawking, Stephen, and Leonard Mlodinow. *The Grand Design*. New York: Bantam. 2010.

Holquist, Michael. "Konstantin Tsiolkovsky: Science Fiction and Philosophy in the History of Soviet Space Exploration." In *Intersections: Fantasy and Science Fiction*, edited by George E. Slusser and Eric S. Rabkin, 74–86. Carbondale: Southern Illinois University Press, 1987.

Ianshin, A. L. *V. I. Vernadskii: Pro et Contra Antologiia literatury oV. I. Vernadskom za sto let (1898–1998)*. St. Petersburg: Russkii Khristianskii Gumanitarnyi Institut, 2000.

Il'in, V. N. "O religiosnom i filosofskom mirovozrenii N. F. Fedorova." *Evrasiiskii Sbornik* 1929, 17–23.

Irwin, Lee. "A World Full of Gods: Panpsychism and the Paradigms of Esotericism." In Versluis et al., *Esotericism, Religion, and Nature*, 27–52.

Ishboldin, Boris. "The Eurasian Movement." *Russian Review* 5, no. 2 (Spring 1946): 64–73.

Ivanov, Vyacheslav. "Towards Noosphere." In *Candles in the Dark: A New Spirit for a Plural World*, edited by Barbara Sundberg Baudet, 187–204. Seattle: University of Washington Press, 2003.

Ivanov, Vyacheslav Vsevolodovich et al. *Noosfera i khudozhestvennoe tvorchestvo*. Moscow: Nauka, 1991.

Kaziutinskii, V. V. "Mirovozzrencheskie orientatsii sovremennogo kosmizma." Nauchnye chteniia pamiati K. E. Tsiolkovskogo, GMIK im. K. E. Tsiolkovskogo, Sektsiia "Kosmonavtika i obshchestvo: Filosofiia K. E. Tsiolkovskogo," 2007.

Kelly, Aileen. "Russian Philosophy." In *Routledge Encyclopedia of Philosophy*, edited by Edward Craig, 8:418–22. London: Routledge, 1998.

Khoruzhii, S. S. *Mirosozertsanie Florenskogo*. Tomsk, Russia: Vodolei, 1999.

Kingsley, Peter. *Ancient Philosophy, Mystery, and Magic: Empedocles and Pythagorean Tradition*. Oxford: Clarendon, 1995.

Kiselev, A. "Nikolaj Fedorov Oggi." *Russia Cristiana* 118 (1971): 7–28.

Kiselev, A. "Uchenie N. F. Fedorova v svete sovremennosti." *Grani* 81 (1971): 122–53.

Kiselev, A. "Varsonofev i N. F. Fedorov." *Novyi Zhurnal* 110 (1973): 296–99.

Kline, George L. *Religious and Anti-Religious Thought in Russia*. Chicago: University of Chicago Press, 1968.

Kline, George L. "Religious Motifs in Russian Philosophy." *Studies on the Soviet Union* 9, no. 2 (1969): 89–91.

Knorre, Boris Kirillovich. *V poiskakh bessmertiia: Fedorovskoe religiozno-filosofskoe dvizhenie; Istoriia i sovremennost'*. Moscow, LKI, 2008.

Koehler, Ludmilla. *N. F. Fedorov: The Philosophy of Action*. Pittsburgh, PA: Institute for the Human Sciences, 1979.

Komarowitsch, W. "Der Vatermord und Fiodoroffs Lehre von der 'Fleischlichen Auferstehung.'" In *Die Urgestalt der Brüder Karamasoff: Dostojewskis Quellen, Entwürfe und Fragmente*, 3–58. Munich: Piper, 1928.

Kornblatt, Judith Deutsch. "Solov'ev on Salvation: The Story of the 'Short Story of the Antichrist.'" In Kornblatt and Gustafson, *Russian Religious Thought*, 68–90.

Kornblatt, Judith Deutsch, and Richard F. Gustafson, eds. *Russian Religious Thought*. Madison: University of Wisconsin Press, 1996.

Kornilov, S. V. "Proekt 'vseobshchevo dela' i preodolenie 'filosofii beznadezhnosti i otchaianiia.'" In Gacheva, Panfilov, and Semenova, *Na poroge griadushchego*, 128–37.

Koutaissoff, E. "Some Futurological Aspects of Fedorov's Philosophy of the Common Cause." *Russian Literature Triquarterly* 12 (Spring 1975): 393–407.

Kozhevnikov, V. A. "Iz pis'ma A. K. Gorskomu o poslednikh chasakh zhizni Fedorova." In Gacheva and Semenova, *Fedorov: Pro et contra*, 1:113–14.

Kozhevnikov, Vladimir Alexandrovich. "Nikolai Fedorovich Fedorov: Opyt izlozheniia ego ucheniia po izdannym i neizdannym proizvedeniiam, perepiske i lichnym besedam" [1908], reprinted in Gacheva and Semenova, *Fedorov: Pro et contra*, 1:231–351.

Kozin, Alexander V. "Iconic Wonder: Pavel Florensky's Phenomenology of the Face." *Studies in Eastern European Thought* 59, no. 4 (2007): 293–308.

Krasheninnikova, Ekaterina. "Krupitsy o Pasternake." *Novyi mir* 1 (1997): 204–13.

Kuprevich, V. F. "Dolgoletie: Real'nost' mechty." *Literaturnaia gazeta*, December 4, 1968, reprinted in Semenova and Gacheva, *Russkii kosmizm*, 347–52.

Laruelle, Marlène. *Russian Eurasianism: An Ideology of Empire*. Translated by Mischa Gabowitsch. Baltimore: Johns Hopkins University Press, 2008.

Lazurskii, V. F. "Dnevnik V. F. Lazurskogo." *Literaturnoe Nasledstvo* 38 (1939): 445–509.

Leighton, Lauren G. *The Esoteric Tradition in Russian Romantic Literature: Decembrism and Freemasonry*. University Park: Pennsylvania State University Press, 1994.

Likhachev, Dmitry S. *Reflections on the Russian Soul: A Memoir*. Translated by Bernard Adams. Budapest: Central European University Press, 2000.

Linnichenko, I. A. "Moi vstrechi s L'vom Tolstym." In Gacheva and Semenova, *Fedorov: Pro et contra*, 1:220–21.

Lord, R. "Dostoyevsky and N. F. Fyodorov." *Slavonic and East European Review* 40 (1962): 408–30.

Lövgren, Håkan. "Sergei Eisenstein's Gnostic Circle." In Rosenthal, *Occult*, 273–97.

Lowrie, Donald A. *Rebellious Prophet: A Life of Nicolai Berdyaev*. New York: Harper, 1960.

Lukashevich, Stephen. *N. F. Fedorov (1828–1903): A Study in Russian Eupsychian and Utopian Thought*. Newark: University of Delaware, 1977.

Makarov, V. G. "Arkhivnye tainy: filosofy i vlast': Aleksandr Gorskii; Sud'ba, pokalechennaia 'po pravu vlasti.'" *Voprosy Filosofii* 8 (2002): 98–133.

Manakin, Aleksei, and Liudmila Engelgardt. "Aleksandr Chizhevskii, Leonardo da Vinchi XX-ogo veka." *Nash Sovremennik* 11 (2002).

Maneev, A. K. "Gipoteza biopolevoi formatsii kak substrata zhizni i psikhikr cheloveka." In Semenova and Gacheva, *Russkii kosmizm*, 354–66.

Marchenko, O. V. "K istorii evropeiskogo Sokratizma: N. F. Fedorova." In *Sluzhitel' dukha vechnoi pamiati: Nikolai Fedorovich Fedorov; 180-letiiu so dnia rozhdenii; Sbornik nauchnykh statei*, 89–94. Moscow: Pashkov Dom, 2010.

Masing-Delic, Irene. *Abolishing Death: A Salvation Myth of Russian Twentieth-Century Literature*. Stanford, CA: Stanford University Press, 1992.

Matich, Olga. "The Symbolist Meaning of Love: Theory and Practice." In Paperno and Grossman, *Creating Life*, 24–50.

McDaniel, Charles. "Sergei Bulgakov's 'Philosophy of Economy': A Resource for Economic Bridge-Building between Islam and the West." *Religion, State, and Society* 36, no. 4 (December 2008): 451–67.

Medvedev, D. A. "The Decisive Role of Science in the Development of Philosophical Ideas in 21st Century." Paper presented at the Sixth International Philosophical and Cultural Congress, October 29–November 2, 2003, St. Petersburg, Section 6: The Prospects of Transhumanism, or the Man in Search of Authenticity, available online at http://danila.spb.ru/papers/sciencerole/sciencerole_summary_ENG.html.

Menzel, Birgit. "The Occult Revival in Russia Today, and Its Impact on Literature." *Harriman Review* 16, no. 1 (Spring 2007): 1–13. Available online at http://www.harrimaninstitute.org/MEDIA/00786.pdf.

Mitrofanova, A. V. "Otrazhenie gnosticheskikh idei v filosofskikh rabotakh K. E. Tsiolkovskogo." Nauchnye chteniia pamiati K. E. Tsiolkovskogo, GMIK im. K. E. Tsiolkovskogo, Sektsiia "Kosmonavtika i obshchestvo: Filosofiia K. E. Tsiolkovskogo," 2002.

Mochul'skii, K. *Vladimir Solov'ev: Zhizn' i uchenie.* Paris: YMCA-Press, 1951.

Moiseev, N. N. "Russkii kosmizm i vosstanovlenie gumanisticheskikh traditsii v nauke i obshchestve." In *Obshchee delo: Sbornik dokladov predstavlennykh na i Vsesoiuznye Fedorovskie chteniia, G. Borovsk 14–15 Maia 1988 goda,* 7–20. Moscow: Komitet Kosmonavtiki DOSAAF SSSR, 1990.

Murav'ev, V. N. "Vseobshchaia proizvoditel'naia matematika." In Semenova and Gacheva, *Russkii kosmizm,* 190–211.

Murav'ev, Valerian N. *Ovladenie vremenem.* Moscow: ROSSPEN, 1998. First published 1924.

Neumann, Erich. *The Origins and History of Consciousness.* Translated by R. F. C. Hull. Princeton, NJ: Princeton University Press, 1995. First published 1954 by Pantheon Books.

Obolensky, Dimitri, ed. *The Penguin Book of Russian Verse.* Baltimore: Penguin Books, 1962.

Odoevskii, V. F. "4338 god." In Semenova and Gacheva, *Russkii kosmizm,* 34–48.

Odoevsky, V. F. *Russian Nights.* Translated by Olga Koshansky-Olienikov and Ralph E. Matlaw. Evanston, IL: Northwestern University Press, 1997.

Onnerfors, Andreas, and Robert Collis, eds. *Freemasonry and Fraternalism in Eighteenth Century Russia.* Sheffield, UK: University of Sheffield, Centre for Research into Freemasonry and Fraternalism, 2009.

Ostrander, Sheila, and Lynn Schroeder. *Psychic Discoveries Behind the Iron Curtain.* Englewood Cliffs, NJ: Prentice-Hall, 1970.

Palmer, G. E. H., Philip Sherrard, and Kallistos Ware, trans. *The Philokalia.* London: Faber & Faber, 1983.

Paperno, Irina, and Joan Delaney Grossman, eds. *Creating Life: The Aesthetic Utopia of Russian Modernism.* Stanford, CA: Stanford University Press, 1994.

Pasternak, L. O. "Iz zapisok Leonida Pasternaka." *Novyi Zhurnal* 77 (1964): 190–214.

Peterson, N. P. *N. F. Fedorov i ego kniga 'Filosofiia obshchego dela' v protivopolozhnost' ucheniiu L. N. Tolstogo . . . 'o neprotivlenii' i drugim ideiam nashego vremeni.* Verny, Russia: Tipografiia Semirechen, 1912.

Peterson, N. P. "Pis'mo k izdateliu Russkogo Arkhiva: Po povodu otzyva F. M. Dostoevskogo o N. F. Fedorove." *Russkii Arkhiv* 6 (1904): 300–301.

Peterson, N. P. "Polemika." *Voprosy Filosofii i Psikhologii* 118 (May–June 1913): 405–11.

Pisareva, Elena F. *The Light of the Russian Soul: A Personal Memoir of the Early Russian Theosophical Society.* Translated by George M. Young; edited by John Algeo. Wheaton, IL: Quest Books, 2008.

Plato. "The Apology." In *The Dialogues of Plato*, translated by Benjamin Jowett. Chicago: Encyclopedia Britannica, 1965. First published 1937 by Random House.

Pobedonostsov, Konstantin Petrovich. *Reflections of a Russian Statesman.* Translated by Robert Crozier Long. London: Grant Richards, 1898.

Priakhin, V. F. "Uchenie N. F. Fedorova kak mirovozzrencheskaia osnova protivostoianiia global'nym vyzovam sovremennosti." In Gacheva, Panfilov, and Semenova, *Na poroge griadushchego*, 314–22.

Pyman, Avril. *Pavel Florensky: A Quiet Genius; The Tragic and Extraordinary Life of Russia's Unknown da Vinci.* New York: Continuum, 2010.

Pyman, Avril. Review of *Pavel Florensky i simvolisty*, by E. A. Ivanova. *Slavic and East European Review* 83, no. 4 (2005): 740–42.

"Repose of the Venerable Sergius, Abbot and Wonderworker of Radonezh," available online on the Web site of the Orthodox Church in America, http://ocafs.oca.org/FeastSaintsLife.asp?FSID=102725.

Richards, Susan. *Lost and Found in Russia: Lives in a Post-Soviet Landscape.* New York: Other Press, 2010.

Roerich, Nicholas. *Shambhala.* New York: Stokes, 1930.

Rosenthal, Bernice Glatzer. "The Nature and Function of Sophia in Bulgakov's Prerevolutionary Thought." In Kornblatt and Gustafson, *Russian Religious Thought*, 154–76.

Rosenthal, Bernice Glatzer. *New Myth, New World: From Nietzsche to Stalinism.* University Park: Pennsylvania State University Press, 2002.

Rosenthal, Bernice Glatzer, ed. *The Occult in Russian and Soviet Culture.* Ithaca, NY: Cornell University Press, 1997.

Ryan, W. F. *The Bathhouse at Midnight: An Historical Survey of Magic and Divination in Russia.* University Park: Pennsylvania State University Press, 1999.

Sabaneeff, Leonid. "Pavel Florensky—Priest, Scientist, and Mystic." *Russian Review* 20, no. 4 (October 1961): 312–25.

Sabaneev, L. L. "Moi vstrechi s Nik. Fed. Fedorovym." In Gacheva and Semenova, *Fedorov: Pro et contra*, 1:222–24.

Saltykov, A. "Pervyi illustrator Maiakovskogo." *Tvorchestvo* 12 (1965): 15.

Scanlan, James P. "The Resurrection of Nikolai Fedorov as a Russian Philosopher." In Tandy, *Death and Anti-Death*, 49–80.

Scanlan, James P., ed. *Russian Thought After Communism: The Recovery of a Philosophical Heritage.* Armonk, NY: M. E. Sharpe, 1994.

Schmemann, Alexander. *Holy Week: A Liturgical Explanation for the Days of Holy Week.* Tuckahoe, NY: St. Vladimir's Seminary Press, n.d., ca. 1960.

Schmemann, Alexander. *Ultimate Questions: An Anthology of Modern Russian Religious Thought.* New York: Holt, Rinehart & Winston, 1965.

Schmidt-Biggemann, Wilhelm. "Salvation through Philology: The Poetical Messianism of Quirinus Kuhlmann (1651–1689)." In *Toward the Millennium: Messianic Expectations from the Bible to Waco*, ed. Peter Schäfer and Mark Cohen, 259–98. Leiden, the Netherlands: Brill, 1998.

Sedgwick, Mark. *Against the Modern World: Traditionalism and the Secret Intellectual History of the Twentieth Century.* Oxford: Oxford University Press, 2004.

Semenova, S. G. *Filosof budushchego veka.* Moscow: Pashkov Dom, 2004.

Semenova, S. G. *Nikolai Fedorov: Tvorchestvo zhizni.* Moscow: Sovetskii Pisatel', 1990.

Semenova, S. G., and A. G. Gacheva, eds. *Russkii kosmizm: Antologiia filosofskoi mysli.* Moscow: Pedagogika-Press, 1993.

Semenova, S. G., A. G. Gacheva, and M. V. Skorokhodov, eds. *Filosofiia bessmertiia i voskresheniia.* 2 vols. Moscow: Nasledie, 1996.

Sergay, Timothy D. "Boris Pasternak's 'Christmas Myth': Fedorov, Berdiaev, Dickens, Blok." Ph.D. diss., Yale University, 2008.

Setnitskii, N. A. *Kapitalisticheskii stroi v izobrazhenii F. F. Fedorova.* Harbin, China: n.p., 1926.

Setnitskii, N. A. *O konechnom ideale.* Harbin, China: Frenkel', 1926.

Setnitskii, N. A. "Ob ideale." In Semenova and Gacheva, *Russkii kosmizm*, 242–58.

Setnitskii, N. A. *Russkie mysliteli o Kitae (V. S. Solov'ev i N. F. Fedorov).* Harbin, China: n.p., 1926.

Shestov, Lev. "N. F. Fedorov" [1934]. In Gacheva and Semenova, *Fedorov: Pro et contra*, 1:714–16.

Shklovskii, Viktor. *Zhili-byli: Vospominaniia, memuarnye zapisi, povesti o vremeni, s kontsa XIXv. po 1962.* Moscow: Sovetskii Pisatel', 1964.

Shostakovich, Dmitri. *Testimony: The Memoirs of Dmitri Shostakovich.* As told to Solomon Volkov. Translated by Antonina W. Bouis. New York: Limelight, 1979.

Siddiqi, Asif A. *The Red Rockets' Glare: Spaceflight and the Soviet Imagination, 1857–1957.* New York: Cambridge University Press, 2010.

Sokolov, Y. M. *Russian Folklore.* Translated by Catherine Ruth Smith. New York: Macmillan, 1950.

Sokolsky, V. N., and A. A. Blagonravov. "From the Editors." In Tsiolkovsky, *Selected Works*, 7ff.

Solov'ev, Vladimir Sergeevich. *Pis'ma Vladimira Sergeevicha Solov'eva.* 4 vols. St. Petersburg: n.p., 1908–23.

Solov'ev, Vladimir Sergeevich. *Sobranie sochinenii.* Edited by S. M. Solov'ev and E. L. Radlov. 12 vols. Brussels: Mysl', 1966–1970. Reprint of 2nd ed., first published 1911–1914 by Prosvieshchenie.

Solovyev, Vladimir. *Lectures on Godmanhood.* London: Dobson, 1948.

Solovyoff, Vsevolod. *A Modern Priestess of Isis*. Abridged and translated by Walter Leaf. London: Longmans, Green, 1895.

Solovyov, Vladimir. *A Solovyov Anthology*. Arranged by S. L. Frank; translated by Natalie Duddington. New York: Scribner, 1950.

Solovyov, Vladimir. *Divine Sophia: The Wisdom Writings of Vladimir Solovyov*. Edited by Judith Deutsch Kornblatt. Ithaca, NY: Cornell University Press, 2009.

Solzhenitsyn, Alexander. *The Gulag Archipelago, 1918–1956: An Experiment in Literary Investigation*. Translated by Thomas P. Whitney. 3 vols. New York: Harper & Row, 1974–1978.

Spinka, Matthew. *Nicolas Berdyaev: Captive of Freedom*. Philadelphia: Westminster, 1950.

Spong, John Shelby. *Resurrection: Myth or Reality? A Bishop's Search for the Origins of Christianity*. San Francisco: HarperSanFrancisco, 1994.

Strémooukhoff, D. *Vladimir Soloviev et son Oeuvre Messianique*. Paris: Les Belles Lettres, 1935.

Stuckrad, Kocku von. *Western Esotericism: A Brief History of Secret Knowledge*. Translated by Nicholas Goodrick-Clarke. London: Equinox, 2005.

Sukhovo-Kobylin, A. V. *Death of Tarelkin and Other Plays: The Trilogy of Alexander Sukhovo-Kobylin*. Translated by Harold B. Segal. Amsterdam: Harwood, 1995.

Sukhovo-Kobylin, A. V. "Filosofiia dukhi ili sotsiiologiia (uchenie Vsemira)." In Semenova and Gacheva, *Russkii kosmizm*, 49–63.

Tandy, Charles, ed. *Death and Anti-Death*, vol. 1, *One Hundred Years after N. F. Fedorov (1829–1903)*. Palo Alto, CA: Ria University Press, 2003.

Tandy, Charles. "N. F. Fedorov and the Common Task: A 21st Century Reexamination." In Tandy, *Death and Anti-Death*, 29–48.

Tchijevsky, A. L. "Physical Factors of the Historical Process." *Cycles*, January 1971, 11–27, available online at http://cyclesresearchinstitute.org/cycles-history//chizhevsky1.pdf.

Terras, Victor, ed. *Handbook of Russian Literature*. New Haven, CT: Yale University Press, 1985.

Tilak, Bal Gangadhar. *The Arctic Home of the Vedas*. Pune, India: Govind, 1903.

Trubetskoi, E. N. *Mirosozertsanie Vl. S. Solov'eva*. Moscow: Put', 1913.

Trubetskoi, Eugene N. *Icons: Theology in Color*. Translated by Gertrude Vakar. Tuckahoe, NY: St. Vladimir's Seminary Press, 1973.

Tsiolkovskii, K. E. "Kosmicheskaia filosofiia." In Semenova and Gacheva, *Russkii kosmizm*, 278–82.

Tsiolkovskii, K. E. "Monism vselennoi" [1925; excerpts]. In Semenova and Gacheva, *Russkii kosmizm*, 264–77.

Tsiolkovskii, K. E. *Put' k zvezdam: Sbornik nauchno-fantasticheskikh proizvedenii*. Moscow: Izd-vo Akademii Nauk SSSR, 1961.

Tsiolkovsky, K. E. *K. E. Tsiolkovsky: Selected Works*. Moscow: Mir, 1968.

Ustrialov, N. V. "O filosofii N. F. Fedorova v svete sovremennosti." *Nashe Vremia* 1934.

Ustrialov, N. V. *Rossiia: U okna vagona*. Harbin, China: Kitaiskoii Vostochnoii Zheleznoii Dorogi, 1926.

Utechin, S. V. "Bolsheviks and Their Allies after 1917: The Ideological Pattern." *Soviet Studies* 10 (1958–1959): 113–35.

van den Broek, Roelof. "Gnosticism and Hermeticism in Antiquity: Two Roads to Salvation." In *Gnosis and Hermeticism from Antiquity to Modern Times*, ed. Roelof van den Broek and Wouter J. Hanegraaf, 1–20. Albany: State University of New York Press, 1998.

Vernadskii, V. I. "Avtrotrofnost' chelovechestva." In Semenova and Gacheva, *Russkii kosmizm*, 288–303.

Vernadskii, V. I. "Neskol'ko slov o noosfere." In Semenova and Gacheva, *Russkii kosmizm*, 303–12.

Vernadsky, George. *The Origins of Russia*. Oxford: Clarendon, 1959.

Versluis, Arthur, Lee Irwin, John Richards, and Melinda Phillips, eds. *Esotericism, Religion, and Nature*. Minneapolis: North American Academic Press, 2010.

Versluis, Arthur, Lee Irwin, John Richards, and Melinda Weinstein, eds. *Esotericism, Art, and Imagination*. East Lansing: Michigan State University Press, 2008.

Vishev, I. "'Filosofiia obshchego dela' N. F. Fedorova i biokosmizm." In Semenova, Gacheva, and Skorokhodov, *Filisofiia bessmertiia i voskresheniia*, 1:179–86.

Vishev, I. V. "Ot Postmortologii k Immortologii i Gomo Immortalis." *Nauka i Tekhnologii* 23 (2003): 13–28.

Volynskii, A. L. "Voskresenie mertvykh." In Gacheva and Semenova, *Fedorov: Pro et contra*, 1:479–517.

Vroon, Ronald. "The Old Belief and Sectarianism as Cultural Models in the Silver Age." In *Christianity and the Eastern Slavs*, vol. 2, *Russian Culture in Modern Times*, edited by Robert P. Hughes and Irina Paperno, 172–90. Berkeley: University of California Press, 1994.

Walicki, Andrzej. *A History of Russian Thought from the Enlightenment to Marxism*. Translated by Hilda Andrews-Rusiecka. Stanford, CA: Stanford University Press, 1979.

Walker, D. P. *Spiritual and Demonic Magic from Ficino to Campanella*. University Park: Pennsylvania State University Press, 2000. First published 1958 by the Warburg Institute, University of London.

Webb, James. *The Harmonious Circle: The Lives and Work of G. I. Gurdjieff, P. D. Ouspensky, and Their Followers*. Boston: Shambhala, 1987. First published 1980 by Putnam.

Wilbur, Ken. *A Theory of Everything: An Integral Vision for Business, Politics, Science, and Spirituality*. Boston: Shambhala, 2000.

Wiles, Peter. "On Physical Immortality: Materialism and Transcendence." *Survey* 56 (1965): 125–43; 57 (1965): 142–61.

Wilson, Colin. *The Occult: A History*. New York: Random House, 1973.

Yates, Frances A. *Giordano Bruno and the Hermetic Tradition*. Chicago: University of Chicago Press, 1964.

Yates, Frances A. *The Rosicrucian Enlightenment*. Boston: Routledge & Kegan Paul, 1972.

Young, George M. "Esoteric Elements in Russian Cosmism." *Rose+Croix Journal* 8 (2011): 127–39, available online at http://www.rosecroixjournal.org/issues/2011/articles/vol8_124_139_young.pdf.

Young, George M. "Fedorov, Nikolai Fedorovich (1829–1903)." In *Routledge Encyclopedia of Philosophy*, edited by Edward Craig, 3:574–75. London: Routledge, 1998.

Young, George M. "Fedorov's Legacy: The Russian Cosmist View of Man's Role in History." In *Death and Anti-Death*, vol. 3, *Fifty Years after Einstein, One Hundred Fifty Years after Kierkegaard*. Palo Alto, CA: Ria University Press, 2006.

Young, George M. "Fedorov's Transformations of the Occult." In Rosenthal, *Occult*, 171–84.

Young, George M. "Mezhdunarodnoe znazhenie idei N. F. Fedorova." In *Sluzhitel' dukha vechnoi pamiati Nikolai Fedorovich Fedorov: 180-letiiu so dnia rozhdenii; Sbornik nauchnykh statei*, 19–22. Moscow: Pashkov Dom, 2010.

Young, George M. *Nikolai F. Fedorov: An Introduction*. Belmont, MA: Nordland, 1979.

Young, George M. "Our Temporary Enemy and Eternal Friend: Nature in the Thaumaturgical Christianity of Nikolai Fedorov." In Versluis et al., *Esotericism, Religion, and Nature*, 93–105.

Young, George M. "The Search for a Practical Immortality: Fedorov and Yoga." In Tandy, *Death and Anti-Death*, 81–100.

Young, George M. "Toward the New Millennium: Ideas of Resurrection in Fedorov and Solov'ev." In Scanlan, *Russian Thought After Communism*, 62–73.

Young, George M. "Vladimir Solovyov's Poems of Wisdom, Mystery, and Love." In Versluis et al., *Esotericism, Art, and Imagination*, 145–61.

Young, George M. "What Will The Immortals Eat?" In *Death and Anti-Death*, vol. 2, *Two Hundred Years after Kant, Fifty Years after Turing*, edited by Charles Tandy, 19–22. Palo Alto, CA: Ria University Press, 2004.

Zenkovskii, V. V. *A History of Russian Philosophy*. Translated by George L. Kline. 2 vols. New York: Columbia University Press, 1953.

Zenkovsky, Serge A. *Medieval Russia's Epics, Chronicles, and Tales*. Rev. ed. New York: Dutton, 1974.

Zernov, Nicolas. *The Russian Religious Renaissance of the Twentieth Century*. New York: Harper & Row, 1963.

Zhegin, L. F. "Vospominaniia o P. A. Florenskom," available online at Biblioteka "Vekhi," http://vehi.net/florensky/zhegin.html.

Znamenski, Andrei. *Red Shambhala: Magic, Prophecy, and Geopolitics in the Heart of Asia*. Wheaton, IL: Quest Books, 2011.

# Index